REFIGURING SELF AND PSYCHOLOGY

Also in the Dartmouth Benchmark Series:

Experiments in Social Interaction
Michael Argyle, University of Oxford

Psychology in Action
David Canter, University of Surrey

Louis Guttman on Theory and Methodology: Selected Writings
Shlomit Levy, The Louis Guttman Israel Institute of Applied Social Research

Human Nature: Selected Writings of Hans J. Eysenck
Graham Powell, University of Surrey

COLLEGE LIBRARY

**Please return this book by the date stamped below
- if recalled, the loan is reduced to 10 days**

- 2 APR 2003

CANCELLED

RETURNED
2 7 JUN 2011

1 8 NOV 2003

- 1 MAR 2004

4 OCT 2011

1 4 JAN 2005

2 0 MAY 2005

2 0 MAY 2005

1 6 APR 2025

Fines are payable for late return

Refiguring Self and Psychology

Edited by

Kenneth J. Gergen

Swarthmore College

Dartmouth

Aldershot · Brookfield USA · Hong Kong · Singapore · Sydney

Published by
Dartmouth Publishing Company Limited
Gower House
Croft Road
Aldershot
Hants GU11 3HR
England

Dartmouth Publishing Company
Old Post Road
Brookfield
Vermont 05036
USA

British Library Cataloguing in Publication Data
Refiguring Self and Psychology. –
(Benchmark Series)
I. Gergen, Kenneth J. II. Series
155.2

Library of Congress Cataloging-in-Publication Data
Gergen, Kenneth J.
Refiguring self and psychology / [written and] edited by Kenneth
J. Gergen.
p. cm. — (Benchmark series)
Includes bibliographical references and index.
ISBN 1-85521-369-9 : £40.00 ($69.95 U.S.)
1. Self. 2. Self—Social aspects. 3. Social psychology.
I. Title. II. Series.
BF697.5.S65G47 1993
155.2—dc20
93-6400
CIP

ISBN 1 85521 369 9

Printed in Great Britain by Galliard (Printers) Ltd, Great Yarmouth

Contents

PART III   SOCIAL CONSTRUCTION AND THE RELATIONAL SELF

Acknowledgements

I gratefully acknowledge the kindness of various editors and publishers who have granted permission to republish the essays included in this collection. These include: *Journal of Personality and Social Psychology* (Chapters 1, 2, 3, 5, 7, 8); *European Journal of Social Psychology* (Chapters 6 & 11), *Psychology Today* (Chapter 4), *McGraw Hill* (Chapter 9), *Academic Press* (Chapter 14), *American Psychologist* (Chapter 10), Springer-Verlag (Chapter 12), *Journal of Mind and Behavior* (Chapter 13), and *Sage Ltd.* (Chapter 15).

Kenneth J. Gergen
Swarthmore College
Pennsylvania

Series Preface

Psychologists publish in a wide variety of outlets; many different journals, chapters of readings, conference proceedings as well as their own monographs and books. Even the work of one distinguished scholar is likely to be spread over many different sources. For the serious student this can make the task of locating all the significant work of a prolific psychologist extremely difficult.

The parsimony with which libraries throughout the world now stock journals, and the rapidity with which publishers cause books to be out of print, can mean that key papers in an seminal opus may be hard to obtain.

Psychology is a discipline in which it is often valuable to read the original papers of major contributors. It is also often of great value to be able to study the development in their ideas over their careers. Psychologists, possibly more than in any other discipline, should be able to benefit from exploring how particular individuals have struggled, through their writings, to make sense of human actions and experience.

As an educational device, the bringing together of the writings of one key figure in a single volume, helps students to understand the development of issues, theories and results, whilst being able to relate them directly to the approach of a particular person.

The *Benchmark Series* brings together the key publications of leading psychologists from right across the discipline. Each volume is edited by the author or a close colleague and includes a full bibliography of the work of the author and a brief biography. An introduction reviews the contribution of the work and sets it in its historical and intellectual context.

The books will be valuable adjuncts to many undergraduate courses in psychology, bringing the discipline alive through a deeper understanding of the people who are shaping it. Psychologists specialising in the areas covered by a particular author will find them to be of especial value.

DAVID CANTER
Series Editor
University of Surrey

Introduction

The present volume was prompted by the invitation of David Canter and Dartmouth Publications to select a set of papers reflecting the growth and development of my ideas since I began publishing over 30 years ago. The task has been accomplished with a considerable mixture of pleasure, nostalgia and anxiety. Memories both sweet and bitter crowd the selection procedure; I cringe at the naïveté of certain views, and try to be forgiving; I muse over the popularity of certain contributions (not always my favourites), and the silence with which some of my more engaging work was greeted. I have included contributions of both kinds, while sadly discarding many once held dear. However, throughout the task there has been a prevailing excitement over the many and varied discussions in which these ideas have found a home.

In an important sense these selections tell a story. At the same time, stories inevitably thrive on what they obscure. Let me address the unstoried first. My professional life has not been 'all of a piece'. I have often been moved by quixotic and sometimes intemperate enthusiasms; I have been drawn into collaborative work out of friendship and/or admiration of others' skills; and a certain thirst for learning has made me vulnerable to invitations to write on subjects about which I knew very little. Thus, in striving for coherence, the present volume makes little mention of various investments in social perception (Jones, Davis and Gergen, 1961; Gergen, 1967); in social exchange theory (Gergen, 1969; Marlowe, Gergen and Doob, 1966); in ageing and lifespan development (Gergen and Back, 1963; Back and Gergen, 1965; Gergen, 1977); in the study of policy formation (Bauer and Gergen, 1968), and in my research programmes concerned with altruism and the effects of foreign aid (see for example, Gergen, Gergen and Meter, 1972; Gergen, Ellsworth, Maslach and Seipel, 1975; Gergen and Gergen, 1979). Also missing is an extended collaboration with dear friends, Margaret and Wolfgang Stroebe, on the effects of personal loss (see for example, Stroebe, Gergen, Stroebe and Gergen, 1981; Stroebe, Gergen, Gergen and Stroebe, 1992). Finally, I have included nothing of recent writings on postmodern culture, or attempts to bring both the profession and the populace into closer dialogue (see for example, Gergen, 1991).

As for the story which is set forth here, I have divided the volume into three sections, each of which may be viewed as a form of chapter. Part I, *Empirical Psychology and the Mutable Self*, includes several early explorations. During these fledgling years, first as a graduate student at Duke University and then at my first job in the Social Relations Department at Harvard, my chief concern was in working towards a conception of human functioning that was compatible with life as I experienced it. As a budding professional, the challenge was also a daunting one. The vast body of psychological theory to which my studies were directed seemed strangely alien – mechanical, lifeless and all too coherent. Most problematic was the common romance with fixedness, with a view of human action as reliably determined by a relatively fixed set of internal dispositions, mechanisms or structures. To be sure, life was not lived inchoately, but the degree of order seemed more flexible than one determined by internal necessity. Rather, I was struck with the degree to which my own actions were embedded within local and ever-changing contexts.

This concern was congenial with the 'situationist movement' then sweeping much of social psychology. However, the narrow models to which the field was committed (e.g. dissonance theory, balance theory) scarcely spoke of the problem of human functioning more generally. I thus found myself drawn in the micro-social direction, first to the work of George Herbert Mead and Harry Stack Sullivan, but most importantly to Erving Goffman's dramaturgic orientation. Goffman's writings seemed to provide a far richer account of human action than more formal theories of psychology and, while suggesting a certain degree of predictability, left room in the human arena for surprise, subterfuge and irony. At the same time, however, Goffman's writings were suffused with cynicism; all actions seemed strategic, crafted for the occasion by an alienated Machiavelli. There was little room in this account for passion, commitment and common experiences of authenticity and genuineness.

The papers comprising this initial section thus represent the attempt to employ an experimental paradigm – deriving from my training as an empirical psychologist – to explore a view of the self congenial to a dramaturgic view of human functioning, but extending its dimensions. The first of these chapters is my doctoral dissertation, conducted under the caring supervision of an enormously talented mentor, Edward E. Jones. As my work unfolded, this study increasingly suggested to me that one's sense of identity is created through action: social engagement yields authenticity as a byproduct, and not the other way around. The second and related study was undertaken while I was still a graduate student, and for me carried with it the compelling conclusion that identity is always and everywhere in motion, geared to very subtle changes in the social ethos. The third study, a product of my Harvard days, owes a great deal to my assistant and subsequent friend and colleague, Stan Morse. Here a special twist is given to the meaning of individual differences (structural determinants), and an attempt is made to generate dialogue with the model builders of mainstream social psychology. Although very brief, the final paper in this section continues the emphasis on mutability. I include it here because, even though never published in a scholarly journal, the piece has generated unceasing interest.

In Part II, *Psychology as Historical and Cultural*, a radical disjunction occurs. Although experimental methodology gave rise to precise formulation and a comforting sense of real-world validation, much remained troubling in the enterprise. One of the major tensions was between the theoretical journey on which I was embarked and the scientific metatheory fortifying the experimental work. If human activity is as mutable as I maintained, then we could view most patterns of social conduct as socio-culturally situated. Yet if our actions are historically contingent, then my experiments were documenting little more than contemporary custom. And if these were simply styles of the times, on what account could it be maintained that empirical work reveals 'principles of behaviour'? What are the grounds for believing that psychology is a cumulative science? These doubts gave rise to the initial chapter of this section.

The argument for social psychology as history proved little less than a bombshell, striking as it did at the foundations of the field and forming a painful interruption in an otherwise optimistic, self-satisfied and energetic enterprise. Together with several other critiques of the time, the article helped to precipitate what came to be known as 'the crisis in social psychology'. Much was said in criticism of my work, and I became the black sheep of my own professional organization, the Society for Experimental Social Psychology; in 1982 the paper became a 'citation classic' according to the standards of the *Science Citation Index*. However, as the debate continued I found my initial views not becoming more tempered by the broad vexation they evoked, but, on the contrary, somewhat understated. When more closely examined, I found that the entire empiricist superstructure lacked convincing, rational warrant. Chapter 6, a critique of experimental methodology, was initially accepted for publication by the *American Psychologist*, but subsequently barred by its editor, a fellow social psychologist, Charles Kiesler. Chapter 7 attempts to explore an alternative to 'empirical validation' as a means of crediting theoretical formulations. It stands as a strong endorsement for theoretical audacity.

One of the most compelling attacks against my thesis in 'Social Psychology as History' (Chapter 5) took the following form: the superficial activities of individuals may vary both historically and culturally, but the proper focus of psychology should be on the underlying principles of mental functioning. They are universal and transhistorical. My answer to this argument is contained in Chapter 8. Here my co-authors and I try to demonstrate the hermeneutic impasse confronted by psychologists attempting to validate propositions about 'mental process' by recourse to behavioural observations. At the time, I thought these arguments were more powerful than those contained in 'Social Psychology as History'. However, it was virtually a decade before I found this paper to be reaching any audience at all. This section is completed with my address to the American Psychological Association on the occasion of the Centennial of the founding of the first psychological laboratory. The paper represents the culmination of my views at the time concerning psychology's development, its problems and its future.

In Part III, *Social Construction and the Relational Self*, the narrative turns in a positive direction. While the papers of the preceding section largely represent a critical challenge to the traditional view of psychological science, the contributions of the present section are attempts to build from this critique towards a positive alternative. This alternative is bidirectional. At the outset it is metatheoretical; I try to grapple with the possibilities of a new conception of the science, its rationale and potentials. To this end, Chapter 10 lays out grounding assumptions for a social constructionist view of knowledge – essentially a more fully developed outgrowth of what I called 'socio-rationalism' in the preceding chapter. Chapter 11 demonstrates the relevance of the constructionist standpoint for social psychology. First I demonstrate shortcomings in the cognitive view of human functioning; then, to illustrate the potential of a constructionist social psychology, I integrate a burgeoning array of studies congenial to this standpoint.

The final four chapters represent attempts to realize the implications of a constructionist psychology. Chapter 12 first deconstructs the concept of aggression as a behavioural descriptor, and goes on to demonstrate how cultural (and scientific) talk about aggression is limited by linguistic tradition. Indeed, the exploration of such traditions becomes a challenging task for a constructionist psychology. Chapter 13 is a response to a second challenge for such a psychology: cultural critique. Resonating with the previous chapter's concerns with linguistic tradition, here I take aim at the profusion of mental deficit terms spawned by the mental health professions. As I attempt to demonstrate, such languages are deeply detrimental to society, and on a trajectory of unlimited growth.

The last two chapters bring the volume full circle. Here I return to my initial concern, the self. Drawing from social constructionist metatheory, I work with my wife, colleague and companion, Mary Gergen, to abandon the traditional conception of the individual as self-contained agent, driven by universal and biologically-based psychological processes. And, as described in Chapter 14, we move towards a view of relationship as the central unit of concern. On this account, individual processes are only significant (or meaningful) as constituents of the more extended process of relationship. We inherit narrative forms from the culture with which we make ourselves mutually intelligible; emotional performances derive their significance from their place in relational scenarios. The final chapter (15) moves the site of concern from the academy into cultural practices. Narrative theory, as outlined in the preceding chapter, has had a substantial impact on recent developments in therapeutic practice. This final chapter supports this development and, using constructionist ideas, explores both its limitations and the possibilities for more fully potentiating practices.

References

Back, K.W. and Gergen, K.J. (1965), 'Time perspective, aging, and preferred solutions to international conflicts', *Journal of Conflict Resolution*, **9**, 177–87.

Bauer, R.A. and Gergen, K.J. (eds) (1968), *The Study of Policy Formation*, New York: Free Press.

Gergen, K.J. (1967), 'The significance of skin color in human relations', *Daedalus*, Spring, 390–406.

Gergen, K.J. (1969), *The Psychology of Behavior Exchange*, Reading, MA: Addison Wesley.

Gergen, K.J. (1977), 'Stability, change and chance in understanding human development', in N. Datan and H. Reese (eds), *Lifespan Developmental Psychology, Dialectic Perspectives*, New York: Academic Press.

Gergen, K.J. (1991), *The Saturated Self, Dilemmas of Identity in Contemporary Life*, New York: Basic Books.

Gergen, K.J. and Back, K.W. (1966), 'Communication in the interview and the disengaged respondent', *Public Opinion Quarterly*, **30**, 386–98.

Gergen, K.J., Ellsworth, P., Maslach, C. and Seipel, M. (1975), 'Obligation, donor resources and reactions to receiving aid in three nations', *Journal of Personality and Social Psychology*, **31**, 390–400.

Gergen, K.J. and Gergen, M.M. (1979), 'The psychological evaluation of international aid' in R. Eels (ed.), *Perspectives on International Aid*, New York: Columbia University Press.

Gergen, K.J., Gergen, M.M. and Meter, K. (1972), 'Individual orientations to pro-social behavior', *Journal of Social Issues*, **28**, 105–30.

Jones, E.E., Davis, K.E. and Gergen, K.J. (1961), 'Role playing variations and their informational value for person perception', *Journal of Abnormal and Social Psychology*, **53**, 302–10.

Marlowe, D., Gergen, K.J. and Doob, A. (1966), 'Opponent's personality, expectation of social interaction, and interpersonal bargaining', *Journal of Personality and Social Psychology*, **3**, 206–13.

Stroebe, M.S., Gergen, K.J., Stroebe, W. and Gergen, M.M. (1981), 'The broken heart, reality or myth?', *Omega*, **12**, 87–105.

Stroebe, M.S., Gergen, M.M., Gergen, K.J. and Stroebe, W. (1992), 'Broken hearts or broken bonds: Love and death in historical perspective', *American Psychologist*, **47**, 1205–1212.

PART I
EMPIRICAL PSYCHOLOGY
AND THE MUTABLE SELF

[1]

Journal of Personality and Social Psychology
1965, Vol. 1, No. 5, 413–424

THE EFFECTS OF INTERACTION GOALS AND PERSONALISTIC FEEDBACK ON THE PRESENTATION OF SELF [1]

KENNETH J. GERGEN

Harvard University

During a 30-min. interview Ss were (a) either exposed to a type of social feedback called reflective reinforcement or not exposed to such feedback, (b) presented this feedback in either a personal or impersonal manner, and (c) instructed either to be accurate about themselves or to make a good impression. As predicted, the positive character of the Ss' self-description increased to a greater extent under feedback than under conditions of no feedback. However, the variation in personalism had minimal consequences. Ss instructed to make a good impression demonstrated a greater increase in positiveness than did accurate Ss. The generalization of the responses produced by these manipulations and the role of awareness were also explored.

The present study was designed to investigate a few of the major conditions affecting the way in which one person presents or describes himself to another. It seems clear that persons do present different self-attributes to meet the functional demands of various social settings (cf. Goffman, 1959). On the other hand it is also clear that persons are concerned with self-consistency, and are repeatedly faced with the dilemma: how to remain "true to self" and yet respond adaptively to varying social demands. This conflict between consistency and social adaptation can be considered a major theme of the present investigation. Thus the study is concerned with the effects of differing social conditions on changes in self-presentation, and with the consequences of having changed for subsequent self-description.

Social reinforcement has long been considered the most important determinant of the self-concept. Such reinforcement, or feedback, seems to be continuously influential in moulding the self-concept in at least two ways: (a) From the standpoint of operant conditioning a person can be *reinforced* by others for providing certain behavior at certain times. Since such responses should then occur with increasing frequency, the person should come to feel that such responses are truly representative of the self. (b) From the viewpoint of classical learning a person can come to associate his overt behavior with descriptions communicated to him by others. It is one version of this process which has been stressed by the "symbolic interactionists" (for example, G. H. Mead and C. H. Cooley). According to this view, a person's self-definition is primarily a *reflection* of the views of significant others about him.

Based on the assumption that persons tend to describe themselves in accord with self-conceptions, the present experiment attempted to exploit both of the above components of social feedback to produce a shift in the self-image, and thus a shift in self-presentation. Subjects described themselves to an attractive interviewer who agreed with their positive statements about self and disagreed with negative self-statements. In this manner the interviewer reflected her opinion of the subject to the subject. However, in that her opinion was also highly gratifying to the subject, it served as a reinforcing agent for certain of the subject's responses. This type of dual feedback can be termed *reflective reinforcement*.

It is thus proposed that social feedback in the form of reflective reinforcement alters the way in which a person views himself in a given situation. These alterations will be reflected in modified presentation of self. The second major intent of the present study was to show that the same feedback can have

[1] This research was supported by Grant MF-14, 799 from the National Institute of Mental Health, United States Public Health Service, and Grant G21955 from the National Science Foundation. The article is based on a dissertation submitted in partial fulfillment for the PhD degree at Duke University. The author is especially indebted to Edward E. Jones, who served as dissertation advisor, for his expert advice and kind encouragement.

quite different consequences depending on whether it is perceived to be personal or impersonal and the goal of the subject in the situation.

One aspect of interpersonal relations which intuitively seems important is the extent to which they are *personalistic* in character. Some relationships we feel to be conducive to the expression of true feelings; others seem to breed insincere expressions of feeling. Although there is certainly a continuum along which such relationships vary, the former type of relationship can be termed "personal" and the latter "impersonal." (Compare Jones & Thibaut's, 1958, notion of "reciprocal contingency" and Jourard's, 1964, concept of "authentic interaction.") In terms of the above discussion, it would seem that impersonal feedback is both nonreflective and nonreinforcing. Impersonal feedback cannot be trusted to be truly representative of another's feelings, and thus cannot be considered valid as a reflection of another's perceptions of us. Second, because impersonal feedback is neither informative nor a meaningful approval cue, it should have less reward value than personal feedback. It was thus hypothesized that impersonal feedback should be less effective in influencing the way a person thinks of himself in a given situation, and, in turn, should have less effect on self-presentation.

A further source of variation in an individual's response to social feedback is the actor's primary goal in the situation. Perhaps the most relevant dimension along which such goals can vary is that inherent in the previous discussion of the self-presentation dilemma. At one extreme of the dimension the salient goal of the actor is to insure consistency between his presented attributes and some core concept of self. At the other extreme, the goal of social adaptation would be salient and self-consistency ignored. In the present study the attempt was made to tap into this continuum at fairly extreme points in order to sample the effects of different interaction goals on self-presentation and subsequent self-description. To this end, one set of subjects was asked to be honest and accurate, a second set was instructed to try to create the most positive impression possible on the inter-viewer. This latter goal can be termed *ingratiation*.

There is an empirical precedent for using the particular interaction goals of accuracy versus ingratiation. In a study by Jones, Gergen, and Davis (1962) subjects attempting to make an interviewer respond favorably to them described themselves more positively than a group instructed to "be themselves." Although such a finding seems rather obvious, there are also conditions under which the opposite is true. In a second study (Jones, Gergen, & Jones, 1963) low-status subjects showed the same tendency as subjects in the above study, but high-status subjects actually became more modest when attempting to ingratiate themselves with lows.

In view of these findings, vis-à-vis the fact that subjects in the present experiment were also in a low-status position relative to the interviewer, it was anticipated that subjects attempting to ingratiate should rate themselves from the onset of the interview more positively than those attempting to be accurate. In addition, they should be more sensitive to the approval cues given by the interviewer. They should be less willing to accept feedback as more or less descriptive of them as a function of the interviewer's personalism. Rather, feedback should function as a notification or signal of the optimal tactic of self-presentation. It was thus predicted that the rate of increase in the positiveness of self-presentation should be greater when subjects are attempting to ingratiate than when attempting to be accurate. In the ingratiation conditions self-presentation should not vary as a function of the personalism of the interviewer.

Generalization of Self-Presentation

In this study generalization was measured after the interview by having subjects fill out a number of items similar to those used in the interview. Based on the assumption that reflective reinforcement is effective in altering a person's feelings about self, it was predicted that subjects who are attempting to be accurate and who receive personal feedback should generalize from the reinforcement experience to a greater extent than those receiving impersonal feedback. However, in the ingratiation conditions the assumptions are quite different in character. Since the instructions specifically invite the subject to ignore his private assessment of self during the interview, there should be little tendency on the part of the subject to make his subsequent self-descriptions consistent with his behavior in the interview. It was thus anticipated that the generalization effects in the ingratiation conditions should show a more complete return to the preexperimental level of positiveness than in the accuracy conditions.

Awareness of Change

It is also of some importance to know the degree to which one is aware of shifts in self-presentation. Recent research on learning without awareness has cast considerable doubt on the earlier findings that learning could be achieved without the subject's being capable of verbalizing the fact. According to several recent sources (cf. Eriksen, 1962) successful learning on the tasks used to date seems to require some type of active hypothesis formation. However, it does seem that if learning without awareness is to be found, it might be advantageous to use methods which do not promote a problem-solving set. Also, it would seem that one might have a better chance of obtaining learning without awareness if the materials used tapped emotional rather than strictly rational resources. The former should be less easily verbalized and, at the same time, more naturally responsive to situational changes. In the present study it was felt that both the informal nature of the experimental situation and the instructions to be honest would operate against the tendency to adopt a problem-solving set. Also, as the materials used in the experiment were primarily evaluative in nature, rationality should not play such a significant role. Subjects in the ingratiation conditions also provide a convenient comparison group, for in these conditions the instructions should shift the subject's focus to one more closely akin to problem solving.

METHOD

The basic design was a 2×2 factorial with four cells reflecting combinations of interviewer personalism and interaction goal of the subject. It was also of importance to assess the effects of the stimulus

conditions in the absence of reinforcement. Thus, additional subjects were interviewed under accuracy-personal or under accuracy-impersonal instructions with no systematic reinforcement provided. The experiment thus involved two overlapping designs, each containing four cells, with the two accuracy cells in common. Nine subjects appeared in each of the six cells.

Self Valuation Triads Test

The Self Valuation Triads test (SVT test), derived from a measure used by Dickoff (1961), consisted of 72 groups of three self-descriptive statements. The statements covered a wide range of attributes and within each triad one statement reflected a positive trait, one a negative trait, and the third a trait more neutral in tone.[2] The positiveness of each statement was established through a group of independent raters. For each triad the subject was to distribute 10 points among the statements in such a way that the most descriptive statement of the three would receive the greater number of points, etc. A subject's SVT score was calculated by summing the points given to positive statements.

Subjects

The subjects were freshman and sophomore females enrolled in an introductory psychology course. Early in the course a group testing session (hereafter called the "neutral" testing period) was held in which all students filled out the following measures: the SVT test, a questionnaire concerning these evaluations, and the deCharms and Rosenbaum (1960) self-esteem measure. Of this initial group, persons scoring in the upper and lower fifths on the SVT measure were excluded from further consideration. Of the remaining group, 56 were subsequently selected and assigned to experimental conditions on essentially a random basis. Attention was given to the equality of initial SVT scores from cell to cell. Two subjects had to be excluded from the final sample because of stated suspicion of the manipulation.

Experimental Procedure

Inasmuch as experimental conditions differed from each other in more than one respect, the procedure for the cell combining accuracy and personal instructions will be outlined first.

Accuracy-personal condition. The experiment was introduced to each subject as part of an interviewing project concerned with obtaining personality information from large numbers of people. Students were being used to aid in training the interviewers prior to the actual carrying out of the survey. The interviewers were said to be carefully chosen from the junior and senior classes. Their central task was

[2] A sample triad, composed of a positive, negative, and neutral phrase, is as follows:

> very accepting and approachable
> resentful of others
> aloof when busy

to get to know the persons interviewed as well as possible during the time available. In doing this, however, the interviewer was to concentrate on being as natural and spontaneous as possible; she was not to adopt a stereotyped "front" but was to consider each person as an individual.

The remainder of the procedure was then briefly outlined for the subject. First, the interviewer would be introduced and in her presence the experimenter would ask a number of questions regarding the subject's background. Meanwhile the interviewer would take notes. Since part of her training included practice in making rapid judgments, she would then leave for a short period to make some preliminary ratings of the subject. Upon returning she would begin the main portion of the interview. The subject was encouraged to be honest and natural throughout the procedure.

The interviewer was then brought in and introduced. She was an attractive, well-dressed, junior-class female, instructed to behave in a standard, pleasant manner at all times. After the questioning the interviewer left the room. Upon her return 5 minutes later the experimenter departed and the interviewer began by asking the subject a number of standard, informal questions about her interests, etc. The subject was then told that the remainder of the interview would center around the items on the SVT test.

Accuracy-impersonal condition. Upon the subject's arrival she was taken to an observation booth from which she could see through a one-way mirror into the same room as used above. The experimenter's explanation of the situation was the same as above until the interviewer's task was described. Here the subject was told that the interviewer had been extensively trained in interviewing techniques. She had been taught what to say, how to smile, how to make the interviewee feel comfortable, etc. Her task was only to practice the techniques she had learned. In order that this might be done without distraction, the subject was told that the interviewer would be looking into a one-way mirror and would not be able to see her.

Although the interviewer in the personal condition was exposed to information about the subject and was given time to think about this information, in the impersonal condition she received no such information. In order to keep all other aspects of the situation constant, however, the experimenter asked the subject the same preliminary questions regarding her background. During this questioning the interviewer moved into a position where she could be seen through the mirror by the subject. It was also clear to the subject that the interviewer could not hear her response. When the questioning was over the microphones were switched on. The subject was introduced only by her first name, and the interview proceeded as in the above condition.

Ingratiation conditions. A third of the subjects in both of the above conditions were instructed to make a positive impression on the interviewer. In all cases these instructions followed the experimenter's pre-

liminary questioning of the subject. In the personal condition they were given while the interviewer was out of the room "rating" the subject. In the impersonal condition they were given just before the microphone was turned on. In each case the subject was told that it was very important for the planners of the project to know how a person would rate herself if she were only attempting to make a good impression. The subject was told that in carrying out her task she could say whatever she pleased about herself.

Nonreinforced conditions. The instructions for the nonreinforced accuracy-personal and the nonreinforced accuracy-impersonal conditions were exactly the same as outlined above for their reinforced counterparts. The only difference in the procedure was that during the presentation of the triads, to be described below, the interviewer gave no reinforcement and confined her conversation to the mechanics of the proceedings.

Procedure for Providing Reflective Reinforcement

Sixty triads of the 72 on the original test had been assembled so that they could be handed one by one to the subject. (In the impersonal conditions, two sets of triads were assembled, one for the subject and another for the interviewer.) The triads had been arranged so that, for scoring purposes, they formed six trial blocks with 12 triads in each block. All but the sixth block (generalization triads) were administered during the interview. The triads had been rearranged, however, so that the subject's previous score for any given block roughly equaled her score on each of the other blocks. In this manner the base-line score of each subject remained similar from one trial block to the next. Care was also taken that each trial block contained the same number of triads of each order of positive, neutral, and negative statements. In addition, it was insured that no triad appeared in a given trial block significantly more often in one experimental condition than in another.

During the experimental procedure the triads were handed one by one to the subject who would then record in pencil by each statement the number of points she decided to assign. She would then hand the triad back to the interviewer. (In the impersonal conditions, the subject would relay the point assignments to the interviewer over the microphone.) The interviewer would then reinforce her according to the following schedule:

1. During the first 24 triads, each time the points assigned to the positive statement equaled or exceeded the subject's previously established average for positive statements, the interviewer would provide positive reinforcement. (The interviewer was preinformed of the subject's previous average for positive statements in each case.)

2. During the first 24 triads, each time the points assigned to the positive statement were less than the subject's previous average for positive statements, the interviewer would reinforce negatively.

3. During the last 36 triads, positive and negative reinforcements were provided only when the subject exceeded or went below her previous average by 2 or more points. Positive statements receiving points which could neither be positively nor negatively reinforced according to this criterion were responded to with silence.

As the reinforcement was also gauged to convey the interviewer's impression of the subject to the subject, it took the form of agreement or disagreement with the subject's self-evaluations. However, in order that the interviewer appear natural, she was allowed to use five types of positive and negative reinforcement. The interviewer expressed positive reinforcement in the following ways:

a. Yes, I would agree with . . .
b. Yes, I think you are . . .
c. Yes, you look like you would be . . .
d. Good
e. Very good

All of these were accompanied by either a smile or a nod of the head. The negative reinforcements were as follows:

a. You don't strike me as being the type who . . .
b. I sort of disagree with . . .
c. I would say you were much more . . .
d. I think you underestimate yourself . . .
e. Oh, really?

Disagreement was accompanied by either a frown or a puzzled expression. In order to check on the comparability of reinforcement type across conditions, approximately half of the interviews in each condition were recorded from a hidden location. In addition to the data obtained during the reinforcement procedure, several other measures were administered by the experimenter after the interview was over. Included were the final 12 triads (generalization triads), the deCharms-Rosenbaum self-esteem test, a series of ratings to be made of the interviewer, and a questionnaire designed to tap awareness and the subjects' reactions to other aspects of the situation.

RESULTS

Validation of Experimental Manipulations

Before assessing the major results it is first necessary to establish whether or not the experimental manipulations were effective.

Variation in perceived personalism. Perceived personalism was measured after the interview by having subjects rate on a 5-point scale both how "natural and spontaneous" the interviewer seemed to be and to what extent her behavior seemed "bound by a set of rules." A 10-point scale of "perceived personalism" was derived by combining subjects' ratings on both items. Under conditions of reinforcement, the interviewer in the personal conditions was seen as significantly ($p < .01$) more personal than in the impersonal conditions. Although the difference between means in the nonreinforced conditions was in the same direction, this difference did not reach significance. However, this failure is not crucial in understanding the results.

Variation in interaction goal. As will be recalled, a third of the subjects were given instructions to make the most positive impression possible on the interviewer and the remainder were encouraged to be natural and honest during the interview. On the final questionnaire all subjects were asked how they came to assign the number of points to the triads during the interview. Without a single exception, all subjects in the accuracy conditions indicated that they gave the interviewer an honest picture of themselves; subjects in the ingratiation conditions indicated that they had described themselves in such a way as to make a good impression.

Variation in reflective reinforcement. In assessing the validity of this variation, it was of importance to know whether subjects in the reinforced conditions perceived the interviewer as feeling more positively about them than subjects in the nonreinforced conditions. The answer to this question could be found in the subjects' predictions of the way the interviewer would rate them. After the interview, each subject filled out a series of antonyms on which she was to predict the way the interviewer would rate her after the interview. Most relevant was the personal attractiveness cluster, formed by such antonyms as "likable" versus "not particularly likable," and "attractive personality" versus "unattractive personality," etc. An analysis of variance of the combined antonym ratings indicated that the reinforced-accuracy groups, as compared with the nonreinforced groups, felt that the interviewer would rate them as more personally attractive ($p < .05$).

Stability of reinforcement type. As there were several ways in which positive and negative reinforcements could be expressed, the question arises as to whether some reinforcing phrases might have been used more often in one condition than in another. However, an analysis of these phrases revealed only that

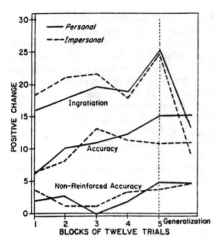

Fig. 1. Mean positive change across blocks of trials for all conditions.

in every condition more of the shorter reinforcing phrases, for example, "good" or "very good," were used than the longer ones. No other systematic differences among types of reinforcement used across the various conditions were discovered.

In summary, with the exception of the failure to find significant differences in perceived personalism in the nonreinforced conditions, there is good evidence that each of the manipulations was perceived or carried out as intended.

TABLE 1

ANALYSIS OF VARIANCE OF POSITIVE CHANGE SCORES
IN THE REINFORCED- AND NONREINFORCED-
ACCURACY CONDITIONS

Source	df	MS	F
Between subjects	(35)		
Personal-impersonal (B)	1	4.05	<1.00
Reinforced-nonreinforced (C)	1	2,936.27	14.46**
B × C	1	22.05	<1.00
Error (b)	31*	202.89	
Within subjects	(144)		
Trial blocks (A)	4	90.02	2.25
A × B	4	32.83	<1.00
A × C	4	81.23	2.03
A × B × C	4	5.36	<1.00
Error (w)	124*	39.92	

* Reduced because of data substituted for one subject.
** $p < .001$.

Changes in Self-Valuation

Effects of reflective reinforcement. It was predicted that reflective reinforcement would produce significant increases in the positiveness of self-ratings under conditions in which the subject was told to be accurate. In order to test this prediction, neutral and experimental SVT scores across the five trial blocks were converted to *positive-change* scores, a higher score reflecting a greater change toward being more positive about oneself. The mean positive change across the five trial blocks for the various conditions appears graphically in Figure 1. In order to test this first prediction a Type III (Lindquist, 1956)

TABLE 2

ANALYSIS OF VARIANCE OF POSITIVE CHANGE SCORES
IN THE REINFORCED CONDITIONS

Source	df	MS	F
Between subjects	(35)		
Personal-impersonal (B)	1	.67	<1.00
Accuracy-ingratiation (C)	1	4,234.05	19.36**
B × C	1	56.67	<1.00
Error (b)	31*	218.66	
Within subjects	(144)		
Trial blocks (A)	4	260.48	6.08*
A × B	4	30.95	<1.00
A × C	4	41.28	<1.00
A × B × C	4	11.92	<1.00
Error (w)	124*	42.85	

* Reduced because of data substituted for one subject.
* $p < .025$.
** $p < .001$.

analysis of variance was carried out in which the change scores of the reinforced- and nonreinforced-accuracy groups were compared. The results of this analysis are summarized in Table 1. As evidenced by the significant main effect due to the variation in reinforcement, it is clear that reflective reinforcement did, indeed, produce a marked increase in the positiveness of self-preservation. Orthogonal comparisons further indicate that the positive change in the reinforced accuracy-personal condition was significantly ($p < .01$) greater than that found in its nonreinforced counterpart; a comparison of the reinforced accuracy-impersonal group and its nonreinforced control also yielded a significant ($p < .025$) difference.

Effects of variations in personalism and interaction goals. Given that reflective reinforcement is effective in altering the positiveness of self-valuation, a second set of predictions concerned the differential effectiveness of reflective reinforcement as a function of the personalism of the stimulus person and the subject's interaction goal. The results of an analysis of variance in which these variations were compared, appear in Table 2. As evidenced, the variation of personalism did not contribute in any significant way.

However, before concluding that variations in personalism had nothing to do with positive change, several other aspects of the data deserve attention. First of all, Figure 1 suggests that there may have been differences in the cumulative effect of reinforcement in the accuracy-personal versus the accuracy-impersonal condition. In the former, self-valuation underwent a monotonic increase throughout the five trial blocks; in the latter the power of the reinforcement seemed to be lost by the end of the third trial block. Although the A × B × C interaction term, which would indicate overall slope differences, was not significant, an orthogonal polynomial test of the components of slope (Ray, 1960) yielded a significant ($p < .005$) linear trend in the personal condition. The same test when applied to the reinforced accuracy-impersonal condition was not significant. When reflective reinforcement is personal in nature, changes in self-rating thus seem to be continuous; when impersonal, reflective reinforcement seems only to have short-lived effects.

Second, it was also apparent that some of the subjects who interacted with the personal stimulus person were not particularly convinced of her spontaneity; on the other hand, some subjects in the accuracy-impersonal condition felt the stimulus person was quite sincere. This fact prompted an investigation of the relationship between perceived personalism and amount of positive increase within each of these conditions. Correlations were computed between perceived personalism scores and the positive-change scores. In the reinforced accuracy-personal condition the resulting correlation was high and just short of reaching significance ($r = .45$); in the reinforced accuracy-impersonal condition the correlation was also high and significant

($r = .58$, $p < .05$). Within the nonreinforced accuracy conditions, however, these correlations did not begin to approach significance. When receiving reflective reinforcement, then, the more personal the agent providing such reinforcement is seen, the greater the tendency to react to this reinforcement.

The effects on self-valuation of the variation in interaction goals can now be examined. It was predicted above that the ingratiation condition subjects would demonstrate positive increases which would exceed those produced by subjects under accuracy instructions. Further, it was predicted that this differential increase would manifest itself from the outset of the interview and would increase throughout the duration of the interview. The first of these predictions was fully confirmed; the positive change manifested in the ingratiation conditions was significantly ($p < .001$) greater than that found in the reinforced-accuracy conditions. An analysis of the first trial block also indicated that the ingratiation subjects manifested a greater initial increase in the positiveness of self-valuation than subjects in the accuracy conditions ($p < .05$). The lack of a significant A × B × C interaction, however, indicates that there was no tendency for the ingratiation groups to increase the positiveness of self-ratings at a faster rate than subjects in the accuracy groups. These results, however, seem to give full support to the importance of interaction goals as a factor in understanding self-presentation.

Generalization. As Figure 1 has shown, the degree of generalization from the conditioning procedure to the subsequent testing period was substantial. A comparison of subjects' scores on the generalization triads with scores for the same triads filled out in the neutral situation indicated all of the reinforced groups with the exception of the ingratiation-impersonal group showed a significant ($p < .05$) increase in the positiveness of self-ratings. Neither of the nonreinforced groups, combined or considered separately, showed a significant increase in positiveness over their scores obtained in the neutral testing. Before drawing any conclusions from these results, however, several additional factors should be considered.

One of the hypotheses developed above was that generalization resulting from personal reinforcement would be greater than that produced by impersonal reinforcement (accuracy-instruction groups only). Although there was no significant difference between the two groups in the degree of decline in the positiveness of self-ratings from the fifth trial block to the generalization triads, a comparison of "generalization gain" scores (i.e., generalization triad scores minus scores on the same triads under neutral conditions) lends support to this hypothesis. Whereas the reinforced accuracy-personal group differed significantly ($p < .05$) from its nonreinforced control in terms of amount of gain in self-valuation produced by the manipulations, the impersonal group did not differ from its non-reinforced control ($F < 1.60$). The difference between the differences, however, was not significant.

A second hypothesis concerned the amount of generalization in the reinforced accuracy groups as compared with the ingratiation groups. Here it was felt that calculated increases in positiveness would wash out more rapidly and completely than the more modest increases occurring in the reinforced-accuracy conditions. A glance at Figure 1 reveals that, indeed, *loss* in positiveness from the fifth learning block to the generalization triads was much greater for the ingratiation groups than the accuracy groups. This difference proved to be significant at beyond the .001 level. However, of equal interest is a comparison of the generalization *gain* produced in these two conditions. A comparison of generalization gain scores indicates that there was no difference in the final level of positiveness reached in the accuracy or the ingratiation groups. It would then seem that calculated changes in self-ratings produce their own demands on personal consistency. This latter finding will receive further attention below.

It could be argued that the subject was merely learning from the interviewer a new norm for the mechanics of filling out the items, and thus the generalization effects were only reflecting this new norm. In order to assess the validity of this argument a comparison was made of subjects' pre- and post-scores on the deCharms and Rosenbaum self-esteem test. This test had been found to correlate .58 with the self-valuation measure, but was quite different in format. This comparison revealed an increase in self-esteem in all of the reinforced groups and the combined pre- versus postdifference was significant at beyond the .01 level. The smallest increases were also found in the impersonal conditions. An analysis of the nonreinforced groups combined yielded no significant difference. These findings would seem to increase one's confidence that, indeed, underlying changes had been produced by the experimental manipulations.

Awareness and changes in self-valuation. Awareness of change in self-ratings was tapped in several ways. First of all, subjects were asked whether they felt they generally filled out the items during the interview more positively, more negatively, or approximately the same as they had in the earlier testing situation. Second, subjects were asked if the interviewer said anything during the administration of the triads, and, if so, what kind of things she said. Finally, they were asked whether they felt that anything the interviewer said might have influenced the number of points assigned to phrases. One of these items failed to discriminate among individuals: all subjects who had been reinforced were fully aware that the interviewer had been positive in her reactions toward them.

Awareness was thus defined in the following ways: for the accuracy conditions (reinforced groups only) all those who felt they were more positive during the interview than earlier and who also felt the interviewer influenced their self-ratings were deemed "aware": those who said that the interviewer's attitude could not have affected their ratings were designated "unaware." These two measures were perfectly correlated. In the ingratiation conditions all subjects said they were more positive in the experimental conditions than in the neutral. Thus awareness in this instance was based on whether the subject felt she had responded to the feedback by creating a more positive image or not. Those who felt they "stressed what she seemed to approve" or "emphasized what seemed to impress her," for example, were

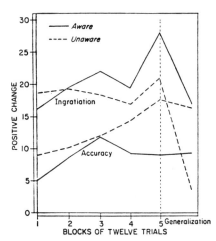

FIG. 2. **Mean positive change for aware and unaware subjects in the reinforced conditions.**

designated "aware." Those who said that the interviewer's remarks had no effect on them were deemed "unaware." Subjects from the personal and impersonal conditions appeared in roughly equal numbers in the four awareness groups.

The positive-change means across the five trial blocks for the four groups are graphically depicted in Figure 2. The findings are of considerable interest. First, in the only group which one could use to test whether learning could take place without awareness, i.e., the unaware-accuracy group, there appears to have been a substantial increase in positiveness. An analysis of variance supports this observation, indicating that the difference between neutral and experimental SVT scores was significant beyond the .001 level. The linear trend was also significant beyond the .005 level. The amount of increase in positiveness demonstrated in the aware-accuracy group as compared with the unaware-accuracy group was not significant ($F < 1.00$). Under reinforced-accuracy conditions, then, unaware subjects demonstrated changes in self-ratings which, if anything, tended to be greater than those found in the aware subjects.

Second, although unaware subjects in the accuracy conditions tended to increase the positiveness of self-ratings to a greater extent than the aware group, in the ingratiation conditions this tendency was *reversed*. Although the total increase in positiveness in the aware-ingratiation condition was not significantly greater than that manifested in the unaware-ingratiation condition, the picture as a whole is one of an interesting interaction: when subjects were told to be accurate, awareness of the fact that they might have been influenced by what the interviewer said seemed to operate against strong shifts in self-ratings. However, when told to make a positive impression, awareness of cue utilization operated in a fashion typical of traditional learning without awareness studies: greater awareness led to greater increments in learning. Although this interaction was not quite significant by the fourth trial block, in the fifth trial block it had reached significance ($p < .05$).

One further finding of interest concerns the relationship between awareness and generalization. As can be seen in Figure 2, under accuracy conditions there seemed to be little relationship between the two. However, in the ingratiation conditions those who were aware of having used the reinforcement to their best advantage maintained a very high level of positiveness after the interview was over: those who said that the interviewer had no effect on their self-ratings dropped back quite substantially. A comparison of the neutral to postexperimental gain in positiveness for the ingratiation-aware group with that found in the unaware group was significant at the .001 level. This finding will receive further attention in the following section.

DISCUSSION

The present study fully supported the contention that social feedback in the form of reflective reinforcement is effective in increasing the positiveness of self-evaluations. The results indicated, however, that the degree of personalism of the agent providing feedback was only minimally related to the amount of increase. The variation in interaction goals produced results by and large in line with predictions. In addition, it was found that the alterations in self-presentation generalized differentially to a subsequent testing period as a function of the conditions producing such changes. Evidence also indicated that self-presentation could be modified without the subject's being aware of such modifications, and that awareness was differentially related to increases in the positiveness of self depending on the goal of the subject in the situation.

Modifying the self-image. The prediction of an increase in the positiveness of self-valuation in the reinforced accuracy conditions was based on the assumption that reflective reinforcement would produce momentary shifts in the subject's feelings about self, and that this enhanced self-image would reflect itself in the subject's public presentation. All the evidence from this experiment was consistent with this supposition. The relevance of this finding to the hypothesis that the self-concept is a result of social learning should be noted. Wylie (1961) has commented that in spite of the importance of this hypothesis, her review of the literature uncovered only two questionable studies which made an explicit connection between the psychology of learning and the development of the self-concept. Although the subjects in this experiment were not necessarily affected in any profound way, the importance of the above findings would not seem to rest on the longevity of the produced effects. Given that the principle is valid, it would follow that with more intense learning experiences more deep-seated effects could be produced.

It was further reasoned, however, that in order to be maximally effective positive feedback should be provided in a personal setting. However, the present study would appear to lend only minimal support to this speculation. In view of the gross differences in procedure and setting between the personal and impersonal conditions, the question arises as to whether subjects in the reinforced accuracy-impersonal condition were manifesting behavior in the interview which resulted from a change in feelings toward self. From all indications the answer would seem to be both "yes" and "no." For one thing, it is known from the ratings of perceived personalism that there were subjects in this condition who failed to see the behavior of the interviewer as impersonal, and these were the subjects who demonstrated the greater increases during the interview.

On the other hand, it has been pointed out that positive feedback in the experiment could also be thought of as serving as a notification to the subject of what the interviewer wanted or expected her to do in the situation. In spite of the admonishment to be accurate during the interview subjects could well have felt that it was simply easier to give in to the pressure of social expectancy. There is at least some evidence that pressures of social expectancy did have a greater effect in the reinforced accuracy-impersonal condition than in the personal condition. First of all, subjects in the impersonal condition, in contrast to those in the personal condition, did not differ from the nonreinforced counterparts in terms of positive increases produced during the generalization period. Second, all subjects were twice asked to rate their degree of sincerity in making their self-ratings, once after the neutral testing session and again after the experimental interview. For both nonreinforced control conditions and the reinforced accuracy-personal condition there was a significant ($p < .05$) increase in the ratings of sincerity, i.e., subjects in all these conditions felt that they were more honest in the experimental procedure than during the neutral testing periods. However, for the reinforced accuracy-impersonal subjects this increase was not found. One is led to speculate that the experimental interview generally caused subjects in the accuracy conditions to feel they were being quite honest *except* in the one condition, the reinforced impersonal, in which subjects felt they were reacting more to social pressures.

Ingratiation and generalization. As indicated above, the effects on self-presentation of the variation in interaction goals were much as anticipated. Subjects in the ingratiation conditions began rating themselves very positively from the initial stages of the interview and continued to do so for the remainder of the interview. However, there was no evidence that subjects in these conditions increased the positiveness of their self-ratings at a more rapid rate than those in the reinforced-accuracy conditions. In view of the extremely positive self-ratings with which the ingratiation subjects began the interview this result is not surprising. An examination of the initial distribution of SVT scores for the entire population of undergraduates tested revealed that the level of positiveness reached by the ingratiation subjects in the first trial block would have been exceeded by only the upper 8% of this population under normal circumstances. It seems clear that the boundaries of credibility were reached much too soon by the ingratiation subjects for the anticipated cumulative increase to manifest itself in response to reinforcement.

Somewhat more intriguing, however, were the results obtained from the ingratiation subjects on the measure of generalization. In terms of positive increase from the neutral testing to the generalization period, subjects in the ingratiation conditions were quite similar to those in the reinforced-accuracy conditions. It seemed, in other words, that some change in covert feelings of self-regard had been produced by the intentional modification of overt self-ratings. Additional information concerning this phenomenon was found in the data on awareness. The ingratiation subjects who were aware of having used the reinforcement provided by the interviewer as cues for modifying their responses, accounted for almost all of the increase in positiveness of self-ratings.

In attempting to account for these results it should be noted that somewhat similar effects have been discussed in the literature on role playing and attitude change. For example, Kelman (1953) and Janis and King (1954) have demonstrated that significant attitude change can be induced by having subjects participate in support of a position towards which they are initially opposed. It is also of importance that these studies have found that the more initiative taken. or the greater the improvisation shown in this participation, the greater the resultant change in attitude. These findings have been explained in two ways. First of all they have been explained in terms of implicit verbal responses which differentially accompany high and low initiative groups. Those who demonstrated more initiative, it was reasoned, thought of many more arguments supporting the side initially opposed and were less hampered by

conflicting thoughts arising from the overt pressures to participate.

Applying this reasoning to the present results, it seems safe to assume that the aware-ingratiation subjects expended more effort in consideration of information which would make a good impression. They seemed to be attuned to the contingencies of the situation and were able to improvise accordingly. On the other hand, the unaware-ingratiation group seemed to respond to the instructions as they would to a flat ultimatum to rate themselves positively. This seems evidenced in the more or less unchanging pattern of responses displayed from the beginning of the interview to its end. It might thus be said that the aware-ingratiation group, in their more vigorous involvement, brought to mind many more positive features of their own personalities. Once out of the interview, they manifested a higher level of positiveness in congruence with their immediately preceding view of the self.

A second interpretation of the effects of role playing on attitude change has been offered by Brehm (1960). Brehm has suggested that subjects in the high initiative groups were committing themselves to a position which was dissonant with their initial attitude. and attitudes were altered in a direction consistent with the commitment in order to reduce dissonance. Although such an explanation would be consistent with the present data, there seems to be no good reason for contending that the ingratiation subjects were in a position which would arouse dissonance. Subjects in these conditions were offered no choice as to whether to be ingratiating or not, and the experimenter's instructions made it clear that falsification of self-ratings was appropriate behavior during the interviewing situations. There would thus seem to be little reason to suppose these subjects felt personally committed to a dissonant position.

These latter findings would seem to have important implications for much everyday behavior. Most of a person's daily activity can be looked at as role behavior. The above results seem to imply that playing out these roles in various social situations may have important reflexive effects on the way a person views himself. Further, it would seem that it is precisely the person who is sensitized to the cues provided by others who is most deeply affected. However, it remains a question as to the amount of change in a person's feelings about self which can be produced in such instances in the absence of social feedback. In addition, it would be interesting to know whether such changes are likely to occur when the role being played is self-deprecating rather than self-enhancing.

REFERENCES

BREHM, J. W. A dissonance analysis of attitude-discrepant behavior. In C. I. Hovland & M. J. Rosenberg (Eds.), *Attitude organization and change*. New Haven: Yale Univer. Press, 1960. Pp. 164–197.

DeCHARMS, R., & ROSENBAUM, M. E. Status variables and matching behavior. *Journal of Personality*, 1960, **4**, 492–502.

DICKOFF, HILDA. Reactions to evaluations by another person as a function of self evaluation and the interaction context. Unpublished doctoral dissertation, Duke University, 1961.

ERIKSEN, C. W. (Ed.) *Behavior and awareness*. Durham: Duke Univer. Press, 1962.

GOFFMAN, E. *The presentation of self in everyday life*. New York: Doubleday, 1959.

JANIS, I. L., & KING, B. The influence of role playing on opinion change. *Journal of Abnormal and Social Psychology*, 1954, **49**, 211–218.

JONES, E. E., GERGEN, K. J., & DAVIS, K. E. Some determinants of reactions to being approved or disapproved as a person. *Psychological Monographs*, 1962, **76**(2, Whole No. 521).

JONES, E. E., GERGEN, K. J., & JONES, R. G. Tactics of ingratiation among leaders and subordinates in a status hierarchy. *Psychological Monographs*, 1963, **77**(3, Whole No. 566).

JONES, E. E., & THIBAUT, J. W. Interaction goals as bases of inference in interpersonal perception. In R. Tagiuri & L. Petrullo (Eds.), *Person perception and interpersonal behavior*. Stanford: Stanford Univer. Press, 1958. Pp. 151–179.

JOURARD, S. M. *The transparent self*. New York: Van Nostrand, 1964.

KELMAN, H. C. Attitude change as a function of response restriction. *Human Relations*, 1953, **6**, 185–214.

LINDQUIST, E. F. *Design and analysis of experiments in psychology and education*. Boston: Houghton Mifflin, 1956.

RAY, W. S. *An introduction to experimental design*. New York: Macmillan, 1960.

WYLIE, RUTH C. *The self concept*. Lincoln: Univer. Nebraska Press, 1961.

(Received September 10, 1963)

[2]

Journal of Personality and Social Psychology
1965, Vol. 2, No. 3, 348–358

OTHERS' SELF-EVALUATIONS AND INTERACTION ANTICIPATION AS DETERMINANTS OF SELF-PRESENTATION [1]

KENNETH J. GERGEN   AND   BARBARA WISHNOV [2]

Harvard University   *Duke University*

Female Ss faced a partner who was either self-centered, self-derogating, or who evaluated herself in an average fashion. ½ of the Ss in each of these groups anticipated further interaction with the partner; ½ expected no further interaction. All Ss then made a number of self-ratings which were to be sent to their partner. As predicted, Ss rating themselves for the self-centered partner became more positive in their self-ratings, and the self-derogating partner caused Ss to emphasize more negative self-characteristics. Contrary to prediction, the average partner caused Ss to emphasize more negative features of self when future interaction was anticipated. Such modifications did not seem to depend on conscious mediation.

The information we present to others about ourselves is seldom selected at random. We constantly face the dilemma of choosing from a vast storehouse of self-knowledge the appropriate items for public display. One of the more crucial periods for such decision making is during the formative stage of a relationship. As Thibaut and Kelley (1959) have pointed out, the fate of any relationship depends to a great extent on the level of outcomes experienced by the respective members during the introductory stages. The present investigation was an attempt to explore the ways in which the attributes of one member of a dyad and the interaction context can modify the self presented by a second member during the initial stages of a relationship.

One principal dimension along which self-referent statements can vary is that of positiveness. The importance of this dimension is well reflected in the abundance of psychological studies using the variable of self-esteem. By far the major portion of the literature on self-esteem has found it convenient to assume relatively stable feelings of self-regard within any individual. Thus many of the studies in this area have been devoted to demonstrating the differential reactions to various situations of persons deemed to be either high or low in self-esteem.

On the other hand, the importance and to some extent the validity of a concept like self-esteem depends largely on the consistency of the overt behavior of the individual. If a person is completely capricious in his expressed feelings of self-regard, any single measure of self-regard would constitute a poor predictive device. And yet, we are all quite aware that persons do indeed vary in what they say about themselves from one situation to another. Many such variations have been discussed by Goffman (1959); others have been more formally exposed in studies like those of Jourard and Lasakow (1958), and Katz (1942). There are two prominent questions which such studies pose: What are the systematic determinants of such variations? Under what circumstances do these overt variations reflect changes in the subjective state of the person? The present study was devoted primarily to shedding light on the former of these questions. In doing so, however, it was hoped that at least some evidence could be generated concerning the latter.

There are a number of studies which have dealt with systematic changes in self-evaluations. Several investigations, for example, have explored the conditions under which success and failure affect a person's evaluations of self (cf. Stotland & Zander, 1958; Videbeck, 1960). From a different vantage point, Jones, Gergen, and Davis (1962) and Jones, Gergen, and Jones (1963) have demonstrated the effects of various interaction goals and status assignments on a person's

[1] This article is based on a thesis submitted by the second author in partial fulfillment for the BA degree with distinction at Duke University.

[2] Now at Brandeis University.

public self-evaluation. In a further study (Gergen, 1965), the effects of social feedback on the positiveness of self-ratings were explored under systematically varied conditions. In this study it was possible to distinguish between those conditions giving rise to public versus private self-evaluations.

However, it also seems apparent that a person's public self-evaluations are highly dependent on personal attributes of others in the same situation. For example, Davis (1962) demonstrated that the degree of interpersonal dominance displayed by one member of a dyad influenced the degree of dominance manifested by the other. In the present study the question was whether one can display the same social identity before another who is seen to be self-centered and egotistical, as before another who is self-effacing or self-demeaning? To shed light on this question subjects were exposed to a person who described herself in a very positive light, revealed both good and bad points, or who was very self-derogating. Each of these situations, it was felt, would pose for subjects a specific kind of problem in impression management (Goffman, 1959) and these problems would be resolved by differential self-evaluations. Before discussing the specific predictions a word must be said about the context of interaction.

The personal attributes of another can seldom be considered in exclusion of the circumstances in which they are encountered. Although there are a number of context factors of relevance in the present case, one of the more intriguing aspects of a social relationship has to do with the participants' perceptions of how long the relationship will last. It has been noted, for example, that when interacting with a stranger a person is often more open and revealing than with a personal friend. Thibaut and Kelley (1959) have termed this the "stranger *passant*" phenomenon and have theorized that in a short-lived relationship the participants are not threatened by problems of dependency. The amount of anticipated interaction would thus seem to have some interesting implications for the present study. The solution to each of the problems mentioned above should be differentially altered as a result of the subjects' perceptions of the duration of the relationship.

We may now turn to a more complete description of the various problems and their probable resolutions. First of all, one major problem for a person finding himself faced with a highly positive other might be termed *power restoration*. Interacting with another who displays an impeccable personality can often be an intimidating experience. Such a person immediately usurps a position of seniority in a dyad and forces the other member into a usually undesirable, low-status position. Given little latitude of behavior, as subjects in the present experiment were, the optimum solution to such a problem would seem to be to counter in kind, that is, to become more positive about oneself. This anticipated self-enhancement should, however, be most dramatic when further interaction is anticipated. When the possibility of future intimidation and dependency is nonexistent, the necessity for redressing a power imbalance should not be as great.

When faced with another who demonstrates that he has at least a number of worthy attributes and enough honesty to admit shortcomings, a different type of problem emerges. It would seem that such a person should cause one to seek out his friendship and the problem can thus be termed one of *acquaintance seeking*. One method of becoming better acquainted in the present experiment would be also to demonstrate both good and bad features of self, that is, "be oneself." However, as Thibaut and Kelley (1959) have suggested, when a long-term relationship is anticipated a person can ill afford to reveal weaknesses. It was thus predicted that subjects would be more positive about themselves when further interaction was anticipated than when no further interaction was expected.

When another is encountered who is self-effacing, still a third problem is generated. The self-derogating other immediately places himself in a position of dependency. The stronger partner in such a dyad is soon faced with the major share of the responsibility for the welfare of the dyad. The weaker member often acts as a parasite, thriving at the expense of the personal resources of the other. The person encountering such another might be said to be faced with the problem of *succorance avoidance*. Before considering the solution to such a problem, it should also be noted that the person who seems to have almost no good qualities often elicits feelings of pity or sympathy. Such feelings greatly complicate the problem of succorance avoidance, for it is usually a very difficult matter to turn a cold shoulder on one who has admitted that you are everything and he is nothing. In such a situation the variation in interaction anticipation should play a very important role. If future dependency is expected, the optimum solution should be to avoid the self-derogating other at all costs. One seemingly effective avoidance tactic would be to emphasize as many differences between yourself and this person as possible. This leads to the prediction that the self-derogating other should cause subjects expecting interaction to become more self-enhancing. However, when the relationship has no future, subjects should be free to express the pity felt for the low self-esteem other. One way of expressing such feelings might be to say, "Don't feel so bad; when you get right down to it none of us are so good." In the present study, such an expression would be manifested in a decreased emphasis on one's positive features.

To summarize, the major predictions of this study can be formally stated as follows:

1. Under conditions of no anticipated interaction, the positiveness of self-presentation will be a linear function of the perceived egotism of the other. A highly positive other will induce self-rating changes in the positive direction and a self-demeaning other will produce changes in the negative direction.

2. Under conditions of anticipated interaction, the positiveness of self-presentation will be a curvilinear function of the other's egotism. A highly positive and highly negative other will elicit positive self-presentation, and the medium other will produce little change.

3. The positiveness of self-presentation under conditions of anticipated interaction will be displaced in a more positive direction than under conditions of no anticipated interaction.

METHOD

Subjects

The subjects were 58 undergraduate females enrolled in an introductory psychology course. During the early stages of the course, all students were required to fill out a self-evaluation measure to be described below. From this initial sample, persons who scored within approximately the upper or lower 15% of the sample were eliminated from further consideration. Of the remaining group, 58 subsequently participated in the experiment. Selection of subjects and assignment to experimental conditions was carried out on a random basis. One subject was excluded from the results because of suspicion of the manipulations and three others were randomly eliminated in order to equalize the cell frequencies.

Self-Evaluation Measure

The 30 items composing the positiveness of self-presentation measure were taken from a measure developed by Dickoff (1961). Each item was in the form of a short self-descriptive phrase, such as "more emotionally mature than average," "inconsiderate of others," etc. Original items had been assigned scale values for their degree of positiveness by a group of independent raters. Fifteen of the items were highly positive and 15 were considered by the raters to represent negative attributes. The instructions required a person to assign any number of points from 0 to 10 to each item according to how representative he felt the item to be of himself. Either a large number of points assigned to positive items or a small number to negative items would thus be indicative of high self-regard.

Experimental Procedure

The experimenter met with groups of 8–10 subjects who were not generally acquainted with each other. He described the experiment as one designed to explore the way in which two people get to know each other. After discussing some remotely related topics, such as, types of status relationships among members of a military hierarchy, subjects were told that they would each be taken to a separate booth. Once in the booth each would communicate in writing to a partner, ostensibly one of the other members of the group, whose identity would be unknown. Such anonymity was said to eliminate the influence of previous acquaintance and to allow a written record of all communications to be obtained.

The subjects were further told that once in the booths, half of them would find a form (the self-evaluation measure and associated questions) on which they were to describe themselves. These descriptions were then to be taken by the experimenter to a partner, a member of the other half of the group. The other half of the group (in actuality, the entire group) were to find magazines in their booths which they could read while waiting. After receiving the communication, the second partner would fill out an identical set of materials which were then to be returned to the first communicator.

Half of the experimental groups were then told that the conditions of anonymity would be broken neither during nor after the communication exchange. Persons in these conditions, in other words, would never get to know the identity of the partner with whom they communicated (no-anticipation condition). The remaining experimental groups were told that they would meet the partner after they had finished the communication exchange. Further, the experimenter expressed his expectation that the various pairs would become much better acquainted with each other during the semester, and that later in the semester they would be asked to participate in additional experimentation together (anticipation condition).

The experimenter then took each subject to a separate soundproof booth, where a new issue of a women's magazine was found. After approximately a 10-minute interval the experimenter brought the stimulus materials to the subjects. There were three different sets of stimulus materials, one of which was delivered to each subject on a random basis. Each set contained the self-evaluation measure and three handwritten paragraphs, ostensibly filled out by actual partners. Regarding the self-evaluation measure, the number of points assigned to items by the partners in the three relevant conditions was based on an assessment of the averages assigned to these items by the initial sample from which subjects were drawn. Whereas the average (medium-positive) partner assigned the same number of points to the items as the average student in the sample, the egotistical (high-positive) other was much more positive than the average and the humble (low-positive) partner differed from the average by the same amount but in the opposite direction. Care was taken that the absolute or total number of points assigned to all items by the fictitious partner was the same for all conditions. In addition, it seemed that high or low numbers of points assigned to a particular item by the partner could introduce unwanted bias. Thus two sets of 15 different numbers, one for positive and one for negative items, were constructed for *each* of the three sets of stimulus materials. Within each of these conditions the sets of numbers were then rotated through the items from subject to subject. Thus each subject received a different number of points on the various items but the total number of points assigned to positive and negative items within any condition remained the same. In order to maintain as much constancy as possible, each particular configuration of digits for each of these conditions appeared twice, once in the anticipation condition and once in the no-anticipation condition.

As noted, in addition to the self-evaluation measure each subject received three paragraphs supposedly written by her partner. These paragraphs were in response to questions concerning high-school or prep-school activities, relationships with peers, and future plans. The content of these paragraphs was also varied for the three partner types. In the high-positive condition, the partner said that she enjoyed high school, got along perfectly with others, and looked forward to the future. The partner in the medium-positive condition, however, felt that she enjoyed high school most of the time, got along with others fairly well, and had at least some doubts about the future. The low-positive partner felt very depressed about her high-school days, her relations with others, and her future. In spite of the differences in feeling tone, the attempt was made to keep various other aspects of the paragraphs as similar as possible. For example, each partner had participated in the very same activities with equal success. In addition, the total number of written words was constant across conditions and all paragraphs were written in the same hand.

After the subjects had an ample opportunity to digest these materials, the experimenter reappeared, bringing with him a fresh set of materials identical to those filled out by the supposed partner. He again reminded each subject that these were to be sent to her partner. After a 10–15 minute interval the experimenter again returned to the booth and picked up the subject's self-ratings and asked her to make a set of ratings of her partner, ratings which the partner was not to see. These ratings were designed to assess the subject's perceptions of the partner. After another 10–15 minute interval, the experimenter again returned and gave the subject an additional questionnaire to fill out. This questionnaire dealt with such matters as the subject's awareness of shifts in self-presentation and other aspects of her behavior in the situation.

Upon completion of the questionnaire each subject was asked to return to the room in which the group had originally met. After all subjects had returned the experimenter attempted to assess suspicion and revealed the rationale behind the experiment. All subjects were asked to cooperate by not divulging the details of the experiment to their classmates.

RESULTS

Validation of the Manipulations

There was good independent evidence that the manipulation of the partner's characteristics was effective. One of the "rating of partner" measures which each subject filled out after communication with her partner consisted of a series of antonyms. Each antonym was separated from its opposite by a 10-point scale, and 4 of the 18 antonyms ("self-centered versus humble," "personally modest versus conceited," etc.) were designed to tap perceived egotism of the partner. Combining each subject's ratings on these

352   KENNETH J. GERGEN AND BARBARA WISHNOV

four items, perceived egotism scores were derived. An analysis of variance revealed that subjects in the high-positive condition saw the partner as significantly ($p < .001$) more egotistical than subjects in the medium-positive condition, and these latter subjects saw their partner as significantly ($p < .001$) more egotistical than those in the low-positive condition.

The validation of interaction anticipation is more difficult to establish. Unfortunately the items on the postexperimental questionnaires could not be used to make a reasonable assessment of the effectiveness of this manipulation. However, in that the major results would be difficult to interpret without assuming that the instructions for the two conditions were perceived differently, it seems safe to assume that the subjects believed what they were told.

Changes in the Positiveness of Self-Presentation

As noted, positiveness of self-presentation was measured with a 30-item scale, of which 15 items were stated in a positive manner and 15 in a negative. Although it might be expected that changes in the number of points assigned to negatively phrased items would be a mirror image of changes found in the positive items, there seemed to be good reason for analyzing the two sets of data separately. For example, the most obvious way a person might indicate that he feels

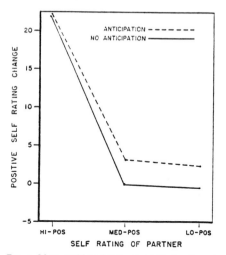

FIG. 1. Mean positive change on positively phrased items for all conditions.

himself to be a "good person" would be to make a direct statement to that effect and assign a large number of points to positive items. However, this same message can be communicated on a more subtle level by saying "I don't feel that I am a bad sort of a person," which would be analogous to assigning a small number of points to negative items. In other words, the two sets of items might be differentially sensitive to varying types of communication.

Positiveness as expressed on positive items. Since the items had been administered twice, once under relatively neutral and once under experimental conditions, the effects of the manipulations could be gauged by comparing the two sets of scores. The group means for change in points assigned to positive items appear in Figure 1. A Type III (Lindquist, 1956) analysis of variance of the neutral and experimental scores is summarized in Table 1.

Turning first to the effects of the various partners on subjects' self-ratings in the no-anticipation conditions, it can be seen that the prediction of a linear relationship is only partially verified. The significant A × B interaction term in the analysis of variance allowed orthogonal comparisons to be made between neutral and experimental scores for

TABLE 1

ANALYSIS OF VARIANCE OF POSITIVENESS AS EXPRESSED
ON POSITIVE ITEMS

Source	df	MS	F
Between subjects	53	338.75	
High, medium, low (B)	2	1,936.15	8.13**
Anticipation versus no anticipation (C)	1	1,365.33	5.73*
B × C	2	562.33	2.36
Error (b)	48	238.18	
Within subjects	54	131.30	
Before-after (A)	1	1,776.33	30.05***
A × B	2	1,220.11	20.64***
A × C	1	10.71	
A × B × C	2	12.70	
Error (w)	48	59.11	

* $p < .05$.
** $p < .01$.
*** $p < .001$.

subjects exposed to the three types of partners. As predicted, subjects interacting with
an egotisical other showed a significant (p
$< .001$) increase in the number of points assigned to positive items. Further, as anticipated, the average partner elicited less positive change than the egotist. An orthogonal
comparison between the experimental-neutral
differences between the two conditions was
significant beyond the .001 level. However,
the low-positive partner failed to elicit any
significant amount of change.

Assessing the changes produced by the
three partners under conditions of anticipated
interaction, it is seen that the curvilinear
prediction was almost verified. The egotist
elicited significant positive change ($p < .001$),
the medium-positive partner elicited significantly less positive change ($p < .01$), and
the humble partner also boosted the positiveness of subjects' self-ratings slightly, though
not significantly.

The prediction that self-presentation would
become more positive under conditions of
anticipated interaction than under conditions where no further interaction was anticipated receives little support from these data.
As can be seen, with each of these partners
the means are in the predicted direction.
However, the lack of a significant A × C
interaction in the analysis of variance indicates that this difference is merely suggestive.

Positiveness as expressed on negative items.
The change means in points assigned to nega-

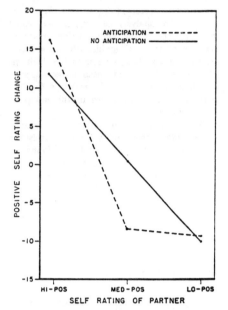

FIG. 2. Mean positive change on negatively phrased
items for all conditions.

tive items appear in Figure 2. As can be
seen, the pattern of change detected with
this measure is appreciably different than
that found using the positive items. Looking
first at the changes found under conditions
of no-anticipated interaction, it is seen that
the hypothesis of a linear relation between
partner's egotism and subject positiveness is
verified. Orthogonal comparisons based on
the analysis of variance summarized in Table
2 indicate that the highly positive partner
produced a significant ($p < .005$) decrease
in the number of points assigned to negative
items, the medium-positive partner had significantly less effect on subjects' self-ratings
($p < .05$), and the humble other produced
a significant ($p < .005$) increase in the
number of points assigned to negative
phrases. This latter increase was also significantly ($p < .05$) different from the change
occurring in the medium-positive condition.

Turning next to self-rating change under
conditions of anticipated interaction, a rather
surprising set of findings emerges. Although
the highly positive other produced a sig-

TABLE 2

ANALYSIS OF VARIANCE OF POSITIVENESS AS EXPRESSED
ON NEGATIVE ITEMS

Source	df	MS	F
Between subjects	53	492.54	
High, medium, low (B)	2	1,956.46	4.67*
Anticipation versus no anticipation (C)	1	1,401.12	3.34
B × C	2	341.45	
Error (b)	48	418.91	
Within subjects	54	99.90	
Before-after (A)	1	7.79	
A × B	2	1,325.39	25.30***
A × C	1	4.89	
A × B × C	2	108.18	2.06
Error (w)	48	52.39	

* $p < .05$.
*** $p < .001$.

nificant ($p < .001$) decrease in the number of points assigned to negative items, the medium-positive partner had exactly the opposite effect. Whereas it was predicted that subjects would become slightly defensive in this condition and thus decrease the number of points assigned to negative items, it was found that there was a significant ($p < .01$) increase. In other words, these subjects gave greater emphasis to their negative characteristics. The low-positive condition furnishes an additional surprise. Although it was predicted that subjects in this condition would decrease the number of points assigned to negative items, it is found that a significant ($p < .01$) *increase* occurred.

Finally, when changes are compared under conditions of anticipated interaction versus no anticipation, it is again found that no significant differences emerge. Although the mean differences are in the expected direction in both the high- and low-positive conditions, Figure 2 reveals that when exposed to the medium partner, subjects tend to become more negative under conditions of anticipated versus no-anticipated interaction. This difference, however, is just shy of reaching statistical significance ($p < .10$).

Self-Presentation and Awareness

The present experiment was based on the assumption that subjects in the various conditions were faced with varying problems of impression management. A secondary concern of this study was with the issue of whether the solutions to such problems are mediated by conscious awareness or are perhaps sufficiently habitual as to take place unconsciously. In order to deal with this question, two measures of awareness were utilized. The first was in the form of a question appearing on the postexperimental questionnaire. The question indicated that no one filled out the answers in the same way each time and asked whether the subject felt she was more or less positive during the communication exchange than she was earlier in the year. It was assumed that a subject who answered in the affirmative was likely to be aware that her self-ratings had been affected in some way by the manipula-

tions. The second measure was derived from the way the subject answered a question appearing first at the end of the neutral testing and again on the postexperimental questionnaire. The question asked was: "To what extent do you feel that the self-rating just completed was *truly* representative of yourself?" and subjects indicated their answers on a 20-point scale. It was felt that any difference in these two ratings would be likely to reflect awareness of shifts in self-ratings from one testing session to the next.

Combining these two measures, each subject was placed into one of three groups. If a subject indicated that she was more or less positive in her self-ratings in the experiment than in the neutral session, and also indicated a difference in feelings of sincerity from one session to the next, she was placed in the high-awareness group. Any subject who demonstrated awareness on one measure but not on the other was placed in the medium-awareness group. Those who showed awareness on neither measure were designated low-awareness subjects. Because some subjects became more positive and others more negative, and because positive and negative items were utilized differentially in the various conditions, the relationship between awareness and change was assessed by converting changes in either direction to absolute change scores. There were 13 subjects in the high-awareness group, 27 in the medium, and 12 in the low-awareness group.

Perhaps the most striking fact revealed by this analysis is that there appears to be virtually no relationship between awareness and amount of change in self-ratings. The mean change for the low-awareness group for both positive and negative items is highly similar to that of both the medium- and high-awareness groups. Statistical analysis of these data revealed no significant differences in absolute change between any awareness groups. In short, there seems to be no evidence that the changes in self-presentation which occurred in this experiment had to be mediated by conscious awareness. At least one implication of these results is that persons can vary markedly in the overt presentation of self and yet feel equally as honest across situations.

DISCUSSION

That a person's public self-evaluations are highly dependent on the way other persons present themselves and on the context in which interaction takes place receives substantial support from the above findings. It seems clear that persons are highly selective concerning the information about self which they provide to others, and that such selection can be systematically explored in a laboratory setting. The task remains, however, of dealing with certain irregularities in the data and of determining the extent to which the above findings can be accounted for by the rationale presented in the introduction.

With regard to the subjects who faced the egotistical other, it was predicted that there would be an increase in the positiveness of self-ratings, and that this increase would be greater when further interaction was anticipated. These predictions were based on a power restoration rationale with the additional specification that when further interaction was anticipated, the need for restoring power would be enhanced. The results fully confirmed the first of these predictions. However, with the exception of the fact that the means were in the expected direction, there was no reliable evidence that the variation in interaction anticipation had any differential effect. It remains a question as to whether such shifts in self-presentation can be attributed to the power restoration rationale. At least one major competing explanation would be that the highly positive other was seen as more attractive and that boosting the attractiveness of one's self-ratings would be a way of ingratiating oneself with this person. There is some evidence bearing on these explanations. First of all it will be recalled that all subjects made a number of ratings of their supposed partner. Conceiving of power as one's ability to drive another person through a range of outcomes (Thibaut & Kelley, 1959), a person who is seen as more powerful would also be seen as less dependent and more self-sufficient. Four antonyms on the rating list, for example, "independent versus dependent," "reliant on others versus self-reliant," had been included to reflect this dimension of perceived dependency. By sum-

ming ratings of the partner on these antonyms, perceived dependency scores were derived for all subjects. The means and standard deviations for the various conditions are contained in Table 3. As can be seen, the highly positive partner was seen as more independent than the partner in either of the remaining conditions. An analysis of variance revealed that the difference between the high- and medium-positive conditions was significant ($p < .001$). Although by no means conclusive, such evidence would at least be consistent with the power restoration rationale.

If the social attractiveness of the highly positive other were the cause of the subjects' self-enhancement, one would expect this also to be reflected in the ratings of the partner. The social attractiveness cluster was formed by antonyms such as "likable versus not particularly likable," "unattractive personality versus attractive personality," etc. The means and standard deviations of the combined social attractiveness scores for the various conditions can also be found in Table 3. There is almost no difference between the means found in the high- and medium-positive conditions. The evidence thus does not seem to indicate that subjects in the high-positive conditions changed their ratings in order to be ingratiating. It should also be noted that one could derive the results in the high-positive conditions from Festinger's (1954) theory of social comparison. These subjects could have simply been attempting to reduce the discrepancy between their own and their partner's self-evaluations. However, this theory would be of little aid in clarifying the total complex of results in the experiment. Findings in both the medium- and low-positive conditions are quite contrary to a social comparison prediction.

Based on a rationale of acquaintance seeking, it was hypothesized that little self-rating change would be produced in the medium-positive condition except when interaction was anticipated. In this latter instance it was predicted that the anticipation group would be more positive than the no-anticipation subjects. The results proved to be highly interesting. With positively phrased items,

KENNETH J. GERGEN AND BARBARA WISHNOV

TABLE 3

MEANS AND STANDARD DEVIATIONS OF PERCEIVED DEPENDENCY AND SOCIAL ATTRACTIVENESS SCORES

	Anticipation		No anticipation	
	Dependency	Social attractiveness	Dependency	Social attractiveness
High-positive				
M	33.33	32.11	33.66	29.22
SD	5.70	3.45	3.67	7.55
Medium-positive				
M	25.11	27.55	25.11	30.00
SD	6.16	5.73	5.75	6.77
Low-positive				
M	14.78	21.78	14.11	26.33
SD	5.78	4.53	5.09	7.73

no significant change in self-ratings was found either within or between groups. However, when the negative items were considered it was found that subjects expecting future interaction became significantly more negative in their self-ratings, whereas subjects who were shielded by anonymity presented essentially the same self-picture as they had at the neutral testing.

This pattern of results raises several issues. First of all, in order to obtain the results which were initially predicted, certain preconditions would have to be established. For example, subjects in the medium-positive no-anticipation condition should have felt least constrained in communicating an honest self-picture. Meeting someone similar to oneself in a relationship with no future, it was felt, would give rise to the feeling of freedom to reveal one's "true self." Evidence bearing on this issue came from questions on the postexperimental questionnaire which dealt with the subjects' feelings of ease in communicating with their partner. On a 7-point scale subjects rated how much their partner "caused me to want to tell her about myself" and how difficult it was to communicate with their partner. On both of these measures subjects in this condition indicated greater ease of communication than subjects in any of the other experimental conditions. A comparison of the mean for this condition with the combined means for the remainder of the conditions was just shy of reaching significance ($p < .10$) for both questions. Given that subjects in this condition did feel fewer constraints in communicating, vis-à-vis the

fact that these subjects were the only ones in the experiment who did not alter their ratings significantly, what conclusion might be drawn? The most likely conclusion would seem to be that subjects' ratings in the neutral or group testing session represented a rather honest self-appraisal (although many have been led to doubt that students give an honest self-picture under such circumstances). Subjects who subsequently found themselves in a situation which allowed honesty, that is, the medium-positive no-anticipation condition, simply repeated the self-ratings made in the earlier circumstance.

The question remains, however, as to why the subjects meeting someone similar to themselves with whom they expected future interaction became more self-derogating. An examination of the possibility that the mean ratings obtained in the neutral situation from these subjects might have differed by chance from the points assigned to these items by the partner revealed no evidence of artifact. Self-evaluation change scores (negative items) were also correlated with each of the ratings of the partner made by subjects in this condition. The only significant correlation emerging was dramatic. Self-rating change in the negative direction in this condition was correlated .66 ($p < .005$) with ratings of the partner on the egotism-humility dimension. In other words, the more self-centered, egotistical, etc., the partner was seen, the more the subjects altered their self-ratings in a negative direction. Furthermore, this correlation is actually in the negative direction, though not significant, in the medium-positive no-anticipation condition.

This finding raises interesting possibilities. First of all it is important to notice that both ends of the egotism rating (see Results section) tend to have a pejorative flavor. A high score would indicate that the partner was seen as self-centered, etc., and a low score would mean that the partner was seen as having feelings of inferiority, etc. It will also be recalled, subjects in the medium-positive condition used neither extreme of the scale in rating their partner. The implication would seem to be that when another person is seen to be neither too self-centered nor too self-derogating, and future interaction is anticipated, the tendency is to *complement* the behavior of this other person. If the other is seen to be rather positive about self, the resulting tendency is to be slightly self-effacing and vice versa. Such a finding raises an interesting question vis-à-vis earlier research showing that dyads in which the members' personalities complement each other tend to be compatible (cf. Schutz, 1958; Winch, 1955). Such studies have generally assumed that complementarity can be determined by an assessment of the pre-established personalities of the prospective members. The present study raises the possibility that when acquaintance seeking is a prominent issue in a dyad, the members may alter their appearance *in order to* complement each other.

In the low-positive conditions, it was reasoned that when no interaction was anticipated, subjects would be free to express sympathy and that such an expression would take the form of self-derogation. However, when interaction is anticipated, avoidance of the relationship would become more salient, and subjects should tend to become more self-enhancing. The findings, however, presented a somewhat more complicated picture. When no further interaction was expected subjects did indeed become more self-derogating on the negatively phrased items. Contrary to expectations, the anticipation-condition subjects demonstrated a similar tendency. On positively phrased items, however, neither group showed any significant change.

Before interpreting this pattern of results,

it is first useful to determine whether the humble partner was felt to be more pitiful, more dependent, and more to be avoided. Data were available concerning all of these dimensions. First of all, subjects were asked to rate on a 7-point scale the degree they felt their partner should be pitied. Subjects interacting with the humble other rated her as significantly ($p < .001$) more to be pitied than subjects dealing with either of the other two partner types. Regarding dependency, it will be recalled that on the perceived dependency measure discussed above (see Table 3) the low-positive partner was seen as most dependent. A comparison of difference between the medium- and low-positive conditions was significant beyond the .001 level. Finally, evidence for avoidance of the self-derogating other would seem to be indicated by the social attractiveness ratings found in Table 3. An analysis of variance revealed that the low-positive partner was seen as less socially attractive ($p < .05$) than either of the other two partner types. It is also the case that for the low-positive conditions attractiveness and dependency are negatively related; this correlation is significant beyond the .05 level in the anticipation condition.

In understanding the results it should first be noted that, as in the high-positive conditions, the manipulation of anticipated interaction produced no significant effects. Considering the extremity of the self-ratings made by the high- and low-positive partners, it seems quite likely that the effectiveness of this manipulation was all but obscured. Since the data in both of the conditions are highly suggestive, a more powerful manipulation of this variable seems in order in further work.

If it is assumed that the two low-positive groups reacted in much the same manner, how might the present results be interpreted? First of all, if the rationale is correct it would seem to be the case that feelings of pity for the partner elicited the increased emphasis of personal shortcomings. Further support for this notion comes from the correlation between self-rating change and ratings of pity. Combining both groups, the correlation is .53 ($p < .025$), indicating that those who saw the partner as more to be pitied revealed more personal shortcomings. One might thus suspect that subjects may have used the negatively phrased items to express pity and the positively phrased items to avoid the partner's dependency. However, the relevant correlation between social attractiveness ratings and change on positive items was in the predicted direction but not significant ($r = -.16$).

It should finally be asked why positively and negatively phrased items should be used differentially, both in these conditions as well as in the medium-positive anticipation condition. At least one explanation would be that the differential usage depends entirely on the fact that the positive items dealt with different content areas than the negatively phrased items. In order to assess whether the experimental effects were dependent on specific item content, a Kuder-Richardson reliability test was conducted on the change scores for both groups of items. The resulting reliability coefficients were within acceptable standards (.85 for positive items and .77 for negative items), and indicate that the effects of the manipulations were general in scope rather than dependent on specific item content.

A more important source of explanation for differential item usage in these conditions would seem to have to do with the subjective meaning attached to the use of positive and negative phrases about the self. In the medium-positive anticipation condition a paraphrase of a subject's thought might be, "I'll show you I'm human by revealing some of my negative attributes, but I will retain my positive characteristics in order to show you that I am attractive." In the low-positive conditions, such a paraphrase might be, "I feel sorry for you so I will show you that I too have difficulties, but I will separate myself from you by showing you that I have many good attributes." In that the results for the two low-positive conditions and the medium-positive anticipation condition were all similar, this approach would suggest an interesting possibility for further research: depending on the social context, similar presentations may be used to communicate quite discrepant information about the self.

REFERENCES

DAVIS, K. E. *Impressions of others and interaction context as determinants of social interaction in two-person discussion groups.* (Doctoral dissertation, Duke University) Ann Arbor, Mich.: University Microfilms, 1962, No. 62-397-398.

DICKOFF, HILDA. *Reactions to evaluations by another person as a function of self-evaluation and the interaction context.* (Doctoral dissertation, Duke University) Ann Arbor, Mich.: University Microfilms, 1961, No. 61-2166.

FESTINGER, L. A theory of social comparison processes. *Human Relations,* 1954, 7, 117–140.

GERGEN, K. J. The effects of interaction goals and personalistic feedback on the presentation of self. *Journal of Personality and Social Psychology,* 1965, 1, 413–424.

GOFFMAN, E. *The presentation of self in everyday life.* New York: Doubleday, 1959.

JONES, E. E., GERGEN, K. J., & DAVIS, K. E. Some determinants of reactions to being approved or disapproved as a person. *Psychological Monographs,* 1962, 76(2, Whole No. 521).

JONES, E. E., GERGEN, K. J., & JONES, R. G. Tactics of ingratiation among leaders and subordinates in a status hierarchy. *Psychological Monographs,* 1963, 77(3, Whole No. 566).

JOURARD, S. M., & LASAKOW, P. Some factors in self-disclosure. *Journal of Abnormal and Social Psychology,* 1958, 56, 91–98.

KATZ, D. Do interviewers bias poll results? *Public Opinion Quarterly,* 1942, 6, 248–268.

LINDQUIST, E. F. *Design and analysis of experiments in psychology and education.* Boston: Houghton Mifflin, 1956.

SCHUTZ, W. C. *FIRO: A three-dimensional theory of interpersonal behavior.* New York: Rinehart, 1958.

STOTLAND, E., & ZANDER, A. Effects of public and private failure on self-evaluation. *Journal of Abnormal and Social Psychology,* 1958, 56, 223–229.

THIBAUT, J. W., & KELLEY, H. H. *The social psychology of groups.* New York: Wiley, 1959.

VIDEBECK, R. Self-conception and the reactions of others. *Sociometry,* 1960, 23, 351–359.

WINCH, R. F. The theory of complementary needs in mate selection: A test of one kind of complementariness. *American Sociological Review,* 1955, 20, 52–56.

(Received March 5, 1964)

[3]

Journal of Personality and Social Psychology
1970, Vol. 16, No. 1, 148–156

SOCIAL COMPARISON, SELF-CONSISTENCY, AND THE CONCEPT OF SELF [1]

STAN MORSE   AND   KENNETH J. GERGEN [2]

University of Michigan   *Swarthmore College*

The social comparison process presents a potential source of instability in self-conception. In this study, job applicants casually encountered a stimulus person whose characteristics were either socially desirable or undesirable. Half the subjects in each of these conditions found the other was competing with them for the same position, and half did not. Preliminary assessments were also made of the subjects' level of self-consistency. The major dependent variable was self-esteem change. As predicted by comparison theory, the socially desirable stimulus person produced a significant decrease in self-esteem, while the undesirable other significantly enhanced subjects' self-estimates. Subjects low in self-consistency were most affected by the presence of the other, while extent of competition had no effect. It was also found that similarity between subject and stimulus person tended to enhance self-esteem, while dissimilarity tended to reduce it.

One assumption which underlies much work on the self-concept is that the individual's picture of himself crystallizes in early childhood and remains relatively stable thereafter. According to the symbolic interactionist position (cf. Cooley, 1902; Mead, 1934), the child learns to see himself as "significant others" in his environment see him, and over time these views become incorporated into a stable view of self. This assumption of stability in self-concept is also supported by clinical observation. Rogers (1961) and Kelly (1955), for example, felt that massive therapeutic efforts are required to produce even slight shifts in how the individual views himself. Armed with such evidence, students of individual differences have felt relatively safe in using variations in self-esteem to predict behavior in a wide range of situations.

In contrast to this view, there is good reason to believe that the categories the individual applies to himself are in a constant state of flux. First, as the person goes through life, the significant others in his environment

may change. Indeed, several studies (cf. Gergen, 1965; Videbeck, 1960) have demonstrated that a person's concept of self at any given moment is dependent on the views others have of him in the situation. It would also seem that self-conception is vitally affected by social comparison. As Festinger (1954) has pointed out, people have a constant need to evaluate their abilities and test the validity of their opinions. Since there are few uniform yardsticks to aid in such evaluations, the person will compare himself with others in order to reach conclusions about himself.

While social comparison theory has generated a considerable amount of research (cf. Latané, 1966), most of it has dealt with the effects of comparison in the evaluation of particular skills and opinions. It also seems clear that people are often concerned with their personal attractiveness and general value as human beings. They may frequently compare themselves with others in their immediate environment (and in the mass media) to judge their own personal worth. Thus, for example, to find oneself disheveled when those around are tastefully dressed may be humiliating. Or, for the typical student to discover that he has obtained the highest score in his class may boost his self-esteem. Rosenberg (1965) reports that high school students from minority ethnic groups have lower self-esteem when living in ethnically mixed neigh-

[1] This research was supported by Grant GS562 from the National Science Foundation to the junior author. The authors would like to thank Elliot Barden, Barbara Cronk, Gerald Gurin, and Alan Philbrook for helping in various ways with this study and the Institute for Social Research, University of Michigan, for providing the facilities.

[2] Requests for reprints should be sent to Kenneth J. Gergen, Department of Psychology, Swarthmore College, Swarthmore, Pennsylvania 19081.

borhoods than when living in homogeneous ones. Likewise Clark and Clark (1939) found that black children attending integrated, northern schools show more self-hatred than those in segregated southern classrooms. In both cases, respondents in the ethnically and racially mixed environments may have had more opportunity to compare themselves with their more affluent and better established neighbors.

Half the subjects in the present study casually encountered an individual whose personal characteristics could be described as socially desirable, while the remaining subjects encountered another whose characteristics were quite the opposite. Based on social comparison theory, it was predicted that the former group would suffer a decrement in generalized self-esteem, while the latter group would experience an increment.

In addition to the personal characteristics of the target, other factors may enhance or mitigate the impact of the comparison process on self-conception. Earlier research has dealt with such factors as the similarity between the person and the target of comparison, the amount of threat in the comparison situation, and subjects' motivation (cf. Latané, 1966). In the present study, attention was directed toward two variables heretofore unexamined. The first resides in the nature of the comparison situation and the second in the personality of the individual.

An individual encounters a large number of others during an average day, and yet it is safe to say that not all of these serve as targets for comparison. One major factor influencing the impact which any one target might have may be called the *utility of comparison*. As Jones and Gerard (1967) have reasoned, the individual engages in social comparison primarily because it is useful for him to do so. The information obtained in some comparison situations is more valuable to a person in assessing his position and planning his behavior than that obtained in other situations. In short, situations vary in the utility of the comparison opportunities they present. A junior executive may be little concerned when he sees a person on a street corner who has all the earmarks of success, but should the same person attend the office party, he

may pay close attention to him and suffer accordingly.

Half the subjects in this study encountered an individual (with either positive or negative characteristics) in a situation where comparison had high utility—one in which they were competing with the other for the same employment opening. The remaining subjects were exposed to the same person in a non-competitive, low-utility setting. Greater self-esteem change was predicted in the former case than in the latter.

In addition to the characteristics of the target of comparison and the utility of comparison, the personality of the individual may also affect the extent to which his self-esteem is altered in such situations. Personality theorists have long recognized that an important determinant of an individual's behavior and psychological adjustment is the extent to which he sees the various components of his self-concept as forming a coherent whole, as being consistent with one another (cf. Erikson, 1946; Lecky, 1945; Rogers, 1961). Gergen and Morse (1967) constructed a scale to assess individual differences along this dimension. They found, for example, that those who showed a high level of perceived inconsistency on this test perceived more disagreement in others' evaluations of them, had more frequently changed their residence, and showed greater maladjustment on subscales of the California Psychological Inventory. The inconsistency scale also predicted extent of dissonance reduction in a replication of the Aronson and Carlsmith (1962) study of performance expectancy. Consistent subjects showed significantly more dissonance reduction (Winer, 1966). This latter finding suggested that persons whose conceptions of self are highly consistent should be *least* susceptible to the effects of social comparison. They should experience greater difficulty in incorporating new and potentially inconsistent information about themselves into their relatively well-ordered and coherent systems of self-conception.

The discussion thus far can be summarized with three hypotheses:

1. The presence of a person perceived to have highly desirable characteristics produces a decrease in self-esteem. If the other's

characteristics are undesirable, self-esteem increases.

2. Both the increment in self-esteem in the former case and the decrement in the latter are greater when the utility of comparison is high rather than low.

3. Both the increment in self-esteem in the former case and the decrement in the latter are greater when the person has an inconsistent self-concept than when he has a consistent one.

Attention was also paid in this study to the degree of difference between the subject's characteristics and those of the target. Festinger (1954) suggested that greater comparison occurs the more similar the two individuals. On the other hand, the greater the difference between the two, the sharper the contrast and the more one's positive (or negative) characteristics are thrown into relief. From this viewpoint, greater self-esteem change seemed likely when the subject and target were dissimilar.

METHOD

The 78 subjects used in this study were male undergraduates at the University of Michigan, assigned randomly to the different experimental conditions. None had actually volunteered to be subjects in an experiment, but had answered an advertisement placed in the campus newspaper and at the student employment office offering two part-time jobs in "personality research." The job paid $3 an hour. When an applicant arrived for his job interview at the University's Institute for Social Research, he was met by a secretary. She seated him at one side of a long table and gave him the job application and a set of self-rating forms to complete. A letter from the project director explained that these forms contained various questionnaires being developed as part of a study of "new ways of selecting people for jobs" and that responses to them would in no way be used to screen current job applicants. These initial forms included the Gergen and Morse (1967) self-consistency scale and half the items from a slightly revised version of the Coopersmith (1959) self-esteem inventory.

Stimulus Persons—Mr. Clean and Mr. Dirty

The secretary could observe the subject through the glass wall of the room in which he was seated. When she saw that he had completed the questionnaires, she entered the office to collect them. She also brought with her "another job applicant" whom she seated opposite the subject, mentioning that she would return shortly with additional forms for the subject to complete.

Half of the subjects found themselves confronted with a person whose personal appearance was highly desirable. He wore a dark suit and appeared well-groomed and self-confident. After he had been seated, he immediately opened an attaché case, pulled out several sharpened pencils, and began to work on his forms diligently. The subject could see that he also had a statistics book, a slide rule, and a copy of a college philosophy text in his case. For descriptive purposes, this stimulus person will be called *Mr. Clean*.

The other half of the subjects were exposed to *Mr. Dirty*, an individual whose appearance was in sharp contrast to Mr. Clean's. He wore a smelly sweatshirt, ripped trousers, no socks, and seemed somewhat dazed by the whole procedure. He placed his worn paperback edition of *The Carpetbaggers* on the table in front of him, and after staring aimlessly around the office for a few seconds, began searching for a pencil, which he finally found on the table. Once he began filling out the application, he would periodically stop, scratch his head, and glance around the office as if looking for guidance. There was absolutely no verbal interaction between the subject and the stimulus person.

Utility of Comparison

The experiment had been designed to create a high-incentive situation for all subjects. It was conducted during the summer when job applicants were much more plentiful than the supply of jobs. The work was relatively attractive, and the pay offered exceeded the going campus rate. It seemed reasonable, then, that if the subject were to encounter another applicant for the same job, face-to-face, he would be inclined to evaluate his prospects by comparing himself with this competitor. Were the other not applying for the same position, the utility of the comparison for the subject would be far less. Thus, when the subject appeared for his interview, the secretary off-handedly asked him whether he was applying for the job in personality research or the one in computer programming. This impressed upon the subject that two different types of jobs were open at the same time. All subjects, of course, replied that they were applying for the position in personality research, the only job for which they had requisite skills. To clarify this distinction between jobs, the personality application had a blue cover containing a sociometric diagram and the computer programming application had a yellow cover with a flow chart on it. Both of these covers were conspicuously taped to the wall next to the table at which the subject sat. When the stimulus person entered with the secretary, half of the subjects in each of the above conditions could clearly see from his application that he was applying for the same position as they (high-utility condition). The remaining subjects could immediately notice that he was applying for an entirely different job (low-utility condition). Subjects could also easily observe that his questionnaire resembled theirs in the first situation, or contained mathematical problems which did not appear on their forms at all in the second.

After 1½ minutes, during which the subject had nothing to do but observe the stimulus person, the secretary returned with the remaining forms. These contained, among other things, the second half of the Coopersmith self-esteem measure. When the subject completed these questionnaires, he left the room, as instructed, and handed them to the secretary. She gave him a final questionnaire to complete, on which appeared a series of rating scales and questions concerning the procedure he had just completed. Among the rating scales were a series of items in semantic differential format which reflected various personal attributes (e.g. confident–anxious, neat–sloppy). The secretary casually asked the subject to use the scales to rate anyone who was present during the assessment procedure. The subject was paid $1.50 for helping with the job selection and was told that he would be notified shortly by mail whether or not he had been chosen for the job. At the completion of the study, two applicants were actually hired—to help analyze the data for the study.

Consistency and Esteem Measures

The Gergen–Morse self-consistency scale was administered prior to the completion of the pretest self-esteem measure. The scale presents the respondent with a list of 17 positive and 17 negative traits and asks him to select those 5 traits from each list which "best describe" him. He next lists these 10 traits down the side and across the bottom of a 10×10 matrix, so that all traits intersect one another. Finally, he rates the degree of "conflict or incompatibility" he perceives between each pair on a 0–5 scale, with 0 indicating that the two traits "don't contradict each other, but tend to go hand in hand or cohere," and a 5 indicating the opposite. The sum of these matrix entries yields a total perceived self-inconsistency score: the higher the score, the greater the level of perceived self-inconsistency. Reliability and validity data for this scale appear in an earlier report (Gergen & Morse, 1967). A median split across all conditions was used to divide the subjects into low- and high-consistency groups.

The Coopersmith inventory has commonly been used to assess what is assumed to be one's basic level of self-esteem. The modified version employed here contained 58 items covering a wide variety of characteristics. Items appear in the form of self-descriptive sentences, such as, "I can make up my mind without too much trouble" and "I'm proud of my work at college so far." Half were administered before the arrival of the stimulus person and half after. On one of these sets of 29 randomly selected items, the respondent checked his agreement or disagreement with each statement on a 6-point Likert scale, ranging from "strongly agree" to "strongly disagree." On the other, he checked one of six boxes going from "almost always true" to "almost never true." The order in which the two sets were used was reversed for half of the subjects in each condition.

In summary, the study has a $2 \times 2 \times 2$ factorial design, with two different types of stimulus persons (Mr. Clean and Mr. Dirty), high and low utility of comparison, and high and low subject self-consistency. Approximately 10 subjects appeared within each of the 8 conditions.

RESULTS

Validation Measures

As will be recalled, the subjects were asked to rate the person who had been present during the testing procedure on a series of semantic differential scales. These ratings showed that Mr. Clean was seen as significantly more handsome, more intellectual, more qualified for the job, stronger, less irresponsible, and less "sloppy" in appearance than Mr. Dirty ($p < .001$, in all cases). In addition, subjects did not see themselves as being more similar to one of the stimulus persons than to the other, as indicated by their ratings of the stimulus person on the "like me–unlike me" dimension. Given the extreme differences in perceived desirability of the stimulus persons, and the fact that each stimulus person was seen by the subjects to differ from them in roughly equal amounts, it is reasonable to conclude that subjects perceived Mr. Clean to be superior to them in certain respects and Mr. Dirty as inferior in these respects.

The utility of comparison manipulation was much less successful. All subjects correctly reported whether the stimulus person had been applying for the same job as they or a different one. However, the variation of his personal appearance was apparently so powerful that it overshadowed the impact of this piece of information. None of the semantic differential ratings reflected significant differences between the competitive (high-utility) and noncompetitive (low-utility) stimulus persons. In fact, on the dimension "competitor-noncompetitor," the only significant difference was produced by variations in the character of the stimulus person. Mr. Clean was seen as significantly more of a competitor than Mr. Dirty ($p < .05$).

High- and low-consistency subjects were not found to differ in their ratings of the stimulus person or the situation. Thus, differences in self-esteem change found for these two groups cannot be attributed to obvious variations in

TABLE 1

MEAN CHANGE IN SELF-ESTEEM

Ss	Mean self-esteem change	
	Mr. Clean	Mr. Dirty
Inconsistent		
High utility	−3.88	2.44
n	8	9
Low utility	−8.20	9.90
n	10	10
Consistent		
High utility	−3.80	2.22
n	10	9
Low utility	−1.89	1.40
n	9	13

how they interpreted their environment and others within it.

Experimental Results

The primary interest of the study was in the effects of the varying conditions on subjects' self-esteem ratings. Mean self-esteem change for each condition is featured in Table 1, and the summary of a four-way analysis of variance comparing prescores versus postscores in self-esteem. in Table 2. As can be seen, the variation in the characteristics of the stimulus person had a pronounced effect on self-esteem ratings. For subjects exposed to Mr. Clean, self-esteem ratings were diminished across varying conditions of utility and consistency. Mr. Dirty produced exactly the opposite effect. Mean

TABLE 2

FOUR-WAY ANALYSIS OF VARIANCE

Source of Variation	df	MS	F
Between Ss	71		
Consistent vs. inconsistent (B)	1	877.77	
High vs. low comparison utility (C)	1	306.24	
Mr. Clean vs. Mr. Dirty (D)	1	34.02	
B × C	1	300.46	
C × D	1	26.71	
B × D	1	64.01	
B × C × D	1	160.43	
Error (b)	63	293.82	
Within Ss	72		
Pre vs. post self-esteem (A)	1	2.24	
A × B	1	4.01	
A × C	1	14.71	
A × D	1	616.56	5.02**
A × B × C	1	14.67	
A × B × D	1	365.99	2.98*
A × C × D	1	111.09	
A × B × C × D	1	53.80	
Error (w)	63	122.82	

* $p < .10$.
** $p < .03$.

change in self-esteem was positive in each of the relevant cells. The analysis of variance [3] in Table 2 indicated that the difference in prepost change between the Mr. Clean and Mr. Dirty conditions was significant beyond the .03 level. Within-conditions comparisons showed that the decrease in self-esteem ratings for subjects encountering Mr. Clean was significant beyond the .05 level, while the increase for those facing Mr. Dirty reached the .07 level. These findings provide sound support for the first of the three hypotheses.

It is also clear from the results that self-esteem change is not uniform across levels of comparison utility and subject self-consistency. In the former case, low utility of comparison appears to contribute heavily to self-esteem change for inconsistent subjects. However, this tendency was reversed for consistent subjects, and neither the main effect for utility of comparison nor its interaction with self-consistency was significant ($F < 1$). Considering that the manipulation of utility of comparison does not seem to have been effective, it is not surprising that this variable failed to account for a significant amount of variance. More is said about this issue in the Discussion section.

However, we cannot rule out the effects of the third variable, self-consistency, in such summary fashion. Self-esteem change for high- versus low-consistency subjects in the Mr. Clean and Mr. Dirty conditions is shown in Figure 1. As can be seen, when exposed to Mr. Clean, high-consistency subjects were less likely than low-consistency subjects to experience a decrement in self-esteem; in the Mr. Dirty condition, they were also less likely to

[3] In order to assess the significance of change within single conditions, pre-post analysis was necessitated. However, because this analysis calls for equal cell frequencies, and the sample sizes for the various cells differed slightly (range 9–13), it was necessary to equalize cell frequencies. A preliminary analysis of prescores across the conditions indicated significant discrepancies between conditions. Thus, in equalizing cell frequencies. subjects were deleted whose prescores most contributed to these discrepancies— regardless of the direction of subsequent change in self-esteem. Mean change by condition remained relatively unaffected by this procedure. and prescore differences were reduced to nonsignificance.

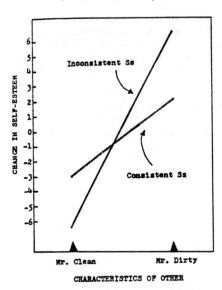

FIG. 1. Changes in self-esteem as a function of characteristics of the other and level of self-consistency.

experience an increment. Although the relevant F ratio did not reach customary standards of statistical significance ($F = 2.98$), the results were in the predicted direction, and the variable did account for a moderate amount of the variance.

Internal analyses of the data support these observations. Inconsistent subjects underwent a significant ($p < .05$) decrease when confronting Mr. Clean and a significant ($p < .05$) increase when exposed to Mr. Dirty. In neither situation did consistent subjects show a significant change in self-esteem. The results thus lend reasonable support to the hypothesized relationship between self-consistency and self-esteem change. Inconsistent subjects were significantly affected by the character of the stimulus person, while consistent subjects were not. Lacking was a significant difference between the two groups.

Similarity of Subject and Stimulus Person

It will be recalled that an additional interest of the study was in the relationship between the similarity of subject and stimulus person and the extent of self-esteem change.

Two measures of similarity were employed. First, the postexperimental questionnaire contained a 7-point rating scale, on which subjects rated the degree of difference they perceived between themselves and the stimulus person. This single rating, however, yielded very low variability in ratings. A more differentiating measure of subject–stimulus person similarity was provided by ratings made of each subject by the secretary. This unbiased and unsophisticated observer independently rated each subject's posture, dress, grooming, manners, overall appearance, speech, and general attitude on a series of a 10-point scale ranging from "very much like Mr. Clean" to "very much like Mr. Dirty." These ratings could then be summed and a mean subject-appearance score derived. Scores did not differ significantly by experimental condition, by level of consistency, or by initial level of self-esteem.[4] Subjects could be divided at the midpoint on this scale into two groups, one evaluated as being more like Mr. Clean, the other more like Mr. Dirty. Approximately half of the subjects in each of these groups had encountered the former stimulus person and half the latter.

Mean self-esteem change for subjects in each similarity group, encountering each stimulus person, appears in Table 3. As can be seen, Mr. Clean elicited the greatest negative change in self-esteem among subjects rated most like Mr. Dirty. Subjects rated as similar to Mr. Clean actually underwent a slight increase in self-esteem. These findings are generally consistent with the notion that a larger self-other discrepancy provides a sharper contrast and thus has greater impact on self-esteem. In the case of Mr. Dirty, however, this reasoning proved unsatisfactory. The results were in the opposite direction. Those subjects rated most like Mr. Dirty experienced an increase in self-esteem, while those dissimilar to him demonstrated a slight

[4] Correlations were carried out within the Mr. Clean and Mr. Dirty conditions between this measure and subjects' single rating of similarity to the stimulus person. Tendencies were found within both conditions for subjects who rated themselves as similar to the stimulus person to have been rated similarly by the observer. However, due to the constricted range of responses in subjects' perceptions, these tendencies were not significant.

154   STANLEY J. MORSE AND KENNETH J. GERGEN

TABLE 3

MEAN SELF-ESTEEM CHANGE AS A FUNCTION OF
RATED SIMILARITY TO STIMULUS PERSON

S's characteristics	Stimulus person	
	Mr. Clean	Mr. Dirty
Resembles Mr. Clean		
$\bar{X}$	3.78	-1.39
n	20	17
Resembles Mr. Dirty		
$\bar{X}$	-10.69	5.13
n	19	22

decrement. A two-way analysis of variance comparing self-esteem change in the four groups yielded an interaction significant beyond the .001 level ($F = 6.32$).

Rather than speculate about separate processes that might be at stake in affecting reactions to Mr. Clean as opposed to Mr. Dirty, it seems more parsimonious to examine possible similarities between the two cases. Specifically, in both situations those subjects rated most like the stimulus person in question underwent an increase in self-esteem; those who were unlike him experienced a decrease. Viewed in this light, the finding is an intriguing one. It suggests that the mere presence of another person who is like oneself may be sufficient to boost one's self-esteem, while a person who is dissimilar may tend to reduce one's self-estimate. When another is seen to be similar to self, he places a stamp of legitimacy on one's conduct or appearance. Interpersonal support of this sort may be particularly important in circumstances, such as those involved here, in which public appraisal is highly salient. Encountering an individual whose characteristics differ from one's own may initiate a process of self-questioning and doubt. We return to this issue shortly.

DISCUSSION

This study indicates that casual exposure to another person is sufficient to produce a marked impact on a person's momentary concept of self. The presence of someone with highly desirable characteristics appears to produce a generalized decrease in level of self-esteem. Exposure to a socially undesirable person produces the opposite effect. These findings are not only consistent with the

proposition that a person may use others to gauge his own self-worth, but extend the range of phenomena to which social comparison theory has been applied. As a result of others' characteristics appearing more desirable or less desirable than his own, a person's generalized self-estimate is displaced downward or upward.

The results raise further questions concerning the long-standing assumption of stability in self-conception. They suggest that rather than possessing a crystallized and enduring identity, a person is subject to momentary fluctuations in self-definition. This view is further supported in studies showing that changes in an individual's presentation of self are often accompanied by subtle shifts in his underlying feelings of who he is within the situation (cf. Gergen, 1965; Gergen & Wishnov, 1965). And yet, it seems unreasonable to abandon completely the assumption of self-concept stability in favor of a view of man as chameleon. An individual probably receives fairly consistent evaluations from others about certain aspects of himself (e.g., sex role), and heterogeneous evaluations concerning others (e.g., his appealingness to others). When such learning experiences are consistent and continuous, a certain degree of stability in self-conception may result. With variability in what is learned about self comes flexibility in feelings of identity from moment to moment. This study demonstrates the ease with which momentary shifts in certain self-conceptions may be brought about for persons at a particular stage in life.

There is much less to be said about the results concerning utility of comparison. Although subjects did discern whether the stimulus person was or was not competing with them for the same job, there is no indication that they felt comparison would be more useful in the competitive as opposed to the noncompetitive situation. One possibility is that their framework for judging competition and, thus, comparison utility, included more than the immediate situation. Subjects may have felt that the noncompetitive stimulus person *could* also apply for the position in personality research, a possibility not specifically ruled out by the procedure. And they may have seen him as a potential competitor for academic marks and other rewards within the university. Finally, as suggested, the personal characteristics of the stimulus person may have been sufficiently demanding that the more subtle effects of utility were obscured. In any case, given the potential importance of this variable, future research might well attempt to test its effects more directly.

The findings concerning self-consistency were not powerful, but they are compatible with the results of previous work in the area and lend further construct validity to the measure. Persons characterized as inconsistent, by virtue of their scale scores, underwent a significant decrease in self-esteem when faced with Mr. Clean, while self-esteem increased significantly in the presence of Mr. Dirty. Consistent subjects were not affected significantly in either condition. It seems quite likely that inconsistent persons, having been subjected to a less homogeneous set of learning experiences related to self (Gergen & Morse, 1967), are more susceptible to situational shifts in feelings of identity. Future work might fruitfully concentrate on fluctuations in, and adaptability of, overt behavior. If the person whose psychological life is dominated by inconsistency is more flexible with respect to self-definition, he might also be more prone to change in outward behavior from one situation to the next.

But nowhere is the need for future research more apparent than in the case of the relationship between interpersonal similarity and self-esteem change. Subjects were subdivided into two groups on the basis of rated similarity between themselves and the two stimulus persons. When subjects were rated as having socially desirable characteristics, their self-esteem was boosted when in the presence of another who shared these characteristics, and was diminished in the presence of one who did not. On the other hand, if the subjects were judged to have undesirable characteristics, they experienced an enhanced state of self-esteem when the undesirable other was present, and a reduced state if not.

One major implication stemming from these findings is that self-esteem may be a unique member of the family of self-assessments to which the comparison process is relevant. In the case of opinions and abilities, comparison effects may be enhanced the more similar the person to the target of comparison. However, in the case of self-esteem, there may be effects over and above those produced by comparison. Superimposed on the comparison effect may be an esteem increment produced by increasing the similarity between the person and the target of comparison.

The findings also have important implications for social attraction. A large number of studies demonstrate a positive relationship between interpersonal similarity and attraction (see Secord & Backman's 1964 review). And it has also been found that people prefer to interact with those whom they perceive to be similar to themselves in attitudes (Newcomb, 1961) and personality (Freedman & Doob, 1968). While balance theory has often been used to explain such findings, the present research suggests an alternative way in which they may be viewed. As indicated, one major reason for an increase in self-esteem in the presence of someone who is similar is that he validates or lends social support to one's manner of being. This increment in self-esteem may be a major intervening mechanism prompting social attraction. Because another is similar, he increases one's esteem for self, and inasmuch as enhanced self-esteem is positively valued, the other may become a target of attraction.

REFERENCES

ARONSON, E., & CARLSMITH, J. M. Performance expectancy as a determinant of actual performance. *Journal of Abnormal and Social Psychology,* 1962, 65, 178–183.

CLARK, K. B., & CLARK, M. P. The development of consciousness of self and the emergence of racial identification in Negro preschool children. *Journal of Social Psychology,* 1939, 10, 591–599.

COOLEY, C. H. *Human nature and the social order.* New York: Scribner's, 1902.

COOPERSMITH, S. A method for determining self-esteem. *Journal of Abnormal and Social Psychology,* 1959, 59, 87–94.

ERIKSON, E. H. *Ego development and historical change, the psychoanalytic study of the child.* New York: International University Press, 1946.

FESTINGER, L. A theory of social comparison processes. *Human Relations,* 1954, 7, 117–140.

FREEDMAN, J. L., & DOOB, A. N. *Deviancy: The psychology of being different.* New York: Academic Press, 1968.

GERGEN, K. J. Interaction goals and personalistic feedback as factors affecting the presentation of self. *Journal of Personality and Social Psychology*, 1965, 1, 413–424.

GERGEN, K. J., & MORSE, S. J. Self-consistency. Measurement and validation. *Proceedings of the 75th Annual Convention of the American Psychological Association*, 1967, 2, 207–208. (Summary)

GERGEN, K. J., & WISHNOV, B. Others' self-evaluations and interaction anticipation as determinants of self-presentation. *Journal of Personality and Social Psychology*, 1965, 2, 348–358.

JONES, E. E., & GERARD, H. B. *Foundations of social psychology*. New York: Wiley, 1967.

KELLY, G. A. *The psychology of personal constructs*. New York: Norton, 1955.

LATANÉ, B. Studies in social comparison. *Journal of Experimental Social Psychology*, 1966, Supplement 1.

LECKY, P. *Self-consistency*. New York: Island Press, 1945.

MEAD, G. H. *Mind, self and society*. Chicago: University of Chicago Press, 1934.

NEWCOMB, T. M. *The acquaintance process*. New York: Holt, Rinehart & Winston, 1961.

ROGERS, C. R. *On becoming a person*. Boston: Houghton Mifflin, 1961.

ROSENBERG, M. *Society and the adolescent self-image*. Princeton, N. J.: Princeton University Press, 1965.

SECORD, P. F., & BACKMAN, C. W. Interpersonal congruency, perceived similarity, and friendship. *Sociometry*, 1964, 27, 115–127.

VIDEBECK, R. Self-conception and the reaction of others. *Sociometry*, 1960, 23, 351–359.

WINER, C. H. Self-perceived consistency and the reduction of dissonance. Unpublished honor's thesis, Harvard University, 1966.

(Received March 13, 1969)

[4]

Deviance in the Dark

by Kenneth J. Gergen, Mary M. Gergen
and William H. Barton

Wanted:
subjects for a psychology experiment.

THE STUDENT SEES THE NOTICE on a bulletin board and on a whim decides to volunteer. He or she learns nothing about the experiment beforehand except that it is about "environmental psychology." He arrives at the appointed hour at an address given over the phone. A man ushers him into an empty room, and leaves him with a series of written tasks to complete. Twenty minutes later, the man reappears and says he is taking the student to a chamber that is absolutely dark. The only light in the chamber will be a pinpoint of red over the door, he says, so the student can find his way out should that be necessary. "You will be left in the chamber for no more than an hour with some other people," the man says. "There are no rules... as to what you should do together. At the end of the time period you will each be escorted from the room alone, and will subsequently depart from the experimental site alone. There will be no opportunity to meet the other participants."

The man asks the student to slip off his or her shoes, empty all pockets and leave whatever he or she is carrying behind. Then he takes the student through a set of double doors into the chamber and leaves him on his own in the pitch black.

Spatial disorientation sets in. Visual contact with the other people is impossible. Perhaps a childhood fear of the dark looms up. The student has no name or face. Conversely, he is freer to project on to others in the chamber the characteristics he chooses. The purpose of this experiment is to find out what the student will do in this environment and what sort of relationships will evolve in this setting. What do people do under conditions of extreme anonymity?

Almost 50 persons participated in our initial exploration. They were between the ages of 18 and 25, and primarily students from colleges and universities in a 10-mile radius of Swarthmore College. They were divided into groups of approximately eight persons, half males and half females. The chamber itself was 10 feet wide and 12 feet long. The floor and walls were padded. The ceiling was above arm's reach.

We tape-recorded all voice communication during each hour's session and used infrared cameras to record how our subjects dispersed themselves around the room. After each hour was over, we asked our subjects to write down their impressions of the experience. We then ran the experiment three more times, but this time we left the lights on. By comparing the behavior of the groups in the darkened chamber with the behavior of groups in the lighted chamber, we hoped to find out what people would do to and with each other when cut away from the normal sanctions governing their lives. Will they try to reestablish life as usual? Or will they willingly forsake the sanctions for another way of interacting?

The logic of our experiment was simple. If it is true, as sociologist Erving Goffman argues, that society channels most of an individual's energy into set patterns as a result of rewards or punishments, then it follows that the behavior of most individuals is routinized. We all come to act in more or less expected ways. During an hour with six or seven strangers in a padded room in the dark, we thought, our subjects would be free from the expectations of friends, family and so on not to act as usual. Even if someone tried to introduce society's norms into the chamber, the dark would make it difficult to reward or punish our subjects appropriately for their behavior. The fact that participants knew they would never meet face to face provided a final guarantee that they could interact the way they wanted to.

The Deafening Silence. The differences in behavior between students in the darkroom and light-room groups proved enlightening. Subjects in the lighted room kept a continuous, focused stream of conversation going from start to finish of the session. In the dark room, talk slacked off dramatically after the first 30 minutes. At one point in a dark-room session that in-cluded a very talkative boy, the conversation had become muted, disjointed, and faltering. Finally, the boy said in a loud voice, "Why isn't anybody talking?" A voice returned the answer softly, "Why don't you shut up?"

Verbal inactivity in the dark chamber, however, was not matched by inactivity at other levels of interaction. Subjects entering the lighted room quickly found a place to sit (seldom closer than three feet to any other subject); and remained seated in the same positions throughout the session. Using photographs, we could predict with better than 90 percent accuracy the individual placement of each subject during the last five minutes of a session from his position during the first five minutes. But in the dark room subjects moved about fluidly. It was difficult to predict with greater than 50 percent accuracy where subjects would be from one five-minute period to the next.

All dark-room participants accidentally touched one another, while less than five percent of the light-room subjects did. More to the point, almost 90 percent of the dark-room participants touched each other on purpose, while almost none of the light-room subjects did. Almost 50 percent of the dark-room participants reported that they hugged another person. Almost 80 percent of the dark-room subjects said they felt sexual excitement, while only 30 percent of the light-room subjects said they did.

The impressions of the hour written by the dark-room subjects give a less cut and dried idea of what went on. "There was tension and nervousness at the beginning," wrote one girl. "A lot of movement. Gradually, a significant change took place. People sat down in smaller groups, a large portion were silent, the darkness no longer bothered me. The last group of us sat closely together, touching, feeling a sense of friendship and loss as a group member left. I left with a feeling that it had been fun and nice. I felt I had made some friends. In fact I missed them."

A boy wrote, "As I was sitting Beth came up and we started to play touchy face and

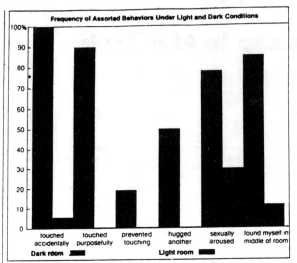

Frequency of Assorted Behaviors Under Light and Dark Conditions

Bar chart with y-axis from 0 to 100%, categories: touched accidentally, touched purposefully, prevented touching, hugged another, sexually aroused, found myself in middle of room. Dark room ■ / Light room ■

touchy body and started to neck. We expressed it as showing 'love' to each other. Shortly before I was taken out, we decided to pass our 'love' on, to share it with other people. So we split up and Laurie took her place. We had just started touchy face and touchy body and kissed a few times before I was tapped to leave."

Another boy wrote, "Felt joy over the possibility of not having to look at people in clichéd ways. Enjoyed feeling of a self-awareness surrounded by a rich environment . . . Enjoyed the wantonness of just crawling around and over other people to get from one place to another." Others wrote they felt more "free" during the session yet more "serious" than normal. The dark-room subjects indicated they were less anxious to be known by others, and less anxious to know the identity of others. With the simple subtraction of light, a group of perfect strangers moved within approximately 30 minutes to a stage of intimacy often not attained in years of normal acquaintanceship.

Intimacy is Natural. The results of these experiments suggested to us that when freed from normative constraints, people at least people between the ages of 18 and 25, develop very immediate and close relations. To check this observation, we joined with Caroline Curtis to run a second set of experiments. We repeated the dark-room sessions with 22 more people, and extended the time in the chamber to an hour and a half. Given the emotional intensity reached in the chamber after 60

minutes, we wanted to see what would happen in 90 minutes.

Our second group of dark-room subjects emulated the behavior of the first group. In the extra 30 minutes, subjects became even more open with each other. Fifteen percent more subjects in the 90-minute sessions said they talked about "important" things. Reports of boredom from the 90-minute subjects dropped by the same percent. In effect, we got the same behavior in the longer sessions that we got in the shorter, but more of it.

We next contrasted the behavior of the three 90-minute groups with three additional 90-minute groups who were told they *would* meet after the session. The purpose was to see what would happen when we reduced the amount of anonymity our subjects could expect, thus increasing the chances that they would be punished or ridiculed for their behavior.

Compared with the subjects who were guaranteed anonymity, the subjects who were told they would be introduced after the session were less likely to explore the chamber, more likely to feel bored, less likely to introduce themselves, less likely to hug, less likely to "feel close to another person," and more likely to feel panicky. By pulling back the cloak of anonymity, we reduced the intensity of relations in the chamber.

The behavior of our subjects in the dark room suggests that we must think anew the question of anonymity. Supposedly, we live in the "Age of Anonymity."

Large-scale accounting systems replace our names with numbers. We use mechanical means to select people impersonally for college entrance, career placement and even marriage. Urban living is so complex that personal idiosyncrasy cannot be tolerated. We are in danger, say the critics, of becoming anonymous creatures with no individual significance.

Psychologists such as Leon Festinger, Albert Pepitone and Philip Zimbardo have added a significant dimension to these ideas. Both laboratory and field studies have demonstrated that when a person is without markers of personal identity, when he or she becomes *deindividuated* in the researchers' terms, the stage is set for increased aggression. Faceless people are more likely to harm each other, a finding with important implications for the high incidence of crime in the anonymous setting of the inner city.

Yet few of our subjects found anything displeasing about the experience of anonymity. Most gained deep enjoyment and volunteered to return without pay. Anonymity itself does not seem to be a social ill. Rather, the state of anonymity seems to encourage whatever potentials are most prominent at the moment—whether for good or for ill. When we are anonymous we are free to be aggressive or to give affection, whichever expresses most fully our feelings at the time. There is liberation in anonymity.

Why did our subjects chose to be so affectionate in the dark room? They were faced with an immense number of alternatives for action, and yet, almost all chose some form of closeness. Were these intimacies based on fear of the unknown threat—an attempt to band together to ward off danger? None of our data support this explanation, and in fact, analysis revealed that those who were most unsettled by the circumstance were least likely to form close relationships. We are struck, instead, by what seemed an essential desire for intimate alliance among our subjects. Of course, our samples were young, and the numbers not large. But it does seem that if the social norms governing our relationships did not keep distance among us—as they did in the case of our light-room subjects—the sharing of intimacy such as in the dark room, would be widespread.

It appears that people share strong yearnings to be close to each other. However, our social norms make it too costly to express these feelings. Our traditions appear to keep us at a distance. Perhaps these traditions have outlived their usefulness. ♫

PART II
PSYCHOLOGY AS HISTORICAL
AND CULTURAL

[5]

Journal of Personality and Social Psychology
1973, Vol. 26, No. 2, 309–320

SOCIAL PSYCHOLOGY AS HISTORY

KENNETH J. GERGEN [1]

Swarthmore College

An analysis of theory and research in social psychology reveals that while methods of research are scientific in character, theories of social behavior are primarily reflections of contemporary history. The dissemination of psychological knowledge modifies the patterns of behavior upon which the knowledge is based. It does so because of the prescriptive bias of psychological theorizing, the liberating effects of knowledge, and the resistance based on common values of freedom and individuality. In addition, theoretical premises are based primarily on acquired dispositions. As the culture changes, such dispositions are altered, and the premises are often invalidated. Several modifications in the scope and methods of social psychology are derived from this analysis.

The field of psychology is typically defined as the science of human behavior, and social psychology as that branch of the science dealing with human interaction. A paramount aim of science is held to be the establishment of general laws through systematic observation. For the social psychologist, such general laws are developed in order to describe and explain social interaction. This traditional view of scientific law is repeated in one form or another in almost all fundamental treatments of the field. In his discussion of explanation in the behavioral sciences, DiRenzo (1966) pointed out that a "complete explanation" in the behavioral sciences "is one that has assumed the invariable status of law [p. 11]." Krech, Crutchfield, and Ballachey (1962) stated that "whether we are interested in social psychology as a basic science or as an applied science, a set of scientific principles is essential [p. 3]." Jones and Gerard (1967) echoed this view in their statement, "Science seeks to understand the factors responsible for stable relationships between events [p. 42]." As Mills (1969) put it, "social psychologists want to discover causal relationships so that they can establish basic principles that will ex-

plain the phenomena of social psychology [p. 412]."

This view of social psychology is, of course, a direct descendent from eighteenth century thought. At that time the physical sciences had produced marked increments in knowledge, and one could view with great optimism the possibility of applying the scientific method to human behavior (Carr, 1963). If general principles of human behavior could be established, it might be possible to reduce social conflict, to do away with problems of mental illness, and to create social conditions of maximal benefit to members of society. As others later hoped, it might even be possible to transform such principles into mathematical form, to develop "a mathematics of human behavior as precise as the mathematics of machines [Russell, 1956, p. 142]."

The marked success of the natural sciences in establishing general principles can importantly be attributed to the general stability of events in the world of nature. The velocity of falling bodies or the compounding of chemical elements, for example, are highly stable events across time. They are events that can be recreated in any laboratory, 50 years ago, today, or 100 years from now. Because they are so stable, broad generalizations can be established with a high degree of confidence, explanations can be empirically tested, and mathematical transformations can be fruitfully developed. If events were unstable, if the velocity of falling bodies or the compounding of chemicals were in continuous flux, the development of the natural sciences

[1] I am much indebted to the following persons for their thoughtful appraisal of various phases of this analysis: Shel Feldman, Mary Gergen, Kenneth Hammond, Louise Kidder, George Levinger, Paul Rosenblatt, Ralph Rosnow, M. Brewster Smith, Siegfried Streufert, Lloyd Strickland, Karl Weick, and Lawrence Wrightsman.

Requests for reprints should be sent to the author, Department of Psychology, Swarthmore College, Swarthmore, Pennsylvania 19080.

would be drastically impeded. General laws would fail to emerge, and the recording of natural events would lend itself primarily to historical analysis. If natural events were capricious, natural science would largely be replaced by natural history.

It is the purpose of this paper to argue that social psychology is primarily an historical inquiry. Unlike the natural sciences, it deals with facts that are largely nonrepeatable and which fluctuate markedly over time. Principles of human interaction cannot readily be developed over time because the facts on which they are based do not generally remain stable. Knowledge cannot accumulate in the usual scientific sense because such knowledge does not generally transcend its historical boundaries. In the following discussion two central lines of argument will be developed in support of this thesis, the first centering on the impact of the science on social behavior and the second on historical change. After examining these arguments, we can focus on alterations in the scope and aims of the field suggested by this analysis.

IMPACT OF SCIENCE ON SOCIAL INTERACTION

As Back (1963) has shown, social science can fruitfully be viewed as a protracted communications system. In the execution of research, the scientist receives messages transmitted by the subject. In raw form, such messages generate only "noise" for the scientist. Scientific theories serve as decoding devices which convert noise to usable information. Although Back has used this model in a number of provocative ways, his analysis is terminated at the point of decoding. This model must be extended beyond the process of gathering and decoding messages. The scientist's task is also that of communicator. If his theories prove to be useful decoding devices, they are communicated to the populace in order that they might also benefit from their utility. Science and society constitute a feedback loop.

This type of feedback from scientist to society has become increasingly widespread during the past decade. Channels of communication have developed at a rapid rate. On the level of higher education, over eight

million students are annually confronted by course offerings in the field of psychology, and within recent years, such offerings have become unexcelled in popularity. The liberal education of today entails familiarity with central ideas in psychology. The mass media have also come to realize the vast public interest in psychology. The news media carefully monitor professional meetings as well as journals of the profession. Magazine publishers have found it profitable to feature the views of psychologists on contemporary behavior patterns, and specialty magazines devoted almost exclusively to psychology now boast readerships totaling over 600,000. When we add to these trends the broad expansion of the soft-cover book market, the increasing governmental demand for knowledge justifying the public underwriting of psychological research, the proliferation of encounter techniques, the establishment of business enterprises huckstering psychology through games and posters, and the increasing reliance placed by major institutions (including business, government, military, and social) on the knowledge of in-house behavioral scientists, one begins to sense the profound degree to which the psychologist is linked in mutual communication with the surrounding culture.

Most psychologists harbor the desire that psychological knowledge will have an impact on the society. Most of us are gratified when such knowledge can be utilized in beneficial ways. Indeed, for many social psychologists, commitment to the field importantly depends on the belief in the social utility of psychological knowledge. However, it is not generally assumed that such utilization will alter the character of causal relations in social interaction. We do expect knowledge of function forms to be utilized in altering behavior, but we do not expect the utilization to affect the subsequent character of the function forms themselves. Our expectations in this case may be quite unfounded. Not only may the application of our principles alter the data on which they are based, but the very development of the principles may invalidate them. Three lines of argument are pertinent, the first stemming from the evaluative bias of psychological research, the second from the liberating effects of knowledge, and the third from prevalent values in the culture.

Prescriptive Bias of Psychological Theory

As scientists of human interaction, we are engaged in a peculiar duality. On the one hand, we value dispassionate comportment in scientific matters. We are well aware of the biasing effects of strong value commitments. On the other hand, as socialized human beings, we harbor numerous values about the nature of social relations. It is the rare social psychologist whose values do not influence the subject of his research, his methods of observation, or the terms of description. In generating knowledge about social interaction, we also communicate our personal values. The recipient of knowledge is thus provided with dual messages: Messages that dispassionately *describe* what appears to be, and those which subtly *prescribe* what is desirable.

This argument is most clearly evident in research on personal dispositions. Most of us would feel insulted if characterized as low in self-esteem, high in approval seeking, cognitively undifferentiated, authoritarian, anal compulsive, field dependent, or close-minded. In part, our reactions reflect our acculturation; one need not be a psychologist to resent such labels. But in part, such reactions are created by the concepts utilized in describing and explaining phenomena. For example, in the preface of *The Authoritarian Personality* (Adorno, Frenkel-Brunswik, Levinson, & Sanford, 1950), readers are informed that "In contrast to the bigot of the older style, (the authoritarian) seems to combine the ideas and skills of a highly industrialized society with irrational or anti-rational beliefs [p. 3]." In discussing the Machiavellian personality, Christie and Geis (1970) noted

Initially our image of the high Mach was a negative one, associated with shadowy and unsavory manipulations. However . . . we found ourselves having a perverse admiration for the high Machs' ability to outdo others in experimental situations [p. 339].

In their prescriptive capacity such communications become agents of social change. On an elementary level, the student of psychology might well wish to exclude from public observation behaviors labeled

by respected scholars as authoritarian, Machiavellian, and so on. The communication of knowledge may thus create homogeneity with respect to behavioral indicators of underlying dispositions. On a more complex level, knowledge of personality correlates may induce behavior to insubstantiate the correlates. Not so strangely, much individual difference research places the professional psychologist in a highly positive light. Thus, the more similar the subject is to the professional in terms of education, socioeconomic background, religion, race, sex, and personal values, the more advantageous his position on psychological tests. Increased education, for example, favors cognitive differentiation (Witkin, Dyk, Faterson, Goodenough, & Karp, 1962), low scores in authoritarianism (Christie & Jahoda, 1954), open-mindedness (Rokeach, 1960), etc. Armed with this information, those persons unflattered by the research might overcompensate in order to dispel the injurious stereotype. For example, women who learn they are more persuasible than men (cf. Janis & Field, 1959) may retaliate, and over time the correlation is invalidated or reversed.

While evaluative biases are easily identified in personality research, they are by no means limited to this area. Most general models of social interaction also contain implicit value judgments. For example, treatises on conformity often treat the conformer as a second-class citizen, a social sheep who foregoes personal conviction to agree with the erroneous opinions of others. Thus, models of social conformity sensitize one to factors that might lead him into socially deplorable actions. In effect, knowledge insulates against the future efficacy of these same factors. Research on attitude change often carries with it these same overtones. Knowing about attitude change flatters one into believing that he has the power to change others; by implication, others are relegated to the status of manipulanda. Thus, theories of attitude change may sensitize one into guarding against factors that could potentially influence him. In the same way, theories of aggression typically condemn the aggressor, models of interpersonal bargaining are disparaging of exploitation, and models of moral development demean those at less than the optimal stage (Kohlberg, 1970). Cognitive dissonance theory (Brehm & Cohen, 1966; Festinger, 1957) might appear to be value free, but most studies in this area have painted the dissonance reducer in most unflattering terms. "How witless" we say, "that people should cheat, make lower scores on tests, change their opinions of others or eat undesirable foods just to maintain consistency."

The critical note underlying these remarks is not inadvertent. It does seem unfortunate that a profession dedicated to the objective and nonpartisan development of knowledge should use this position to propagandize the unwitting recipients of this knowledge. The concepts of the field are seldom value free, and most could be replaced with other concepts carrying far different valuational baggage. Brown (1965) has pointed to the interesting fact that the classic authoritarian personality, so roundly scourged in our own literature, was quite similar to the "J-type personality" (Jaensch, 1938), viewed by the Germans in a highly positive light. That which our literature termed rigidity was viewed as stability in theirs; flexibility and individualism in our literature were seen as flaccidity and eccentricity. Such labeling biases pervade our literature. For example, high self-esteem could be termed egotism; need for social approval could be translated as need for social integration; cognitive differentiation as hair-splitting; creativity as deviance; and internal control as egocentricity. Similarly, if our values were otherwise, social conformity could be viewed as pro-solidarity behavior; attitude change as cognitive adaptation; and the risky shift as the courageous conversion.

Yet, while the propagandizing effects of psychological terminology must be lamented, it is also important to trace their sources. In part the evaluative loading of theoretical terms seems quite intentional. The act of publishing implies the desire to be heard. However, value-free terms have low-interest value for the potential reader, and value-free research rapidly becomes obscure. If obedience were relabeled alpha behavior and not rendered deplorable through associations with Adolph Eichman, public concern would un-

doubtedly be meagre. In addition to capturing the interest of the public and the profession, value-loaded concepts also provide an expressive outlet for the psychologist. I have talked with countless graduate students drawn into psychology out of deep humanistic concern. Within many lies a frustrated poet, philosopher, or humanitarian who finds the scientific method at once a means to expressive ends and an encumbrance to free expression. Resented is the apparent fact that the ticket to open expression through the professional media is a near lifetime in the laboratory. Many wish to share their values directly, unfettered by constant demands for systematic evidence. For them, value-laden concepts compensate for the conservatism usually imparted by these demands. The more established psychologist may indulge himself more directly. Normally, however, we are not inclined to view our personal biases as propagandistic so much as reflecting "basic truths."

While the communication of values through knowledge is to some degree intentional, it is not entirely so. Value commitments are almost inevitable by-products of social existence, and as participants in society we can scarcely dissociate ourselves from these values in pursuing professional ends. In addition, if we rely on the language of the culture for scientific communication, it is difficult to find terms regarding social interaction that are without prescriptive value. We might reduce the implicit prescriptions embedded in our communications if we adopted a wholly technical language. However, even technical language becomes evaluative whenever the science is used as a lever for social change. Perhaps our best option is to maintain as much sensitivity as possible to our biases and to communicate them as openly as possible. Value commitments may be unavoidable, but we can avoid masquerading them as objective reflections of truth.

Knowledge and Behavioral Liberation

It is common research practice in psychology to avoid communicating one's theoretical premises to the subject either before or during the research. Rosenthal's (1966) research indicated that even the most subtle cues of experimenter expectation may alter the behavior of the subject. Naive subjects are thus required by common standards of rigor. The implications of this simple methodological safeguard are of considerable significance. If subjects possess preliminary knowledge as to theoretical premises, we can no longer adequately test our hypotheses. In the same way, if the society is psychologically informed, theories about which it is informed become difficult to test in an uncontaminated way. Herein lies a fundamental difference between the natural and the social sciences. In the former, the scientist cannot typically communicate his knowledge to the subjects of his study such that their behavioral dispositions are modified. In the social sciences such communication can have a vital impact on behavior.

A single example may suffice here. It appears that over a wide variety of conditions, decision-making groups come to make riskier decisions through group discussion (cf. Dion, Baron, & Miller, 1970; Wallach, Kogan, & Bem, 1964). Investigators in this area are quite careful that experimental subjects are not privy to their thinking on this matter. If knowledgeable, subjects might insulate themselves from the effects of group discussion or respond appropriately in order to gain the experimenter's favor. However, should the risky shift become common knowledge, naive subjects would become unobtainable. Members of the culture might consistently compensate for risky tendencies produced by group discussion until such behavior became normative.

As a general surmise, sophistication as to psychological principles liberates one from their behavioral implications. Established principles of behavior become inputs into one's decision making. As Winch (1958) has pointed out, "Since understanding something involves understanding its contradiction, someone who, with understanding, performs X must be capable of envisioning the possibility of doing not X [p. 89]." Psychological principles also sensitize one to influences acting on him and draw attention to certain aspects of the environment and himself. In doing so, one's patterns of behavior may be strongly influenced. As May (1971) has stated more passionately, "Each of us

inherits from society a burden of tendencies which shapes us willy-nilly; but our capacity to be conscious of this fact saves us from being strictly determined [p. 100]." In this way, knowledge about nonverbal signals of stress or relief (Eckman, 1965) enables us to avoid giving off these signals whenever it is useful to do so; knowing that persons in trouble are less likely to be helped when there are large numbers of bystanders (Latané & Darley, 1970) may increase one's desire to offer his services under such conditions; knowing that motivational arousal can influence one's interpretation of events (cf. Jones & Gerard, 1967) may engender caution when arousal is high. In each instance, knowledge increases alternatives to action, and previous patterns of behavior are modified or dissolved.

Escape to Freedom

The historical invalidation of psychological theory can be further traced to commonly observed sentiments within western culture. Of major importance is the general distress people seem to feel at the diminution of their response alternatives. As Fromm (1941) saw it, normal development includes the acquisition of strong motives toward autonomy. Weinstein and Platt (1969) discussed much the same sentiment in terms of "man's wish to be free," and linked this disposition to the developing social structure. Brehm (1966) used this same disposition as the cornerstone of his theory of psychological reactance. The prevalence of this learned value has important implications for the long-term validity of social psychological theory.

Valid theories about social behavior constitute significant implements of social control. To the extent that an individual's behavior is predictable, he places himself in a position of vulnerability. Others can alter environmental conditions or their behavior toward him to obtain maximal rewards at minimal costs to themselves. In the same way that a military strategist lays himself open to defeat when his actions become predictable, an organizational official can be taken advantage of by his inferiors and wives manipulated by errant husbands when their behavior patterns are reliable. Knowledge thus becomes power in the hands of others. It follows that psychological principles pose a potential threat to all those for whom they are germane. Investments in freedom may thus potentiate behavior designed to invalidate the theory. We are satisfied with principles of attitude change until we find them being used in information campaigns dedicated to changing our behavior. At this point, we may feel resentful and react recalcitrantly. The more potent the theory is in predicting behavior, the broader its public dissemination and the more prevalent and resounding the reaction. Thus, strong theories may be subject to more rapid invalidation than weak ones.

The common value of personal freedom is not the only pervasive sentiment affecting the mortality of social psychological theory. In western culture there seems to be heavy value placed on uniqueness or individuality. The broad popularity of both Erikson (1968) and Allport (1965) can be traced in part to their strong support of this value, and recent laboratory research (Fromkin, 1970, 1972) has demonstrated the strength of this value in altering social behavior. Psychological theory, in its nomothetic structure, is insensitive to unique occurrences. Individuals are treated as exemplars of larger classes. A common reaction is that psychological theory is dehumanizing, and as Maslow (1968) has noted, patients harbor a strong resentment at being rubricated or labeled with conventional clinical terms. Similarly, blacks, women, activists, suburbanites, educators, and the elderly have all reacted bitterly to explanations of their behavior. Thus, we may strive to invalidate theories that ensnare us in their impersonal way.

Psychology of Enlightenment Effects

Thus far we have discussed three ways in which social psychology alters the behavior it seeks to study. Before moving to a second set of arguments for the historical dependency of psychological theory, we must deal with an important means of combatting the effects thus far described. To preserve the transhistorical validity of psychological principles, the science could be removed from the public domain and scientific understanding reserved for a selected elite. This elite would, of course, be co-opted by the state, as no government could risk the existence of a private establishment developing tools of public control. For most of us, such a prospect is repugnant, and our inclination instead is to seek a scientific solution to the problem of historical dependency. Such an answer is suggested by much that has been said. If people who are psychologically enlightened react to general principles by contradicting them, conforming to them, ignoring them, and so on, then it should be possible to establish the conditions under which these various reactions will occur. Based on notions of psychological reactance (Brehm, 1966), self-fulfilling prophecies (Merton, 1948), and expectancy effects (Gergen & Taylor, 1969), we might construct a general theory of reactions to theory. A psychology of enlightenment effects should enable us to predict and control the effects of knowledge.

Although a psychology of enlightenment effects seems a promising adjunct to general theories, its utility is seriously limited. Such a psychology can itself be invested with value, increase our behavioral alternatives, and may be resented because of its threats to feelings of autonomy. Thus, a theory that predicts reactions to theory is also susceptible to violation or vindication. A frequent occurrence in parent–child relations illustrates the point. Parents are accustomed to using direct rewards in order to influence the behavior of their children. Over time, children become aware of the adult's premise that the reward will achieve the desired results and become obstinate. The adult may then react with a naive psychology of enlightenment effects and express disinterest in the child's carrying out the activity, again with the intent of achieving the desired ends. The child may respond appropriately but often enough will blurt out some variation of, "you are just saying you don't care because you really want me to do it." In Loevinger's (1959) terms, ". . . a shift in parentmanship is countered by a shift in childmanship [p. 149]." In the popular idiom, this is termed reverse psychology and is often resented. Of course, one could counter with research on reactions to the psychology of enlightenment effects, but it is quickly seen that this exchange of actions and reactions could be extended indefinitely. A psychology of enlightenment effects is subject to the same historical limitations as other theories of social psychology.

PSYCHOLOGICAL THEORY AND CULTURAL CHANGE

The argument against transhistorical laws in social psychology does not solely rest on a consideration of the impact of science on society. A second major line of thought deserves consideration. If we scan the most prominent lines of research during the past decade, we soon realize that the observed regularities, and thus the major theoretical principles, are firmly wedded to historical circumstances. The historical dependency of psychological principles is most notable in areas of focal concern to the public. Social psychologists have been much concerned, for example, with isolating predictors of political activism during the past decade (cf. Mankoff & Flacks, 1971; Soloman & Fishman, 1964). However, as one scans this literature over time, numerous inconsistencies are found. Variables that successfully predicted political activism during the early stages of the Vietnam war are dissimilar to those which successfully predicted activism during later periods. The conclusion seems clear that the factors motivating activism changed over time. Thus, any theory of political activism built from early findings would be invalidated by later findings. Future research on political activism will undoubtedly find still other predictors more useful.

Such alterations in functional relationship are not in principle limited to areas of immediate public concern. For example, Festinger's (1957) theory of social comparison and the extensive line of deductive research (cf. Latané, 1966) are based on the dual assumption that (a) people desire to evaluate themselves accurately, and (b) in order to do so they compare themselves with others. There is scant reason to suspect that such dispositions are genetically determined, and we can easily imagine persons, and indeed societies, for which these assumptions would not hold. Many of our social commentators

are critical of the common tendency to search out others' opinions in defining self and they attempt to change society through their criticism. In effect, the entire line of research appears to depend on a set of learned propensities, propensities that could be altered by time and circumstance.

In the same way, cognitive dissonance theory depends on the assumption that people cannot tolerate contradictory cognitions. The basis of such intolerance does not seem genetically given. There are certainly individuals who feel quite otherwise about such contradictions. Early existentialist writers, for example, celebrated the inconsistent act. Again, we must conclude that the theory is predictive because of the state of learned dispositions existing at the time. Likewise, Schachter's (1959) work on affiliation is subject to the arguments made in the case of social comparison theory. Milgram's (1965) obedience phenomenon is certainly dependent on contemporary attitudes toward authority. In attitude change research, communicator credibility is a potent factor because we have learned to rely on authorities in our culture, and the communicated message becomes dissociated from its source over time (Kelman & Hovland, 1953) because it does not prove useful to us *at present* to retain the association. In conformity research, people conform more to friends than nonfriends (Back, 1951) partly because they have learned that friends punish deviance in contemporary society. Research on causal attribution (cf. Jones, Davis, & Gergen, 1961; Kelley, 1971) depends on the culturally dependent tendency to perceive man as the source of his actions. This tendency can be modified (Hallowell, 1958) and some (Skinner, 1971) have indeed argued that it should be.

Perhaps the primary guarantee that social psychology will never disappear via reduction to physiology is that physiology cannot account for the variations in human behavior over time. People may prefer bright shades of clothing today and grim shades tomorrow; they may value autonomy during this era and dependency during the next. To be sure, varying responses to the environment rely on variations in physiological function. However, physiology can never specify the nature of the stimulus inputs or the response context to which the individual is exposed. It can never account for the continuously shifting patterns of what is considered the good or desirable in society, and thus a range of primary motivational sources for the individual. However, while social psychology is thus insulated from physiological reductionism, its theories are not insulated from historical change.

It is possible to infer from this latter set of arguments a commitment to at least one theory of transhistorical validity. It has been argued that the stability in interaction patterns upon which most of our theories rest is dependent on learned dispositions of limited duration. This implicitly suggests the possibility of a social learning theory transcending historical circumstance. However, such a conclusion is unwarranted. Let us consider, for example, an elementary theory of reinforcement. Few would doubt that most people are responsive to the reward and punishment contingencies in their environment, and it is difficult to envision a time in which this would not be true. Such premises thus seem transhistorically valid, and a primary task of the psychologist might be that of isolating the precise function forms relating patterns of reward and punishment to behavior.

This conclusion suffers on two important counts. Many critics of reinforcement theory have charged that the definition of reward (and punishment) is circular. Reward is typically defined as that which increases the frequency of responding; response increment is defined as that which follows reward. Thus, the theory seems limited to post hoc interpretation. Only when behavior change has occurred can one specify the reinforcer. The most significant rejoinder to this criticism lies in the fact that once rewards and punishments have been inductively established, they gain predictive value. Thus, isolating social approval as a positive reinforcer for human behavior was initially dependent on post hoc observation. However, once established as a reinforcer, social approval proved a successful means of modifying behavior on a predictive basis (cf. Barron, Heckenmueller, & Schultz, 1971; Gewirtz & Baer, 1958).

However, it is also apparent that reinforcers do not remain stable across time. For example, Reisman (1952) has cogently argued that social approval has far more reward value in contemporary society than it did a century ago. And while national pride might have been a potent reinforcer of late adolescent behavior in the 1940's, for contemporary youth such an appeal would probably be aversive. In effect, the essential circularity in reinforcement theory may at any time be reinstigated. As reinforcement value changes, so does the predictive validity of the basic assumption.

Reinforcement theory faces additional historical limitations when we consider its more precise specification. Similar to most other theories of human interaction, the theory is subject to ideological investment. The notion that behavior is wholly governed by external contingency is seen by many as vulgarly demeaning. Knowledge of the theory also enables one to avoid being ensnared by its predictions. As behavior modification therapists are aware, people who are conversant with its theoretical premises can subvert its intended effects with facility. Finally, because the theory has proved so effective in altering the behavior of lower organisms, it becomes particularly threatening to one's investment in autonomy. In fact, most of us would resent another's attempt to shape our behavior through reinforcement techniques and would bend ourselves to confounding the offender's expectations. In sum, the elaboration of reinforcement theory is no less vulnerable to enlightenment effects than other theories of human interaction.

IMPLICATIONS FOR AN HISTORICAL SCIENCE
OF SOCIAL BEHAVIOR

In light of the present arguments, the continued attempt to build general laws of social behavior seems misdirected, and the associated belief that knowledge of social interaction can be accumulated in a manner similar to the natural sciences appears unjustified. In essence, the study of social psychology is primarily an historical undertaking. We are essentially engaged in a systematic account of contemporary affairs. We utilize scientific methodology, but the results are not scientific principles in the traditional sense. In the future, historians may look back to such accounts to achieve a better understanding of life in the present era. However, the psychologists of the future are likely to find little of value in contemporary knowledge. These arguments are not purely academic and are not limited to a simple redefinition of the science. Implied here are significant alterations in the activity of the field. Five such alterations deserve attention.

Toward an Integration of the Pure and Applied

A pervasive prejudice against applied research exists among academic psychologists, a prejudice that is evident in the pure research focus of prestige journals and in the dependency of promotion and tenure on contributions to pure as opposed to applied research. In part, this prejudice is based on the assumption that applied research is of transient value, while it is limited to solving immediate problems, pure research is viewed as contributing to basic and enduring knowledge. From the present standpoint, such grounds for prejudice are not merited. The knowledge that pure research bends itself to establish is also transient; generalizations in the pure research area do not generally endure. To the extent that generalizations from pure research have greater transhistorical validity, they may be reflecting processes of peripheral interest or importance to the functioning of society.

Social psychologists are trained in using tools of conceptual analysis and scientific methodology in explaining human interaction. However, given the sterility of perfecting general principles across time, these tools would seem more productively used in solving problems of immediate importance to the society. This is not to imply that such research must be parochial in scope. One major shortcoming of much applied research is that the terms used to describe and explain are often relatively concrete and specific to the case at hand. While the concrete behavioral acts studied by academic psychologists are often more trivial, the explanatory language is highly general and thus more broadly heuristic. Thus, the present arguments suggest an

intensive focus on contemporary social issues, based on the application of scientific methods and conceptual tools of broad generality.

From Prediction to Sensitization

The central aim of psychology is traditionally viewed as the prediction and control of behavior. From the present standpoint, this aim is misleading and provides little justification for research. Principles of human behavior may have limited predictive value across time, and their very acknowledgment can render them impotent as tools of social control. However, prediction and control need not serve as the cornerstones of the field. Psychological theory can play an exceedingly important role as a sensitizing device. It can enlighten one as to the range of factors potentially influencing behavior under various conditions. Research may also provide some estimate of the importance of these factors at a given time. Whether it be in the domain of public policy or personal relationships, social psychology can sharpen one's sensitivity to subtle influences and pinpoint assumptions about behavior that have not proved useful in the past.

When counsel is sought from the social psychologist regarding likely behavior in any concrete situation, the typical reaction is apology. It must be explained that the field is not sufficiently well developed at present so that reliable predictions can be made. From the present standpoint, such apologies are inappropriate. The field can seldom yield principles from which reliable predictions can be made. Behavior patterns are under constant modification. However, what the field can and should provide is research informing the inquirer of a number of possible occurrences, thus expanding his sensitivities and readying him for more rapid accommodation to environmental change. It can provide conceptual and methodological tools with which more discerning judgments can be made.

Developing Indicators of Psycho-Social Dispositions

Social psychologists evidence a continuous concern with basic psychological processes, that is, processes influencing a wide and varied range of social behavior. Modeling the experimental psychologist's concern with basic processes of color vision, language acquisition, memory, and the like, social psychologists have focused on such processes as cognitive dissonance, aspiration level, and causal attribution. However, there is a profound difference between the processes typically studied in the general experimental and social domains. In the former instance, the processes are often locked into the organism biologically; they are not subject to enlightenment effects and are not dependent on cultural circumstance. In contrast, most of the processes falling in the social domain are dependent on acquired dispositions subject to gross modification over time.

In this light, it is a mistake to consider the processes in social psychology as basic in the natural science sense. Rather, they may largely be considered the psychological counterpart of cultural norms. In the same way a sociologist is concerned with measuring party preferences or patterns of mobility over time, the social psychologist might attend to the changing patterns of psychological dispositions and their relationship to social behavior. If dissonance reduction is an important process, then we should be in a position to measure the prevalence and strength of such a disposition within the society over time and the preferred modes of dissonance reduction existing at any given time. If esteem enhancement appears to influence social interaction, then broad studies of the culture should reveal the extent of the disposition, its strength in various subcultures, and the forms of social behavior with which it is most likely associated at any given time. Although laboratory experiments are well suited to the isolation of particular dispositions, they are poor indicators of the range and significance of the processes in contemporary social life. Much needed are methodologies tapping the prevalence, strength, and form of psychosocial dispositions over time. In effect, a technology of psychologically sensitive social indicators (Bauer, 1969) is required.

Research on Behavioral Stability

Social phenomena may vary considerably in the extent to which they are subject to historical change. Certain phenomena may be closely tied to physiological givens. Schachter's (1970) research on emotional states appears to have a strong physiological basis, as does Hess's (1965) work on affect and pupillary constriction. Although learned dispositions can overcome the strength of some physiological tendencies, such tendencies should tend to reassert themselves over time. Still other physiological propensities may be irreversible. There may also be acquired dispositions that are sufficiently powerful that neither enlightenment nor historical change is likely to have a major impact. People will generally avoid physically painful stimuli, regardless of their sophistication or the current norms. We must think, then, in terms of a *continuum of historical durability*, with phenomena highly susceptible to historical influence at one extreme and the more stable processes at the other.

In this light, much needed are research methods enabling us to discern the relative durability of social phenomena. Cross-cultural methods could be employed in this capacity. Although cross-cultural replication is frought with difficulty, similarity in a given function form across widely divergent cultures would strongly attest to its durability across time. Content analytic techniques might also be employed in examining accounts of earlier historical periods. Until now, such accounts have provided little except quotations indicating that some great thinker presaged a pet hypothesis. We have yet to tap the vast quantities of information regarding interaction patterns in earlier periods. Although enhanced sophistication about behavior patterns across space and time would furnish valuable insights regarding durability, difficult problems present themselves. Some behavior patterns may remain stable until closely scrutinized; others may simply become dysfunctional over time. Man's reliance on a concept of deity has a long history and is found in numerous cultures; however, many are skeptical about the future of this reliance. Assessments of durability would thus have to account for potential as well as actual stability in phenomena.

While research into more durable dispositions is highly valuable, we should not therefore conclude that it is either more useful or desirable than studying passing behavior patterns. The major share of the variance in social behavior is undoubtedly due to historically dependent dispositions, and the challenge of capturing such processes "in flight" and during auspicious periods of history is immense.

Toward an Integrated Social History

It has been maintained that social psychological research is primarily the systematic study of contemporary history. As such, it seems myopic to maintain disciplinary detachment from (a) the traditional study of history and (b) other historically bound sciences (including sociology, political science, and economics). The particular research strategies and sensitivities of the historian could enhance the understanding of social psychology, both past and present. Particularly useful would be the historian's sensitivity to causal sequences across time. Most social psychological research focuses on minute segments of ongoing processes. We have concentrated very little on the function of these segments within their historical context. We have little theory dealing with the interrelation of events over extended periods of time. By the same token, historians could benefit from the more rigorous methodologies employed by the social psychologist as well as his particular sensitivity to psychological variables. However, the study of history, both past and present, should be undertaken in the broadest possible framework. Political, economic, and institutional factors are all necessary inputs to understanding in an integrated way. A concentration on psychology alone provides a distorted understanding of our present condition.

REFERENCES

ADORNO, T. W., FRENKEL-BRUNSWIK, E., LEVINSON, D. J., & SANFORD, R. N. *The authoritarian personality.* New York: Harpers, 1950.
ALLPORT, G. W. *Pattern and growth in personality.* New York: Holt, Rinehart & Winston, 1965.
BACK, K. W. Influence through social communication. *Journal of Abnormal and Social Psychology,* 1951, 46, 9–23.
BACK, K. W. The proper scope of social psychology. *Social Forces,* 1963, 41, 368–376.
BARRON, R., HECKENMUELLER, J., & SCHULTZ, S. Differences in conditionability as a function of race of subject and prior availability of a social reinforcer. *Journal of Personality,* 1971, 39, 94–111.
BAUER, R. (Ed.) *Social indicators.* Cambridge, Mass.: M.I.T. Press, 1969.
BREHM, J. W. *A theory of psychological reactance.* New York: Academic Press, 1966.
BREHM, J. W., & COHEN, A. R. *Explorations in cognitive dissonance.* New York: Wiley, 1966.
BROWN, R. *Social psychology.* Glencoe, Ill.: Free Press, 1965.
CARR, E. H. *What is history?* New York: Knopf, 1963.
CHRISTIE, R., & JAHODA, M. (Eds.) *Studies in the scope and method of "The authoritarian personality."* Glencoe, Ill.: Free Press, 1954.
CROWNE, D. P., & MARLOWE, D. *The approval motive: Studies in evaluative dependence.* New York: Wiley, 1964.
DION, K. L., BARON, R. S., & MILLER, N. Why do groups make riskier decisions than individuals? In L. Berkowitz (Ed.), *Advances in experimental social psychology.* Vol. 5. New York: Academic Press, 1970.
DIRENZO, G. (Ed.) *Concepts, theory and explanation in the behavioral sciences.* New York: Random House, 1966.
ECKMAN, P. Communication through non-verbal behavior: A source of information about an interpersonal relationship. In S. S. Tomkins & C. Izard (Eds.), *Affect, cognition and personality.* New York: Springer, 1965.
ERICKSON, E. Identity and identity diffusion. In C. Gordon & K. J. Gergen (Eds.), *The self in social interaction.* Vol. 1. New York: Wiley, 1968.
FESTINGER, L. *A theory of cognitive dissonance.* Evanston, Ill.: Row, Peterson, 1957.
FROMKIN, H. L. Effects of experimentally aroused feelings of undistinctiveness upon valuation of scarce and novel experiences. *Journal of Personality and Social Psychology,* 1970, 16, 521–529.
FROMKIN, H. L. Feelings of interpersonal undistinctiveness: An unpleasant affective state. *Journal of Experimental Research in Personality,* 1972, in press.
FROMM, E. *Escape from freedom.* New York: Rinehart, 1941.
GERGEN, K. J., & TAYLOR, M. G. Social expectancy and self-presentation in a status hierarchy. *Journal of Experimental and Social Psychology,* 1969, 5, 79–92.
GEWIRTZ, J. L., & BAER, D. M. Deprivation and satiation of social reinforcers as drive conditions. *Journal of Abnormal and Social Psychology,* 1958, 57, 165–172.
HALLOWELL, A. I. Ojibwa metaphysics of being and the perception of persons. In R. Tagiuri & L. Petrullo (Eds.), *Person, perception and interpersonal behavior.* Stanford: Stanford University Press, 1958.
HESS, E. H. Attitude and pupil size. *Scientific American,* 1965, 212, 46–54.
JAENSCH, E. R. *Der Gegentypus.* Leipzig: Barth, 1938.
JANIS, I. L., & FIELD, P. B. Sex differences and personality factors related to persuasibility. In I.

320   KENNETH J. GERGEN

Janis & C. Hovland (Eds.), *Personality and persuasibility.* New Haven: Yale University Press, 1959.

JONES, E. E., DAVIS, K. E., & GERGEN, K. J. Role playing variations and their informational value for person perception. *Journal of Abnormal and Social Psychology,* 1961, 63, 302–310.

JONES, E. E., & GERARD, H. B. *Foundations of social psychology.* New York: Wiley, 1967.

KELLEY, H. H. *Causal schemata and the attribution process.* Morristown, N.J.: General Learning Press, 1971.

KELMAN, H., & HOVLAND, C. "Reinstatement" of the communicator in delayed measurement of opinion change. *Journal of Abnormal and Social Psychology,* 1953, 48, 327–335.

KOHLBERG, L. Stages of moral development as a basis for moral education. In C. Beck & E. Sullivan (Eds.), *Moral education.* Toronto: University of Toronto Press, 1970.

KRECH, D., CRUTCHFIELD, R. S., & BALLACHEY, E. L. *Individual in society.* New York: McGraw-Hill, 1962.

LATANÉ, B. Studies in social comparison—Introduction and overview. *Journal of Experimental Social Psychology,* 1966, 2(Suppl. 1).

LATANÉ, B., & DARLEY, J. *Unresponsive bystander: Why doesn't he help?* New York: Appleton-Century-Crofts, 1970.

LOEVINGER, J. Patterns of parenthood as theories of learning. *Journal of Abnormal and Social Psychology,* 1959, 59, 148–150.

MANKOFF, M., & FLACKS, R. The changing social base of the American student movement. *Journal of the American Academy of Political and Social Science,* 1971, 395, 54–67.

MASLOW, A. H. *Toward a psychology of being.* New York: Van Nostrand-Reinhold, 1968.

MAY, R. Letters to the Editor. *New York Times Magazine,* April 18, 1971, p. 100.

MERTON, R. K. The self-fulfilling prophecy. *Antioch Review,* 1948, 8, 193–210.

MILGRAM, S. Some conditions of obedience and disobedience to authority. In I. D. Steiner & M. Fishbein (Eds.), *Current studies in social psychology.* New York: Holt, Rinehart & Winston, 1965.

MILLS, J. *Experimental social psychology.* New York: Macmillan, 1969.

REISMAN, D. *The lonely crowd.* New Haven: Yale University Press, 1952.

ROKEACH, M. *The open and closed mind.* New York: Basic Books, 1960.

ROSENTHAL, R. *Experimenter effects in behavioral research.* New York: Appleton-Century-Crofts, 1966.

RUSSELL, B. *Our knowledge of the external world.* New York: Menton Books, 1956.

SCHACHTER, S. *The psychology of affiliation.* Stanford: Stanford University Press, 1959.

SCHACHTER, S. The interaction of cognitive and physiological determinants of emotional states. In L. Berkowitz (Ed.), *Advances in experimental social psychology.* Vol. 1. New York: Academic Press, 1970.

SKINNER, B. F. *Beyond freedom and dignity.* New York: Knopf, 1971.

SOLOMAN, F., & FISHMAN, T. R. Youth and peace: A psycho-social study of student peace demonstrators in Washington, D.C. *Journal of Social Issues,* 1964, 20, 54–73.

WALLACH, M. A., KOGAN, N., & BEM, D. J. Diffusion of responsibility and level of risk taking in groups. *Journal of Abnormal and Social Psychology,* 1964, 68, 263–274.

WEINSTEIN, F., & PLATT, G. M. *The wish to be free.* Berkeley: University of California Press, 1969.

WINCH, P. *The idea of a social science and its relation to philosophy.* New York: Humanities Press, 1958.

WITKIN, H. A., DYK, R. B., FATERSON, H. F., GOODENOUGH, D. R., & KARP, S. A. *Psychological differentiation.* New York: Wiley, 1962.

(Received April 17, 1972)

[6]

European Journal of Social Psychology, Vol. 8, 507–527 (1978)

Experimentation in social psychology: A reappraisal*

KENNETH J. GERGEN

Swarthmore College

Abstract

Psychological inquiry into social phenomena has become virtually indistinguishable from controlled experimentation. Although the assets and liabilities of psychological experiments have been subject to periodic debate, a continued increase in the reliance placed on experiments is evidenced. The present paper re-examines the adequacy of experimentation in light of major features of social interaction. Significant failures of the experiment emerge when the following characteristics of social events are considered: their imbeddedness in broader cultural patterns, their position within extended sequences, their open competition within real-life settings, their reliance on psychological confluences, and their complex determination. The additional consideration of social phenomena within historical context indicates that all reasonable hypotheses are valid and that critical testing between hypotheses about social behaviour is fruitless. Criteria for the productive usage of experiments are detailed.

INTRODUCTION

During the past three decades the practice of social psychology has become unmistakably identified with the experimental method. For many this development has been welcomed and much effort has been devoted to sustaining its hegemony. In contrast to the earlier methodologies of social psychologists, the merits of the experi-

*This article is based on an invited address to Division 8 at the 1975 meetings of the American Psychological Association in Chicago, Illinois. I wish to thank Curt Banks, Michael Basseches, Donald Campbell, Uriel Foa, Mary Gergen, Robert Helmreich, Clyde Hendricks, Ian Lubek, Serge Moscovici, Franz Samelson, Paul Secord, Philip Shaver, Siegfried Streufert, Karl Weick, and Ricardo Zuniga for their valuable commentary on an earlier draft of this paper. Special appreciation is also expressed to Robert Pages for making the facilities of the Laboratoire de Psychologie Sociale, Université de Paris VII, available for completing the final manuscript.

Requests for reprints should be sent to Kenneth J. Gergen, Department of Psychology, Swarthmore College, Swarthmore, Pennsylvania, 19081.

0046-2772/78/0408-0507$01.00

Received 2 March 1977
Revised 17 July 1978

mental approach have been readily apparent. Through experimentation one could move from sheer speculation to the level of empirically grounded theory. No longer was it necessary to rely on the wholly unreliable accounts of a single observer, nor was the scientist fettered by correlational techniques and their shaky grasp of causal sequence. Through experimentation, it seemed possible to test ideas against reality and to accumulate a repository of fundamental knowledge. Inroads could also be made into the control of social phenomena. In addition experimentation ensured that social psychologists could lay claim to the respectability increasingly enjoyed by their colleagues in the more traditional areas of psychology (e.g. sensory, learning, and physiological). Social psychology could finally link itself securely with the logical positivist orientation to scientific conduct (Koch, 1959).

The results of this line of development are widely apparent. The percentage of experimental studies appearing in the *Journal of Personality and Social Psychology*, the most prestigious voice in the field, increased from approximately 30 per cent in 1949 to 83 per cent in 1959, and then to 87 per cent in 1969 (Higbee and Wells, 1972). The *Journal of Experimental Social Psychology* and the *European Journal of Social Psychology* are commonly viewed as competitors in respectability. Their contributions are almost entirely experimental. Even in the more peripheral journals such as the *Journal of Research in Personality* and the newer *Journal of Applied Social Psychology*, the vast majority of the present contributions rely on experimentation. Simulation methodologies are rarely employed in these journals; survey research is almost exclusively limited to the field of sociology and political science (Fried, Gumper and Allen, 1973); and in Weick's (1968) review of observational methodology in social psychology, only 15 per cent of the 300 references are taken from the four major journals of the field and less than half of this group from the five year period prior to publication of the review. The one elite organization within the field is aptly named the *Society for Experimental Social Psychology*. Within psychology the pursuit of social understanding has become virtually synonymous with the experimental method.

Criticisms of the experimental approach have emerged over the years. Classic is Orne's (1962) discussion of demand characteristics within the laboratory setting. Closely related is Rosenthal's (1966) extensive research on experimenter bias. However, the primary effect of this work has been to enhance experimental rigor. Numerous critics have called attention to the artificiality of the laboratory setting and to our inability to generalize from laboratory experiments to conventional settings (Kelman, 1972; McGuire, 1967; Tajfel, 1972; Harré and Secord, 1972; Bickman and Henchey, 1972). Such criticisms have given rise to a plethora of experiments in field settings, but as McGuire (1973) has argued the field experiment has operated as a 'tactical evasion' of more basic problems. The ethical suppositions and implications of experimentation have also been seriously questioned (cf. Kelman, 1968) and Jourard and Kormann (1968) as well as Harré and Secord (1972) have argued that experimentation is limited to the study of superficial and highly defensive relationships among virtual strangers. Hampden-Turner (1970) has further taken experimental research to task for the misleading picture it paints of human motives and action. Yet, in spite of the emerging doubts, the experimental tradition has continued unabated. To be sure, greater sensitivity to potential biases and to ethical improprieties has been generated. And doubting graduate students may have paused fitfully before pushing on with an experimental thesis that would ensure passage to a secure professional niche. However, with the lack of convincing alternatives to experimentation, in combination with immense institutional inertia, business has continued more or less as usual.

Perhaps it is futile to raise the tattered colors and once again lay seige to the bastion of tradition. Yet, in light of the crisis-like atmosphere currently pervading the field (cf. Israel and Tajfel, 1972; Armistead, 1974; Elms, 1975), the moment may be propitious for a reassessment of the enterprise. While a recounting of the earlier criticisms does not seem particularly fruitful, renewed perspective may be gained by evaluating the experimental paradigm against the crucible of social life as commonly observed. That is, when paramount features of social existence are brought into focus, what increment in understanding may we anticipate in the employment of the experimental paradigm? Is experimentation an adequate means of generating knowledge of ongoing social behaviour? Our initial concern will be with the distinct features of the experimental method. We shall then turn to a consideration of experimentation within the range of techniques commonly used to test hypotheses about the relationship among variables. Our concern in this case will be with the utility of hypothesis testing within the context of historical change. The concluding section of the paper will elaborate on the specific ends which experimentation might effectively serve. Experimentation may be an invaluable technique under certain circumscribed conditions. However, the continued presumption that experimentation is the single best means by which we can attain knowledge of social behaviour seems both mistaken and of injurious consequence to the field and to those who look to the profession for enhancement of understanding.

EXPERIMENTATION IN CONTEMPORARY CONTEXT

Our initial task is to determine the sensitivity of the experiment to major features of social life. To what extent does experimental knowledge accurately map the contours of contemporary conduct? This question presumes, of course, that one has a preliminary grasp of the major aspects of such conduct. Unfortunately no such assurances can be provided. However, our ability to survive in the contemporary world does suggest that we are not wholly ignorant on such matters, and that as an initial approximation it would not be unwise to make use of an explicated form of common knowledge. The present treatment will be selective, and it is possible that an alternative treatment of social life might yield a more satisfactory appraisal of experimental knowledge. However, should such an account emerge, special effort must be given to discrediting the following lines of argument.

Social events as culturally imbedded

Common observation informs us that behavioural events typically occur within and are intimately related to a highly complex network of contingencies. That is, few stimulus events considered independently have the capacity to elicit predictable social behavior; our response to most stimuli seems to depend on a host of attendant circumstances. For example, a clenched fist has little inherent stimulus value. Responses to the fist alone would be extremely varied and difficult to predict. However, as we add additional features to the situation response variability is typically decreased. When we know the age, sex, economic, marital, educational, and ethnic characteristics of the person whose fist is in question, when we know about what others are present in the situation, the surrounding physical circumstances, and the events preceding the raising of the fist, we are able more accurately to predict responses to the stimulus. In another sense we may say that it is only by taking into account the range of attendant circumstances that the stimulus gains 'meaning' for members of the culture. If the fist is that of a child of three in response to his mother's admonishment in the privacy of their own home, the response has far different social significance than if the fist is that of a thirty year old Puerto Rican on a street in Spanish Harlem. In effect, social stimuli are typically imbedded in broader circumstances, and reactions to the stimulus complex depend importantly on the cultural meanings which they evoke.

The experimental method is not fundamentally incapable of capturing the effects of complex stimulus configurations. However, in this case one must distinguish between the method and its ideological framework. While the method itself may permit the manipulation of complex sets of events, the ideological orientation currently pervading the discipline strongly favors rigor over reality. That is, the ideal experimenter delimits his or her concerns to independently delineated variables. The rigorous experiment is one which 'disimbeds' the stimulus from its surroundings, and examines its independent effects on a given behaviour. One may examine the effects of noise level on helping, jury size on the harshness of the verdict, communicator credibility on attitude change, the presence of weapons on aggression, and so on. To the extent that a particular stimulus may be decomposed into more discrete units, the research may be denigrated and further studies mounted in an attempt to form a more precise statement regarding necessary and sufficient conditions. For example, if crowding is one's independent variable, and crowds tend to generate a higher noise level and greater heat, the rigorous experimenter will attempt to control these latter factors. Crowding is thus disimbedded so that its effects may be ascertained independent of noise level, heat and other 'extraneous' factors. Although the logic of this practice is compelling, profound difficulties emerge as a result.

The initial difficulty is no stranger to the social psychological literature and need not be belabored (cf. Tajfel, 1972; McGuire, 1973). In the attempt to isolate a given stimulus from the complex in which it is normally imbedded, its meaning within the normative cultural framework is often obscured or destroyed. When subjects are exposed to an event out of its normal context they may be forced into reactions that are unique to the situation and have little or no relationship to their behaviour in the normal setting. In more dramatic terms, Harré (1974) has termed the experimentalist, 'tragically deceived' and has concluded that 'experiments are largely worthless, except as descriptions of the odd way people carry on in trying to make social sense of the impoverished environment of laboratories.' (p. 146).

In addition to this unsettling problem, a concern with the imbedded character of social events raises additional issues of equal significance. Within the current ideological framework, the formulation of an hypothesis concerning the relationship between two or more isolated variables (along with an explanatory rationale) is sufficient grounds for mounting an empirical test. If we believe communicator credibility, forced compliance, or crowding influence a given behaviour, and we can develop a theoretical rationale for such effects, we may immediately submit our ideas to the crucible of experimental test. However, in the facile employment of experiments to test isolated relationships among variables, account is seldom taken of the actual circumstances surrounding the manipulation of the stimulus, circumstances which may be essential to its effects. In spite of the fact that the experimental ideology encourages the investigator to think of variables in isolated form, the experiment itself provides a context in which the stimulus is actually imbedded and which may play an integral role in determining its effects. In testing communicator credibility effects, for example, one typically insures that the subject must attend to the message and is not angered by doing so, that the message is relevant to the subject's realm of interest or knowledge and does not personally offend him, that the subject is in no way threatened by the presence (or absence) of the communicator, and so on. Such circumstances are wholly obscured in the concentration on the disimbedded stimulus, and yet may be absolutely essential to the effects of communicator credibility. What passes for knowledge within the discipline may thus rest on an immense number of unstated assumptions and obscured conditions. Knowledge, in the form of independent statements of relationship among variables, may be wholly misleading.

To extend the argument further, in the attempt to isolate particular variables for experimental test, an aggressive insensitivity to limiting or boundary conditions is invited. Consideration of a stimulus as it may be imbedded in various circumstances typically reveals that it may evoke a wide range of reactions depending on the character of these circumstances. Thus, if a broad analysis were to be made of wide-ranging cultural circumstances, the investigator would typically find numerous negations of his or her hypothesis. The preliminary location of such negations would eliminate the need for test of the initial hypothesis. To take only one example, Brehm and his colleagues (cf. Brehm, 1966; Wicklund, 1974) have carried out an extended set of experiments attempting to demonstrate that people in general react negatively to reductions in their freedom, and under such conditions strive to re-establish their initial set of behaviour options. In concentrating on the pure test of the simple reactance hypothesis, preliminary attention to the broad cultural patterns in which such tendencies may be enmeshed was disregarded. Yet, there are numerous instances in which people have readily relinquished their freedom and have pressed toward increasing controls over their own behaviour (cf. Müller, 1963; Weinstein and Platt, 1969). If research had commenced with a careful consideration of the cultural circumstances in which its occurrences are imbedded, it is unlikely that experimental tests of the general reactance hypothesis would have been conducted.

It might be countered that the success of the experimental demonstration is sufficient grounds to justify the effort. It is appropriate to rely on the results of the 'general test' until further experimental evidence contradicts the initial assumption. This rebuttal has little merit. At the outset it would be a myopic and self-deceived science that failed to admit evidence collected on less than experimental grounds. More importantly, the success of the 'general test' is not obstructed by countervening circumstance because in the subtle and unspoken decisions concerning the choice of experimental context, the content of the situation and measures employed, such deterrents can be obscured. In this sense, hypotheses are not so much tested as the experimenter searches for (or is aware of) the appropriate social context in which the validity of what is purported to be a general hypothesis can be demonstrated. As McGuire (1973) has put it, we have learned to be 'finders of situations in which our hypotheses can be demonstrated as tautologically true' (p. 449). If one were to commence with a consideration of the extended culture and its patterned complexity, testing unbridled hypotheses about general reactions to cognitive dissonance,

512   *Kenneth J. Gergen*

imbalance, group pressures, social attraction, bystanders in an emergency, inequity, aggression and so on would seldom occur.

Social events as sequentially imbedded

In addition to its linkages to the broader social context at any given time, most social events appear as integral parts of sequences occurring over time. The exchange of smiles at a first meeting is of a far different character than that occurring after a bitter fight, primarily because the sequence in which an event is imbedded is of utmost importance in understanding its social significance. In effect, the major parameters of relevance to any given behaviour are likely to depend on where it falls within a given sequence. Let us consider the experimental sequence within this light.

In the application of fundamental standards of rigor, the experimentalist attempts to ensure that variations in the dependent variables can be traced unequivocally to variations in one or more independent variables, each of which can be isolated independently or considered in combination with others. Normally this entails limiting oneself to very brief behavioural sequences, as the greater the interval separating the manipulation of the independent variable and the assessment of the dependent variable, the greater the difficulty in interpreting one's data. As the period intervening between the onset of the stimulus conditions and the assessment of the effects is increased, the number of uncontrolled processes or extraneous factors that can intrude to cloud the chain of causality responsible for the results is also increased. For this same reason most research in social psychology takes pains to ensure that after exposure to the major manipulation subjects do not speak with anyone whose behaviour is not standardized. It is partly out of the same interest in rigor that the psychology of group process has floundered so during the past two decades (cf. Steiner, 1974), and well-trained social psychologists often avoid research on programs of social change. In both cases it has proved impossible to accurately trace causal connections among variables.

With such intensive concentration on brief sequences, extended patterns of social interaction are virtually non-existent in the social psychological literature. In spite of the immense importance of such phenomena, our texts have almost nothing to say about the social psychology of family relationships, the development of intimacy, professionalism, career trajectories, the aging process, or the development of extended negotiations or armed conflict.[1] All would require an analysis of interaction patterns across extended periods. In the same way, experimentation too often commits itself to the dangerous assumption that initial reactions to a given stimulus are valid predictors of reactions to the same stimulus on subsequent occasions. For example, an immense amount of experimental research has shown that increases in similarity produce increases in attraction (cf. Clore and Baldridge, 1968; Byrne, 1969, 1971; Lamberth and Craig, 1970). In the interests of ruling out extraneous variables almost all of this research has utilized a stranger's attitude protocol as stimulus. Yet, as Kirckhoff and Davis (1962) have shown, similarity may have little predictive value at later points in a relationship. In the same way our reactions to another's inconsistency, inequity, positive regard, opinion statements, non-verbal cues, or leadership

---

[1] Refreshing exceptions to the general case do exist. Both Levinger and Snoek (1972) and Altman and Taylor (1973) have developed models of growth in intimacy and Osgood's (1962) GRIT model for reducing international tensions has fruitful implications for problems of sequence.

tendencies may be far different when encountered for the first time in a brief relationship than when imbedded in long-term interaction sequences. Because long-term relationships embody numerous confounds, 'late-stage' phenomena are not amenable to precise experimentation and thus may vanish from consideration.

Social events as openly competitive

We have already seen that the function form relating any two variables may be highly dependent on the specific context in which the variables are examined. Over and above this problem, it may be ventured that the magnitude of response produced by a given stimulus depends importantly on the array of simultaneously occurring stimuli. In particular, the potency of any given stimulus to elicit a response (either at a psychological or behavioural level) is clearly related to the potency of its competitors at that moment. Thus, for example, whether a male's smile elicits a similar response in the female likely depends on what other factors demand psychological engagement. If an infant is crying or a jealous lover is looking on, the smile may have little effect. Let us consider the psychological experiment in light of this self-evident surmise.

Experimentation is primarily designed to assess whether or not a given variable has *any* discernible effects on a specified behaviour. However, because of the isolated circumstances of the normal experiment, we are left ignorant concerning the power of any independent variable in comparison with its competitors in the normal circumstances of daily life. For example, in spite of the several hundred dissonance experiments, it is not at all clear what importance dissonance reduction has in contemporary society. Given the immense amount of inconsistency to which people seem generally exposed each day, it is possible that the psychology of dissonance reduction is primarily limited to the more intellectually prone college student who cannot otherwise escape its presence in the experiment. Or, as Lubek[2] has suggested, dissonance may only be a problem for the privileged class, those able to afford the luxury of an ordered world in which their decisions are important in controlling their destiny. In broader terms, the experimentalist may have little to say concerning the major problems of the day, and what he does have to offer may be grossly misleading.

Several counter arguments to this thesis may be posed and each deserves attention. First, it may be ventured that experiments enable us to plot the relationship between a specified set of variables, independent of competing circumstances. In effect, they allow us to glimpse the *pure* relationship between the variables, uncontaminated by competing factors. Unfortunately this argument proves of little merit. For one, if social psychology is to be concerned with normally recurring patterns of social behaviour, then concentrating on behaviour in the uncontaminated setting is of little predictive value. If our essential task is that of understanding behaviour in naturally contaminated settings, it is not clear that findings in the pure condition will prove generalizable. Cronbach's (1975) discussion of the inability of experimenters to export basic 'laws' of perception and learning from the laboratory into the real world should be sufficiently sobering.

In addition to our inability to generalize from the 'pure' case, the argument that the traditional experiment provides an uncontaminated estimate of a variable's effects is ill-considered at the outset. Experimental settings are also composed of a complex

[2]Personal communication from Ian Lubek.

514   *Kenneth J. Gergen*

variable array, and those affects which do emerge in any given experiment are inextricably linked to the particular character of this array. Research on experimenter effects in psychological research (cf. Rosenthal & Rosnow, 1969) has already informed us of the immense influence of the experimenter on research findings. We are now well aware that we cannot discuss experimental results as if the experimenter were absent from the scene. However, this research only scratches the surface. Experimental results may also depend on the fact that the research is conducted within the trusted confines of the university, that the aim of research is scientific knowledge, that the circumstances are short-lived and non-recurring, that one will not be held responsible for his or her behaviour once outside the confines of the experiment, and so on. A unique composite of stimulus features is apparent within any given experiment, and in no way can the effects of a given variable be demonstrated independent of such supporting conditions.

Field experiments provide one important palliative for this condition. In such circumstances the independent variable must compete on the open market place. However, this singular advantage of the field experiment does not compensate for the other substantial problems with which we are here concerned.

Social events as final common pathways

If our attempt is to understand social life as it naturally occurs, we must further be sensitive to the confounded psychological basis of most social acts. It seems clear that social events are typically influenced by a number of simultaneously occurring psychological factors. In this sense, any given social act may be viewed as 'the final common pathway' for a confluence of interacting psychological states. To return to our simple case, the male's smile may evoke simultaneous feelings of excitement, sensual pleasure, anxiety, and repulsion in the female. The response evoked by the smile will depend on the confluence of these various psychological states.

If this surmise is accurate, severe problems emerge. For the experimentalist, understanding behaviour requires a delineation of both the independent and interactive effects of isolated antecedents. The chief advantage of the experiment is that it purportedly allows for a precise tracing of causal sequence, from the antecedent stimuli through the intervening processes to the behaviour of interest. The promise primarily hinges on the capacity of the experimenter to single out specific variables and manipulate them independently while all other factors are either controlled or held constant. Unfortunately, this promise relies on the assumption that discrete events in the 'real' world are linked in one-to-one fashion with particulate experiences or processes internal to the organism. The guiding ideal is possibly Weberian in origin, in which the relationship between variations in a given stimulus are mapped to alterations in experience via a mathematical formulation (Weber, 1834). The experimentalist seldom approximates this goal, of course, and typically we settle for establishing two (and sometimes three) points along a stimulus continuum of unknown parameters. In this way we attempt to create states of high and low dissonance arousal, fear, communicator credibility, crowding, perceived intentionality, self-esteem, task effort and so on. Or, in the more rudimentary case, we compare the individual's behaviour when alone versus with others, when explanations are available for his actions or not, and so on.

This approach seems quite reasonable until we begin to examine the typical trajectory of research interests in the field. In the normal case initial hypotheses linking conceptually distinct variables are proposed and experimental results almost uncannily provide support for the propositions. Dissonance arousal is said to result in X, crowding in Y, and group discussion in Z. Once the formulation gains interest the argument is invariably made that the initial manipulation of independent variables did not properly alter the specific internal mechanism, state or process. The dissonance manipulation in reality manipulated self-observation, the crowding manipulation inadvertently altered the ambient temperature, and the group discussion engendered riskier decisions for a variety of compounded reasons. The alternative explanations are explored and support is again forthcoming; further critics note the impurity of these manipulations and attempt further purifications; successful alternatives are discovered, and over time the battle for explanatory prominence becomes, in Bem and McConnell's (1971) words, just 'a matter of taste'.

One major conclusion suggested by this common pattern is that wherever precise manipulation is paramount, the research enterprise is destined for the shoals of ennui.. In dealing with human beings in a social setting it is virtually impossible to manipulate any variable at the psychological level in isolation of all others. Even the most elemental variations in an independent variable have the capacity to elicit a host of intervening reactions. While increasing shock is often used to increase fear, it may also affect generalized arousal, hostility toward the experimenter, feelings of obligation, desire for escape, desire for nurturance, and a host of other factors. Similarly, increasing the amount of material reward, often used to manipulate motivation, may alter feelings of generalized arousal, sentiments toward the experimenter, desire to please the experimenter, feelings of obligation toward the experimenter, relief, and so on. In addition to all the reactions specific to a given stimulus, additional confounds stem from the self-reflexive capacities of the human subject. At all times the subject may remove himself from the immediate press of events to conceptualize himself as a respondent. A person's reactions to the cognition of his own being in the situation may depend on a host of additional factors, including personal values, self-estimate, philosophical predilections and so on. In sum, it is virtually impossible to manipulate any variable in simple degree or amount. *Real world variations in quantity inevitably become psychological variations in quality.* The assumption that experiments allow precise tracing of causal sequence dwindles into whimsy.

Social events as complexly determined

The preceding argument depended on the acceptance of psychological constructs into one's theoretical network. Of course, we need not do so. Reasonably reliable theories can be developed without recourse to intervening variables. We may develop a theory of attitude change which includes communicator credibility, one-sided vs. two-sided communication, and recency and primacy as predictor variables, for example, without reference to underlying psychological processes. From this standpoint, we might anticipate the development of theories composed of a wide variety of predictor variables which account for both the independent and interactive effects of these variables on the behaviour in question. Attitude change research in the Hovland tradition, in fact, begins to approximate this end. So too does the spate of research on help-giving in emergencies. Based on the available literature one can begin to construct a model in which such factors as the number of bystanders, the character-

516   *Kenneth J. Gergen*

istics of the victim, the salience of the helping norm, the sex of the bystander, and so on are all taken into account as they combine to determine helping behaviour in any given situation. Such an approach is demanded by the common observation that behaviour in most situations is determined not by one factor but by a complex set of interrelated factors.

From this perspective, the psychological experiment proves highly problematic. In social psychology, experiments employing more than three or four independent variables are very rare. Because of the extreme difficulties in experimental execution, location of large samples and interpretation of results, few investigators venture into the wilderness of multi-factor manipulation.[3] As Thorngate (1976) has shown, even with our increased sophistication in experimental technique, the size of multi-factor experimental designs has leveled off during the past five years. Even if optimistic in our estimate of expansion over the next decade, it is difficult to imagine experimental designs employing more than six independent variables. These pragmatic limits in experimental design place significant restrictions over our capacity to generate knowledge via this means. Several of these limitations have been extensively discussed by Thorngate (1976). As he points out, experiments place an upper limit on the number and types of function forms which can be used to capture events in nature. If the state of nature is sufficiently complex that high order interactions among variables are most prevalent, knowledge accumulated through experimentation will always remain a crude approximation to its subject matter. This also means that highly complex explanations (involving large numbers of variables) cannot adequately be tested through experimental means. The explanation might be tested piece-meal, but never would the investigator be able to explore all possible interactions within the design.[4]

Such pragmatic limitations become especially onerous in light of arguments emerging from other areas of the field. As McGuire has pointed out in his 1968 review of attitude research, the number of factors operating to enhance or impede change is immense, and the potential interactions among these factors truly formidable. Mischel (1973) has reached a similar conclusion in his discussion of personality and social behaviour. Likewise, Cronbach (1975) has shown how the delimitation of variables in experimentation conceals higher order interactions which contribute to bloated main effects, erroneous lower order interactions, and null effects where true effects actually exist.

In general it may be ventured that the search for higher order interactions is presumed by the serious application of the experimental method. In order to accumulate knowledge in the experimental tradition, the solid demonstration of a main effect is ample reason to commence searching for factors that enhance, reduce or reverse the effect. The demonstration of first order interaction is sufficient to trigger

---

[3] Not the least of these difficulties is insuring that each independent variable can be manipulated with just enough efficacy that subjects are aware of it, but not so much that it will obscure the effects of variables competing for attention. In addition, with multiple variables it is very likely that manipulation cannot occur independently; variations in one variable often interact with variations in others, thus raising extremely difficult problems of interpretation.

[4] Various research designs (e.g., Latin squares, latticed designs, multivariate analysis of variance) can be used to off-set the difficulties of large numbers of variables. However, none of these alternatives fully alleviates the problems described here. Cronbach's (1975) words provide the most onerous warning. "Once we attend to interactions, we enter a hall of mirrors that extends to infinity. However far we carry our analysis – to third order or fifth order or any other – untested interactions of still higher order can be envisioned."

a search for second order interactions, and so on. However, because of pragmatic limitations it is clear that the attempt to construct understanding in this way rapidly reaches an upper limit.

In sum, we find that in significant degree the social psychological experiment is interposed between the investigator and the phenomena he or she hopes to understand. Rather than elucidating the phenomena the experiment more often serves as a fun house mirror in which reality is served up in distorted or ludicrous form. Such need not be the case, and later we shall consider several potential solutions to these dilemmas. Such indulgence must be postponed, however, for consideration of an additional issue of some importance. The argument in this case concerns not only the experiment, but the more general attempt to accumulate social knowledge via the hypothetico-deductive process.

EXPERIMENTATION IN HISTORICAL CONTEXT

In the main, social psychology is concerned with the exploration of the lawful aspects of interpersonal behaviour. However, it is also clear that the lawful properties of human relations are subject to continuous modification (Gergen, 1973). Thus, laws or principles of social behaviour developed and supported at one point in time do not necessarily retain their validity. To the extent that natural, social, or subjective circumstances are altered, empirical findings may fluctuate. Theoretical statements resting on such a shifting data base may thus be of circumscribed validity across time. When we view the common practice of testing hypotheses in this perspective, fundamental difficulties emerge. Such difficulties are relevant not only to the experimental method, but to the entire range of techniques utilized for purposes of hypothesis testing. In light of existing controversy over this general line of thinking (cf. Schlenker, 1974; Manis, 1975; Cronbach, 1975), careful elaboration of the problem is required.

To elucidate, let us consider a more or less established principle in contemporary social psychology, one for which there is immense experimental support and for which the claims of transhistorical validity could most convincingly be made. This proposition, found in virtually all the major texts of the field, is that attraction toward another is a positive function of O's similarity to P. At least 50 separate studies now support this general proposition (cf. discussions by Newcomb, 1961; Byrne, 1971; Berscheid and Walster, 1969). To be sure, there are conditions under which such results fail to emerge or may be reversed (cf. Mettee and Wilkins, 1972; Senn, 1971; Taylor and Mettee, 1971; Novak and Lerner, 1968), but few could doubt that over wide-ranging social and behavioural conditions, similarity does breed attraction.

For purposes of analysis let us further break the proposition down into independent, intervening and dependent variables and consider each in more detail. In the case of the independent variable, interpersonal similarity, it is initially clear that there may be many different types of similarity, and that not all types may have the same relationship with attraction. At a minumum, one might wish to distinguish between similarity in opinions and in personality. Most of the data supporting the general proposition have indeed been generated in the former area, and doubts have been cast about the generality of the proposition in the latter case (cf. Lipetz, *et al.*, 1970). However, for purposes of inquiry, further distinctions may be useful between political opinions and those concerning values and morality. There may also be a virtual infinity of personality dimensions, along with innumerable differences in

518   *Kenneth J. Gergen*

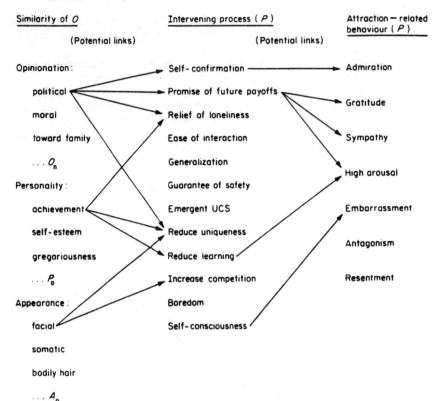

Figure 1.   Elaboration of the Similarity-Attraction Proposition*

physical appearance along which one may be judged similar or dissimilar. For convenience, these distinctions are portrayed in graphic form in Figure 1.

Let us further expand the model to consider a range of intervening variables or processes that might link one or more types of similarity with resulting attraction. For one, another's similarity provides confirmation of one's own perceptions or beliefs; it may also suggest that the other will provide positive payoffs on further occasions; another's similarity can also relieve feelings of isolation or loneliness, or it may ease the course of interaction and thus make one feel more comfortable with the other. Another's similarity may also guarantee one's safety (criticisms are unlikely), or one may be attracted to a similar other as a by-product of attraction to self (the similar other being closer to self on a generalization gradient). Similarity may also function as a secondary stimulus within the classical conditioning paradigm and simply lend itself to attraction on an automatic basis. All of these intervening mechanisms have been added to Figure 1.

However, such an analysis would be altogether biased without considering as well a number of processes that might engender a *negative* relationship between similarity

* Entries in each category are intended as examples, and not to be exhaustive. Virtually all linkages are possible between entities.

and attraction. For example, as Fromkin has shown in a number of studies (1970, 1972) there may be a prevalent desire for uniqueness, such that the presence of someone who is similar could evoke a negative reaction. Another's similarity might further imply a constricted set of learning experiences; if the other is similar to self then one can learn little that is new. The presence of a similar other might also suggest stronger competition for scarce resources, or engender self-consciousness, a state that Duval and Wickland (1972) contend is negative in character. Finally, a similar other may simply be more boring. Each of these various processes or tendencies should also be taken into account (See Figure 1).

In turning to the dependent variable, social attraction, analytic differentiation is also required. There is little reason to suspect that feelings of admiration, sympathy, gratitude and so on all operate in the same way (Marlowe and Gergen, 1968). Thus, we might wish to consider the relationship between varying types of similarity and varying qualities of attraction. For example, we might admire another whose qualities were the same as our own, feel anticipatory gratitude for the rewards we expect to receive from them, or feel increased sympathy with their positive disposition (Stotland, 1969). By the same token, we might experience a low level of general arousal in anticipation of reduced learning, or an embarrassed antagonism in the case enhanced self-consciousness. The formulation in Figure 1 reflects these minimal distinctions.

Having glimpsed a variety of distinctions that may all bear on the validity of the general similarity-attraction proposition we can consider the types of alteration we may anticipate as a function of changes in the social, physical or subjective context over time. Three types of alteration are of cardinal significance:

1. Alterations in entity frequency

Each entity in each sector of our model is subject to variations in its frequency of occurrence in society. For example, whether strong political opinionation is present in a culture depends on the historical climate. Where democracy prevails and differing parties compete for scarce positions, political opinionation may be highly prevalent; at other times or in other places poltical opinionation may play a very modest role in social life. In the same way, whether strong needs for self-esteem or uniqueness exist is also primarily a matter of whether the society provides the necessary learning experiences. For example in traditional Japanese culture needs for uniqueness did not seem to prevail among the common people (Benedict, 1946). Similarly, desires for uniqueness may change in our own society as patterns of family life are altered and the society becomes more or less homogeneous. Likewise, feelings of empathy, admiration, boredom and so on may also fluctuate in their relevance over time. Principles of behaviour developed at one point in time may thus be irrelevant at later periods in history. There may simply be no particulars for which the general principle holds true.

2. Alterations in independent-intervening variable bonds.

More importantly, we find that the articulation between the independent variables and intervening processes is subject to fluctuation over time. Whether a given type of similarity elicits feelings of self-esteem, whether it promises rewards for the future, whether it bodes ill for one's desire for stimulation or information, all seem highly dependent on the prevailing context of experience. Certainly there is little reason to suspect genetically preferred connections between varying types of similarity and varying types of internal processes. From this standpoint it is clear that virtually any type of similarity has the capacity to elicit, trigger or stimulate any type of intervening process. As indicated by the arrows in Figure 1, depending on the learning experiences of the individual, prevalent beliefs or values, or structural constraints, political similarity could have strong consequences for self-esteem, or none at all. It could also indicate the likelihood of future rewards or it could play into one's needs for uniqueness. All such bonds are reasonable and variations in the type and strength of the various bonds can well be expected within any given culture.

3. Alterations in intervening-dependent variable bonds

In the same way that marked variation may be anticipated between independent and intervening variables, the relationships between intervening processes and dependent variables are also subject to the vicissitudes of history. For example, in the case of the linkage between anticipation of positive payoffs and gratitude, it is not at all clear that one's reaction will be positive. Gratitude is not always enhanced when one expects to be showered with positive outcomes; indeed, gifts, aid or help can often evoke hostility (Gergen and Gergen, 1971). In cultures such as Japan such reactions to gifts may be exceedingly complex (cf. Befu, 1966; Benedict, 1946). Similarly one may feel a lack of gratitude for another who has boosted his esteem; many people within our own culture view esteem enhancement as synonymous with pride or egotism. Uniqueness may not always be a congenial state as well, and there may be important historical periods (e.g. during World War II in the U.S.) in which finding oneself in a unique political position could be extremely threatening. In sum, a myriad of differing connections between internal process and resulting effect are both reasonable and probable. Which connections exist and in what degree are matters of historical concern.

Before elaborating on the implication of these various types of change, it is important to note that almost all contemporary research and theory in social psychology is subject to such analysis. Not only may the prevalence of tendencies to reduce inconsistency, achieve balance, or attribute casualty wax and wane over time, but so may the prevalence of opposing tendencies to create inconsistency, to negate balance and to view behaviour as environmentally rather than willfully determined. Likewise, the relationship between variables such as demands for obedience and obedient behaviour (Milgram, 1963), aggressive attack and aggressive response (Geen, 1968; Gentry, 1970), a leader's task capabilities and willingness to follow (Hollander, 1964), and so on, are subject to alteration in strength and prevalence within society. And for each of these relationships there are several good reasons to suspect a function form opposite in direction from that now accepted as lawful. Over time, as the bonds among the variables are molded anew, such tendencies could well increase in strength and/or prevalence.

It is additionally important to consider the possibility that these various alterations may fluctuate over very brief periods of time. Thus far we have viewed relations among variables much as one would a personality trait: as relatively enduring but subject to slow transitions or modifications over the years. However, it is also quite possible that such relations are subject to momentary fluctuations and thus approximate situationally induced states. For example, in examining one's own experience it should be possible to verify the existence of virtually all the bonds relating independent variables with intervening processes in the illustration above. We may carry with us the potential for all such relationships. Depending on the situational cues or constraints, one or more of the bonds may become activated. Thus, if the individual participates in an experiment where self-esteem is threatened, the bond between similarity and esteem may become relevant; in a situation threatening one with boredom, stimulus needs might become more salient. To the extent that such momentary fluctuations can be documented, the problems stemming from the following arguments reach staggering proportions.

Having specified the major types of alterations within and between the various components of our model, the prospects and limitations of social psychological experiments, along with ancillary techniques, become apparent. The following conclusions are especially cogent:

(1) *All reasonable hypotheses are likely to be valid.* Given the fluctuations within and between entities in the model, there is no reasonable hypothesis about social activity that is not likely to contain truth value for at least some persons at some time. Placing hypotheses under experimental test is thus primarily a challenge to the experimenter's skill in discerning the proper time location, and population in which the support for the hypothesis may be generated. The results of such tests seldom tell us anything we did not already know to be possible. Not only does this argument question the utility of our primary stock in trade, it further implies that for every hypothesis occupying the literature of the field, the contradiction is also valid. Such implications are indeed disturbing as they suggest that all that has passed in our texts and from our podia as knowledge is no more accurate than its negation. Matters may indeed be more critical, as it is possible that the number of persons and situations for which the negation is valid may be more prevalent than the instances in which the particular theories may be confirmed. In the case of the more stimulating theories of the field, those which predict the non-obvious, there is ample reason to believe this is so. Yet, so long as the experiment is the chief instrument for gaining knowledge we shall not be able to escape this dilemma. As we have seen, the experiment tells us only that a particular hypothesis has demonstrable truth value. It does not inform us of the proportion of the population, or the range of instances in which the hypothesis is valid.

(2) *The 'critical experiment' as expendable.* Traditionally the experiment has played a key role in ruling between competing hypotheses. It is commonly assumed that the experiment can be used as the crucible against which the validity of alternative or competing explanations may be determined. Such thinking continues to pervade contemporary social psychology. The past decade has witnessed, for example, an exhausting number of attempts to displace the cognitive dissonance formulation by demonstrating alternative explanations for its supporting evidence. Chapanis and Chapanis (1964), Bem (1967), Janis and Gilmore (1965) and Silverman (1964) and many others have contributed to this colloquy. Similarly, numerous demonstrations have been made of alternatives to initial equity theory findings (cf. Lawler, 1968; Gergen, Morse and Bode, 1974), demonstrations of risky shift (cf. Cartwright, 1971; Pruitt, 1971) and so on. From the present standpoint there is little to be gained from such efforts. To the extent that a given stimulus may elicit a variety of different

processes or internal reactions, and the strength and prevalence of such bonds are subject to historical fluctuation, critical tests contain little information value. When perfectly executed, they tell us only that some other process *could* account for the observed patterns of behaviour at the present time. Given the premise that most reasonable hypotheses are likely to be valid at some time or place, and that most behaviour represents a final common pathway for many antecedent processes, such demonstrations may be viewed as unproductive.

THE CRITICAL EMPLOYMENT OF EXPERIMENTATION

The foregoing arguments strongly suggest that a continued commitment to the experimental paradigm will eventuate in a psychology that is both myopic in its vision and irrelevant to the continuously emerging character of social conduct. This is by no means to argue for a termination of the paradigm, but rather for the adoption of more critical standards in its application. In no way do I wish to see the death of the experimental enterprise, but rather its transfiguration. While the wholesale employment of experiments to test all manner of delimited hypotheses is virtually a dead-end, experimentation can productively be employed in several ways. Most important would appear to be the following:

(1) Explicating bio-social relationships. Due to the relative stability and simplicity of the biological system (as contrasted with the vicissitudes of social history), experimental inquiry into its various relationships to social behaviour would seem reasonable. An understanding of the impact of biological process on social behaviour (e.g., behaviour genetics, generalized arousal, specific motivational states), the effects of social factors on biological process (e.g. perception of emotion, socialization of hunger, psychosomatics), and interdependencies between biological and social factors would seem much enhanced through continued experimentation. To be sure, many of these inter-relationships can be altered by time and circumstance; for example, affective, motivational and genetic contributions to behaviour can be wholly submerged by strong cultural norms. However, in contrast to the plasticity of the social arena, in which virtually any relationship between variables is possible, the biological system would seem to furnish an enduring backdrop for the shadow-show of mores, style and custom.

(2) Experimentation for alteration of consciousness. It has been argued that most social psychological experiments primarily furnish us with an indication of what is possible in social life. Since common experience also furnishes us with a vast repository of knowledge concerning what is possible, most experiments do little more than validate some facet of common knowledge. Continuation of such efforts hardly seems merited. However, upon occasion the experiment can be used to unsettle our common understanding of 'the way things are'. They may generate a constructive self-consciousness, an enhanced awareness of various inequities or irrationalities built into our institutionalized ways of viewing things, or an increased caution before commitment. Some excellent examples of experimentation in the service of such 'consciousness raising' would include Asch's (1956) research on conformity, Milgram's (1963) initial study on obedience to authority, the early work of Festinger (1957) on cognitive dissonance, Deutsch's classic (1969) research on conflict

resolution, Darley and Latané's (1970) early research on bystander intervention, and initial demonstrations of causal attribution and perceptual defense. Such research has played a vital role in sensitizing us to little-considered possibilities in social life. Although these studies have been extremely valuable in their sensitizing function, we can be far less sanguine about their sequelae. In each case, hundreds of additional studies have been spawned: conceptual replications, attempts to find alternative explanations for the initial studies, and attempts to isolate additional factors that supposedly round out our understanding of the phenomenon. Each of these latter pursuits presumes the possibility of constructing transhistorically valid and comprehensive principles of social behaviour on the basis of accumulated experimentation. As we have seen, such an assumption is indeed problematic. These classic studies contribute virtually nothing to such a theory, and the confluence of processes permitting the findings to emerge is subject to the tides of history. In their sensitization function, the classic experiments share the positive alerting function of various events of current history. Like Mai Lai, Watergate, or political assassination, they stimulate widespread reassessment of our condition, our potential, or the future. The experimental social psychologist is in a favourable, if not critical position, however, as he may create the event which stimulates the dialectic. In this sense, the experimentalist's task is not so much to reflect the character of contemporary behaviour, as to *create* it.

(3) Increasing theoretical impact. As argued elsewhere (Gergen, 1973) and as implied in the foregoing, there is little to be gained in attempting through experimentation to validate a series of general laws of social behaviour. With intelligence, all general theories of social behaviour (e.g. behaviourism, phenomenology, field theory, etc.) could probably be extended or elaborated to account for virtually all social phenomena. As we have also seen, there is little way of selecting among such theories on empirical grounds. This is not to say that general theories have no place in the field. They may have immense value in generating coherency, synthesizing disparate facts, sensitizing us to various factors affecting our lives, and demonstrating the shortcomings of conventional truth. However, these functions are not generally served by generating experimental proofs. Experimental data have neither enhanced nor detracted significantly from the contributions of Darwin, Marx, Durkehim, Freud, Parsons, Goffman, Lewin, Skinner or Heider. This is not to argue that experimental data are irrelevant to the impact or acceptance of such theories. Certainly in the case of Lewin, Skinner and Heider, experimental data have increased our concern for the widespread implications of the theorizing. However, where general theory is concerned, enhancement of viewpoint may indeed be the primary function of experimentation. While the formal testing of theories seems a chimerical goal, the occasional use of experiments to demonstrate the viability of a viewpoint insures that we remain in a healthy state of conceptual conflict.

(4) Experimentation in the service of social reform. A vital role may finally be played by experiments in testing the effects of varying social policies. Campbell (1969) has outlined a variety of ways in which various social reforms may be treated as natural experiments and the effects systematically documented. Such experimentation might be employed on both the national level (as in the case of new tax reforms or Presidential pleas for energy conservation) as well as on the local scene (as in the case of alterations in local traffic regulations or school busing). The same logic applies, of course, in the pretesting of various reforms. As Rivlen (1973) concludes in her discussion of problems and prospects in this domain, social experiments in areas such

524   *Kenneth J. Gergen*

as performance contracting, negative income tax, and compensatory education have been highly enlightening and may engender far wiser legislation than otherwise. Riecken and Boruch (1974) have pinpointed additional cases in which experimentation may be utilized in social intervention. If we view such investigations in historical perspective, however, it must be concluded that experimentation may not yield answers of long-term validity. Simply because Program A is superior to B at t^1, we cannot assume that it will remain so; with changing social conditions, the opposite results might also emerge. Thus, where social experimentation is concerned we must be prepared for periodic reassessment of competing policy alternatives.

It would be appropriate to complete this analysis with a strong endorsement of McGuire's (1973) exhortation for a broad liberalization of methodology in social psychology. Experimentation does not provide a solid foundation on which to build social knowledge. However, in light of the present arguments, it would appear an auspicious time for a serious shift of our attentions to the area of methodology. Our major methods of inquiry have remained essentially unchanged over the past three decades and its seems a propitious moment to turn our attention from the 'what' of social life to the 'how' of knowing. Not only do we require better means of understanding naturally occurring behaviour, embedded in historical sequence, but we must develop ways of regenerating knowledge as the character of social conduct emerges anew.

REFERENCES

Altman, I. and Taylor D. (1973). *Social penetration*, Holt, Rinehart and Winston, New York.

Armistead, N. (Ed.) (1974). *Reconstructing social psychology*. Penguin Books, Middlesex, England.

Asch, S. (1956). 'Studies of independence and conformity: A minority of one against a unanimous majority', *Psychological Monographs*, 70: Whole No. 416.

Befu, H. (1966). 'Gift giving and social reciprocity in Japan', *France-Asia*, 188: 161–177.

Bem, D. J. (1967). 'Self-perception: An alternative interpretation of cognitive dissonance phenomena', *Psychological Review*, 74, 183–200.

Bem, D. J. and McConnell, H. K. (1970), 'Testing the self-perception explanation of dissonance phenomena: On the salience of premanipulation attitudes. *Journal of Personality and Social Psychology*, 14, 23–31.

Benedict, R. (1946). *The chrysthanemum and the sword*. Houghton Mifflin, New York.

Berscheid, E. and Walster, E. (1969). *Interpersonal Attraction*, Addison-Wesley, Reading Mass

Bickman, L. and Henchey, T. (1972). *Beyond the Laboratory: Field Research in Social Psychology*, McGraw Hill, New York.

Brehm, J. W. (1966) *A Theory of Psychological Reactance*, Academic Press, New York.

Byrne, D. (1971). *The Attraction Paradigm*, Academic Press, New York.

Byrne, D. (1969). Attitudes and attraction. *In* Berkowitz, L. (Ed.), *Advances in Experimental Social Psychology*, Vol. 4. Academic Press, New York.

Campbell, D. T. (1969). 'Reform as experiments', *American Psychologist*, 24: 409–429.

Cartwright, D. (1971). 'Risk taking by individuals and groups: An assessment of research employing choice dilemmas', *Journal of Personality and Social Psychology*, 20: 361–378.

Chapanis, N. and Chapanis, A. (1964). 'Cognitive dissonance: Five years later,' *Pscyhological Bulletin*, 61: 1–22.

Clore, G. L. and Baldridge, B. (1968). 'Interpersonal attraction: The role of agreement and topic interest,' *Journal of Personality and Social Psychology*, 9: 340–346.

Cronbach, L. J. (1975). 'Beyond the two disciplines in scientific psychology', *American Psychologist*, 30: 116–127.

Darley, J. and Latané, B. (1970). *The unresponsive Bystander: Why Doesen't he Help?* Appleton-Century-Crofts, New York.

Deutsch, M. (1969). 'Socially relevant science: Reflections on some studies of interpersonal conflict.' *American Psychologist,* 24, 1076-1092.

Duval, S. and Wicklund, R. A. (1972). *A Theory of Objective Self-awareness.* Academic Press, New York.

Elms, A. C. (1975). 'The crisis in confidence in social psychology', *American Psychologist,* 30: 967-976.

Festinger, L. A. (1957). *A Theory of Cognitive Dissonance.* Row, Peterson, Evanston, Illinois.

Fried, S. B., Gumper, D. C. and Allen, J. C. (1973). 'Ten years of social psychology: Is there a growing commitment to field research?' *American Psychologist,* 28: 155-156.

Fromkin, H. L. (1970). 'Effects of experimentally aroused feelings of undistinctiveness upon valuation of scarce and novel experiences', *Journal of Personality and Social Psychology,* 16: 521-529.

Fromkin, H. L. (1972). 'Feelings of interpersonal undistinctiveness: An unpleasant affective state' *Journal of Experimental Research in Personality,* 6: 178-185.

Geen, R. G. (1968). 'Effects of frustration, attack and prior training in aggressiveness upon aggressive behaviour', *Journal of Personality and Social Psychology,* 9: 316-321.

Gentry, W. D. (1970). 'Effects of frustration, attack and prior aggressive training on overt aggression and vascular processes', *Journal of Personality and Social Psychology,* 16: 718-725.

Gergen, K. J. (1973). 'Social psychology as history', *Journal of Personality and Social Psychology,* 26: 309-320.

Gergen, K. J. and Gergen, M. M. (1971). 'Understanding foreign assistance through public opinion', *Yearbook of World Affairs,* Vol. 25. pp. 87-103, Institute of World Affairs, London.

Gergen, K. J., Morse, S. J. and Bode, K. (1974). 'Overpaid or overworked: Cognitive and behavioural reactions to inequitable payment', *Journal of Applied Social Psychology,* 4: 259-274.

Hampden-Turner, C. (1970). *Radical man.* Schenkman, Cambridge, Mass.

Harré, R. (1974). 'Some remarks on 'rule' as a scientific concept'. *In* Mischel, T. (Ed.), *Understanding Other Persons.* Blackwell, Oxford.

Harré, R. and Secord, P. (1972). *The Explanation of Social Behaviour.* Blackwell Press, Oxford, England.

Higbee, K. L. and Wells, M. G. (1972). 'Some research trends in social psychology during the 1960s', *American Psychologist,* 27: 963-966.

Hollander, E. P. (1964). *Leaders, Groups and Influence.* Oxford University Press, New York.

Israel, J. and Tajfel, H. (1972). (Eds.) *The Context of Social Psychology: A Critical Assessment.* Academic Press, London.

Janis, I. J. and Gilmore, J. B. (1965). 'The influence of incentive conditions on the success of role playing in modifying attitudes', *Journal of Personality and Social Psychology,* 1: 17-27.

Jourard, S. M. and Kormann, L. (1968). 'Getting to know the experimenter and its effect on psychological test performance', *Journal of Humanistic Psychology,* 8: 155-160.

Kelman, H. C. (1968). *A Time to Speak.* Jossey Bass, San Francisco.

Kelman, H. C. (1972). The rights of the subject in social research: An analysis in terms of relative power and legitimacy. *American Psychologist,* 27, 989-1016.

Kerckhoff, A. and Davis, K. E. (1962). 'Value consensus and need complementarity in mate selection', *American Sociological Review,* 27: 295-303.

Koch, S. (1959). 'Epilogue'. *In* Koch, S. (Ed.), *Psychology: A Study of a Science,* Vol. III, pp. 729-788, McGraw Hill, New York.

Lamberth, J. and Craig, L. (1970). 'Differential magnitude of reward and magnitude shifts using attitudinal stimuli', *Journal of Experimental Research in Personality,* 4: 281-285.

Lawler, E. E. (1968). 'Effects of hourly overpayment on productivity and work quality', *Journal of Personality and Social Psychology,* 10: 306-314.

Levinger, G. and Snoek, J. D. (1972). *Attraction in Relationships: A New Look at Interpersonal Attraction.* General Learning Press, Morristown, N. J.

Lipetz, M. E., Cohen, I. H., Dowrin, J. and Rogers, L. S. (1970). 'Need Complementarity,

526   *Kenneth J. Gergen*

marital stability and Material satisfaction'. *In* Gergen, K. and Marlowe, D. (Eds.), *Personality and Social Behaviour.* Addison-Wesley, Reading, Mass. pp. 201–212.

Manis, M. (1975). 'Comment on Gergen's "Social Psychology as History"'. *Personality and Social Psychology Bulletin,* 1: 450–455.

Marlowe, D. and Gergen, K. J. (1968). 'Personality and social interaction'. *In* Lindzey G. and Aronson E. (Eds.), *The Handbook of Social Psychology,* 2nd Ed. Vol. 3, pp. 590–665, Addison-Wesley, Reading, Mass.

Marx, M. H. and Hillix, W. A. (1973). *Systems and theories in psychology.* McGraw Hill, New York.

McGuire, W. J. (1973). The yin and yang of progress in social psychology', *Journal of Personality and Social Psychology,* 26: 446–456.

McGuire, W. J. (1967). 'Some impending reorientations in social psychology', *Journal of Experimental Social Psychology,* 3: 124–139.

Mettee, D. R. and Wilkins, P. C. (1972). 'When similarity "hurts": Effects of perceived ability and a humorous blunder on interpersonal attraction'. *Journal of Personality and Social Psychology,* 22, 246–258.

Milgram, S. (1963). 'Behavioural study of obedience', *Journal of Abnormal and Social Psychology,* 67: 371–378.

Mischel, W. (1973). 'Toward a cognitive social learning reconceptualization of personality'. *Psychological Review,* 80, 252–283.

Müller, H. J. (1963). *Freedom in the Western World.* Harper Row, New York.

Newcomb, T. (1961). *The acquaintance process.* Holt, Rinehart and Winston, New York.

Novak, D. W. and Lerner, M. J. (1968). 'Rejection as a consequence of perceived similarity'. *Journal of Personality and Social Psychology,* 9, 147–152.

Orne, M. T. (1962). 'On the social psychology of the psychological experiment: With particular reference to demand characteristics and their implications', *American Psychologist,* 17: 776–783.

Osgood, C. E. (1962). *An Alternative to War or Surrender.* University of Illinois Press, Urbana, Ill.

Pruitt, I. G. (1971). 'Choice shifts in group discussion: An introductory review', *Journal of Personality and Social Psychology,* 3: 339–360.

Riecken, H. W. and Boruch, R. F. (1974). (Eds.), *Social Experimentation.* Academic Press, New York.

Rivlin, A. M. (1973). 'Social experiments: The promise and the problems', *Evaluation,* 1, 13–24.

Rosenthal, R. (1966). *Experimenter effects in behavioural research.* Appleton-Century-Crofts, New York.

Rosenthal, R. and Rosnow, R. L. (1969). *Artifact in behavioral research.* Academic Press, New York.

Schlenker, B. R. (1974). 'Social psychology and science', *Journal of Personality and Social Psychology,* 29: 1–15.

Senn, D. J. (1971). 'Attraction as a function of similarity-dissimilarity in task performance'. *Journal of Personality and Social Psychology,* 1971, 18, 120–123.

Silverman, I. (1964). 'Self-esteem and differential responsiveness to success and failure. *Journal of Abnormal and Social Psychology,* 69, 115–119.

Steiner, I. (1974). 'Whatever happened to the group in social psychology', *Journal of Experimental Social Psychology,* 10: 94–108.

Stotland, E. (1969). 'Exploratory investigations of empathy'. *In* Berkowitz, L. (Ed.), *Advances in Experimental Social Psychology,* Vol. IV. Academic Press, New York.

Tajfel, H. (1972). 'Experiments in a vacuum'. *In* Israel, J. and Tajfel, H. (Eds.), *The Context of Social Psychology: A Critical Assessment.* Academic Press, London.

Taylor, S. E. and Mettee, D. R. (1971). 'When similarity breeds contempt. *Journal of Personality and Social Psychology,* 20, 75–81.

Thorngate, W. (1976). 'Possible limits on a science of man.' *In* Strickland, L., Aboud, F. and Gergen, K. J. (Eds.), *Social Psychology in Transition,* Plenum, New York.

Weber, E. H. (1834). *De pulsu, resorptions, auditu et tactu: Annotationes anatomical et physiological.* Koehler, Leipzig.

Experimentation: a reappraisal   527

Weick, K. E. (1961). 'Systematic observational methods'. *In* Lindzey, G. and Aronson, E. (Eds.), *Handbook of Social Psychology*, Vol. II. Addison-Wesley, Reading, Mass.

Weinstein, G. and Platt, G. (1969). *The Wish to be Free*. University of California Press, Berkeley, California.

Wicklund, R. (1974). *Freedom and reactance*, Wiley, New York, 1974.

RÉSUMÉ

En psychologie la recherche concernant les phénomènes sociaux est devenue pratiquement synonyme d'expérimentation contrôlée. Bien que ses avantages et ses inconvénients aient été périodiquement l'objet de débats, on peut observer qu'on fait de plus en plus confiance à l'expérimentation. Celle-ci peut-elle rendre compte des traits les plus importants de l'interaction sociale? On voit qu'il existe des échecs importants lorsqu'on prend en considération quelques caractéristiques des événements sociaux : leur insertion dans des ensembles culturels plus larges; leur position dans des séquences d'événements; leur poids relatif dans différentes situations; le fait qu'ils dépendent d'un grand nombre de facteurs psychologiques simultanés; leur détermination complexe. Si de plus l'on tient compte du fait que les phénomènes sociaux ont un contexte historique on peut dire que toutes les hypothèses raisonnables sont valides et que les expériences destinées à choisir entre plusieurs hypothèses sont stériles. L'article examine quelles sont les conditions d'une expérimentation féconde.

ZUSAMMENFASSUNG

Psychologische Erforschung sozialer Erscheinungen scheint fast untrennbar mit kontrolliertem Experimentieren verknüpft. Obwohl Vor- und Nachteile des psychologischen Experiments immer wieder erörtert werden, läßt sich leicht nachweisen, daß die Forschung sich in noch immer steigendem Maße auf Experimente stützt. Dieser Artikel prüft, ob das Experiment die wesentlichen Aspekte sozialer Interaktion erfassen kann. Deutlich erweist sich das Versagen des Experiments, wenn man die folgenden Charakteristika sozialer Ereignisse betrachtet: Soziale Ereignisse sind in breitere kulturelle Rahmen eingebettet; sie sind Bestandteil langer Ereignisketten; ihr Einfluß konkurriert mit dem anderer Ereignisse in vielschichtigen Situationen; sie beruhen auf dem Zusammengehen vielfältiger psychologischer Faktoren; und schließlich sind sie mannigfach determiniert. Betrachtet man zusätzlich die soziale Erscheinung im historischen Zusammenhang, wird deutlich, daß jede vernünftige Hypothese ihre Gültigkeit hat und daß das vergleichende Testen von Hypothesen sozialen Verhaltens ein fruchtloses Unterfangen darstellt.

[7]

Journal of Personality and Social Psychology
1978, Vol. 36, No. 11, 1344-1360

Toward Generative Theory

Kenneth J. Gergen
Swarthmore College

Much contemporary theory appears to lack generative potency, that is, the capacity to challenge prevailing assumptions regarding the nature of social life and to offer fresh alternatives to contemporary patterns of conduct. This deficit may be traced primarily to the commitment of the field to traditional positivist assumptions that (a) give preeminent weight to "the fact," (b) demand verification of theoretical ideas, (c) encourage disregard for the temporal dependency of social pattern, and (d) recommend dispassionate comportment in scientific affairs. Shortcomings are demonstrated in each of these cases, and the groundwork is laid for developing generative theory, liberated both from the press of immediate fact and the necessity for verification. Such theory may properly function to sustain value commitments and to restructure the character of social life.

When inquiry is made into the function of social theory, the typical response points to its essential contribution to "understanding, prediction, and control." If one were to inquire further into what is meant by "understanding" in this case, the answer might well be framed in terms of the scientist's role in "apprehending clearly the character, nature or subtleties" of social life (Urdang, 1968). From this standpoint, social conduct is granted a preeminent ontological status: It furnishes the essential mysteries for the scientist to unlock. Yet, there is a contrasting sense in which one may understand, a sense that does not take nature for granted. Understanding may also entail "assigning a meaning" to something, thus creating its status through the employment of concepts. Whereas the former sense of meaning finds its roots in empiricist philosophy, the latter may be traced primarily to the rationalist writings of Kant & Hegel. The rationalist orientation, while long entrenched in European

intellectual life, has gradually given way in the social sciences to the positivist-empiricist approach so central to present-day activities.

This distinction in orientations furnishes important insight into the ironic discrepancy between the seminal theoretical contributions emerging within the recent European, as opposed to the contempory American, context. In spite of the relatively vast professional ranks and supporting resources within the latter context, theoretical contributions have generally been far less provocative in their effects. Few American contemporaries have been able to match the intellectual ferment furnished by such figures as Freud, Durkheim, Marx, Mannheim, Piaget, Levi-Strauss, Weber, Köhler, Veblen, and Keynes, among others. American social psychology appears to suffer the same malady. Most general treatments of theory in the field typically devote primary attention to Freud and Lewin; for many, Fritz Heider's richly suggestive work is deserving of equal status. Role theory has played a historically important part in the development of American social psychology, yet its roots may propertly be traced to the early contributions of Durkheim. Similarly, the symbolic interactionist perspective may be traced to the early European training of its initial spokesmen (Jones & Day, 1977). In

I am indebted to Peter Dachler, Mary Gergen, Carol Gould, Diana Kaplin, Ann Kimura, Jacob Meskin, Ralph Rosnow, Barry Schwartz, and Wolfgang Stroebe for critical appraisal of this work in its earlier stages.

Reprint requests should be addressed to Kenneth J. Gergen, Department of Psychology, Swarthmore College, Swarthmore, Pennsylvania 19081.

terms of general perspectives, only learning theory may be indigenous to American scientific soil. In effect, the strength of contemporary social psychology does not seem to lie in its capacity for engendering theory of major scope and challenge. More generally, it would appear that correspondent with the hegemony of the positivist–empiricist orientation has been a diminution in catalytic theorizing.

This is hardly to say that social psychology has been devoid of significant theoretical work. Although occasionally conjoined, two major forms of endeavor may be distinguished: (a) the *construction of minimal models* and (b) *the isolation of significant theoretical variables*. In the former case, theorists have attempted to account for a delimited range of phenomena with a minimal set of theoretical assumptions.[1] Festinger's (1957) theory of cognitive dissonance may be paradigmatic in this respect; its simple set of pivotal assumptions has engendered well over a thousand empirical inquiries during the past 20 years. Similar with respect to their parsimonious construction and limited explanatory ends are Brehm's (1966) theory of psychological reactance; Schachter's (1964) two-factor theory of emotion; Osgood and Tannenbaum's (1955) congruity model; Kelley's (1972) three-factor theory of causal attribution; Jones and Davis's (1965) theory of correspondent inference; Walster, Walster, and Berscheid's (1978) equity formulation; Byrne's (1971) similarity–attraction hypothesis; Anderson's (1974) integration model; Duval and Wicklund's (1972) self-awareness theory; and Ajzen and Fishbein's (1972) attitude–behavior theory, to name but a few. The second major theoretical endeavor has been that of isolating variables thought to be vital in their effects on a circumscribed range of social activity.[2] Paradigmatic in this case is perhaps the work of the Hovland school of attitude change, in which investigators differentiated among source, message, medium, and recipient factors believed to influence attitude change (cf. McGuire's 1969 review). Schachter's (1959) attempt to isolate key processes responsible for affiliative activity furnishes a second classic example. More recently, variables such as physical attractiveness (Ber-

scheid & Walster, 1974); actor versus observer differences in causal attribution (Jones & Nisbett, 1971); internal versus external control (Phares, 1976); and "mere exposure" (Zajonc, 1968) have all received similar attention.

Yet, there is one vital difference separating such theoretical endeavors from those of "prescientific" European origin. Whereas the central thrust of American social psychology theory has been that of stimulating research within an elite, professional circle, the theories of Freud, Marx, Durkheim, and others often challenged the assumptive bases of social life, with profound catalytic effects both within the profession and without. The primary debates emerging from contemporary social psychological theory are generally limited to questions of alternative explanation (cf. Bem, 1972; Cartwright, 1971).[3] In contrast, the earlier offerings have often fostered colloquy among scientists of diverse origin along with philosophers, historians, theologians, politicians, and so on. As Asch wrote in 1952,

It has to be admitted that social psychology lives today in the shadow of great doctrines of man that were formulated long before it appeared, that it has borrowed its leading ideas from neighboring regions of scientific thought and from the social philosophies of the modern period. It is paradoxical but true that social psychology . . . has as yet not significantly affected the conceptions it has borrowed. (p. viii)

And, as Tajfel (1972) has more recently commented, "Social psychology has certainly not succeeded in creating an intellectual revolution in the sense of deeply affecting our views of human nature" (p. 106). One may wish to defend contemporary theory by pointing to its superior testability and its related capacity to

---

[1] Such models correspond to Hendrick's (1977) "miniature theories."

[2] This form of endeavor corresponds with Moscovici's (1972) concept of "taxonomic" theorizing.

[3] As Silverman (1977) has commented, "Apparently we have nothing to offer in terms of general theoretical or empirical evolutions or revolutions; nothing to discuss that would represent the basic issues or questions of our field and the paths taken toward their resolution" (p. 354). In effect, substantive debate appears largely eclipsed by methodological quarreling.

1346   KENNETH J. GERGEN

yield reliable bodies of social knowledge. Yet, it is difficult to fault the earlier theories for the lack of research that they have generated (cf. Blum's 1964 summary of empirical research on psychoanalytic theory), nor can one distill from the immense contemporary effort at hypothesis testing a body of highly reliable propositions (cf. Cartwright, 1971; Gergen, in press-a; Greenwald, 1975). In effect, the contemporary alternatives are not demonstrably superior in other respects.

It may be useful, then, to consider competing theoretical accounts in terms of their *generative capacity, that is, the capacity to challenge the guiding assumptions of the culture, to raise fundamental questions regarding contemporary social life, to foster reconsideration of that which is "taken for granted," and thereby to furnish new alternatives for social action.*[4] It is the generative theory that can provoke debate, transform social reality, and ultimately serve to reorder social conduct. It is the contention of the present article that the generative weaknesses of contemporary social psychological theory may be traced primarily to the discipline's steadfast commitment to the traditional positivist–empiricist paradigm.[5] Although the paradigm has furnished a guiding rationale for many decades, it is essential to monitor continuously the paths along which it has led, as well as those which have been foreclosed. Four fundamental deterrents inherent in the positivist paradigm will be singled out for attention, and in each case serious weaknesses will be elucidated. Further, the critical rationale will be employed in each instance to lay the groundwork for generative theoretical pursuits.

The Preeminence of Objective Fact

From the traditional positivist standpoint, it is the scientist's initial task to observe the state of nature and to document with accuracy the systematic relationship among observables. On the basis of such preliminary observation, it is said, the scientist may build inductively toward general theoretical statements describing and explaining the phenomena in question. Progress from the level of particulars to that of theoretical generalization is to be made by employing canons of inductive logic, such as those proposed by John Stuart Mill in 1846. Classical astronomy is often considered exemplary in this respect. The science commenced, it is said, when serious individuals began to record systematically the movements of the heavenly bodies. On the basis of such records, theoretical descriptions and explanations could be formulated and subsequently tested against continuing observation. In effect, observable fact is of preeminent concern.

The general acceptance of the traditional position within contemporary social psychology seems widely evident. As Shaw and Costanzo (1970) state the case,

Modern social psychology has largely been empirical in nature, basing its propositions and conclusions upon observations in controlled situations. . . . As a result of the empirical approach, a considerable amount of data about social behavior has accumulated. To be useful, such data must be organized in a systematic way so that the meaning and implications of these data can be understood. Such systematic organization is the function of theory. (p. 3)

In keeping with this orientation, graduate training is commonly centered on the process of systematic observation. Extensive knowledge of methodology and statistics is normally required, and the thesis typically insures that the candidate has mastered the skills of sound observation. Training in the process of theory construction is a rarity. The primary journals of the field are also devoted almost exclusively to the establishment of fact. Freedman's (Note 1) recent comment on the state of the art appears to capture the modal thinking of the discipline,

----

[4] The generative criterion may be contrasted with the traditional concept of "heuristic." The latter typically refers to the capacity of a theory to generate research or solutions to practical problems. In these senses, generative theory may or may not be heuristically valuable, and vice versa. Whether generative theory need be contrary to common assumptions may also be questioned. However, it would appear that the formulation of new alternatives is inevitably counterposed to some set of existing agreements. Creativity and conflict may be inseparable.

[5] Clearly, not all social psychologists wholly ascribe to all four of the assumptions here set forth. Yet, a family of congenial assumptions can be discerned in the public documents of the field, and it is to this "metatheoretical representation" that the present arguments are directed.

Since research [on crowding] has only been going on for a few years, and since the findings are rather inconsistent and confused, it seems that people should be doing research rather than worrying about theories. The idea that there would already be a review of the theories in the field is certainly depressing. It is perfectly all right for people to offer hunches or tentative explanation or what might be called mini-theories of any area of social psychology, but to start presenting theories when we don't even know what the facts are is an exercise in futility.

Yet, the common belief that social theory should ideally be premised on sound fact seems to have continued undaunted by significant misgivings within the philosophic realm. It has first become apparent that the scientist cannot approach nature as an unsophisticated or unbiased observer of the facts. Rather, he or she must already harbor conceptions of "what there is to be studied" in order to carry out the task of systematic observation. From this perspective, scientific astronomy did not begin with the process of documenting existing fact. Required were preliminary conceptual distinctions between the earth and the heavens and among entities existing within the heavens. In effect, scientists must share certain theoretical assumptions in order to carry out meaningful investigation. Or, to put it more formally, "It is the theory that determines what is to count as a fact and how facts are to be distinguished from one another" (Unger, 1975, p. 32).

It has further been recognized that canons of inductive logic are inadequate to describe the process by which the scientist typically moves from the concrete to the conceptual level. The most careful observation and cataloguing of all the stone formations on earth, combined with the most assiduous employment of inductive logic, would not yield contemporary geological theory (cf. Medawar, 1969). Neither the facts nor the logic can furnish the questions to be asked of the data or a metaphor for conceptual organization. Concepts such as "the ice age" or "geosynclinal stage" appear to require some form of creative or intuitive act that is as yet poorly understood. Again, it appears that a premium is to be placed on theoretical imagination and that a preeminent commitment to establishing "the facts" is inimical to such investments.

The case is particularly potent with respect to generative theory. If "commonsense assumptions" concerning, for example, the units of behavior, their labels, or their relationships are allowed unconsciously to guide one's observations and hypotheses, then the resulting theoretical models are very likely to reflect those assumptions. Resulting theory will approximate "commonsense," a problem with which social psychologists have been struggling for several decades. When one "begins with the facts" one has already incorporated an implicit theory, and the potential for a generative outcome may thereby be reduced. Or, as Moscovici (1972) has more forcefully concluded, "social psychologists have done no more than to operationalize questions and answers which were imagined elsewhere. And thus the work in which they are engaged—in which we are all engaged—is not the work of scientific analysis but that of engineering" (p. 32).

Psychological Theory and the Shaping of Social Phenomena

Although early astronomical investigation was surely guided by preformal theoretical conceptions, it is difficult to argue that such preconceptions have operated at an obvious disadvantage in this domain. If such is the case, one may well ask why social investigation cannot proceed along similar lines; what problems are incurred by allowing "normative preconceptions" to channel social psychological investigations? The answer to this query lies in the far greater potential for such preconceptions to shape the phenomena for study in the social, as opposed to the natural, sciences. That is, the social scientist appears to be in a far more precarious position with respect to generating theory that serves to fulfill itself. There are two important respects in which social theory actively creates the phenomena to be investigated, neither of which appears as germane to most investigation in the natural sciences.

In the initial case, social theory may *determine the investigatory scanning process*, thus focusing attention on particular patterns while obscuring others. In determining the investigator's focus of attention, the theory establishes in advance the form of observation. To appreciate this point we must return to the earlier argument, that in order to recognize "the facts" one must already possess some form of conceptual knowledge. Such preliminary knowledge is required in order for a discrimination to be made between "facts" and "nonfacts" or events and their surrounding context. Yet, it may be further asked, what is the basis of the preliminary conceptual orientation? While the possibility for a priori conceptual structure awaits thorough study, it does appear that sensory inputs must frequently play some part in shaping these preliminary conceptual schemata. At the same time, the extent of their impact may depend on the character of these inputs as related to the physiology of the organism. At one extreme we may consider experiential inputs which readily lend themselves to "natural categorization" (Rosch, 1977). In particular, stimulation that significantly disturbs the nervous system may frequently give rise to conceptual distinctions. For example, the difference between the size and luminosity of the star against the background of the night sky, the sound of thunder versus the preceding quiet, the shape of fish as opposed to fowl may prompt the development of conceptual distinctions in virtually all cultures. These categories might later come to fix the range of preconceptions operating within the relevant branches of the natural sciences.

In contrast, we may consider a range of experiences dominated by continuous movement and ambiguous repetition. In observing the ocean waves, for example, it is exceedingly difficult to discriminate one wave from another or to form more than the roughest of category schemata (e.g., "wave height"). In this case, natural categories may not be readily forthcoming, and "what sorts of waves" one sees may largely be determined by one's visual focus. Such focus could be directed toward the wave slope, the amount of emerald green, the amount of foam, and so on. With each new focus, one's experience of pattern may be altered. The "pattern of study" thus depends very importantly on the cognitive set of the observer (cf. Neisser, 1976; Posner & Snyder, 1975; Shiffrin & Schnieder, 1977). In this

case, the category system serves to direct attention and, in doing so, "creates" the phenomenon for observation. It may further be argued that the great abundance of human social activity is of this second order.[6] That is, such activity appears in a state of near continuous motion, its forms are infinitely variable, and fresh patterns may emerge at any point. Under such conditions, the conceptual standpoint of the observer may become an extremely powerful determinant of what is perceived. Preliminary understandings of "what there is" may well prove self-supportive. It is in just such conditions that competing conceptual perspectives are most required. Each perspective may operate as a lens through which experience is served up in differing form. With each new lens one increases sensitivity to the whole.

In addition to determining the scanning process through which social experience is fashioned, the social theorist may create his or her subject matter by actively *changing its composition.* Such alterations may be effected in a variety of ways, one of which may be singled out for its special importance. It would appear that people do not generally respond to social stimuli on a purely sensory basis. Intervening between the impinging stimulus and subsequent action is a conceptual or symbolic reconstruction of the stimulus, and it is to this "world as symbolically translated" that one's actions most typically correspond. Thus, unlike structurally undifferentiated organisms such as protozoa, echinoderms, and flatworms, the human being is not "stimulus bound." Little in the way of response reliability can be anticipated. The same proximal stimulus may engender a virtual infinity of reactions depending on its

---

[6] It would be cavalier to assert that what the natural scientist senses is not frequently influenced by preliminary conceptions. One must learn "what to see," for example, through the aperture of a microscope, and this learning is typically conceptual in character. The present argument must thus be considered one of degree. It is also possible that as a natural science exhausts the gains to be made on the basis of "natural categories," it becomes increasingly dependent on social agreement within the field for specifying "what there is to be studied."

"meaning" for the recipient. This line of reasoning is, of course, consistent with major assumptions underlying much contemporary research in social psychology. However, virtually unexamined by the field is the potential of the science to shape the meaning systems of the society and thus the common activities of the culture. Following the traditional positivist model, the social psychologist has remained primarily concerned with the tasks of reliable description and explanation. However, unlike the natural scientist, the social psychologist uses descriptive and explanatory terms that have the capacity to shape the character of social activities about which accounts are fashioned.

In the case of Freudian theory, such shaping effects already seem broadly apparent. In previous times, aberrant, exotic, or deviant activity was frequently viewed as an expression of "witchcraft," "inferior character," or "lack of willpower." Resulting reaction patterns were often punitive. With the advent of psychoanalytic theory, the same activities came to be seen as products of personality dynamics over which the individual had little control. From this perspective, the actor is deserving of "treatment" or "cure." In effect, the development and dissemination of psychoanalytic theory succeeded in altering widespread patterns of social activity (Moscovici, 1961). Similar effects may be traced to social psychologists' attempts to explain such phenomena as prejudice, obedience, social protest, and ghetto revolution. To elaborate, it appears from the broad literature on causal attribution that the culture frequently distinguishes between behavior that is under the individual's control ("internally caused") and behavior that is under environmental control ("externally caused"). Further, the literature makes it clear that patterns of blame and praise are often related to the locus of causal attribution (cf. Kelman & Lawrence, 1972; Newtson, 1974). In particular, for devalued behavior (e.g., murder) we may assign increasing amounts of blame or punishment to the extent that action seems internally, as opposed to externally, caused. Similarly, for valued acts (e.g., heroism in battle) we typically assign lesser amounts of praise or

reward to the extent that the act seems externally, as opposed to internally, caused. Thus, as the common explanation for a given action shifts from one causal locus to another, behavioral reactions may shift as well.

In this light, we seee that the social psychologist's choice of explanation for a given action may either sustain or alter the common attribution patterns of the culture and thus the common patterns of blame and praise. For example, when prejudice is explained in terms of authoritarian personality dynamics (Adorno et al., 1950), the prejudiced person is treated as the causal source of his or her own actions. Person blame is enhanced through such explanation, and one may feel justified antipathy toward the prejudiced person. A similar argument may be made in the case of obedient behavior, as described by Milgram (1974). When such behavior is traced, as it is, to the subject's divesting him- or herself of responsibility, to primitive thought patterns, to narrowing of moral concerns, and to lack of inner resources, then public scorn for the obedient individual can be justified. On the other side of the ledger, social protest is generally viewed in a positive light by the liberal wing of the profession. When such behavior is explained in terms of the individual's conscience, personal values, or intelligence (cf. Flacks, 1969; Keniston, 1968), it gains increasing value. In the case of ghetto riots, scientific explanation has frequently centered on society's oppression of the ghetto black. Such explanation functionally shifts blame from the rioter to the society. In all such instances social psychological theory has operated much like instructions in a reattribution experiment (cf. Dienstbier, 1972; Storms & Nisbett, 1970). They shift the attributed locus of causality for a given range of activity and, in doing so, alter common reations to such activity.

From the positivist perspective, one might view such shaping effects with dismay. They constitute inappropriate violations of the traditional roles assigned to the scientist, namely those of observation, description, and explanation. Yet, from the present standpoint we find that in the process of description and explanation, the scientist is inevitably engaged in the creation of social phenomena, both in the fashioning of the theoretical lenses through which social action is observed and in the reconstitution of the culture's systems of meaning. Theoretical terms, the range of activities to which they are applied, and the form of explanation may all enter the common systems of constructed reality and, in doing so, may determine "what there is" and the appropriate manner of responses. Yet, rather than viewing such effects as nettlesome "incidents de parcours," we may appropriately consider them among the foremost of our assets. The capacity of the discipline to effect social change need not depend on quixotic alliances with the public official or professional change agent. Rather, the theorist may directly alter patterns of social action as his or her mode of conceptualization is incorporated into the common understandings of the culture. This possibility stands as a major challenge to generative theorizing. Not only is the theorist urged to free him- or herself from the shackles of prevailing conceptual agreements, but is asked to consider alternative social forms that may be created through theory.

The Demand for Theoretical Verification

From the traditional scientific perspective, a close relationship should ideally be maintained between theory and data. Not only should theories emerge from initial observation, but once developed, they should be subjected to thorough and systematic empirical test. Through empirical assessment, theories of high predictive validity may be sustained and those which fail to correspond with fact excluded from the corpus of "acceptable knowledge." This general line of argument forms the basis of the traditional hypothetico-deductive system for advancing scientific understanding (cf. Koch, 1959) and serves as the underlying rationale for the major line of scholarly work in the discipline, namely, hypothesis testing. The demand for verification has not remained unchallenged over the years. For example, Popper (1959) has argued that there is little to be gained from increasing the amount of empirical support for a given the-

ory. It is primarily failures of verification that push understanding forward in significant degree. Popper's protegé, Thomas Kuhn (1962) has further argued that shifts in theoretical paradigm do not generally depend on the empirical status of the relevant conceptual systems. Yet, Kuhn's thesis is not generally viewed as prescriptive in implication. There are more damaging arguments at stake, and it is to these we must now attend. There are at least three major reasons for believing that the goal of verification in social science is largely a chimerical one.

The Negotiated Character of Social Fact

Social actions appear to carry little in the way of intrinsic meaning; the conceptual categories or meaning systems into which they are placed appear primarily to be products of social negotiation. The fact that a given stimulus pattern falls into the category of "humor," "aggression," "dominance," or "manipulativeness," for example, depends not on the intrinsic properties of the relevant pattern but on the development of a community of agreement. As a result, the labeling of any given action is forever open to negotiation among interested parties, and the legitimacy of any observation statement is continuously open to challenge. "What is the case" in social life may thus be viewed largely as a matter of social influence.

In the natural sciences, this potential for challenging the existing meaning systems does not appear to pose serious threat. Two important reasons for this relatively sanguine state will concern us here. First, the major proportion of the theoretical terms in the natural sciences are tied rather closely to specific empirical operations or measurements. Such terms as *temperature, weight, velocity,* and *electical energy* may often be defined in terms of empirical operations about which broad agreement can easily be reached. Second, the theoretical terms employed in the natural sciences are developed within a relatively closed social system, the constituents of which are typically confronted by similar functional problems. Conflict of interest is not the general rule.

In contrast to this relatively optimistic state of affairs, theoretical terms in the social sciences are only loosely connected to specific operations. As Katz and Stotland (1959) put it,

In physics the concept of atmospheric pressure is fairly close to its operational measure. In physiological psychology many concepts are similarly tied to their operational measurement. In personality theory and social psychology, however, concepts like ego strength, defense mechanisms, role systems and role conflict are so remote from their measurement that we have no single, clearly required set of operational measures. (p. 471)

Although it might appear that this problem is only symptomatic of the youthfulness of the field, closer examination suggests that it may be intrinsic to the language of social interaction. Any given behavior or concrete action may be defined in numerous ways, depending on its function within a given social context. Thus, there is no one transcontextual operation to which the investigator can afford to tie a given theoretical term. The pointing of a finger, for example, may signify aggression in certain contexts, but in others may be used to indicate an altruistic giving of information, a positive or negative attitude, egocentrism, or high achievement motivation. In short, any behavior might, on a given occasion, serve as the operational definition for virtually any general term. On no occasion can one be certain what theoretical categories are relevant (cf. Wilson, 1970). Second, for the social scientist, the mode of theoretical description and explanation is intimately related to the common meaning systems within the culture. For the scientist to "make sense" about human behavior, he or she must do so in ways that are ultimately intelligible to members of the culture (or a subculture). Thus, a continuous, dialectical interplay may take place between the meaning of specific theoretical terms within the sciences and the culture more generally, such that the meaning of specific theoretical terms may evolve over time (e.g., the scientist may borrow a term such as *aggression* from the vernacular, alter its meaning through theoretical and empirical analysis, and in turn, alter the resulting meaning system of the culture). As a result, the range of particulars to which any theoretical term

applies may be in a state of continuous emergence. What "counts" as aggression, for example, may vary from one individual to another and for the same individual over time.

Because of the ambiguous and continuously negotiated meaning of social actions, an immense impediment is placed in the way of theoretical verification. If all stimulus conditions and all subject actions are open to multiple interpretation, then a given hypothesis may be sustained only so long as other investigators refrain from challenging the meaning of the data base. For example, much empirical support has been generated for the simple proposition that people are attracted to those whose opinions are similar to their own (cf. Byrne, 1971). Yet, in any given experimental situation, what the investigator takes to be a "similar" opinion may be viewed by a subject or another investigator as a "correct opinion," "brave opinion," "judicious opinion," "helpful opinion," "moral opinion," "appropriate opinion," and so on. The hypothesis thus retains a patina of verification because the discipline has generally allowed the independent variable to be negotiated as a manipulation of similarity. At any time one wishes to renegotiate such meaning, the support drops into obscurity.

It is also for this reason that attempts to solve debates among competing theories in social psychology so often end in an impasse. Freudian theory, for example, has been able to maintain a brisk following in spite of the legions of studies that have attempted to discredit it. It may continue to do so as long as there are intelligent defenders who can demonstrate the "misleading" character of the many operations used to its detriment. Similarly, the hundreds of careful experimental studies that have attempted to solve the riddle of the risky shift (cf. Cartwright, 1971) or that have pitted dissonance theory against a phalanx of challengers (cf. Elms, 1969)

---

[7] Relevant here is Quine's (1969) surmise that most attributive terms of daily discourse belong to a "dim domain" of meaning, not worthy of science. One might hope for a social science terminology free of person language (Ossorio & Davis, 1968), but it is difficult to envision such an accomplishment.

have left us with no abiding answers. Nor, from the present standpoint, would an indefinite continuation of such efforts. Multiple alternatives in interpretation may be located for virtually any set of empirical findings, as no observation can be unambiguously linked to a general conceptual term.

The Self-Fulfilling Character of Hypothesis Testing

A second major impediment to theoretical verification is closely related to the first. To the extent that the relationship between theoretical terms and empirical operations is an ambiguous one, the investigator's latitude of choice for testing any given hypothesis is increased. Given a broad latitude of choice in selecting how a given hypothesis is to be tested, the investigator seeking to sustain a given hypothesis can scarcely select a set of empirical operations in a way that is not likely to render support for the hypothesis. For example, much common thinking relates stress with a variety of negative consequences (cf. Glass & Singer, 1972; McGrath, 1970). At the same time, given the intrinsic ambiguity of a term such as *stress*, the number of operational possibilities is virtually infinite. The investigator attempting to demonstrate a negative reaction to stress may thus choose to induce stress by exposing subjects to a threat to their physical well-being, as opposed to a challenging sports event or the presence of a superior. The choice is based neither on theoretical considerations nor on guile, but on the fact that the investigator is aware, by virtue of his or her immersion in the culture, that threat to physical well-being often produces a negative reaction. The alternative means of inducing stress may be avoided because the common experience suggests that many people respond positively in such situations. From this standpoint, securing anticipated results speaks far less to the empirical status of the hypothesis than it does to the investigator's familiarity with the shared meanings and mores of the subjects under test. With sufficient cultural knowledge it should be possible to generate support for any reasonable hypothesis, along with its antithesis.

The A Priori Truth of Sensible Theory

To the extent that people's behavior does conform to their common conceptions of the world, then theories that are intelligible within the framework of such conceptual systems may be endowed with truth value without regard to empirical test. If people generally maintain themselves within normally accepted limits of sensibility and avoid acting nonsensically, then any theory that reflects common conceptions of what is sensible may be supported by at least a portion of the population at some time. To draw from Ossorio and Davis (1968), setting out to test the balance theory hypothesis that people will be attracted to those who express liking toward them is equivalent to testing the hypothesis that twice two is four. In the same way that people generally accept this particular conception of numbers and their relations as correct, they also believe that liking is an appropriate reaction to another's regard. Of course, one need not employ this particular arithmetic system, and there are numerous instances in which people do not. Similarly, one need not conform to the particular balance conception of relations, and on any occasion may select other intelligible ways of responding to positive regard. The major point is that so long as one's theory "makes sense" within the culture, it may be assumed without test that its conceptual basis will, on occasion, be put to use in everyday life.

Given the substantial if not insuperable problems underlying the traditional demand for theoretical verification, the chief efforts of the discipline, namely those of testing hypotheses, are thrown into severe question.[8] The immense resources presently directed toward testing formal hypotheses may be rechanneled. The responsible scholar need not hesitate to develop and disseminate his or her ideas for lack of empirical test; the massive hours absorbed in the process of executing such tests

---

[8] This is not in the least to argue that empirical research has no place in the science. As argued elsewhere (Gergen, in press-a) such work may play a number of vital roles (e.g., social prediction, catalytic illustration, evaluation) other than the traditional one of verification.

may be reinvested in significant intellectual work. The discipline may thereby more fully realize its potential contribution to the history of thought.

The Assumption of Temporal Irrelevance

From the traditional positivist standpoint, the scientist's task is one of developing theory of transhistoric validity. Thus, in developing limited theoretical models and isolating major variables, social psychologists normally assume the transtemporal applicability of their formulations. Dissonance theory, balance theory, integration theory, the two-factor theory of emotional experience, attribution theory, and so on are not generally viewed as mere reflections of contemporary life styles. As many have argued (cf. Manis, 1976; Schlenker, 1974; Triandis, 1978), such formulations should be valid across time. From this perspective, one need not be concerned with the transient peculiarities of contemporary life; all may ultimately be subsumed by more basic theoretical principles.

As argued elsewhere (Gergen, 1976), the case for cross-time applicability of social theory is largely limited to matters of *post hoc interpretation*. Given the complexity of most social activity, a theorist may typically look back and discern some manner in which his or her theory may apply. General theoretical formulations can almost never be threatened by past history. However, when one turns to the problem of *prediction*, the case for cross-time applicability of social theory seems far less convincing. Either by choice or good fortune, the natural sciences have largely concerned themselves with a subject matter that is relatively stable or replicable (cf. Scriven, 1956). Astronomical theory continues to provide reasonably accurate predictions over time because the movements of the specified entities are relatively reliable. In contrast, the social scientist is confronted with an organism that is both sensitive to wide-ranging influences and capable of immense variations in behavior. Further, because of the individual's symbolic capacities, the range and type of inputs to which he or she may be responsive, along with the resulting forms of conduct, may all

be rapidly altered over time. In effect, patterns of human activity may be in a continuous state of emergence, *aleatoric* in the sense that they may largely reflect contemporary contingencies (Gergen, 1977). Such capacities place severe restrictions over the social scientist's efforts at predicting ongoing interaction.

In part, this line of argument suggests that traditional social psychology has suffered from a historical myopia. This possibility is well dramatized by recent investigation into life-span development. Developmentalists have become increasingly aware that patterns of childhood development may vary from one historical period to another. For example, as van den Berg (1961) has demonstrated, from the 15th to the 17th century, the child was viewed as an adult in miniature, fully developed in terms of mental capacities and lacking only in experience. Thus, a child in the wealthy classes might be expected to master four separate languages, to translate Plato from the original, and to hold serious discussions on death, sex, and ethics before the 7th year. More recently, however, research employing cohort methodology (cf. Buss, 1974) has greatly strengthened the case. Such techniques have enabled investigators to trace developmental trajectories in intelligence, mental and physical skills, personality traits, and other variables within contrasting historical periods (Baltes & Nesselroade, 1973; Baltes & Reinert, 1969; Schaie & Strother, 1968; Woodruff & Birren, 1972). As these analyses typically demonstrate, developmental trajectories appear highly dependent on historical circumstance; any given pattern of development may be limited to a particular period. As Looft (1972) has concluded from such work, "no longer should developmental psychologists focus so exclusively on ontogenetic age functions; each new generation will manifest age trends that are different from those that preceded it" (p. 51).[9]

_____

[9] Such work does not suggest that there are no transhistorically reliable patterns of development. The genetically programmed pattern of physiological maturation, for example, should insure a limited degree of reliable change. Parallels to the arguments made within the life-span arena may also be found in the fields of cognition (Jenkins, 1974) and personality theory (Sarbin, 1976).

This line of argument harbors two important implications for the development of generative theory. First, we find that the theorist may be liberated from the press of contemporary events. If the theorist considers current social pattern as fragile, temporary, and capable of alteration, theoretical analysis need not be circumscribed by a consideration of "what now exists." Rather, the theorist may be freed to consider alternatives, the advantages and disadvantages of relationships as yet unseen. To illustrate, traditional theory of aggression has confined itself largely to making sense of existing patterns of aggression. The effects of such factors as frustration, modeling, generalized arousal, the presence of models, the presence of weapons, and so on have all been explored (cf. Bandura's 1973 review). Yet, if we view all such accounts as relevant primarily to contemporary sociohistorical circumstances and take seriously the individual's capacity for wide-ranging change, then we may begin to consider alternative patterns and to evaluate their comparative assets. It seems clear that many reactions other than aggression may be adopted in frustrating circumstances or in response to aggressive models or weapons. One may choose to relax oneself, to divert one's attention, to behave altruistically, and so on, and each such reaction may have certain specifiable advantages and shortcomings. In exploring such alternatives, the theorist operates generatively to undermine common assumptions about social life. The theorist thus breaks the stranglehold of what people accept as "human nature" and paves the way to alternative social arrangements.

In addition to liberating the theorist from the press of contemporary pattern, the present thesis buttresses the initial line of argument regarding the shaping of social phenomena through theory. To the extent that observed patterns of behavior are historically limited, the invitation for generative theorizing is intensified. The theorist may view him- or herself as a potential contributor to the historical situation and thus as capable of altering it in such a way as to engender change. If the theorist is faced with virtually infinite possibilities for human change, then he or she may challenge the desirability of contemporary patterns as against envisioned alternatives and consider theoretical vehicles for reaching desired ends.

The Dispassionate Bystander Versus the Participant Theorist

In confronting the potential for transforming society through generative theory, the question of functional endpoint rapidly comes to the fore. What forms of action are to be shaped or supported through theory? Who is to make such decisions? From the traditional perspective, this issue is all but obscured from attention: The scientist's task is chiefly that of *description*, while matters of *prescription* are not within the purview of the scientist *qua scientist*. As commonly claimed, the scientist is concerned with *what is*, and there is no way of deriving "ought propositions" from the results of such activities. Further, when the scientist harbors vested interests in the endpoint of his or her investigation, one cannot trust the results. Passionate involvement may bias the ultimate product. Theorists in social psychology have thus tended to remain remote and aloof from what may be seen as the "squalid bickering over matters of the good."

The extent to which value investments shape scientific knowledge has long been the subject of debate (cf. Nagel, 1961; Rudner, 1953; Weber, 1949; Lacey, Note 2). While the range of implications remains unclear, such debate does indicate that the scientist's values are almost inevitably linked to the phenomena selected for study, the labels attached to those phenomena, the manner of interpreting new findings, the amount of confirming evidence required for a conclusion, and the manner of applying social theory. For present purposes, the most significant implication of such debate is that all such *valuational influences serve as "ought expressions" for the recipient of knowledge.* As such, they have the potential to shape the society; they may favor certain forms of social conduct at the expense of potential alternatives. As its implications and applications are borne out, every theory becomes an ethical or ideological advocate.

Perhaps the first social scientists to take seriously such valuational shaping effects were those forming the Frankfurt School (cf. Jay, 1973). In the 1930s, Max Horkheimer began his attack on the negative social effects of the more general positivist paradigm (see Horkheimer, 1972). On the one hand, he argued, the scientific paradigm treats the individual solely as an object to be acted upon, thus denying him his subjecthood or status as a free agent. Further, general scientific description of society is one that justifies by implicit assumption the hierarchical organization of society; such theory thus supports the continued oppression of certain classes by others. It was this latter line of argument that Jürgen Habermas (1971) elaborated with special force. As Habermas argued, in their underlying epistemology, positivist formulations obliterate the critical issues of social ethics; such formulations appear to be nonevaluative and, as such, resist questioning on ethical or ideological grounds. Thus, with fundamental questions of value obscured, the critical problem of ends is replaced with the relatively superficial concern with means; society is left primarily with problems of technical application. For reasons of social utility, both the scientist and the technician also tend to be absorbed by the decision-making institutions of the state. Thus, the scientific institution as a whole contributes to the maintenance of the existing power structure. The power structure, in turn, operates to the disadvantage of many people, primarily those occupying the lower classes. In short, positivist social science contributes to the continued oppression of the "have-nots." Such concerns have been echoed more recently in American sociology by Alvin Gouldner (1970). As Gouldner has demonstrated, even such seemingly dispassionate analyses as Parsonian functionalism provide a rationale for maintaining the status quo and, in doing so, serve the advantaged strata in society.

Within social psychology, concern with the valuational implications of normative theory has been relatively late in developing. Perhaps the earliest cries of alarm were European in origin. As Moscovici, Israel, and others pointed out (cf. Israel & Tajfel, 1972), by one means or another, American social psychological theory renders implicit support to ideological commitments of an indigenous character. This theme is reflected again in Apfelbaum and Lubek's (1977) attack on normative theories of conflict; as they contend, such theories do not take sufficient account of conflict from the standpoint of the "have-nots" in society and, in failing to incorporate their concerns into mainstream theory, render such groups "invisible." Sampson's (1977) recent analysis of social psychological theory represents perhaps the boldest statement to emerge within the American context. As he argued, much contemporary theory places strong implicit value on "self-contained individualism" and thus stands opposed to a collectivist or interdependent mode of orientation. As he points out,

Psychology plays an important role, even more so as it has become the new popular ideology, religion, and justifier for a variety of social programs. That role can continue to serve an isolating, atomizing, individualizing, and alienating function, or it can help refocus us on the fundamental interdependencies that need nurturance as well. (p. 779)

For present purposes it is largely irrelevant whether one agrees with the thrust of these various critiques: it is sufficient that ethical or ideological objection is publicly expressed over theory ostensibly lacking in valuational investment. It is also unimportant whether the majority of those exposed to such theories find their values either supported or questioned; precisely *how many* people are influenced at any given time is largely of historical concern and may reflect such practical exigencies as packaging and dissemination. The important point is that regardless of the traditional attempt to remain ethically neutral, the social theorist is inevitably favoring certain forms of social activity over others, certain strata of society as opposed to others, and certain values over their antitheses.

The answer to our initial query concerning the functional endpoint of generative theory is now apparent. Heretofore, the social psychologist has largely avoided questions of value by hiding behind the mask of "dispassionate observer." Yet, in spite of such attempts, we find that the fruits of neutrality are passionate in their consequences. This fact stands as an active challenge for the scientist to throw off the mask of neutrality and to confront more directly and honestly the valuational implications of his or her work. It would appear far more desirable for the theorist to give self-conscious consideration to matters of value in the development of theory than to stumble upon them some time after dissemination. The theorist need not fear the expression of values in a given formulation; they are inevitable. The major problem is to avoid expressions of value that, upon reflection, are disagreeable to the theorist. In effect, personal values or ideology may properly serve as a major motivational source for generative theorizing. In this way, the theorist becomes a full participant in the culture, fundamentally engaged in the struggle of competing values so central to the human venture.[10]

Continuing Controversy

To recapitulate the central thesis, it appears that in the commitment to traditional positivist assumptions, social psychology has substantially curtailed its capacity for generative theorizing. The attempt to build theory inductively from "what is known," the demand for verification of theoretical ideas, the disregard for the temporally situated character of social events, and the avoidance of valuational entanglements all prove detrimental to the kind of catalytic theorizing that throws into question the commonly shared assumptions of the culture and points to fresh alternatives for action. Further analysis reveals significant weaknesses in each of the traditional assumptions, thus paving the way for a liberalization of future theory. Yet, this analysis raises a variety of additional questions concerning the aims and potential for generative theorizing. Two of these deserve continuing attention.

The Desirability of Generative Theory

One major assumption underlying the present analysis is that undermining confidence in commonly shared assumptions represents a positive goal for scientific theory. In its departure from traditional aims, this goal is surely moot. Other than for reasons of intellectual zest, why should the scientist strive to create altered forms of social reality? In some

measure the present argument rests on the constricting character of the traditional scientific perspective. As we have seen, the traditional role of the scientist as an accurate reflector of social events is gravely misleading; scientific reflection inevitably lends support to certain assumptions about social life while denigrating others. As assumptions are sustained or rejected, social life may be altered in ways that may be judged "good" or "bad" from some standpoint. Given the choice of whether one's theoretical work will support the common assumptions of the society or not, there are important reasons for building toward contranormative theory.

On the most pragmatic level, it is not clear that the field may sustain itself if its major theoretical outcomes primarily perpetuate the commonsense understandings of the culture. Neither will the intellectual issues be sufficiently engaging to capture the interests of intelligent professionals, nor will the research fruits appear of sufficient importance to merit public funding. The field may wither out of ennui, and its efforts may be curtailed because it offers few new insights. Such problems are hardly new ones in social psychology. The lament that the field too often duplicates common sense has long been echoed, and from the present standpoint, it may continue, so long as the traditional mold for "doing science" prevails.[11] With the loosening of such strictures and the development of generative theory, the long-standing lament may recede.

There are additional reasons for favoring generative theory that are based on the potential of the discipline for broad social bene-

---

[10] Many may question the "right" of the psychologist to speak to matters of moral good. As we see from the present arguments, the scientist does so whether he or she wishes it or not. Further, as Brewster Smith (Note 3) has pointed out, the psychologist possesses a "privileged window on human experience," which may enable him or her to make a distinct contribution to such controversies.

[11] It has been argued elsewhere (Gergen, in press-b) that positivist metatheory dictates in large measure the components of substantive theory in social psychology. In adopting the metatheory, one simultaneously accepts a particular image of human functioning. Thus, a full liberation of theoretical options will depend on the search for alternative metatheory.

fit. In the act of theorizing, one translates experience into symbol, and the conceptual replica is inevitably a distortion of such experience. By nature a concept treats separate entities as equivalent, entities that may vary in numerous ways unrecognized by the concepts in question; any conceptual system is by nature incomplete. In addition, concepts are ill fitted to continuous motion or to stimuli of extreme complexity. Concepts do not adequately account for the complicated and continuous movements of a ballet dancer or a tumbler in action. Because of such inherent shortcomings, one may justifiably remain suspicious of any conceptual system. All theories remain partial, distorted, and biased. Thus a special premium is to be placed on generative theories, that is, theories that have the capacity to unseat the comfortable truths of wide acceptance. Such theories may generate controversy and doubt and, in doing so, reduce the strangling biases imbedded in any particular conceptual system. In effect, generative theory engenders a flexibility that may enhance the adaptive capacity of the society.

Such concerns have been linked to ideological ends by members of the Frankfurt School. The concept of "critical theory" was elaborated by Horkheimer, Adorno, Habermas, and others as a form of undermining the conceptual basis for the contemporary social order, an order that they viewed as inimical to the interests of the laboring classes. The critical orientation would isolate inconsistencies in the prevailing system of beliefs (scientific and otherwise), problems within the social structure, as well as discrepancies between prevailing beliefs and relevant fact. In this way, critical theory was to serve *emancipatory* interests (Rommetveit, 1977). Although such critiques of knowledge may seem uncongenial to those committed to the traditional maxim "no criticism without alternatives," critical theorists maintained that through criticism, choice was restored. Through critical appraisal, a given course of action (or manner of doing science) was no longer taken for granted, adopted without reflection. Rather, the critical awareness gave one the choice of doing other than treading time-worn paths. Although the ultimate aims

of the critical school were to see the capitalist structure of the society give way to a Marxist form, it becomes apparent that the central thrust of their argument is relevant to anyone concerned with changing any aspect of the prevailing order.

The Quicksand of Committed Theorizing

Serious pragmatic questions may also be raised with the present arguments for valuational advocacy in theorizing. It may well be maintained that such activity equates the scientist with the political ideologue or religious proselytizer and will eventually create widespread public suspicion. If theories become conscious expressions of value, then whatever trust has accrued to the field by virtue of its attempts at objectivity may be lost. These are grave issues indeed and should be subject to continued study. However, it is important in this case to distinguish between problems of prediction versus explanation, on the one hand, and the principles versus the practices of valuational expression, on the other. In the case of scientific explanation, it seems clear that scientific theory may well lose its status as an essentially objective enterprise. However, as we see, this status was ill acquired at the outset, and it is far preferable that the discipline revitalize its aims on an indigenous basis than remain vulnerable to attack over its duplicity or self-deception. At the same time, important distinctions must be made between the task of theorizing and that of predicting (Toulmin, 1961). Prescriptive investments at the theoretical level do not prevent the science from offering useful predictive services. The objectivity of predictive formulae need be no less suspect than those of the insurance actuarial. A similar case may be made for contemporary economic theory. Although macroeconomic theory is inevitably value based and prescriptive in implication, the economic forecaster may offer reasonably reliable predictions of certain economic activities.

Turning to the problem of principle versus practice, we find that the present arguments do suggest that social psychological theory is inevitably biased on ideological grounds, even in its most ardent attempts at "realistic description." However, this fact need not have adverse practical consequences. The impact of Marxist theory has been diminished in no obvious way by virtue of its ideological commitments; one might even argue the contrary. It is simply not clear that the society searches for dispassionate theoretical accounts, especially when such accounts appear to have personally beneficial consequences. The question is deserving of continued exploration.

Other issues remain. For example, certain forms of theoretical work in contemporary social psychology may have generative potential as yet unexplored. Consistency theories contain strong valuational implications that remain to be fully elaborated; the two-factor theory of emotion contains the seeds for a major challenge to the liberal political tradition (Unger, 1975); should attribution theory be extended, it could unseat the epistemological basis for contemporary social science. In effect, we have too frequently stopped short of realizing the generative potential of present pursuits. At the same time, we have little encouraged creative theorizing and have scarcely begun to take advantage of theory as a means to social reconstruction.

Reference Notes

1. Freedman, J. *Social psychology*. Presentation to the 1975–76 meetings of the Psychology Section, New York Academy of Sciences, New York.
2. Lacey, H. *Fact and value*. Unpublished manuscript, Swarthmore College, 1977.
3. Smith, M. B. *Psychology and values*. Gordon Allport memorial lecture, Harvard University, 1978.

References

Adorno, T., Frenkel-Brunswick, E., Levinson, D., & Sanford, N. *The authoritarian personality*. New York: Harper, 1950.

Ajzen, I., & Fishbein, M. Attitudes and normative beliefs as factors influencing behavioral intentions. *Journal of Personality and Social Psychology*, 1972, *21*, 1–9.

Anderson, N. H. Cognitive algebra: Integration theory applied to social attribution. In L. Berkowitz (Ed.), *Advances in experimental social psychology* (Vol. 7). New York: Academic Press, 1974.

Apfelbaum, E., & Lubek, I. Resolution versus revolution? The theory of conflicts in question. In L. Strickland, F. Aboud, & K. Gergen (Eds.), *So-cial psychology in transition*. New York: Plenum Press, 1976.

Asch, S. *Social psychology*. New York: Prentice-Hall, 1952.

Baltes, P. B., & Nesselroade, J. R. The developmental analysis of individual differences on multiple measures. In G. R. Nesselroade & H. W. Reese (Eds.), *Life-span developmental psychology: Methodological issues*. New York: Academic Press, 1973.

Baltes, P. B., & Reinert, G. Cohort effects in cognitive development of children as revealed by cross-sectional sequences. *Developmental Psychology*, 1969, *1*, 169–177.

Bandura, A. *Aggression: A social learning analysis*. Englewood Cliffs, N.J.: Prentice-Hall, 1973.

Bem, D. J. Self-perception theory. In L. Berkowitz (Ed.), *Advances in experimental social psychology* (Vol. 6). New York: Academic Press, 1972.

Berscheid, E., & Walster, E. Physical attractiveness. In L. Berkowitz (Ed.), *Advances in experimental social psychology* (Vol. 7). New York: Academic Press, 1974.

Blum, G. S. *Psychoanalytic theories of personality*. New York: McGraw-Hill, 1964.

Brehm, J. W. *A theory of psychological reactance*. New York: Academic Press, 1966.

Buss, A. R. Generational analysis: Description, explanation and theory. *Journal of Social Issues*, 1974, *30*, 55–71.

Byrne, D. *The attraction paradigm*. New York: Academic Press, 1971.

Cartwright, D. Risk taking by individuals and groups: An assessment of research employing choice dilemmas. *Journal of Personality and Social Psychology*, 1971, *20*, 361–378.

Dienstbier, R. A. The role of anxiety and arousal attribution in cheating. *Journal of Experimental Social Psychology*, 1972, *8*, 168–179.

Duval, S., & Wicklund, R. A. *A theory of objective self-awareness*. New York: Academic Press, 1972.

Elms, A. C. *Role-playing, reward and attitude change*. New York: Van Nostrand, 1969.

Festinger, L. *A theory of cognitive dissonance*. Evanston, Ill.: Row, Peterson, 1957.

Flacks, R. The liberated generation: An exploration of the roots of student protest. *Journal of Social Issues*, 1969, *23*, 52–75.

Gergen, K. J. Social psychology, science and history. *Personality and Social Psychology Bulletin*, 1976, *2*, 373–383.

Gergen, K. J. Stability, change and chance in understanding human development. In N. Datan & H. Reese (Eds.), *Life-span developmental psychology: Dialectical perspectives on experimental research*. New York: Academic Press, 1977.

Gergen, K. J. Experimentation in social psychology: A reappraisal. *European Journal of Social Psychology*, in press. (a)

Gergen, K. J. The positivist image in social psychological theory. In A. R. Buss (Ed.), *The social context of psychological theory*. New York: Irvington, in press. (b)

Glass, D. C., & Singer, J. E. *Urban stress.* New York: Academic Press, 1972.

Gouldner, A. W. *The coming crisis in western sociology.* New York: Basic Books, 1970.

Greenwald, A. G. Consequences of prejudice against the null hypothesis. *Psychological Bulletin,* 1975, *82,* 1–20.

Habermas, Jürgen. *Knowledge and human interest.* Boston: Beacon Press, 1971.

Hendrick, C. Social psychology as an experimental science. In C. Hendrick (Ed.), *Perspectives on social psychology.* Hillsdale, N.J.: Erlbaum, 1977.

Horkheimer, M. *Critical theory: Selected essays.* (Translated by M. J. O'Connell and others.) New York: Seabury Press, 1972.

Israel, J., & Tajfel, H. (Eds.). *The context of social psychology: A critical assessment.* New York: Academic Press, 1972.

Jay, M. *The dialectical imagination.* London: Heinemann, 1973.

Jenkins, J. Remember that old theory of memory? Well, forget it. *American Psychologist,* 1974, *29,* 785–794.

Jones, E. E., & Davis, K. E. From acts to dispositions: The attribution process in person perception. In L. Berkowitz (Ed.), *Advances in experimental social psychology* (Vol. 2). New York: Academic Press, 1965.

Jones, E. E., & Nisbett, R. *The actor and the observer: Divergent perceptions of the causes of behavior.* Morristown, N.J.: General Learning Press, 1971.

Jones, R. A., & Day, R. A. Social psychology as symbolic interaction. In C. Hendricks (Ed.), *Perspectives on social psychology.* Hillsdale, N.J.: Erlbaum, 1977.

Katz, D., & Stotland, E. A preliminary statement to a theory of attitude structure and change. In S. Koch (Ed.), *Psychology: A Study of a science.* New York: McGraw-Hill, 1959.

Kelley, H. H. *Causal schemata and the attribution process.* Morristown, N.J.: General Learning Press, 1972.

Kelman, H. C., & Lawrence, L. H. Assignment of responsibility in the case of Lt. Calley: Preliminary report on a national survey. *Journal of Social Issues,* 1972, *28,* 177–212.

Keniston, K. *Young radicals: Notes on committed youth.* New York: Harcourt, Brace & World, 1968.

Koch, S. Epilogue. In S. Koch (Ed.), *Psychology: A study of a Science* (Vol. 3). New York: McGraw-Hill, 1959.

Kuhn, T. S. *The structure of scientific revolution.* Chicago: University of Chicago Press, 1962.

Looft, W. R. Egocentrism and social interaction across the life span. *Psychological Bulletin,* 1972, *78,* 73–92.

Manis, M. Is social psychology really different? *Personality and Social Psychology Bulletin,* 1976, *2,* 427–436.

McGrath, J. E. (Ed.). *Social and psychological factors in stress.* New York: Holt, 1970.

McGuire, W. J. Personality and susceptibility to social influence. In E. F. Borgatta & W. W. Lambert (Eds.). *Handbook of personality theory and research.* Chicago: Rand McNally, 1969.

Medawar, P. B. *Induction and intuition in scientific thought.* London: Methuen, 1969.

Milgram, S. *Obedience to authority.* New York: Harper & Row, 1974.

Mill, J. S. *A system of logic: Ratiocinative and inductive.* New York: Harper, 1846.

Moscovici, S. *La psychanalyse, son image et son public.* Paris: Presses Universitaires de France, 1961.

Moscovici, S. Society and theory in social psychology. In J. Israel & H. Tajfel (Eds.), *The context of social psychology: A critical assessment.* New York: Academic Press, 1972.

Nagel, E. *The structure of science.* New York: Harcourt, Brace & World, 1961.

Neisser, U. *Cognition and reality.* San Francisco: Freeman, 1976.

Newtson, D. Dispositional inference from effects of actions: Effects chosen and effects forgone. *Journal of Experimental Social Psychology,* 1974, *10,* 489–496.

Osgood, C. E., & Tannenbaum, P. H. The principle of congruity in the prediction of attitude change. *Psychological Review,* 1955, *62,* 42–55.

Ossorio, P. G., & Davis, K. E. The self, intentionality, and reactions to evaluations of the self. In C. Gordon & K. Gergen (Eds.), *The self in social interaction.* New York: Wiley, 1968.

Phares, E. J. *Locus of control in personality.* Morristown, N.J.: General Learning Press, 1976.

Popper, K. R. *The logic of scientific discovery.* London: Hutchinson, 1959.

Posner, M. I., & Snyder, C. R. R. Facilitation and inhibition in the processing of signals. In P. M. A. Rabbitt & S. Dornic (Eds.), *Attention and performance V.* New York: Academic Press, 1975.

Quine, W. V. *Ontological relativity and other Essays.* New York: Columbia Univ. Press, 1969.

Rommetveit, R. On "emancipatory" social psychology. In L. Strickland, F. Aboud, & K. Gergen (Eds.), *Social psychology in transition.* New York: Plenum, 1976.

Rosch, E. Human categorization. In N. Warren (Ed.), *Studies in cross-cultural psychology* (Vol. 1). London: Academic Press, 1977.

Rudner, R. No science can be value-free. *Philosophy of Science,* 1953, *20,* 1–6.

Sampson, E. E. Psychology and the American ideal. *Journal of Personality and Social Psychology,* 1977, *35,* 767–782.

Sarbin, T. Contextualism: A world view for psychology: In Alvin Landfield (Ed.), *Nebraska Symposium on Motivation* (Vol. 24). Lincoln: University of Nebraska Press, 1976.

Schachter, S. *The psychology of affiliation.* Stanford, Calif.: Stanford University Press, 1959.

Schachter, S. The interaction of cognitive and physiological determinants of emotional states. In L. Berkowitz (Ed.), *Advances in Experimental Social Psychology* (Vol. 1). New York: Academic Press, 1964.

1360 KENNETH J. GERGEN

Schaie, K. W., & Strother, C. R. The effects of time and cohort differences on the interpretation of age changes in cognitive behavior. *Multivariate Behavioral Research*, 1968, *3*, 259–294.

Schlenker, B. R. Social psychology and science. *Journal of Personality and Social Psychology*, 1974, *29*, 1–15.

Scriven, M. A possible distinction between traditional scientific disciplines and the study of human behavior. In H. Feigl & M. Scriven (Eds.), *Minnesota studies in the philosophy of science: Vol. 1. The foundations of science and the concepts of psychology and psychoanalysis*. Minneapolis: University of Minnesota Press, 1956.

Shaw, M. E., & Costanzo, P. R. *Theories of social psychology*. New York: McGraw-Hill, 1970.

Shiffrin, R. M., & Schnieder, W. Toward a unitary model for selective attention, memory scanning and visual search. In S. Dornic (Ed.), *Attention and performance VI*. Hillsdale, N.J.: Lawrence Erlbaum Assoc., 1977.

Silverman, I. Why social psychology fails. *Canadian Psychological Review*, 1977, *18*, 353–358.

Storms, M. D., & Nisbett, R. E. Insomnia and the attribution process. *Journal of Personality and Social Psychology*, 1970, *16*, 319–328.

Tajfel, H. Experiments in a vacuum. In J. Israel and H. Tajfel (Eds.), *The context of social psychology*. New York: Academic Press, 1972.

Toulmin, S. *Foresight and understanding*. London: Hutchinson, 1961.

Triandis, H. Some universals of social behavior. *Personality and Social Psychology Bulletin*, 1978, *4*, 1–16.

van den Berg, J. H. *The changing nature of man*. New York: Norton, 1961.

Unger, R. M. *Knowledge and politics*. New York: Free Press, 1975.

Urdang, L. (Ed.). *Random House dictionary of the English language*. New York: Random House, 1968.

Walster, E., Walster, G. W., & Berscheid, E. *Equity, theory and research*. Boston: Allyn & Bacon, 1978.

Weber, M. *The methodology of the social sciences*. Glencoe, Ill.: Free Press, 1949.

Wilson, T. P. Normative and interpretive paradigms in sociology. In J. D. Douglas (Ed.), *Understanding everyday life*. London: Routledge & Kegan Paul, 1970.

Woodruff, D., & Birren, J. E. Age changes and cohort differences in personality. *Developmental Psychology*, 1972, *6*, 252–259.

Zajonc, R. B. Attitudinal effects of mere exposure. *Journal of Personality and Social Psychology Monograph*, 1968, *9*(2, Pt. 2).

Received March 3, 1978 ∎

[8]

Journal of Personality and Social Psychology
1986, Vol. 50, No. 6, 1261–1270

Hermeneutics of Personality Description

Kenneth J. Gergen
Swarthmore College

Alexandra Hepburn
University of Pennsylvania

Debra Comer Fisher
Yale University

Theories concerning the interpretation of human action call attention to the importance of context in assigning meaning to any given action. Yet, most researchers of personality use measures that are taken out of context. As a result, interpretations of findings are without apparent constraint. To explore these and related arguments, we focused on the Rotter internal–external (I–E) scale. We found that sophisticated language users could demonstrate how responses on any item of the scale could plausibly be used as indicators of virtually any common trait term within the English language. Multiple items could be viewed as an indicator of the same trait, or multiple traits could be plausibly explained as indicators of the same I–E response. Furthermore, identical traits (other than I–E) could be linked to opposing items, and logically opposing traits could both be understood as giving rise to the same I–E response. These and additional findings suggest that interpretations of personality research data may depend primarily on social processes within the science. Further implications are examined.

Personality psychologists share a focal interest in the internal mechanisms, processes, or dispositions believed to govern human behavior. As many contend, one of the chief hallmarks of psychological science is the use of psychological terms for purposes of behavioral explanation. However, this focus on the psychological realm has confronted investigators with a formidable range of conceptual and mensurational problems. For example, what is the origin of knowledge about psychological entities or states? How is one to determine what terms are to be used in psychological description? How are valid and reliable indicators of the psychological realm to be developed? For personality psychologists, valid measurement of psychological dispositions is often a principal end point of research; for most other domains, such measurement typically serves as a means for testing hypotheses about more general processes such as learning, information processing, development, or the like. It is this critical connection between overt behavior and what is taken to be the psychological realm that we addressed in this research. It is personality research, with its rich history of mensurational exploration, that serves as the proper crucible for the arguments to be advanced.

The classic papers of MacCorquodale and Meehl (1948) and Cronbach and Meehl (1955) largely furnished the rationale for using hypothetical constructs in research on personality traits. As reasoned, if psychology is to become an objective science, statements about the hypothetical realm of the interior must ultimately be grounded in observation. Thus statements about hypothetical constructs should be linked through definitional means to publicly observable events. These linkages must be such that, depending on the character of observed events, one's

statements about the hypothetical constructs are subject to empirical evaluation. For example, in the case of Rosenberg's (1979) measure of the hypothetical construct of self-esteem, a condition of high self-esteem is defined or indicated by one's agreement with such statements as "On the whole, I am satisfied with myself." This linkage is validated to the degree that the individual responds similarly to other items indicative of the same disposition or behaves in various other ways believed to be expressive of this state. Confidence that the item enables one to measure a state of high self-esteem would be threatened to the extent that agreement with this item is negatively correlated with other indicators of high self-esteem.

Although this general line of reasoning has been virtually foundational for the past 50 years of personality study, emerging arguments in neighboring disciplines suggest that a contemporary reassessment is in order. Of particular concern are developments within the hermeneutic or interpretive domain. Hermeneutic study emerged during the 17th century as a discipline devoted to establishing guidelines for the proper interpretation of Biblical scripture. By what criteria, it was asked, is one interpretation to be held superior to another? Hermeneutic study has since evolved into a more general line of inquiry, shared by theologians, philosophers, literary analysts, social scientists, and others. Such inquiry is primarily concerned with the processes by which human beings interpret or discover the meaning of human action in general and linguistic expressions in particular (see Bleicher, 1980; Palmer, 1969). The question of the grounds of accurate or adequate interpretation remains paramount. As is readily apparent, the task of the hermeneuticist parallels that of the personality psychologist: Both are critically concerned with the justification of inferences about particular psychological conditions (intention or meaning in the one case and personality dispositions in the other) from behavioral indicators (typically linguistic in both cases).

Within the present century a major line of thinking has emerged within hermeneutic thought, one of far-reaching con-

This article has benefited greatly from constructive reactions furnished by Marianthi Georgoudi, Mary Gergen, Linda Harris, Dean Peabody, and John Shotter to an earlier draft.

Correspondence concerning this article should be addressed to Kenneth J. Gergen, Department of Psychology, Swarthmore College, Swarthmore, Pennsylvania 19081.

sequence for the realm of psychology. As has become increasingly clear to interpretation theorists, the linkages connecting overt utterances and the hypothetical realm of meaning or intention are vitally dependent on historically located conventions. It is these interpretive conventions (sometimes termed *forestructures of understanding*) that determine how a text is interpreted and not the author's intention in itself. Thus text or utterance may properly be expected to convey different meanings within various subcultures and across history. From this perspective, the concept of "true meaning" is rendered problematic. Thus, for example, Gadamer (1975) argued that one does not confront a text in a historical vacuum. Rather, people dwell within a comtemporary "horizon of understandings," and these understandings inevitably fashion their interpretation of texts. Or, as Ricoeur (1971) proposed, "with written discourse, the author's intention and the meaning of the text cease to coincide . . . the text's career escapes the finite horizon lived by the author" (p. 532).

We extend the implications of this line of thinking to the classic questions confronting the psychologist. Responses to personality assessment devices, verbal and otherwise, stand in an equivalent relation to psychological dispositions as language does to meaning. Thus from the hermeneutic standpoint, any conclusions reached about the nature of psychological constructs on the basis of observation may be governed principally by the contemporary conventions of interpretation. For example, describing oneself as independent and decisive is often viewed as a sign of masculinity at the psychological level, whereas characterizing oneself as emotional and aware of others' feelings is said to indicate a feminine disposition. Yet, the warrant for using such utterances to infer such dispositions depends principally on whether it makes sense in contemporary culture to say that such self-descriptions are legitimate expressions of gender makeup (Spence, 1983; Tellegen & Lubinski, 1983). As language usage within the culture evolves, the legitimacy of such connections may wax and wane. Investigators who use the F scale have already confronted this problem. As Ghiselli (1974) and Lake, Miles, and Earle (1973) argued, the F scale of the 1940s may today be obsolete. The meaning of answers to questions such as "Homosexuals are hardly better than criminals and ought to be severely punished" and "Nowadays more and more people are prying into matters that should remain personal and private" would be far different to the contemporary sensibility than in earlier decades.

One can argue that a certain degree of temporal decay in the meaning or proper interpretation of various personality indicators can be tolerated. As long as there is widespread agreement by investigators and subjects alike that a given utterance means, indicates, or stands for a given disposition, then one might legitimately proceed (at least for a time) on this basis. Yet, there is good reason to suspect that the problem of proper interpretation is more acute. Two major difficulties must be confronted. As long recognized within the hermeneutic tradition, the warrant for interpreting the meaning of any given word or phrase usually depends on one's reference to the context in which it is embedded. Thus in written discourse one typically clarifies the intention behind a given word, phrase, or sentence by demonstrating how it figures within the corpus of the work as a whole. If a character in a novel addresses another as "a fool," the meaning of this term significantly depends on whether the two have been described, for instance, as friends or as enemies, as given to jocu-

larity or as formal, and so on. As traditionally maintained, the constraints that may be placed over the interpretation of any particular utterance derive primarily from the elaboration of context. Thus to know what is meant by a given sentence is essentially to find the sentence predictable, by conventional standards, from the context in which it occurs.

In the case of personality assessment, it is precisely the extended context that is unavailable, either to the test taker or to the investigator; that is, the assessee is typically confronted by items (questions, statements of value, self-ratings, etc.) that lack the kind of context that would enable him or her to make a meaningful reply. To describe oneself as "loving," for example, without taking into account the conditions (e.g., in battle, at a wedding, on the street), the potential targets (e.g., men, women, crocodiles), and the agent of the question (e.g., one's children, one's ex-love, a drill sargeant) is to furnish a response that is essentially openended in its psychological and social significance. Similarly, for the assessor, an array of responses that are taken out of the kind of context that would elucidate or constrain their meaning essentially furnishes a blank slate upon which a potentially immense variety of interpretive preferences may be inscribed.

An additional problem with reaching a convincing consensus with regard to personality description arises from pragmatic demands of psychological explanation in everyday interchange (cf. Gergen & Gergen, 1982). Normal relationships place a considerable demand on participants to make their actions intelligible—that is, to furnish meanings or interpretations for their conduct (cf. Harré, 1981; Shotter, 1981; Tedeschi & Reiss, 1981). Such phrases as "What I mean by this is . . . ," "Don't take this wrong, but . . . ," "If you see it my way," or "This is a token of . . ." are among the many signals that interpretive instructions are to follow. The speaker is to inform the listener of the proper means of interpreting his or her actions. In a major degree the success of one's social trajectory is dependent on one's capacity to manage the interpretations made of his or her conduct (Pearce & Cronen, 1980). However, the exigencies of interpretation management often militate against the stabilization of interpretive conventions. Rather, practical demands suggest that cultural participants frequently strive to alter, bend, or reshape existing rules of interpretation and to create novel means of demonstrating the desired meaning of their acts. For example, it appears that considerable ingenuity has been devoted within the culture to ensure that the words "I love you" do not fix or unambiguously designate a given psychological state. When one's words unequivocally fix one's psychological condition, flexibility of action is decreased. The struggle toward ambiguity may leave people free to claim a wide range of indicators as expressions of a particular psychological state, and to claim any given utterance or activity to be an expression of wide-ranging states.

For the psychologist, the result of both the "decontextualization" of measurement and the elasticity in rules for linking psychological state terms to language use may be nontrivial. As the conventions for making such linkages are obscured, it becomes increasingly difficult to justify any particular interpretation of a behavioral indicator. If any indicator is subject to an indeterminate number of interpretations, then the warrant for any selected interpretation is open to question. Normally such questions are not open to debate. This is primarily so because once the meaning of a test item response has been framed within a given perspective, its sense appears transparent. For what reason should one wish to challenge the eminently sensible? For example, one may discern many possible motives for a person's saying "I often wish I were someone else." However, once the item is included within a battery of items said to enable one to measure self-esteem, its meaning seems to be disambiguated. One is loath to question the interpretation without special justification. Over time the received interpretation becomes "objectified," a constituent of the common sense reality of the discipline. Of unfortunate consequence, this means that on the professional level the range of explanatory alternatives becomes restricted; theoretical possibilities are truncated rather than expanded. On the applied level, people's lives may be vitally affected by the sustaining interpretation. Depending on their scores on various mental tests, people's options may be denied, paths discouraged, or remedial training recommended. Such policies may be implemented without the affected persons being given access to the process of interpretation in which they are implicated.

We attempt to explore the limits of interpretive flexibility within the sphere of personality assessment. What constraints, if any, may be placed over the range of possible interpretations of responses to personality trait indicators? As a test vehicle, an assessment device was selected on the grounds that it (a) had been subjected to intensive study, (b) continues to be in broad usage, and (c) has achieved generalized agreement regarding proper interpretation. The Rotter (1975) measure of perceived locus of control appears to meet all of these criteria. Evidence regarding predictive validity has accumulated for almost two decades (cf. Findley & Cooper, 1983; Lefcourt, 1976, 1981; Phares, 1976; Strickland, 1976). The measure continues to play a prominent role in wide-ranging research endeavors. Largely because of the high degree of face validity of the 23 items that constitute the measure, minimal question has been raised over what psychological disposition that the items are enabling one to measure. We place into question the warrant for the received view. The specific attempt is to explore what limits may be placed over the options for interpreting the research data on which existing conclusions rest. What limits, if any, may be placed over the range of meanings that may be assigned to scale outcomes and thus the range of existing research in this domain?

Study 1: Can Any Response Express Any Trait?

Method

In contrast to most research in which the ideal is to procure an average sample from the population at large, inquiry into the potentials of language use requires a sample of highly skilled practitioners. The attempt is to challenge sophisticated language users to interpret items that ostensibly enable one to measure locus of control in a variety of alternative ways. Initial participants in the research were thus 24 students enrolled in the University of Pennsylvania Graduate School of Education. Each participant was furnished with a small booklet of "Interpretation Puzzles." In the initial section of the booklet they were told that they would be presented with a series of opinion statements, each coupled with a single personality trait. It was their task to show how it would make sense to say of someone who agreed with the opinion statement that he or she possessed the trait in question, or, as it was said, if someone had the trait in question, whether an explanation as to why he or she would agree with the opinion statement could be furnished. If no sensible explanation could be found, participants were to try to indicate why. The opinion items were drawn from the Rotter internal–external (I–E) locus of control mea-

sure; all items from the measure were used. The trait terms were taken from Anderson's (1968) list of 555 common personality-trait terms. Each booklet contained five separate interpretation puzzles; each puzzle was represented by a randomly selected I–E item (without regard to whether the item was scored on the internal or the external direction) along with a randomly selected trait term (e.g., *relaxed, moral, cautious*). In total, the participants were exposed to 120 separate trait–item combinations.

Results

The results of this inquiry into the flexibility of explanatory conventions were clear-cut. Of the array of 120 combinations, only 4 failed to make sense to the participants. Two of the four were found incoherent by the same subject. In most cases, the solutions to the puzzles were achieved with little apparent effort. Typically, only a single sentence was required in order to demonstrate how agreement with an I–E item served as a plausible indicator of a randomly selected trait. The flavor of the participants' solutions is best demonstrated with several examples:

1. A person who is *shy* says, "There is a direct connection between how hard I study and the grades I get" (scored as internal on the Rotter scale) because "Such a rationale excuses the shy person from too much socializing and allows him to secrete himself in his room."

2. A person who is *impulsive* says, "Unfortunately, an individual's worth often passes unrecognized no matter how hard he tries" (scored as external) because "An impulsive person might very well need to justify his feelings of staying too short a time with one project or another by believing that no matter how persevering or committed he remains, he won't be acknowledged anyway."

3. A person who is *logical* says, "In the long run people get the respect they deserve in this world" (scored as internal) because "People don't get respect randomly; some prior events determine how much respect people get. Thus, the logical person can use his logic to make predictions."

It is possible, of course, that under the duress of solving such problems, the participants may have furnished answers that were incoherent or nonsensical. Thus, we made a separate inquiry into the plausibility of the various solutions. In this case, ratings were made by a panel of 7 additional graduate students, each asked independently to judge the plausibility of a series of approximately a dozen interpretations selected at random from the protocols of the 24 participants. Judgments were made on a 4-point scale ranging from 1 = *nonsense* to 4 = *highly plausible* (2 = *doubtful rationale* and 3 = *plausible*). The overall mean evaluation of the 84 accounts made by the participants proved to be 3.25 (*SD* = 0.84), which indicated that the solutions to the challenges were generally quite plausible. Four of the judges were then furnished with additional puzzles to solve, among which were the four cases that members of the original sample were unable to solve. In this case, a solution was readily found to each.

In summary, the results of this initial study suggest that contemporary language conventions permit virtually any item of the I–E scale to be plausibly interpreted as an expression of virtually any common trait disposition.

Study 2: Multiple Traits and Responses

Given the high degree of interpretive flexibility found in the initial study, we made additional attempts to press for possible limits. In the first of these queries, we raised the question of whether any given item from the I-E measure could be plausibly interpreted as an indicator of a variety of different underlying traits. In order to explore this possibility, a group of 7 undergraduate volunteers from Swarthmore College was exposed to a series of interpretation puzzles, among which were seven items from the I-E scale (four indicating an external orientation and three an internal). For each item, three different trait terms were randomly drawn. Thus each of the seven items appeared three different times on the protocols, in each instance with a separate trait term. Each participant confronted each item only once, but there was no duplication across participants in the trait term associated with the item. The instructions for this task were identical to those for the first study.

The results of this inquiry demonstrated first that there were no trait-item pairings for which participants failed to furnish a solution. Thus, for example, the participants could demonstrate that the item "How many friends you have depends upon how nice a person you are" (internal) could serve as a reasonable indicator of *responsibility, loyalty,* and *shyness;* in addition, according to participants, the item "Who gets to be boss depends on who was lucky enough to be in the right place first" (external) could sensibly be seen as an expression of a person's *oversensitivity, practicality,* or *boldness.* A later panel of five judges also found these interpretive solutions plausible. In this case the average plausibility rating was 3.04 ($SD = 1.12$).

To extend this inquiry, we then attempted to explore whether a variety of items could all serve as signifiers for the same trait, a trait other than locus of control. Most cogently, we asked, are the rules of intelligibility sufficiently flexible to permit various traits to be plausibly expressed in logically opposing statements? To explore this possibility, we embedded eight trait-item pairs within the booklets to which subjects in the first study were exposed. Four traits (e.g., *broad-minded, optimistic, fearful, jealous*) were randomly selected (two from the positive and two from the negative pole of Anderson's 1968 list), and each was paired with two I-E items, one traditionally used to assess an internal and the other an external orientation. Each of the 8 participants in this study were exposed to all four traits, but to only one of the two pairings (i.e., either an internal or an external pairing).

The results of this exploration revealed that participants were successfully able to develop linking rationales for all pairings. The same trait could successfully be related to expressions of both internally and externally scored items. For example, one participant wrote that a *broad-minded* person would say, "In the case of the well-prepared student, there is rarely if ever such a thing as an unfair test" (scored as internal) because "A broad-minded person is willing to admit that if one is well prepared, tests will rarely be unfair. A narrow-minded individual would be more suspecting and defensive." On the other hand, wrote another participant, a *broad-minded* person would say, "As far as world affairs are concerned, most of us are the victims of forces we can neither understand or control" (scored as external) because "A broad-minded person wouldn't try to 'blame' world events on a particular politician or groups." The average plausibility of the explanations proved acceptable ($M = 3.21$, $SD = .98$).

To strengthen the case still further, 12 additional students were furnished with the same task but this time were asked whether they could demonstrate how opposite traits (i.e., *broad-minded* and *narrow-minded; optimistic* and *pessimistic; fearful* and *brave*) could be expressed in the same response. In this case, half the participants were asked to demonstrate how *broad-minded, optimistic,* and *fearful* were expressed in a series of internal and external items, whereas the remaining half were asked to develop rationales for linking *narrow-minded, pessimistic,* and *brave* to the same statements. The results of this analysis paralleled the first. All pairings were explained by the participants. One may obtain a flavor of the results by comparing the previous accounts of how broad-mindedness would be expressed in both internal and external items, with explanations of how narrow-mindedness would be revealed in the same items. In the case of the internal statement concerning the well-prepared student who did not believe in an unfair test, one student wrote, "A narrow minded person would say this because he would not take into account all the many reasons a test could be unfair." In the case of the external statement concerning being victims of forces that one cannot understand or control, another student wrote, "a narrow-minded person is one who doesn't want to look too deeply inside himself to see how he is really responsible for what happens to him." The average plausibility of these various explanations was 3.16 ($SD = 1.03$).

As these studies indicate, intelligent language users can construct a plausible rationale for interpreting randomly selected items from the I-E scale as indicators of a multiplicity of traits. Furthermore, any single trait may be seen as expressed in multiple items from the I-E scale. Of particular note is that the rules of interpretation appear sufficiently flexible that both internal and external statements can both be understood as revealing the same basic trait. Such statements can be interpreted satisfactorily as indicators of both a given trait and its opposite.

Study 3: Multiplicity of Individual Trait-Item Linkages

Method

If a given trait could be linked to a given item in only one intelligible way, important limits might then be placed over the possible interpretations made of various personality measures. Items could be expanded or altered so as to enable one to rule out or be maximally attuned to a given interpretation as required. To explore the range of linking rationales, we carried out a further study with 10 volunteers from Swarthmore College. In this case, four randomly selected traits were paired with I-E items (two scored in the internal and two in the external direction). We used the same research format as that described earlier. This allowed us to assess the number of rationales by which an item might be used as an indicator of a given psychological trait (other than that trait purportedly measured via the item.)

Results

The results of this study first indicated that all of the possible trait-item linkages could be performed. Inspection of the conventions used to relate trait to item also revealed that for no such linkage was the same rationale used by all 10 participants. Rather, for each pair, a variety of linkages was offered by the participants. When these rationales were subclassified, we found that the number of ways of relating a given trait term to an I-E item varied between three to six (for 10 subjects). A fuller appreciation of the results may be derived from the following example: Participants were asked to explain why a *lonely* person would say, "Who gets to be boss often depends on who was lucky enough to be in the right place first" (scored as external). The 10 explanations (largely paraphrased) could be grouped as follows:

Compensation. (a) A person may say this to explain why he or she has no relationships with others, in order "to cover up other, less acceptable explanations." (b) A lonely person probably isn't a boss; he or she does not want to attribute this to himself or herself, and so attributes it to luck. (c) A lonely person has a difficult time in personal relations and "may rationalize to the point of denying" that his or her actions have anything to do with it. (d) A lonely person is poor at social relations, and never got to be a boss; this is said "to protect" himself or herself.

Logic of loneliness. (a) A lonely person lacks self-confidence and thus believes that his or her actions will make no difference in the outcome. (b) A lonely person is unmotivated and detached, and thus believes in the luck of the situation. (c) A lonely person feels left out and isolated, and therefore believes that luck has most to do with success. (d) Becoming a boss is a great deal of work for the lonely person, so he or she "demeans the boss-choosing process."

Incapacity. A person's loneliness stems from his or her lack of understanding of personal relations. This lack of understanding is also revealed in his or her perception of how people get to be leaders.

The 10th participant in this case simply used a "common sense claim": to wit, lonely people believe that "exterior forces such as luck have more control over persons' conditions than [do] persons themselves."

As indicated in this study, then, there appear to be a multiplicity of explanatory means by which people can demonstrate how a given utterance is an expression of various common traits. A group of 10 language users in this case could typically locate between three to six rationales for making such connections. One may well anticipate that by increasing the pool of participants, or locating participants with greater linguistic sophistication, one could expand even further the number of intelligible links.

Study 4: Making Sense of Multiple Items

Thus far the results suggest an impressive degree of flexibility in contemporary conventions for linking terms referring to various psychological states with various self-descriptive statements. How might the weight of these results be diminished? What counterarguments may be posed? At least one possibility derives from the logic of personality assessment: namely, the rationale for using multiple items. As it is reasoned, any given item may be influenced by a variety of psychological factors, and one would thus be ill advised to trust single-item measures of any trait. Rather, it is essential to use multiple items that have a demonstrated relation to each other. In this way, extraneous factors that influence responses on any single item will be obscured, and the contribution of the focal trait will be maximized in the summary score. Applying this logic to our results thus far, one may argue that the flexibility of interpretation has been demonstrated only with single items. Although any single item may be interpreted in several ways, significant constraints over interpretation may derive from the use of multiple items.

Method

To explore this possibility, we carried out two studies, the first as a preliminary to the second. The initial study was prompted not only by the concern just stated, but also by the fact that the I–E scale traditionally demands of respondents that they select between pairs of self-descriptive items, one treated as an expression of an internal and the other an external orientation. Yet, in all studies described thus far, traits have been linked to either an internal or an external statement. Thus in order to explore whether plausible linkages could be constructed when both items appeared simultaneously, 8 Swarthmore students were given six pairs of statements randomly selected from the I–E measure. For each pair a trait was randomly drawn from the Anderson (1968) list, and the participant asked to explain why a person who possesses that trait (e.g., *insecure, independent, inquisitive*) would agree with one of the statements (selected at random) rather than the other. In all, 12 different traits were matched with 12 different item pairs; subjects were challenged to construct half of the linkages to internal and half to external choices.

Results

We found that participants were able to construct all linkages with which they were challenged. The addition of the second statement, said to be "not chosen" by the test taker, produced no barrier to the effective exercise of interpretive capacities. Furthermore, we found that when these linkages were given to an additional sample of 6 students, that the average plausibility rating was 3.32 (*SD* = .97).

These results furnished a useful prelude to a more stringent assessment of interpretive flexibility. In this case, 24 graduate students at the University of Pennsylvania were exposed to a series of "Triple Puzzles"; that is, they were asked to explain how an individual who possessed a single trait, which was selected at random, might agree with three separate statements (also randomly selected) from the I–E measure (also randomly selected). Thus, for example, a participant might be asked how a *fearful* person could agree with all three of the following statements:

1. In any case, getting what I want has little or nothing to do with luck. (Internal)

2. As far as world affairs are concerned, most of us are the victims of forces we can neither understand nor control. (External)

3. Many times we might just as well decide what to do by flipping a coin. (External)

Each participant was presented with three triple puzzles. Nine different traits were used with nine corresponding item triads.

As the analysis of these data demonstrated, of the 72 interpretive challenges, 68 were executed. Because the triple puzzles were included in a larger battery of tasks, and required a greater degree of effort than other sections of the questionnaire, the slightly elevated number of failures to complete might be anticipated. However, insofar as these failures could also be viewed as a signal of interpretive inflexibility, it was possible to examine whether any trait-triple-item pair was insoluble for the other 7 participants exposed to the same pairing. As this analysis revealed, there was no trait-triple-item pair for which at least 7 of the 8 relevant participants could not furnish linkages. Thus, for example, for the triad just presented, one participant said that the initial statement would express fearfulness because "The fearful person believes he controls his own situation by watching out for all things he fears." Such a person was said to endorse the second statement because "A fearful person recognizes the limits of his vigilance." And the third item would be endorsed because "A fearful person gets depressed when confronted with the limits of his vigilance."

In order to assess the intelligibility of these interpretations. a further sample of 8 college students was asked to rate, in the same manner just reported. the reasonableness of a selection of rationales from a random group of 18 trait–item pairs. On the same 4-point rating as that mentioned earlier, the mean of the evaluations was 3.04 ($SD = 1.11$), which indicated that the interpretations furnished by participants were well within the bounds of reason.

In summary, relatively sophisticated language users could develop intelligible reasons for viewing agreement with randomly selected statements from the I–E battery. in the context of disagreement with a contrasting trait. as indicative of wide-ranging traits. Furthermore. randomly selected traits could be seen as intelligibly and simultaneously expressed by as many as three separate I–E items.

Study 5: From Face Validity to Generic Trait

A further argument against this analysis again derives from fundamental views of the assessment process. Although it may be possible for sophisticated language users to show how a handful of items may be expressions of traits other than the one initially designated, such interpretive demonstrations might wear thin if applied to the battery of 23 items. In effect, one may venture that each of these items possesses face validity. The most obvious interpretation to be made of the claim to seeing oneself as internally controlled is that the individual believes himself or herself to be internally controlled. If the various interpretations constructed within these exercises were pitted against the designated interpretation. the latter might well be found the superior in plausibility. Alternative interpretations possess varying degrees of plausibility (as is evident in the magnitude of the standard deviations). but on the face of it they will be less plausible than the designated interpretation.

In inspecting this line of defense. one must confront two major issues. First, in such a defense one makes the fundamental error of presuming that "face validity" reflects the degree to which a response accurately indicates the underlying disposition. In fact. in arguing for face validity. the researcher essentially asks that one accept the most conventional interpretation (typically for a given subculture) rather than the most accurate one. It is true that one's acceding to convention enables social life (or life within scientific subcultures) to proceed more smoothly. As Garfinkel (1967) showed when people are consistently asked to clarify what their utterances "really mean." relationships rapidly deteriorate. However, to capitulate to the demand for smooth relationships does not thereby enhance the accuracy of the interpretations. Under many circumstances (e.g., when people wish to create a good impression, avoid attention, seek help) there may be good pragmatic reason for casting aside the convention of face validity. If one is concerned with generating "an enlightened view," "fresh insight," or a catalytic conceptualization within the sciences, an appeal to convention may be counterproductive.

Yet, there is a deeper difficulty at stake in the argument for face validity. When the argument is explored, one confronts an indeterminacy of interpretation that is even more extended than that suggested thus far. The problem is essentially that of locating the generic source for item responses. One assumes in the case of face validity that the linguistic expression reflects an immediately underlying intention or disposition. However, this assumption does not warrant the further assertion that the intention or disposition is the generic source of the expression. Such intentions or dispositions may be only superficial vehicles for the expression of deeper or more fundamental motives. In the case of the I–E measure. an individual may indicate as many as 23 times that he or she is not in control of outcomes. Yet, one may ask, what is the psychological basis for such patterns? The individual may be giving voice to his or her immediate intentions, but what lies behind the intentions? Mere intentions are uninformative until one discerns their underlying determinants. It is at this point that myriad possibilities are confronted. A wide range of motives or traits could plausibly give rise to the more superficial or proximal intention.

Method

In order to explore the implications of this argument more concretely, Swarthmore undergraduates were first given questionnaires in which they were asked to make conjectures about the goals or needs that might underlie a person's saying (in various ways) that he or she either (a) viewed himself or herself as in control of outcomes or (b) viewed outcomes as largely a result of circumstances beyond his or her control. As this inquiry demonstrated. most participants could furnish a variety of generic sources for such statements. For example, it was said of those who generally see outcomes as outside of their control that they are expressing a need for others to help them succeed (nurturance), a need to excuse their current position, a complacency over their condition, basic cynicism, a state of serenity, pessimism, need for others' reassurance, and so on.

Even if all items on the I–E scale are taken as face-valid indicators of what people desire to communicate. multiple assertions that the world is controlling (or not) do not themselves permit one to designate the underlying motivational or dispositional source. Common linguistic conventions permit such assertions to be interpreted as motivated, driven, stimulated, or otherwise influenced by a wide variety of "deeper" psychological sources. But push the analysis a step further: To say that a person's utterances are the result of needs for nurturance, drive for success, basic cynicism. and the like still leaves open the question of psychological basis. What motivates a person to seek nurturance, to strive for success, and so on? More generally. this is to say that every candidate for a generic source trait or disposition might be dislodged from such candidacy by means of inquiring into its genesis. Each generic trait or stimulus becomes an effect or a "superficial manifestation" when its source is considered.

The implications of this argument were explored in two additional studies. In the preliminary study the free responses generated by participants in the preceding exercise were examined. Four traits or dispositions that were said to be the cause of people's claims that they were in control of their outcomes were selected on the basis of their frequency. Eight undergraduates were then exposed to a set of "psychological speculation puzzles" in which they were asked how it is that persons who characterized themselves as possessing one trait might actually be demonstrating an underlying (or more basic) alternative trait. For example, a participant was asked how a person who expressed a need to be superior could actually be demonstrating a more basic need for control. Thus each of the four traits (need for *superiority. control. freedom from anxiety.* and *self-esteem*) was featured in both a generic and a surface position. and each related to all others.

Results

As the results demonstrated, participants experienced no difficulty in forming intelligible connections among all surface and source traits. For example, as one participant wrote, "A person who indicates his need for superiority may actually be expressing a need for control because those who want control need superior positions in order for them to be able to control." And as another participant indicated, "One who expresses freedom from anxiety is more basically a person who feels good about himself, i.e., has high self-esteem." As this exercise indicates, then, each manifest disposition could be intelligibly interpreted as a result of another more generic psychological disposition. And each of these dispositions could be viewed, in turn, as the surface manifestation of a more basic source. All four layers of explanation could be traversed. In effect, the explanatory base could thus be rendered fully circular insofar as the most basic trait could be viewed as an effect or manifestation of the surface disposition with which the search began. Expressions of internality can be seen to reflect a need for superiority, which is intelligibly viewed as the result of the individual's need for self-esteem, which functions to reduce anxiety. However, the state of reduced anxiety may be viewed as a byproduct of the more basic tendency to see one's outcomes as contingent upon one's actions. The explanatory circle is complete.

These results raise a more general question: Are the linguistic conventions sufficiently flexible that virtually any psychological disposition may be understood as a reasonable cause for any other disposition? In order to explore this possibility, 18 Swarthmore undergraduates were exposed to four different pairs of trait terms drawn randomly from the Anderson (1968) list. For each pair the student was asked how a particular characteristic of the person (Trait 1) could be motivated or caused by a second attribute (Trait 2). Thus, for example, the students were asked how a person's *practicality* might be motivated or caused by his or her *hopefulness*, how being *comical* could be caused by *resentfulness*, how being *foolish* could be caused by the person's desire to be *charming*, and so on. In all, 40 different trait combinations were used.

The results of this study largely duplicated the previous patterns. Linkages were successfully constructed for all of the 40 different trait combinations. (Three such linkages were not executed by certain participants, but whereas one participant failed to make the linkage, another or others successfully did so.) In order to assess general plausibility, each questionnaire was then evaluated by one other participant in the group. The average plausibility rating for all trait combinations in this case was 3.31 (*SD* = .74), a mean that closely approximates the pattern revealed in earlier studies and indicates a high degree of plausibility.

As this series of explorations thus suggests, contemporary language conventions are sufficiently flexible to permit most common trait designations to be plausibly understood as surface manifestations of many other traits at a "deeper level." Trait dispositions operating at the deeper level may intelligibly be understood as a manifestation of still more remote generic sources. Is it possible, one may ask, that any pattern of action, such as claims made to see one's outcomes as under chance or personal control, could be compellingly traced to the full range of common trait dispositions extant within the culture?

Study 6: The Negotiability of Predictive Validity

A final means of combating the implications of our line of argument must be addressed. Traditional assessment theory holds that the validity of a measure is established in important degree through predictive study (Lanyon & Goodstein, 1971; Mischel, 1968; Sundberg, 1977). To achieve validity, any given measure should be predictive of various behaviors to which it is conceptually related (convergent validity) and should not be predictive of those behaviors from which it is conceptually independent (discriminant validity). Thus far our analysis has dealt chiefly with the indeterminacy of interpretation of personality tests. However, using the argument for predictive validity, one may propose that such indeterminacy may be constrained by predictive study. Although test items, either individually or collectively, may be subject to an indefinite number of interpretations, many of these interpretations will be rendered untenable as the measure is correlated with or used to predict other patterns of behavior.

This line of argument seems compelling enough until one returns to the fundamental line of reasoning with which our analysis began. As outlined, from the hermeneutic standpoint, utterances stand in need of interpretation. What may be said of underlying intention, meaning, or motivation must be framed within contemporary conventions of intelligibility; otherwise the utterance is simply nonsense. Yet various behavioral patterns stand in the same relation to underlying dispositions as do linguistic utterances. What can be said of their relation also depends on historically located conventions of making sense. For example, what underlying disposition does "smoking behavior" reveal? It is conventional in some sectors to interpret such behavior as indicating "oral needs"; others see it as an anxiety indicator, or as an anxiety reducer; yet the conventions do not currently permit one to interpret smoking as a sign of "spirituality." To the extent that behavior patterns are considered in a decontextualized manner and the meanings of such patterns are rendered flexible through usage, behavioral observations may be subject to the same flexibility of interpretation as personality test data.

In order to explore the implications of this reasoning, an additional 16 Swarthmore undergraduates were given a fresh set of interpretation puzzles to solve. In this case, they were asked to explain how various behavior patterns could indicate that a person possesses a given trait (drawn from Anderson's 1968 list). The behavior patterns in this case were drawn from the annals of research on the I-E test. Such predictive studies have demonstrated, for example, that the test is successfully predictive of joining social movements (Gore & Rotter, 1963), of social persuasiveness (Phares, 1965), of assertiveness (Doherty & Ryder, 1979), of perception of others' friendliness (Holmes & Jackson, 1975), of task solving (Lefcourt, 1976), of experience of anger (Holmes & Jackson, 1975), and so on. The questionnaires were further arranged so that four of the trait-behavior-pattern pairs were repeated, but in this case participants were asked to explain how the trait in question could be expressed in a pattern that was the opposite of the pattern in question. Thus, for example, participants were asked how joining a social movement is a good indicator of a person's underlying *hostility* and then, later, how deciding against joining a social movement is a good indicator of the same trait. In this way a more stringent assessment could be made of the flexibility of interpretive conventions: Are the conventions sufficiently flexible that various behavior patterns and their contradictions can be used as "evidence" for a given trait?

As this exploration first revealed, of the 240 trait–behavior-pattern combinations, there was none that participants failed to render intelligible. Second, the participants located multiple linkages between trait and pattern. Thus, for example, a person who is *helpful* fails "to be persuasive" because, as one participant put it, "Helpful people are so eager to be accepted that their actions are unnatural and therefore unpersuasive," or, as another wrote, because "Helpful people are interested in others' welfare and not in manipulating them through persuasion." and, as a third asserted, because "Helpful people are likely to offer a variety of alternatives to people in their effort to help and therefore don't persuade others to take any one position." For the 16 participants the modal number of explanatory rationales generated for each trait–pattern pair was three. As a third finding, in each of the four reversals the participants were able to show how a given trait could account for both a given pattern and its contradiction. Thus, for example, a *hostile* person might join a social movement "as a way of finding an expressive outlet for his emotions" and would decide against joining a social movement because "by nature people who are hostile to others are loners." A *logical* person would "fail to be assertive in a relationship" because "people who are logical spend most of their time trying to figure out what is happening in a relationship rather than taking action," and the same type of person would be "very assertive in a relationship" because "they can see clearly what is going on and would thus want to assert themselves." A further check was made of the general plausibility of the participants' solutions. The mean plausibility ratings assigned by a group of 5 raters, exposed to 20 randomly selected solutions, was 3.32 (SD = .86), on the same 4-point scale used in the earlier studies.

In summary, predictive validity does not appear to offer an objective crucible for interpreting trait measures. Behavior patterns, such as being persuasive, active, assertive, and so on are, like assertions on personality tests, subject to a high degree of interpretive indeterminacy. Each may be compellingly viewed as the overt result of myriad source dispositions.

Discussion

As a whole, our findings reveal a remarkable flexibility in the explanatory conventions linking both verbal utterances and other patterns of behavior to psychological dispositions. In brief, the findings indicate the following:

1. Most statements from the I–E inventory can be plausibly interpreted as a reflection of an indeterminate number of common psychological trait terms.

2. Single statements from the I–E inventory can be plausibly understood as an indicator of many different trait dispositions, and differing trait dispositions may be revealed in single I–E statements.

3. Logically opposing statements (avowals of either an internal or an external orientation) are found to be plausible expressions of the same underlying trait disposition. Furthermore, logically opposing dispositions may be found revealed in the same I–E item.

4. There are multiple ways for making intelligible the relation between various trait dispositions and self-descriptive statements. Within a group of 10 language users, from three to six different explanatory rationales can typically be formulated for why agreement with an I–E statement is a good indicator of a randomly selected trait.

5. As many as three different items from the I–E measure (scored in either the internal or external directions) can be plausibly traced to the same underlying trait.

6. Any immediate cause of one's overt activity may also be seen as an effect of more basic motives. Thus dispositions toward control may plausibly be viewed as the localized effect of more fundamental trait dispositions. In this case, language users can spontaneously generate a large number of underlying dispositions that foster a disposition toward control. Furthermore, these dispositions may be traced to still more fundamental dispositions. Ultimately it may be possible to make a plausible case for explaining virtually any psychological trait as an effect of virtually any other kind of psychological disposition.

7. Behavior patterns that are traditionally correlated with the I–E scale (for purposes of generating construct validity) can be plausibly interpreted as expressions of an indeterminate number of trait dispositions within the common vernacular.

Let us consider the limitations of the findings and their implications for personality study and psychological inquiry more generally. To be sure, results such as those reported here can hardly be considered conclusive. The research was confined to items from a single personality measure, and it is possible that items from this measure are unusual in the degree to which they permit such wide-ranging interpretations; more research would be useful in this regard. One might argue as well that the communication process is not as chaotic or relativistic as these findings suggest. People are not forced to consider an immense range of alternatives each time another speaks; unproblematic understanding seems the rule rather than the exception. Yet, it is important to be clear about what is and is not being said in this analysis. Our analysis does not deny that much communication proceeds with relative ease. As long as one participates within the accepted conventions, and as long as there is a relatively unambiguous context of communication, social interchange may proceed smoothly. However, we maintain that which respect to items on personality tests, there are multiple conventions available for interpretation and there is little in the way of a context for constraint. Test items are not embedded within the kinds of contexts that would constrain interpretation. As a result, any given subculture (including scientists themselves) should be able to sustain a given "construction of personality" without threat of empirical falsification.

With respect to the implications of our work for the field of personality study, our findings raise significant questions concerning the role of scientific investigation. Typically, researchers in the discipline have assessed their outcomes in terms of their contribution to understanding, prediction, and control. Our findings suggest that the range of such concerns must be expanded to include both social and moral issues. Traditional researchers have largely treated descriptive accounts of personality pattern as value neutral. Thus it is widely assumed that one can carry out research on the I–E dimension, self-esteem, sensation seeking, self-monitoring, and the like without acting as a moral agent within the culture. The scientist merely attempts to describe what is the case, it is argued, and it is up to others to decide what valuational ends such accounts are to serve. Yet, from the standpoint of our study, descriptive accounts of personality do not appear to be significantly constrained by actual patterns of behavior. As we see, each interpretive account represents a choice among an immense array of alternatives, and this choice is not grounded in the evidence itself. In our case, the putative measure of orientations toward control was found to be intelligible as an indicator of an indeterminate number of alternative traits. Furthermore, all that could be said about the correlates of I–E could be justified as statements about the correlates of optimism, shyness, cautiousness, impulsivity, and the like (or their opposites).

In our analysis we do not deny the predictive utility of various personality measures. Patterns of correlation may be useful for a variety of practical purposes, and we do not question such pursuits. However, the moment that such correlational patterns are linked to a descriptive language, the investigator has entered into what might be called the *performative arena* (Austin, 1962); that is, he or she has reinforced, extended, or altered the arrangement of linguistic conventions within the culture, and thus acted as an agent for "good" or "bad" according to some standard. Persons who score high on the internal end of the Rotter scale ("internals") are often characterized as potent, assertive, and effective persons, whereas "externals" are generally described as helpless, retiring, and incompetent (Lefcourt, 1981). Such characterizations must be viewed primarily as expressions of evaluative commitments rather than objectively warranted reports of fact. To maintain that one's results demonstrate that internals perform better in educational systems, for example, does not appear to be an accurate reflection of reality as much as it is a rhetorical sanction for the value of internality. When any valued activity (e.g., generosity, political participation, nonsmoking) is said to result from a sense of internal control, the scientist is essentially serving as a sanctioning agent: designating certain people as superior and others as deficient. In effect, in our arguments we confront the personality psychologist with an enormous moral responsibility, the proportions of which have only begun to be appreciated in recent years (cf. Apfelbaum & Lubek, 1976; Argyris, 1980; Hogan & Emler, 1978; Morawski, 1982; Sampson, 1977, 1981).

With respect to psychological study more generally, our findings contain wide-ranging implications. As indicated, personality assessment was selected as a test case for the general class of research strategies directed at understanding psychological processes. It is in the personality domain that most assiduous attention is typically paid to the problem of establishing mensurational validity. As our inquiries indicate, many test items within the personality realm may be plausibly explained in terms of an indeterminate number of underlying processes or dispositions. Further data, in terms of correlated patterns, do not improve on the validity of interpretation because each correlate is similarly open to a broad array of interpretations. The question that must now be confronted is whether other domains of psychology are similarly vulnerable. Are research findings in the domains of social, cognitive, perceptual, learning, developmental, and other arenas similarly without interpretive anchors? Our rationale along

with our associated findings, suggests such a conclusion. So do various commentators within these domains who have lamented the lack of cumulative knowledge (cf. Cartwright, 1973; Hathaway, 1972; Koch, 1959; Mayo, 1977; Newell, 1973; Sechrest, 1976). Yet, the difficult but essential task of exploration has yet to be undertaken.

Inquiry into such matters may include extensions of our form of study, along with historical study of knowledge accumulation in the various disciplines. However, such exploration would benefit substantially from a broadening of analytic concern. Serious attempts have been made within philosophy (cf. Mandelbaum, 1967; Taylor, 1971), sociology (Habermas, 1971), literary study (Hirsch, 1967; Ricoeur, 1976), and hermeneutic inquiry more generally to locate limitations over explanatory flexibility and to transcend the historical boundedness of human communication. Debate continues to take place over the success of such arguments (cf. Bleicher, 1980; Gauld & Shotter, 1977; Gergen, 1982). If psychological study is to remain robust, it would be advantageous for psychologists not only to join in such colloquy but to articulate and extend whatever relevant insights have been garnered through psychological study.

References

Anderson, N. H. (1968). Likableness ratings of 555 personality trait words. *Journal of Personality and Social Psychology, 9,* 272–279.

Apfelbaum, E., & Lubek, I. (1976). Resolution vs. revolution? The theory of conflicts in question. In L. Strickland, F. Aboud, & K. Gergen (Eds.), *Social psychology in transition* (pp. 71–74). New York: Plenum.

Argyris, C. (1980). *Inner contradictions of rigorous research.* New York: Academic Press.

Austin, J. L. (1962). *How to do things with words.* Cambridge, MA: Harvard University Press.

Bleicher, J. (1980). *Contemporary hermeneutics.* London: Routledge & Kegan Paul.

Cartwright, D. (1973). Determinants of scientific progress: The case of research on the risky shift. *American Psychologist, 28,* 222–231.

Cronbach, L. J., & Meehl, P. E. (1955). Construct validity in psychological tests. *Psychological Bulletin, 52,* 281–302.

Doherty, W. J., & Ryder, R. G. (1979). Locus of control, interpersonal trust, and assertive behavior among newlyweds. *Journal of Personality and Social Psychology, 37,* 2212–2220.

Findley, M. J., & Cooper, H. M. (1983). Locus of control and academic achievement: A literature review. *Journal of Personality and Social Psychology, 44,* 419–427.

Gadamer, H. G. (1975). In G. Barden & J. Cumming (Eds.), *Truth and method.* New York: Seabury.

Garfinkel, H. (1967). *Studies in ethnomethodology.* Englewood Cliffs, NJ: Prentice-Hall.

Gauld, A., & Shotter, J. (1977). *Human action and its psychological investigation.* London: Routledge & Kegan Paul.

Gergen, K. J. (1982). *Toward transformation in social knowledge.* New York: Springer-Verlag.

Gergen, K. J., & Gergen, M. (1982). Form and function in the explanation of human conduct. In P. Secord (Ed.), *Explaining human behavior* (pp. 127–154). Beverly Hills, CA: Sage.

Ghiselli, E. E. (1974). Some new perspectives for industrial psychology. *American Psychologist, 29,* 80–87.

Gore, P., & Rotter, J. (1963). A personality correlate of social action. *Journal of Personality, 31,* 58–64.

Habermas, J. (1971). *Knowledge and human interest.* Boston, MA: Beacon Press.

Harré, R. (1981). *Social being*. Oxford, England: Basil Blackwell.

Hathaway, S. R. (1972). Where have we gone wrong? The mystery of the missing progress. In J. Butcher (Ed.), *Objective personality assessment* (pp. 27–43). New York: Academic Press.

Hirsch, E., Jr. (1967). *Validity in interpretation*. New Haven, CT: Yale University Press.

Hogan, R., & Emler, N. (1978). The biases in contemporary social psychology. *Social Research, 45*, 478–534.

Holmes, D., & Jackson, T. (1975). Influence of locus of control in interpersonal attraction and affective reactions in situations involving reward and punishment. *Journal of Personality and Social Psychology, 31*, 132–136.

Koch, S. (1959). Epilogue. In S. Koch (Ed.), *Psychology: A study of a science* (Vol. III, pp. 729–788). New York: McGraw-Hill.

Lake, D., Miles, M., & Earle, R. (Eds.) (1973). *Measuring human behavior*. New York: Teachers College, Columbia University.

Lanyon, R. I., & Goodstein, L. (1971). *Personality assessment*. New York: Wiley.

Lefcourt, H. M. (1976). *Locus of control: Current trends in theory and research*. Hillsdale, NJ: Erlbaum.

Lefcourt, H. M. (1981). Overview. In H. M. Lefcourt (Ed.), *Research with the locus of control construct* (pp. 3–27). New York: Academic Press.

MacCorquodale, K., & Meehl, P. (1948). On a distinction between hypothetical constructs and intervening variables. *Psychological Review, 55*, 95–107.

Mandelbaum, M. (1967). *The problem of historical knowledge*. New York: Harper Torchbooks.

Mayo, C. (1977, November). *Toward an applicable social psychology*. Presidential address to the New England Psychological Association, Worcester, MA.

Mischel, W. (1968). *Personality and assessment*. New York: Wiley.

Morawski, J. (1982). Assessing psychology's moral heritage through our neglected utopias. *American Psychologist, 37*, 1082–1095.

Newell, A. (1973). You can't play 20 questions with nature and win. In W. G. Chase (Ed.), *Visual information processing* (pp. 283–310). New York: Academic Press.

Palmer, R. (1969). *Hermeneutics: Interpretation theory in Schleiermacher, Dilthey, Heidegger and Gadamer*. Evanston, IL: Northwestern University Press.

Pearce, W., & Cronen, V. (1980). *Communication, action and meaning*. New York: Praeger.

Phares, E. J. (1965). Internal–external control as a determinant of amount of social influence exerted. *Journal of Personality and Social Psychology, 2*, 642–647.

Phares, E. J. (1976). *Locus of control in personality*. Morristown, NJ: General Learning Press.

Ricoeur, P. (1971). The model of the text: Meaningful action considered as a text. *Social Research, 38*, 520–542.

Ricoeur, P. (1976). *Interpretation theory: Discourse and the surplus of meaning*. Fort Worth: Texas Christian University Press.

Rosenberg, M. (1979). *Conceiving the self*. New York: Basic Books.

Rotter, J. B. (1975). Some problems and misconceptions related to the construct of internal versus external control of reinforcement. *Journal of Consulting and Clinical Psychology, 43*, 56–67.

Sampson, E. (1977). Psychology and the American ideal. *Journal of Personality and Social Psychology, 35*, 767–782.

Sampson, E. (1981). Cognitive psychology as ideology. *American Psychologist, 36*, 730–743.

Sechrest, L. (1976). Personality. In M. R. Rosenzweig & L. W. Porter (Eds.), *Annual Review of Psychology* (Vol. 27, pp. 1–28).

Shotter, J. (1981). Telling and reporting: Prospective and retrospective uses of self-ascriptions. In C. Antaki (Ed.), *The psychology of ordinary explanations*. London: Academic Press.

Spence, J. T. (1983). Comment on Lubinski, Tellegen, and Butcher's "Masculinity, femininity, and androgyny viewed and assessed as distinct concepts." *Journal of Personality and Social Psychology, 44*, 440–446.

Strickland, B. R. (1976). Internal–external control of reinforcement. In T. Blass (Ed.), *Personality variables in social behavior* (pp. 212–231). Hillsdale, NJ: Erlbaum.

Sundberg, N. D. (1977). *Assessment of persons*. Englewood Cliffs, NJ: Prentice-Hall.

Taylor, C. (1971). Interpretation and the sciences of man. *Review of Metaphysics, 25*(1).

Tedeschi, J., & Reiss, M. (1981). Verbal strategies in impression management. In C. Antaki (Ed.), *The psychology of ordinary explanations* (pp. 271–309). New York: Academic Press.

Tellegen, A., & Lubinski, D. (1983). Some methodological comments on labels, traits, interaction, and types in the study of "femininity" and "masculinity": Reply to Spence. *Journal of Personality and Social Psychology, 44*, 447–455.

Received June 14, 1983

Revision received November 15, 1985 ■

[9]
23

Social Psychology and the Phoenix of Unreality*

KENNETH J. GERGEN

Swarthmore College

And every natural effect has a spiritual cause, and not a natural: for a natural cause only seems, it is a delusion.

> William Blake
> *Milton.* Plate 26:46.

If one surveys the vast corpus of Wilhelm Wundt's contributions to psychology, one is struck by what appears to be a significant evolution in orientation. In his early work, such as the *Principles of Physiological Psychology* (1874/1904) and *Lectures on Human and Animal Psychology* (1863–1864/1894), Wundt helped to chart the terrain that was later to become the private reserve of American experimental psychology. It is to this work that Boring's (1929) classic history devotes such singular attention. Yet, during the culminating years of his career, Wundt turned from the task of isolating biologically based mechanisms of psychological function-

*The preparation of this paper was facilitated by a grant from the National Science Foundation (#7809393). For their critical appraisal at various stages of preparation, grateful acknowledgment is extended to Erika Apfelbaum, Michael Basseches, Mary Gergen, Horst Gundlach, Marianne Jaeger, Hugh Lacey, Ian Lubek, Alexandre Métraux, Jill Morawski, Barry Schwartz, and Wolfgang Stroebe. Although relieved of responsibility for its failings, Sigmund Koch must be credited for furnishing both the initial inspiration and final clarification of the paper.

ing to the problems raised by social pattern. The bases of such patterns do not lie primarily within the nervous system, argued Wundt, but are essentially human creations. Patterns of religious activity and governance, for example, along with such culturally significant concepts as honor or truth, are products of people at particular points in history. As such, they demand forms of exploration that differ from those of the experimentalist (Blumenthal, 1975, 1979; Mischel, 1975). *Völkerpsychologie* (1900–1920), the ten-volume work that was to occupy Wundt for the last twenty years of his career, represents his exploration into this alternative form of inquiry. As is apparent from the history of American social psychology, it is Wundt the experimentalist, and not the author of *Völkerpsychologie*, to which the discipline turned for a model of investigation.

Wundt's concept of social psychology is an interesting one and much deserving of contemporary scrutiny. For Wundt the guiding metaphor for social psychology was not that of natural science but, rather, that of historical analysis (*Geschichte*). Rather than searching for general laws of psychological functioning, the task of the social psychologist was to render an account of contemporary behavior patterns as gleaned from the culture's history. Toward this end the laboratory experiment could contribute very little. The method for social psychology developed from the documentation and explanation of historical patterns as they emerged over time. The function of social psychology was not that of making predictions. Consistent with Popper's (1957) views of behavioral science, Wundt did not believe in the inevitability of social patterning. Rather than prediction, the goal of the social psychologist was to render the world of human affairs intelligible. This task was to be carried out by examining the etymology of contemporary patterns.

Yet, in spite of the enticing implications of this line of thought, it is Wundt's conflict between fundamental conceptions of science that furnishes us with a base for examining social psychology's history and its critical standing today. For Wundt's conflict may be viewed as but a localized instance of an antinomy of longstanding and profound consequence both within the intellectual sphere and without. Like many of his contemporaries, Wundt was grappling with competing metatheoretical assumptions concerning human knowledge and its relationship to the natural world.[1] Although these competing assumptions may be characterized in many ways, it will prove useful to center our attention on the critical conflict between environmental versus person-centered theories of knowledge. On the one hand, human knowledge in ideal form may be viewed as a reflection of the real world or a map of nature's contours. From this standpoint, empirical entities are granted preeminent status in the generation of human knowledge; the human mind

---

[1] For further analysis of Wundt's paradigmatic conflict see Blumenthal (1975) and Danziger (1980). Wundt's attempt to distinguish two forms of psychological science, the one concerned with natural process and the other with human artifacts, was paralleled by many others, including Dilthey, Rickert, Troeltsch, and Windelband.

II. THE SPECIAL FIELDS OF PSYCHOLOGY

best serves the interests of knowledge when it operates as a pawn to nature. In contrast, the human mind can be viewed as the origin of knowledge, a font of conceptual construction, or a source of thought-forms that frame both the questions that may be put to nature and the answers derived therefrom. It is the former view that spurred Wundt's concern with the physiological mechanisms driven by or reliably dependent on variations in the natural environment; it is the latter view which sustained Wundt's inquiry into the historically relative patterning of ideas. Elements of this antagonism now insinuate themselves into all aspects of psychological inquiry, including the development of theory, choice of methods, and mode of application.

It is an account of this conflict as it has developed over the past century and its repercussions in contemporary social psychology that I wish to examine. I choose this task for purposes of enlightened self-consciousness and also because I believe not only that we have witnessed a profound shift in the balance of power between these antagonistic views but that we are currently on the threshold of moving beyond them. The redistribution of power is one to which social psychologists have indeed contributed, and it is also one that now promises to thrust the discipline into a pivotal position vis-à-vis the broad intellectual community. My first task, then, is to sketch out an account of the role played by this conflict over epistemic assumptions during the past century, both in psychology more generally and social psychology in particular. This historical résumé will function as a necessary prolegomenon to the central concern of this paper, namely the critical shift taking place in contemporary psychology.

To appreciate properly the historical context of the antagonism, a brief précis is required concerning the protagonists. Let us first employ the term *exogenic* to refer to theories of knowledge granting priority to the external world in the generation of human knowledge, and *endogenic* to denote those theories holding the processes of mind as preeminent.[2] Although one can scarcely locate a pure exemplar of either variety, many philosophic writings may be singled out for the inspiration they have furnished to those of one or the other persuasion. Surely John Locke's arguments against innate ideas, along with his analysis of the means by which elementary sensations give rise to the development of complex ideas, has played a major role in the history of exogenic thought. Similarly, Hume's tracing of compound ideas to the association of simple impressions and Mill's view of the mind as an accumulation of sensations driven automatically by physical inputs have contributed substantially to the exogenic polarity. Although one may draw a meaningful parallel between traditional empiricist philosophy and what is here termed exogenic

---

[2] The distinction between the exogenic and endogenic views may be usefully compared with such analytic distinctions including mechanistic versus organismic views (Reese & Overton, 1970); plastic versus autonomous (Hollis, 1977); structuralist versus functionalist (Rychlak, 1977); and mechanistic versus person-centered (Joynson, 1980).

thought, the relationship between endogenic thinking and either rationalist or idealist philosophy is more clouded. However, certain rationalist arguments, including Spinoza's attempt to derive knowledge not from experience but deductively from propositions and Kant's theory of a priori constructs of time, space, causality, and so on, must surely be viewed as seminal contributions to endogenic thought. However, lodged against these rationalist arguments and sustaining the endogenic line are Schopenhauer's later tracing of knowledge to the wellsprings of will and Nietzsche's arguments for knowledge not as a reflection of fact but as an outgrowth of motives for power.

Lest this metatheoretical antagonism seem pallid, let us glimpse a number of localized conflicts of more pungent familiarity. As an ideal typification, it may be said that:

1. Those who favor an exogenic world view are likely to argue that because the external environment drives the senses in predictable ways, objectively grounded knowledge about this environment is possible. In contrast, those who take an endogenic perspective are likely to argue against the possibility of objective knowledge. Because knowledge is primarily a product of the processing agent, traditional criteria of objectivity are rendered suspect.

2. The exogenic thinker tends to believe that because there are objectively correct and incorrect answers about the world, people of sound mind should reach common agreement. Science should thus ideally strive for consensus among practitioners. For the endogenic thinker, however, multiple interpretations of experience are usually held to be both legitimate and desirable. Thus, if total accord exists within a group, it may be a signal either of oppressed minority views or shallow conformity. The process of generating knowledge, from this standpoint, holds conflict to be superior to consensus.

3. The exogenic thinker, arguing that reality is independent of the observer, may frequently argue for scientific neutrality. If the scientist allows his or her values to guide the course of observation, the result may be a faulty recording of the state of nature. For the endogenic thinker, however, recordings of reality are not so much correct or incorrect as they may be held to be creations of the observer. If scientific statements are not data driven but psychologically generated, then in what sense can one be neutral or independent of what is known? The possibility for scientific neutrality is thus obscured.

4. For the exogenic thinker, it is often argued that the empirical world impinges on the senses and may thus be considered the determinant of psychological states. Such environmental determinism may be direct, in terms of immediate sensory input, or indirect, as in the case of the continuing effects of previous learning experiences. The causal locus for human action is thus placed in the environment: human behavior is dependent on or determined by antecedent environmental events. In contrast, for the endogenic thinker, the individual may be viewed as free

II. THE SPECIAL FIELDS OF PSYCHOLOGY

to construct or interpret sense data furnished either from the environment or from memory. The causal locus of human action thus tends to be placed within the individual: for the endogenic thinker, environmental determinism is often replaced by voluntarism.

5. Because of the emphasis on environmental determinism and the related belief in a separation of fact and value, the exogenic theorist is likely to view questions of moral value as beyond the scope of the discipline. From the endogenic perspective, with its emphasis on personal constructions of reality and the inseparability of fact and value, moral issues often seem inescapable. To declare them irrelevant may itself be morally culpable.

6. The exogenic thinker is likely to place strong emphasis on methods of measurement and control because it is through such methods that one may obtain unbiased assessments of the facts. For many endogenic thinkers, however, "correct assessments" are suspect. Thus, empirical methods may be seen as means of sustaining theoretical positions already embraced. Given a particular theoretical standpoint, methods may be anticipated that will yield support. Methods thus furnish rhetorical rather than ontological support for the scientist.

With the lines of battle thus drawn, let us follow the example set by Wundt and attempt an understanding of the present complexion of the discipline by examining its historical development.

Exogenic-Endogenic Détente: The Reality of the Internal

It is no intellectual accident that psychology as a science was given birth at the close of the nineteenth century. One might indeed ask if it was not a sign of lassitude that it was so late beginning.[3] The foundations had long been laid. The concept of an empirical science had been well developed since the time of Newton, and the function of laboratory experimentation had been impressively demonstrated by Lavoisier, Berzelius, the Curies, and Rutherford. Coupled with this self-conscious attempt to unlock nature's secrets through systematic empirical study was a longstanding belief in mind as an empirical entity. Thinkers from Plato to Descartes had granted the mind ontological status, and by the late nineteenth century, philosophers such as John Locke, David Hume, David Hartley, and J. S. Mill had supplied rather detailed theories of mental processes. For almost a century, German thinkers

---

[3] Kirsch (1976) has argued that the emergence of psychology as an empirical science can largely be attributed to developments in German physiology, where attention was being directed to the physiological basis of experience. Mackenzie (1976) maintains that the development of Darwinism was the essential catalyst for the emergence of an empirically oriented psychology. Ben-David and Collins (1966) trace the impetus to the shifting structure of German academic institutions of the time.

had also given careful thought to the relationship between mental elements and the physiological system. In effect, there existed in the 1900s an auspicious conjunction between the exogenic and endogenic perspectives: mind was an empirical entity that could be studied with no less rigor and precision than the surrounding environment. There remained only the task of welding the belief in the palpability of mental entities with the experimental orientation of the natural sciences to give birth to the science of psychology. This was fully accomplished in late-nineteenth-century Germany.[4]

Yet, while the late 1800s were optimal years for the growth of psychology as a science, they were simultaneously unfavorable to the development of a social psychology. If the mind was the focus of empirical study, if mental operations and their biological coordinates furnished the essential questions, there was little obvious role for a uniquely social psychology. Social stimuli had no distinctive properties; they were essentially patterns of light, sound, and so on to be processed like any other stimuli. Neither was it necessary to develop a special category for social as opposed to nonsocial behavior. An understanding of all behavior patterns should ultimately be derived from thorough knowledge of basic psychological process.[5]

As a result, to develop his *Völkerpsychologie* Wundt had to begin an entirely separate enterprise. Virtually none of his experimental work, nor the contributions of Fechner, Helmholtz, Weber, and the like, made their way into his historical account of social institutions. And when the first two American texts on social psychology appeared in 1908 (one by William McDougall; the other by E. A. Ross), neither drew significantly from the empirical study of mind. McDougall's book relied heavily on an evolutionary perspective, while Ross's work drew sustenance from earlier sociological thinking. For neither of them was it possible to

---

[4] The concept of a détente between the exogenic and endogenic views falls far short of representing the full range of opinion during this period. Indeed, the concept of an empirical science of mind was hotly debated in many circles. Dilthey, Windelband, Rickert, Hensel, and others all carried out strong attacks against the empiricist position. In the same way, pockets of strong endogenic thought continued to exist during the hegemony of American behaviorism. In the latter case, for example, Havelock Ellis's 1923 volume, *The Dance of Life*, presents science as an aesthetic creation no more objectively valid than religion, dance, or literature. As Morawski (1979) points out, Ellis here followed Vaihinger's doctrine of fictions. "Matter is a fiction, just as the fundamental ideas with which the sciences generally operate are mostly fictions, and the scientific materialization of the world has proved a necessary and useful fiction, only harmful when we regard it as a hypothesis and therefore possibly true" (Ellis, 1923, pp. 91–92).

[5] The exogenic-endogenic détente is also evident in Comte's analysis of the social sciences. As Samelson (1974) points out, in *la morale* ("the sacred science") the subject and the object coincide. In this composite is reached "the definitive stage of human reason . . . the establishment of a subjective synthesis" (Comte, 1854; quoted by Samelson, 1974, p. 203). And, consistent with the endogenic position, Comte saw a close relation between value and science. Science was to be used in the service of reforming society. In the United States, Hugo Münsterberg was also attempting to synthesize the laws of nature with social idealism (Hale, 1980). As Münsterberg wrote in his diary of 1900, his aim was "the harmonization of a positivistic study of human life with an ethical idealism in the direction of Kant's and Fichte's philosophy" (Hale, 1980, p. 71).

II. THE SPECIAL FIELDS OF PSYCHOLOGY

discern useful connection between social activity and the laboratory study of mental process.[6]

It was primarily William James who carved out a niche for social psychology within the domain of psychology proper.[7] As he reasoned, there might be certain psychological processes that were distinctly social in their implications. His discussion of the basic senses of self, along with his formula for determining the individual's self-esteem (by dividing success by pretension), informed later generations of social psychologists that if they wished a place in psychology, they must identify mental processes that are uniquely social in implication. From this standpoint, the very most social psychologists could anticipate was a small piece of the mental pie. As we shall soon begin to see, however, there is good reason to believe that social psychology may serve a far more pivotal role in understanding human action. Indeed, the mental pie may be viewed primarily as a social creation.

The Exogenic Succession: Toward Public Reality

The conjunction between the exogenic and endogenic perspectives that served to give birth to early psychology was not to last. Within the robust realism of the American climate assumptions concerning the character of "the mind" soon became targets of attack. American culture, faced with the zesty promises of an expansive environment, was yielding up a philosophy of its own, namely pragmatism. For the pragmatist, nothing was considered real unless it made a difference in practice. With such major thinkers as John Dewey, William James, and Charles Pierce contributing both to the philosophy of pragmatism and to theoretical psychology, American psychology could hardly remain unaffected. There were also seemingly insoluble theoretical squabbles emerging in German circles regarding the nature of mind, and the introspective method allowed no hope of solution. Simultaneously there were the impressive experiments of Pavlov that demonstrated systematic behavioral changes without reliance on experiential analysis. Finally, the

---

[6]Texts are, of course, only one marker for an emerging discipline. However, even in the 1860s journal *Zeitschrift für Völkerpsychologie und Sprachenwissenschaft* and in the French "protosocial psychologies" of the mid-nineteenth century (along with the later works of the Tardes), virtually no mention was made of developments in experimental psychology (Apfelbaum, 1979; Lubek, 1979).

[7]It would be a mistake either to view James as a full proponent of the exogenic-endogenic détente or to assume that the détente was enthusiastically endorsed in all circles. For James, along with Josiah Royce, Henri Bergson, and others the central intellectual problem of the age was to identify "a transcendental source of values and purpose in a world where science had transformed nature into the blind interaction of atoms and where history had relativized all cultural standards of beauty, morality and truth" (Hale, 1980, p. 70). For James this search ultimately led to his severing of his connections with psychology and to the publication of *The Varieties of Religious Experience* (1902/1961).

mentalistic concerns so strongly represented in German psychology must surely be counted among the casualties of World War I.[8]

It was thus in 1924 that J. B. Watson could boldly contrast the "old psychology" which viewed "consciousness" as its subject matter with the "new" psychology of behaviorism which

> holds that the subject matter of human psychology is the behavior or activities of the human being. Behaviorism claims that "consciousness" is neither a definable nor a usable concept; that it is merely another word for the "soul" of more ancient times. The old psychology is thus dominated by a kind of subtle religious philosophy (p. 6).

This shift toward an exogenic psychology was further stimulated by the rise of logical positivist philosophy. Based on the writings of Schlick, Neurath, Ayer, Frank, and others, behaviorist psychologists could draw sustenance from the early positivist argument that assertions closed to empirical verification are without positive function in a mature science. Thus, concepts of psychological process, whether driven by environmental stimuli or autonomously operative, were all subject to disapprobation. Further, the psychologist could draw comfort from the logical positivist arguments for the unity of science. If all theoretical statements in psychology could be linked to an observation language, and all observation language could ultimately be translated into the language of physics, then psychology could anticipate ultimate assimilation into the family of natural sciences.

Social psychologists of the time had much to gain by joining the exogenic succession. Social activity was, after all, publicly observable and could therefore be placed at the center of scientific concern rather than serving as a peripheral derivative of mental process. Social psychology had also been criticized as "hopeless, speculative and verbose,"[9] and a shift of emphasis to observable entities held out promise for greater scientific respectability.[10] Floyd Allport wrote in the preface to his important text, *Social Psychology* (1924): "There are two main lines of scientific achievement which I have tried to bring within the scope of this volume. These are the *behavior viewpoint* and the experimental method" (p. 12). It was largely through

---

[8]For amplification see Blumenthal (1977) and Rieber (1980).

[9]See E. B. Holt's 1935 essay on the "whimsical condition" of social psychology.

[10]In his 1930 review of "recent social psychology," Sprowls argues that the establishment of prediction and control of human behavior as chief aims of social psychology was largely in response to the demands of American politics, philanthropy, industry, and other social institutions. He also agrees with the dominant view of the time that "behavior patterns" should take "first place" among the concerns of the profession. See also Murchison (1929) for a reiteration of the behavioral viewpoint in social psychology.

II. THE SPECIAL FIELDS OF PSYCHOLOGY

his efforts that the scattered social experimentation of Triplett and others became amalgamated into a "scientific discipline."[11]

Exogenic Liberalization: Personal Reality as Hypothetical Construction

The hegemony of radical empiricism proved short-lived within psychology. As logical positivist philosophy flourished and became extended in the 1930s and 1940s, it became increasingly clear that the demand for science without reference to unobservables was far too stringent. In physics, concepts such as "energy," "wave," and "field" were usefully employed, none of which could be directly represented by empirical operations. There appeared no good reason for excluding such terms in psychology. Terms that did not refer to immediate observables thus came to be viewed as "hypothetical constructs" (MacCorquodale & Meehl, 1948). They were to be admitted into the science provided that one could ultimately tie them, through a series of linking definitions, to public observables. Under these conditions it was possible to readmit internal or psychological states into proper study as hypothetical constructs. Personal experience once again had scientific credentials—only on a hypothetical level.[12]

This loosening of the criteria for mature science was enthusiastically received in many quarters of psychology. Many influential thinkers, including Woodworth, Tolman, Cattell, and Gordon Allport had never been moved by radical behaviorism and had continued to place a major emphasis on psychological process.[13] The 1940 publication of *Mathematico-Deductive Theory of Rote Learning*, reflecting the efforts of Clark Hull and his colleagues in both psychology and philosophy, also demonstrated the seeming precision with which such hypothetical terms could be used. And finally, the 1930s exodus from Germany of Gestalt thinkers Köhler, Wertheimer, and Koffka sparked an innervating romance with endogenic thought. To the extent that autochthonous psychological processes enabled the organism to create figure, ground, form, groupings, and movement from a stimulus array that did not itself contain such properties, then a concept of self-directing, internal process seemed inescapable. The liberalization of the positivist-behaviorist orientation was in full force.[14]

---

[11] In their challenging analysis of the Triplett study, Haines and Vaughan (1979) argue that contrary to common belief, the research does not occupy a unique place in the history of social psychology, and that the claim for Triplett's being the first experiment functions only as an "origin myth."

[12] Koch's 1959 analysis of this liberalization is perhaps definitive.

[13] Critical reactions to the inception of the behaviorist movement have been nicely documented by Samelson (1981).

[14] For an analysis of the Gestalt movement as a revolt against positivist science, see Leichtman (1979).

Had the empiricist liberalization not occurred, Kurt Lewin might today be an obscure and lonely figure. Arriving in the United States in 1933, Lewin was indeed in treacherous waters. With philosophers Husserl and Cassirer as his intellectual forebears, his endogenic commitment was not easily reconciled with the dominant empiricist temper of the times.[15] For Lewin, the chief subject of attention was the mental world of the individual, not the world of surrounding nature. Empirical reality of the positivist variety indeed occupied a nebulous position in Lewinian theory—never quite absorbed but not entirely rejected. This ambivalence was also reflected in Lewin's use of the term "external reality." At times the concept referred to public observables, but at others to the internal or psychological construction of the world (Deutsch, 1958). This ambiguity in the status of empirical reality is nicely illustrated in Lewin's 1935 essay on environmental forces. At times he argues for an independent reality capable of altering the psychological field. As he points out,

> The mere knowledge of something (e.g., of the geography of a foreign country . . .) does not necessarily change the child's life-space more than superficially. On the other hand, psychologically critical facts of the environment, such as the friend-liness of a certain adult, may have fundamental significance for the child's life-space . . . (p. 74).

But are these "critical facts" to be viewed as existing entities? Lewin's explication is fully equivocal: "The environment is for all its properties (directions, distances, etc.) to be defined . . . according to its quasi-physical, quasi-social, and quasi-mental structure" (p. 79). Further comment proves equally ambiguous: "Environment is understood psychologically sometimes to mean *momentary situation* of the child, at other times to mean the *milieu*, in the sense of the chief characteristics of the permanent situation" (p. 71). To further complicate the argument, Lewin then speaks as if the psychological world is the empirical world. "These imperative environmental facts—we shall call them valences—determine the direction of the behavior" (p. 77). As the present analysis makes apparent, Lewin's classic equation, $B = f(P, E)$—behavior is a function of the personal construction *and* the environ-ment—represents his attempt to conjoin two fundamental epistemologies. In trac-ing behavior to psychological process, he reflects his longstanding immersion in endogenic thought; in tracing behavior to environmental determinants, he caters to exogenic interests.[16]

It was left to Lewin's students, Back, Cartwright, Deutsch, Festinger, Kelley, Pepitone, Schachter, Thibaut, and others to reconcile fully Lewin's endogenic

---

[15] As Koch has pointed out (personal communication), Lewin finally capitulated to the dominant empiricist metatheory in his (1940) article, "Formalization and Progress in Psychology," where he attempts to elucidate hypotheses for experimental evaluation.

[16] For further discussion, see Miriam Lewin's 1977 paper.

II. THE SPECIAL FIELDS OF PSYCHOLOGY

leanings with mainstream empiricist psychology. This was accomplished first by the adoption of the hypothetico-deductive form of exposition so impressively represented by Hull and his colleagues. Within this mode, the task of the scientist is that of developing and testing hypotheses about the world of observable fact.[17] Festinger's (1954) widely heralded theory of social comparison furnished an impressive model for social psychology. Here Festinger layed out a series of formal assumptions, each accompanied by supportive research findings. The reconciliation with empirical psychology was further achieved through the virtually exclusive adoption of the experimental method.[18] Importantly, this modus operandus also resembled that developed by the major competition—the Hullian satellites. Thus the theories and experiments of the Lewinians, along with such publications as *Frustration and Aggression* (Dollard et al., 1939) and *Communication and Persuasion* (Hovland, Janis, & Kelley, 1953) furnished a univocal model for scientific conduct. It was in this mold that social psychological inquiry was contentedly, if not enthusiastically, cast until the present era. In effect, by the late 1960s social psychology had witnessed the apotheosis of neobehaviorism.

But let us observe more carefully the fate of the endogenic perspective during this period. Clearly the scientists themselves were following empiricist doctrine with respect to their own conduct. From the guild standpoint, they were attempting to map reality as accurately and systematically as possible and to test such maps against reality in dispassionate fashion. However, the endogenic perspective so strongly represented in Lewin's orientation remained. Where? Essentially it became embodied in the theories under empirical study. People other than scientists were said to be dominated by cognitive construction, motives, needs, and so on. *They* lived in a world of mental process. It is this ironic duality—the scientist employing an exogenic theory to guide his or her own conduct, while assuming an endogenic basis for others' actions—that now returns to haunt us.

[17] Social psychology was hardly independent in the development of its central paradigms. In fact, its form may be viewed as an emulation of mainstream experimental psychology, which by 1938 was characterized as *empirical, mechanistic, quantitative, nomothetic,* and *operational* (Bills, 1938). In their 1940 review of the preceding fifty years of social psychology, Bruner and Allport largely agree that such a designation had also come to be applicable to the social domain as well. The only important deviation appeared to be in the concomitant concern of social psychologists with research on social problems.

[18] The Yale group, with its close attachment to the exogenic roots of learning psychology, tended to place a strong emphasis on the manipulation and measurement of observables with a secondary emphasis on mental processes, while the endogenically oriented Lewinians tended to emphasize mental process and place secondary emphasis on accounting for a multiplicity of stimulus or behavioral variables. This difference in epistemological orientations explains McGuire's description of convergent versus divergent forms of research (Chapter 24, this volume). However, the differential emphases were not sufficiently radical to prevent relatively easy transition from one camp to the other. Lewin's student, Harold Kelley, could thus become an important contributor to the Hovland program in attitude change (see Hovland, Janis, & Kelley, 1953) and to later accounts of internal process (see Kelley, 1967). Festinger (1954) incorporated both exogenic and endogenic bases into his theory of social comparison by distinguishing between two realities, the one physical and the other social.

Exogenic Deterioration and the Cognitive Revolution: The Return of Subjectivity

In order to appreciate recent developments in social psychology, it is again necessary to take account of the intellectual ethos. As we have seen, an important interplay has taken place between psychological thought and contributions to exogenic and endogenic thinking more generally. The recent past seems no exception. In particular, one cannot but be impressed with what appears to be a broad-scale disenchantment with exogenic assumptions in philosophy. This disenchantment appears to be highly correlated with both the cognitive revolution in psychology and with what has been termed "the crisis" in social psychology. Let us deal first with the deterioration of the exogenic position in philosophy and the growth of cognitive psychology. We may then turn more directly to the position of social psychology today.

The contemporary deterioration in exogenic epistemology may be traced to three major lines of thought. The first is the *broad reassessment of empiricist philosophy of science*. At the outset, those philosophers most closely identified with the founding of logical positivism themselves retreated over time from the bold and invigorating promise of certainty in science. By 1932 Neurath was prepared to argue that verification is a relation between propositions and not between propositions and experiences; Carnap ultimately gave up his early argument that meaning in the sciences was to be identified as translatability into experience; and Ayer finally argued that sense data cannot be conclusively used to prove assertions about the physical world.

In the meantime, Karl Popper (1957) argued persuasively against the classic view that scientific knowledge can be built up from pure observations and against the positivist view that empirical confirmation of a theory constitutes a proper means of accumulating knowledge. (In effect, Popper's arguments militate against the common practice in psychology of verifying hypotheses.) It is usually possible to find some evidence in favor of a given theory, argued Popper; the critical question is whether the theory can withstand evidence brought against it. Yet, even the falsification thesis has not resisted deterioration. As Quine (1953) demonstrated, along with Duhem (1906/1954) long before, falsification is a problematic process. For one, the defender of a given theory can typically locate auxiliary theoretical assumptions to discredit or absorb the disconfirming evidence. Further, because what counts as data relevant to a theory's falsification cannot easily be specified outside the language of the theory itself, the range of potential threats to a theory may be severely truncated. In effect, what counts as a fact cannot be separated easily from theoretical premises.

The break with empiricist philosophy of science became fully apparent with Kuhn's (1962/1970) account of scientific progress. As Kuhn argued, shifts from one major theoretical paradigm to another in the sciences do not generally depend on

II. THE SPECIAL FIELDS OF PSYCHOLOGY

either confirmation or falsification. Rather, what appears to be "progress" in science represents a shift in perspectives based on a confluence of social factors, along with the generation of anomalies that are simply irrelevant to previously favored theories. The new theories are not improvements over the old in terms of predictive power: primarily they represent differing frameworks of understanding. More polemically, Feyerabend (1975) has argued that rules for induction and deduction, along with methods of hypothesis testing are basically irrelevant to scientific progress. Necessary for a flourishing science is procedural anarchy, argued Feyerabend, where hypotheses contradicting well-confirmed theories should be championed, and social and ideological persuasion should be given equal footing with evidence. To be sure, brisk argument continues in virtually all these sectors. The major point is that the weight of the argument has shifted substantially over the past forty years, so that the chorus of lusty voices that once sang hosannas to empiricist rules of science has now been replaced by a cacophony of dissidents.

A second major contribution to the erosion of the exogenic commitment has been made by *ordinary language philosophy*. Stimulated largely by the work of Moore, Russell, and Wittgenstein, concern shifted away from the problem of relating experience to knowledge, to the way in which claims about knowledge and experience functioned within the language. As it was argued, problems within both philosophy and everyday life are often created by the language, and their solution may thus require an analysis and possibly purification of that language. Of particular concern for the behavioral sciences, increasing attention was given by philosophers such as Ryle, Anscombe, Hamlyn, and Austin to the language of person description.

And, as such concepts as mind, motivation, intention, and behavior were scrutinized, increasing attention was paid to the forms of discourse used in the behavioral sciences. From such analyses a fundamental critique of the empiricist-behaviorist orientation emerged. In particular, it is argued (Hamlyn, 1953; Hampshire, 1959; Peters, 1958; Taylor, 1964; Winch, 1958) that human action cannot be rendered intelligible in strictly physical terms—that is, by referring to the physical properties of the stimulus, physiological process, or resulting behavioral events. To take account of the temperature, the wind velocity, the pitch and magnitude of vocal tones, and so on to which John Jones is exposed on a given occasion, and to relate these systematically and precisely to subsequent movements of his arms, legs, mouth, and so on is not to "make sense" of his behavior. Such an account would indeed leave one mystified. However, this form of empirically based discourse, often termed *causal*, may be contrasted with another which enables immediate comprehension. If we simply point out in this case that John Jones is "greeting his neighbor," we have informatively explained his actions. This level of discourse, often termed *reasoned*, typically requires that reference be made to reasons, motives, purposes, or intentions. When we know what the person is trying or intending to do, his or her actions are typically made intelligible.[19] Thus it could be concluded that endogenic concepts of reason, intention, motive, and so on are fundamentally indispensable to a behavioral science. Concomitantly, the role of environmental stimulus and response became increasingly unclear. If intention is built into our language of understanding, then environmental stimuli cannot easily be viewed as the cause of action. And, if action can only be identified by knowing its intentional basis, then behavioral observation plays an ancillary role to symbolic interpretation (Gergen, 1980).

Coupled with these two important philosophic movements has been a third force antagonistic to the traditional exogenic commitment in behavioral science, that is, the flourishing of "the critical stance" within the social sciences. In part because of hostility toward the U.S. military deployment in Vietnam, a wide variety of potentially culpable institutions, such as government, industry, and education, have undergone critical scrutiny within the past decade.[20] Among the institutions under fire was the scientific establishment. Of particular importance, questions have been raised concerning the ideological implications of what appeared, on the surface, to be value-free description. It is argued, for example, that in exploring the various personal characteristics of participants in race riots the investigator implies that the rioters are responsible for their actions. It is to assume that their character must be changed if rioting is to be reduced. Such a position removes responsibility from institutions practicing racial discrimination, and such institutions are thus protected by what the investigator may assume is nothing but an attempt to study existing correlations. One of the most powerful arguments of this sort was contained in Alvin Gouldner's *The Coming Crisis in Western Sociology* (1970). Gouldner demonstrates how structural-functional theory in sociology, although impeccably neutral in its scientific credentials, lends strong implicit support to the status quo and is inimical to social change. Other accounts have demonstrated the ideological underpinnings of historical accounting (Zinn, 1970) along with behavioral theory in political science (see Surkin & Wolfe, 1970). Such queries also rekindled interest in the earlier writings of Habermas, Adorno, and other members of the Marxist-oriented Frankfurt School (Jay, 1973). As the critical mode became increasingly well-developed, it also became apparent that the empiricist assumption of a value-neutral social science was deceptively misleading (see Unger, 1975). Social science knowledge is not an impartial reflection of "the way things are," as the empiricists would have it, but reflects the vested interests, ideological commitments, and value preferences of the scientists themselves.

---

[19]To clarify, one could not "make sense" of language through an exhaustive study of its phonetics. It is only when such sounds are transformed into morphemes that we understand the language.

[20]Leo Marx (1978) has argued that indeed the current era is witnessing a "neo-romantic" revolution against the cold formalism of "science" more generally.

II. THE SPECIAL FIELDS OF PSYCHOLOGY

It is difficult to ascertain precisely how and where these shifts in philosophic perspective influenced the course of psychological thought, or even whether such influence was unidirectional in its effects. However, it does seem clear that the three major developments just outlined are quite compatible with what is now viewed in psychology as the "cognitive revolution." Several reasons may be offered for this compatibility. Among them, the philosophy of science ceased to offer encouragement and guidance to those who wished to purify the language of psychology of mentalist terms. The door was open for what now may be seen as a wholesale reification of mental process. Terms such as "concept," "memory," and "decoding" have come to acquire an ontic status similar to that granted to the "facts of consciousness" by the nineteenth-century German mentalists. A second fillip to cognitive study was furnished by the philosophic shift toward linguistic analysis. Such work furnished a basis for useful interchange between philosophers and psychologists. The boundaries between the disciplines were often obscured. In some of the work of Noam Chomsky (1968), for example, one finds the reincarnation of the nineteenth-century philosopher-psychologist. And as the present analysis makes clear, the debate between Chomsky (1959, 1964) and Skinner (1957) was not only a scientific disagreement over which theory best fits the data (see also Dixon & Horton, 1968), it was also a recapitulation of the fundamental conflict between exogenic and endogenic worldviews.

This same shift from the exogenic to the endogenic perspective is evident throughout the cognitive domain. Ittelson (1973) has nicely traced the subtle but significant change in the concept of stimulus in the history of perceptual study. As he shows, the traditional view is one that views the stimulus as "physical energy outside the organism which, when it impinges on the organism, initiates processes, the end product of which is a response wholly determined, and predictable from the nature of the stimulus" (p. 8). Exogenic thought could have no clearer exemplar. However, this line of argument has gradually been eroded. For example, Gibson (1950) stated that "the term 'stimulus' will always refer to the light change on the retina" (p. 63) but, by 1966, he had reconsidered this position, stating that his early definition "fails to distinguish between stimulus *energy* and stimulus *information* and this difference is crucial" (p. 29). In effect, information is a concept that recognizes the autonomous processing capacities of the organism; it assumes an organism that is in search of and uses stimulation to fulfill its goals. The quandary over exogenic and endogenic views has now become a focal point of discussion. In his popular text on cognition, we find Neisser (1976) agonizing, "No choice is ever free of the information on which it is based. Nevertheless, that information is selected by the chooser himself. On the other hand, no choice is ever determined by the environment directly. Still, that environment supplies the information that the chooser will use" (p. 182). Finally, we must consider the work of Piaget (1952, 1974). From the present perspective we find Piaget undertaking the titanic challenge of integrating both the exogenic and endogenic worldviews in a single theory.

He wished simultaneously to accept a real world about which true knowledge could be obtained, along with an active organism that formulates and interprets. Thus, Piaget's concept of accommodation yields to exogenic assumptions, while the concept of assimilation emphasizes his commitment to endogenic thought. Development becomes an epistemological see-saw.

To be sure, social psychological thinking has been much influenced by the shift toward cognitive formulations in the field more generally. However, social psychologists were amply prepared. As we have seen, early formulations of the Lewin group planted important seeds for endogenic thought within the discipline. The more general deterioration of the behaviorist-empiricist orientation furnished a context in which such thought could reach fruition. Thus, with Schachter's two-factor theory of emotional labeling (Schachter, 1964; Schachter & Singer, 1962), cognitive processes replaced biological determinism as the basis of behavioral explanation. Festinger's (1957) theory of cognitive dissonance, which began with the supposition that people's actions are driven by inherent cognitive tendencies, came to serve as the battle cry for virtually a small army of social psychologists (see Brehm & Cohen, 1962; Wicklund & Brehm, 1976). Yet, few investigators bothered themselves with the earlier empiricist demand for an independent behavioral anchoring of hypothetical constructs. Balance formulations (Abelson et al., 1968; Heider, 1946; Newcomb, 1961) also came to demand equally wide attention. Again, such formulations assumed the existence of autonomous tendencies toward cognitive equilibrium, tendencies that were not clearly products of previous environmental influences.[21] This variety of formulation continues to the present day. Reactance (Brehm, 1966; Wicklund & Brehm, 1976), equity (Adams, 1965; Walster, Walster, & Berscheid, 1978), self-awareness (Duval & Wicklund, 1972), uniqueness striving (Snyder & Fromkin, 1980), and many similar concepts have all been added to the arsenal of cognitive tendencies.

Heider's (1958) theory of causal attribution also demonstrated its origins in German endogenic thought. For Heider the experience of causality was not given in the movement of relationships among environmental entities: it was rather a phenomenological necessity inherent in mental functioning. Although an overwhelming number of studies were inspired by Heider's formulation, much of this work has attempted a reconciliation with the empiricist roots of experimental social psychology. That is, the inherent mental tendencies so fundamental to the endogenic basis of the theory gave way to traditional exogenic thinking. In the Jones and Davis (1965) and Kelley (1972) formulations, both pivotal to attribution inquiry,

---

[21] It is of historical interest to note the shift from exogenic to endogenic assumptions in the Yale volumes on attitude change. Although early volumes were largely concerned with isolating external determinants of attitude change, with the 1960 publication of *Attitude Organization and Change* the endogenic metamorphosis was virtually complete: concern had shifted almost entirely from external determinants to internal process.

II. THE SPECIAL FIELDS OF PSYCHOLOGY

internally driven cognitive tendencies are largely eschewed. Instead the perceiver becomes a rational being weighing the evidence supplied by the senses. Indeed the Kelley formulation uses as its basis John Stuart Mill's canons of logical inference, long a mainstay in empiricist philosophy.

In adopting a cognitive basis of explanation, social psychologists have also been successful in linking their interests with adjacent domains. Beginning with the attempt of dissonance researchers to account for biological motives (see Brehm & Cohen, 1962), of research relating psychological states of helplessness and control to health related actions and symptoms (see Seligman, 1975; Rodin & Langer, 1977), and of more recent work on stress and coping strategies (see Glass, 1977; Glass & Singer, 1972), social psychologists have helped form the basis for what has become behavioral medicine. And, with the more recent work on cognitive processes underlying social decision-making (see Nisbett & Ross, 1980) and on person memory (Hastie et al., 1980), social psychology has allied itself once again with traditional experimental psychology. So enthusiastically have such enterprises been pursued that many social psychologists have come to fear that concern with fundamental social process may be relegated to a secondary position. Social psychology may become an ancillary discipline whose concerns will be dictated by either applied or experimental psychology.

The Struggle Toward a New Psychology:
Mind as a Social Creation

That which we call the world, the objective world, is a social tradition.

Miguel de Unamuno
The Tragic Sense of Life

Thus far we have seen that the breakdown of empiricist metatheory has been a congenial context for the flourishing of cognitive theory. However, of greater importance, this breakdown has also been accompanied by widespread reconsideration of the nature of behavioral inquiry. Within the fields of sociology and political science, philosopher Richard Bernstein (1978) has spoken of an "emerging new sensibility" in respect to the aims and functions of such disciplines, one that holds promise for fundamental transformation. It is apparent that this new sensibility, so widely evident in our adjoining disciplines, is abundantly manifest within the central ranks of psychology. For example, Meehl's 1978 critique of traditional hypothesis testing along with the Popperian view of science, Cronbach's (1975) lament over the cumulativeness of experimental findings, Sarbin's (1977) argument for a contextualist orientation to understanding human action, Neisser's (1976) misgivings about the predictive capability of cognitive research, Bronfenbrenner's (1977) concern over the ecological irrelevance of much developmental research, Argyris's (1975) elucidation of the manipulative implications of much social theory, Riegel's (1972) attack on traditional developmental psychology for its historical and ideological insensitivity, Fiske's (1978) dismay with the meager progress of personality research, along with recent portrayals of research on learning and memory as both ideologically and historically bound (Schwartz, Lacey, & Schuldenfrei, 1978; Meacham, 1977; Kvale, 1977) are all indicative of a major evolution in thinking.[22] Such generalized ferment has not taken place in psychology since the advent of radical behaviorism in the 1920s.

It is also apparent that what has been termed "the crisis" (Elms, 1975; Lewin, 1977; Sherif, 1977; Graumann, 1979; Silverman, 1971; Mertens & Fuchs, 1978) in recent social psychology is not a matter of localized dyspepsia. Within the manifest discontent with the experimental method (see McGuire, 1973; Gergen, 1978; Gadlin & Ingle, 1975), misgivings concerning the capacity of present research to solve pressing social problems (Helmreich, 1975), arguments against the generation of transhistorical predictions (Gergen, 1973; Hendrick, 1976), arguments for breaking the link between understanding and prediction (Thorngate, 1976), the exploration of the human image implied by social theory (Shotter, 1975), doubts about the cumulativeness of programmatic research (Smith, 1972; Cartwright, 1973), and concern with the ethical foundations underlying psychological research (Kelman, 1972; Mixon, 1972; Schuler, 1980; Smith, 1974), social psychologists are critically confronting the empiricist tradition. Further, in the questioning of the value bases implicit within descriptive theories (Archibald, 1978; Apfelbaum & Lubek, 1976; Sampson, 1977, 1978, Hampden-Turner, 1970), in our growing concern with the effects of social context on social psychological knowledge (Buss, 1979), in our probing the extent to which scientific theory creates social phenomena (Gergen, 1979), in our exploration of the rule following basis of social action (Harré & Secord, 1972; Harré, 1979; Ginsburg, 1979), in the probing of dialectic theory (Buss, 1979; Cvetkovich, 1977) and the interpretive bases of social life (Gauld & Shotter, 1977), in the exploration of the extent to which people may voluntarily escape the predictive efforts of the science (Scheibe, 1978), in the search for biases underlying the discipline's history (see Morawski, 1979; Samelson, 1974; Baumgardner, 1977), and in the various conferences and colloquia devoted to the nature

---

[22] Such citations are only representative of a much broader array of critical self-appraisals within recent psychology. Sigmund Koch's (1959) work may be viewed as prophetic in this regard. However, many others must be added to the list, including Allport, 1975; Bakan, 1969; Campbell, 1969; Chein, 1972; Deese, 1972; Hermann, 1976; Holzkamp, 1976; Hudson, 1972; Israel & Tajfel, 1972; Lorenz, 1967; Mahoney, 1976; McKeachie, 1974; Mishler, 1979; Morawski, 1979; Petrinovich, 1979; Rychlak, 1975; Sampson, 1978; and Shotter, 1975.

II. THE SPECIAL FIELDS OF PSYCHOLOGY

of the discipline and its potential (see Armistead, 1974; Strickland, Aboud, & Gergen, 1976; Israel & Tajfel, 1972), we are breaking clear of a tradition that, for all its solidifying capacities, had become strangulating in its singularity. Such metatheoretic analysis may be viewed, then, as a salutory sign that the field is healthily linked to the broader intellectual community and is making a serious attempt to reach solutions in its own terms.

In this attempt at solutions can one anticipate the emergence of a "new psychology"? This is indeed a momentous question, and its answer will ultimately depend on a confluence of many factors, including intellectual, political, and economic ones. Although criticisms of the empirical tradition seem virtually lethal, assumptions on which such criticisms are based have not been sufficiently tested against the crucible of counterattack. Such assumptions require more complete elaboration and examination. Further, the critics have been unable in most cases to offer compelling alternatives for everyday activity in the science. One often encounters the comment that although traditional practices seem problematic, they are comfortably programmatic and have reward value within the profession. Regarding professional politics, those committed to the empiricist traditions currently occupy most positions of authority and control within the discipline. If the continuation of critical probing succeeds in alienating rather than inviting dialogue, movement toward alternative forms of inquiry may be vitally impeded. And, with respect to economics, as the availability of academic positions continues to recede, many institutions may prefer to select a traditional candidate over one searching, but uncertain. Those who wish to fly on new wings may continue to dream of fairer weather.

Should these and other complex problems be solved, what form of psychology might one anticipate? As an initial answer one might conjecture that no single form will emerge; rather, a variety of competing alternatives will be developed, each of which will vie for centrality. In effect we may see a fragmentation of paradigms. To support this view one might point to the steadily increasing number of social psychologists pursuing the ethogenic orientation, dialectic theory, philosophical psychology, interpretive (hermeneutic) analysis, the critical orientation, historical-social psychology, metatheoretical and historical analysis of social psychology, and ethnomethodology. Scholars in each of these areas have criticized the traditional hypothesis-testing orientation in social psychology and are now searching for viable alternatives for research. Yet it is my belief that there are certain metatheoretical assumptions that would elicit substantial agreement among scholars in each of these seemingly disparate enterprises. That is, when carefully examined, one may find sufficient accord among these orientations that one could, on an abstract level, envision a unified alternative. It will prove useful to elucidate several of these key assumptions about which agreement might be secured. The reader who wishes to trace the assumption back to specific works may consult an earlier paper (Gergen & Morawski, 1980).

Knowledge as Socially Constituted

From the traditional empiricist standpoint, the investigator ideally serves as a passive recording device, sensitive to the patterns of nature. Theoretical description properly serves to map the existing pattern. As we have seen, this view of the scientist has come under brisk attack, both within the philosophy of science and within the behavioral sciences themselves. At the same time, within both circles attention is being increasingly directed toward the relationship between what is taken for knowledge at any point and processes of social interchange. As the reasoning goes, knowledge systems are fundamentally linguistic systems, sounds or markings that are used by people in relationships. In this respect, knowledge would appear vitally dependent on the vicissitudes of social negotiation. Its constraints would not essentially be experiential but social. From this standpoint, the existence of aggression, altruism, attitude change, conformity, reciprocity, socioeconomic class, and the like are not matters of ontological significance; statements about them are not fundamentally subject to empirical test. Rather, statements employing such terms may or may not be supported by observation depending on how one chooses to relate such terms to observation. Typically such relationships depend importantly on the usage of the terms within social interchange. However, it may be ventured that because such usage depends on coordinated actions among people, or "joint action" in Shotter's (1980) terms, knowledge in its linguistic sense can be viewed as fundamentally a social product.

While sensitive to the many persuasive arguments for the "social construction of reality" this view does not simultaneously commit the scientist to the endogenic extreme: reality as subjective. That is, one may accept the empiricist assumption of a real world, or reliable sensory experiences, as one might have it. However, one may simultaneously separate the construction of knowledge systems, or the way one communicates about experience, from the experience itself. One may experience without communication about an entity and communicate without benefit of experience. Knowledge about social life is not to be viewed as a "reflection" of what there is, but as a "transformation" of experience into a linguistic ontology. To reiterate, from this perspective the constraints on knowledge as a language are not furnished by reality but by social process.

This line of argument would apply no less strongly to statements about psychological states or processes (see Coulter, 1979). That is, one may argue that what we take to be psychological knowledge is not fundamentally dependent upon self-experience but is a system of talking governed by continuously evolving rules. In the case of talk about psychological states, however, we may anticipate a particularly elastic set of rules with a high degree of terminological negotiation. This is because the process of pointing, or saying, *"That's* what I mean by X" cannot be easily accompanied by shared experience. In saying "he possesses a *concept* of writing," for example, one cannot conveniently point to what we take to be an object as a way

II. THE SPECIAL FIELDS OF PSYCHOLOGY

of furnishing an experiential anchor for the term "concept." One can usually do so when saying, *"That* is a book."

As this discussion suggests, under favorable circumstances the social psychologist could come to play a critical role in the intellectual community. To the extent that the generation of knowledge is a social process and the social psychologist is committed to an understanding of such processes, then social psychological inquiry does not parallel that of the physicist, chemist, historian, or economist, for example; rather, the social psychologist could become indispensable in elucidating the grounds upon which physical, chemical, historical, or economic knowledge is based. In no way is the discipline prepared for such an undertaking at the present time. However the seeds for such an enterprise are sown both within the discipline and its adjoining domains.

Order as Socially Constituted

Exogenic thought has often placed a strong emphasis on the determined order of events in nature, and such thought sustains the scientist's concern with tracing relationships between antecedents and consequents. Social psychologists have fallen heir to this legacy, and the tradition has thus been committed to generating "basic principles" or "laws" of human interaction. Much of the critical literature cited above has found this view problematic. Rather, on both ontological and humanistic grounds it has been argued that the vast share of human activity is not fruitfully assumed to possess an order favored by nature. The range and variations of human activity seem enormous. Although biology may set limits on human potential, within these limits lies a virtual infinity of possible patterning. And at any point virtually any action within the available repertoire may be used as a "response" to any "antecedent stimulus." On this account there is little necessary connection between a given antecedent, in terms of an environmental event, and any subsequent action. To the extent that this line of thinking can be sustained, it becomes useful to view the ordered activity of human beings not as governed by natural law but as conforming in various degrees to localized and historically situated rules. Rules may be developed within the culture to reduce the threat of chaos and to secure needed ends. However, people remain fundamentally free to obey the rules, break them, or to attempt their alteration. In this respect, the new psychology might replace the mechanistic with a voluntaristic base of human activity.[23]

Within this argument one may also discern the germ of what could become a

---

[23] Even in the domain of cognitive psychology the search for fundamental principles of cognition seems to be ebbing. Such concepts as "cognitive heuristics," "scripts," and "plans" suggest that the range of cognitive orientations could be virtually infinite. Thus, the existing configuration or distribution of cognitive dispositions within the culture must be viewed primarily as a matter of historical concern. Contemporary cognitive research may tell us what people can do; it tells us little about what they must do.

liberation of theoretical explanation in social psychology. When order is assumed to be under human control, the causal power previously granted to the environment (stimulus or reinforcement) within the traditional exogenic framework is thereby diminished. The environment ceases to be "responsible" for human activity, and one cannot thus continue to "scan the landscape of observables" to answer the question of "why" a given pattern occurs. In this context the theorist is granted broad liberties with respect to explanation—where causal power is placed and how it is to be understood. Many of the theoretical departures within the cognitive movement may be viewed as precursors of what could become a far-reaching enrichment of the explanatory vocabulary. Of particular promise is the form of explanation suggested in Wundt's *Völkerpsychologie*, that is, historical or diachronic explanation. Contemporary social psychology is based almost entirely on a logic of efficient cause; it searches for the immediate antecedents, both necessary and sufficient, for a given action. Yet the same action may also be understood in terms of its place in an historical process, both with respect to the individual and the culture. How and why have such patterns been developed in the life of the individual or within the society more generally? What transformations have such patterns undergone over time, and what functions have these transformations served? Such questions open an exciting range of new theoretical possibilities.

Theory as Agency

As we have seen, the empirical tradition has typically considered theoretical description and explanation as mapping devices. From this standpoint, social theory serves society by furnishing reliable predictions in the world as given. However, we have also seen that this characterization of theory appears critically flawed. It may be more fruitful to view theories as linguistic signals with a negotiable relationship to experience. If we further accept the argument for a socially constituted order and grant a functional link between the linguistic practices of the culture and its other patterns of conduct, then alterations in linguistic practices have implications for the social order. In this way social psychological theory acquires an "agentive" role in social life. It can serve as a linguistic tool to be employed by the theorist or others to strengthen, sustain, or obliterate various forms of human activity. As such terms as *equity, reciprocity, conformity, reactance,* and so on enter the scientific vocabulary, they also enter the ontological system in its linguistic aspect. When such terms are then used to "describe" various actions, one's dispositions toward such actions may be vitally altered. For example, to say that one pattern of action is equitable and another inequitable, one is conforming and another autonomous, and so on is to have implications for the continuation of such actions.

This line of argument places the social psychologist in a position at once enviable and precarious. To the extent that society furnishes the means by which the psychologist gains special proficiency within language and communication, it also

II. THE SPECIAL FIELDS OF PSYCHOLOGY

grants him or her enhanced power to alter or sustain patterns of social life. The public thus entrusts to the psychologist skills that may affect its well-being. Further, when the psychologist is looked to for authoritative descriptions and explanations of human activity, he or she is being granted license to employ that skill. The theorist may thus acquire what could in some cases become enormous powers of influence in society. The theorist's hope "to be useful" in the culture need not await the practitioner's attempt to derive predictions in applied settings; the chief lever of social change may lie in the theoretical interpretation of social life.

At the same time, this position confronts social psychologists with a range of formidable problems—in fact, those which many exogenic thinkers had misleadingly argued were irrelevant to behavioral inquiry. These are problems of value—what forms of social life are to be favored, which are to be discouraged? If the language of theoretical description and explanation inevitably carries with it implications for action, as widely and persuasively argued, then the scientist can no longer take refuge in the Shangri-La of "pure description." To describe is inherently to prescribe. The social psychologist is thus invited, if not compelled, to return to the moral concerns so central to Auguste Comte's view of the science. Moral debate may thus come to play an increasingly important role in the new psychology.

Research as Vivification

If these various arguments are sustained and amplified over time, we may also anticipate fundamental alterations in the place of research. Since the 1930s the discipline has primarily been devoted to the empirical testing of hypotheses. The hope has been that with the accumulation of enough reliable facts, one might build inductively toward a fully general and empirically grounded theory. Yet, as critics of this orientation have argued, induction in the sciences is misconceived, the facts of social life are seldom stable, and factual data are negotiable. In effect, the place of empirical work in the sciences must be reassessed.

At the outset, it is clear from these suppositions that within the scholarly setting empirical study may be viewed as ancillary to theory construction. It is the theoretical interpretation of experience that has the capacity to transform social life and not the empirical evidence itself. The data themselves are mute. Further, it can be argued, it is the theory that gives rise to the empirical study and not the other way around. Within this setting the empirical study gives up its former, ill-claimed role as crucible for theoretical accuracy. Rather, research may be viewed as a means of enhancing the efficacy of theoretical communication. In a certain sense the researcher may be considered an artist who fashions the world in such a way that a theory is made palpable, dramatic, or life-like. And, as implied by the earlier arguments, researchers may wish to concern themselves not only with the ethics of observation, but with the ethics of communication about observation. The experiment, once interpreted, enters the common consciousness—to favor and threaten various forms of activity. In effect, the empirical study becomes an instrument for altering or sustaining social patterns—an instrument for good or ill according to moral or ideological criteria.

What does this mean for the researcher in the applied setting—one who wishes to assess the probability of suicide, auto accidents, needs for therapy, or the success of a public policy? In many cases such a researcher may not wish to escape conventional definitions. That is, the applied researcher may agree to common definitions of such terms along with their associated value investments and to furnish data within this framework. However, as the present arguments indicate, the researcher should be aware of the extent to which he or she is acceding to convention. The applied researcher does not at all escape the moral repercussions of "mere description," but joins the scholar as an artisan of symbols.

Should social-psychological study shift in the direction adumbrated by these assumptions, it may find enthusiastic support within other academic domains: vital movements within philosophy (see Taylor, 1971; Gadamer, 1975; Ricoeur, 1970), sociology (Bauman, 1978; Berger & Luckmann, 1966; Giddens, 1976; McHugh, 1970), anthropology (Geertz, 1973; Douglas, 1975), political science (Hirschman, 1970), and literary analysis (Fish, 1979; Hirsch, 1976; Burke, 1966). Ethnomethodological inquiry (see Garfinkel, 1967; Cicourel, 1968; Kessler & McKenna, 1978) must be singled out as well for its pivotal focus on the negotiation process through which verbal constructions become objectified. In effect, should a relatively unified reconstruction in social psychology occur along the lines suggested above, a rich exchange might be anticipated within the broader intellectual milieu.[24]

To conclude, during the past century social psychology has participated in one of humankind's greatest intellectual adventures. It has, in J. L. Austin's (1962) terms, joined in the "pursuit of the incorrigible," or certain knowledge, a pursuit that has challenged thinkers from Heraclitus to the present. Early in this century it appeared that the means had been discovered for gaining certainty in the behavioral sciences. Yet, subsequent examination has found such means sadly wanting. The search for certainty is a child's romance, and as in most romances, one holds fast to even the most fragile shard attesting to continued life. The question that must now be confronted is how to pass successfully into the maturity of a second century. A new romance may be required to extinguish the old, and possibly the signals of its inception are at hand.

REFERENCES

Abelson, R. P., Aronson, E., McGuire, W. J., Newcomb, T. M., Rosenberg, M. J., & Tannenbaum, P. H. (Eds.). *Theories of cognitive consistency: A sourcebook*. Skokie, Ill.: Rand McNally, 1968.

[24] For a more extended analysis of the development of a transformed psychology see Gergen, 1982.

II. THE SPECIAL FIELDS OF PSYCHOLOGY

Adams, J. S. Inequity in social exchange. In L. Berkowitz (Ed.), *Advances in experimental social psychology* (Vol. 2). New York: Academic Press, 1965.

Allport, D. A. The state of cognitive psychology. *Quarterly Journal of Experimental Psychology,* 1975, 27, 141–152.

Allport, F. H. *Social psychology.* Boston: Houghton Mifflin, 1924.

Apfelbaum, E. Some overlooked early European social psychologies. Paper presented at the 1979 meeting of the American Psychological Association, New York.

Apfelbaum, E., & Lubek, I. Resolution vs. revolution? The theory of conflicts in question. In L. Strickland, F. E. Aboud, & K. J. Gergen (Eds.), *Social psychology in transition.* New York: Plenum, 1976.

Archibald, W. P. *Social psychology as political economy.* New York: McGraw-Hill, 1978.

Argyris, C. Dangers in applying results from experimental social psychology. *American Psychologist,* 1975, 30, 469–485.

Armistead, N. (Ed.). *Reconstructing social psychology.* Harmondsworth: Penguin, 1974.

Austin, J. L. *Sense and sensibilia.* London: Oxford University Press, 1962.

Bakan, D. *On method.* San Francisco: Jossey-Bass, 1969.

Bauman, Z. *Hermeneutics and social science.* New York: Columbia University Press, 1978.

Baumgardner, S. R. Critical studies in the history of social psychology. *Personality and Social Psychology Bulletin,* 1977, 3, 681–687.

Ben-David, J., & Collins, R. Social factors in the origins of a new science: The case of psychology. *American Sociological Review,* 1966, 31, 451–465.

Berger, P., & Luckmann, T. *The social construction of reality.* Garden City, N.Y.: Doubleday, 1966.

Bernstein, R. J. *The restructuring of social and political theory.* Philadelphia: University of Pennsylvania Press, 1978.

Bills, A. G. Changing views of psychology as a science. *Psychological Review,* 1938, 45, 377–394.

Blumenthal, A. L. A reappraisal of Wilhelm Wundt. *American Psychologist,* 1975, 30, 1081–1086.

Blumenthal, A. L. Wilhelm Wundt and early American psychology: A clash of two cultures. *Annals of the New York Academy of Sciences,* 1977, 291, 13–20.

Blumenthal, A. L. The founding father we never knew. *Contemporary Psychology,* 1979, 24, 547–550.

Boring, E. G. *A history of experimental psychology.* New York: Century, 1929.

Brehm, J. W. *A theory of psychological reactance.* New York: Academic Press, 1966.

Brehm, J. W., & Cohen, A. R. *Explorations in cognitive dissonance.* New York: Wiley, 1962.

Bronfenbrenner, U. Toward an experimental ecology of human development. *American Psychologist,* 1977, 32, 513–531.

Bruner, J. S., & Allport, G. W. Fifty years of change in American psychology. *Psychological Bulletin,* 1940, 37, 757–776.

Burke, K. *Language as symbolic action: Essays on life, literature and method.* Berkeley, Calif.: University of California Press, 1966.

Buss, A. R. (Ed.). *Psychology in social context.* New York: Irvington, 1979.

Campbell, D. T. A phenomenology of the other one: Corrigible, hypothetical and critical. In T. Mischel (Ed.), *Human action: Conceptual and empirical issues.* New York: Academic Press, 1969.

Cartwright, D. Determinants of scientific progress: The case of research on the risky shift. *American Psychologist,* 1973, 28, 222–231.

Chein, I. *The science of behavior and the image of man.* New York: Basic Books, 1972.

Chomsky, N. A review of B. F. Skinner's *Verbal Behavior, Language,* 1959, 35, 26–58.

Chomsky, N. Current issues in linguistic theory. In J. A. Fodor & J. J. Katz (Eds.), *The structure of language.* Englewood Cliffs, N.J.: Prentice-Hall, 1964.

Chomsky, N. *Language and mind.* New York: Harcourt, Brace, 1968.

Cicourel, A. V. *The social organization of juvenile justice.* New York: Wiley, 1968.

Coulter, J. *The social construction of the mind.* London: Macmillan, 1979.

Cronbach, L. J. Beyond the two disciplines of scientific psychology. *American Psychologist,* 1975, *30,* 116–127.

Cvetkovich, G. Dialectical perspectives on empirical research. *Personality and Social Psychology Bulletin,* 1977, *3,* 688–698.

Danziger, K. Wundt and the two traditions of psychology. In R. W. Rieber (Ed.), *Wilhelm Wundt and the making of scientific psychology.* New York: Plenum, 1980.

Deese, J. *Psychology as science and art.* New York: Harcourt, Brace, 1972.

Deutsch, M. Field theory in social psychology. In G. Lindzey (Ed.), *Handbook of social psychology.* Reading, Mass.: Addison-Wesley, 1958.

Dixon, T. R., & Horton, D. L. (Eds.), *Verbal behavior and general behavior theory.* Englewood Cliffs, N.J.: Prentice-Hall, 1968.

Dollard, J., Doob, L., Miller, N. E., Mowrer, O. H., & Sears, R. R. *Frustration and aggression.* New Haven: Yale University Press, 1939.

Douglas, M. *Implicit meanings.* London: Routledge & Kegan Paul, 1975.

Duhem, P. *The aim and structure of physical theory* (P. Wiener, trans.). Princeton, N.J.: Princeton University Press, 1954. (Originally published, 1906.)

Duval, S., & Wicklund, R. A. *A theory of objective self-awareness.* New York: Academic Press, 1972.

Ellis, H. *The dance of life.* Boston: Riverside, 1923.

Elms, A. C. The crisis in confidence in social psychology. *American Psychologist,* 1975, *30,* 967–976.

Festinger, L. A theory of social comparison process. *Human Relations,* 1954, *7,* 117–140.

Festinger, L. *A theory of cognitive dissonance.* Evanston, Ill.: Row, Peterson, 1957.

Feyerabend, P. K. *Against method.* London: Humanities Press, 1975.

Fish, S. Normal circumstances, literal language, direct speech acts, the ordinary, the everyday, the obvious, what goes without saying, and other special cases. In P. Rabinow & W. Sullivan (Eds.), *Interpretive social science: A reader.* Berkeley, Calif.: University of California Press, 1979.

Fiske, D. W. *Strategies for personality research.* San Francisco: Jossey-Bass, 1978.

Gadamer, H.-G. *Truth and method* (G. Barden and J. Cumming, Eds.). New York: Seabury, 1975.

Gadlin, H., & Ingle, G. Through the one-way mirror: The limits of experimental self-reflection. *American Psychologist,* 1975, *30,* 1003–1009.

Garfinkel, H. *Studies in ethnomethodology.* Englewood Cliffs, N.J.: Prentice-Hall, 1967.

Gauld, A., & Shotter, J. *Human action and its psychological investigation.* London: Routledge & Kegan Paul, 1977.

Geertz, C. *Interpretation of cultures.* New York: Basic Books, 1973.

Gergen, K. J. Social psychology as history. *Journal of Personality and Social Psychology,* 1973, *26,* 309–320.

Gergen, K. J. Experimentation in social psychology: A reappraisal. *European Journal of Social Psychology,* 1978, *8,* 507–527.

Gergen, K. J. The positivist image in social psychological theory. In A. R. Buss (Ed.), *Psychology in social context.* New York: Irvington, 1979.

Gergen, K. J. Toward intellectual audacity in social psychology. In R. Gilmour & S. Duck (Eds.), *The development of social psychology.* London: Academic Press, 1980.

Gergen, K. J. *Toward transformation in social knowledge.* New York: Springer-Verlag, 1982.

Gergen, K. J., & Morawski, J. An alternative metatheory for social psychology. In L. Wheeler (Ed.), *Review of personality and social psychology.* Beverly Hills, Calif.: Sage, 1980.

Gibson, J. J. *The perception of the visual world.* Boston: Houghton Mifflin, 1950.

Gibson, J. J. *The senses considered as perceptual system.* Boston: Houghton Mifflin, 1966.

Giddens, A. *New rules of sociological method.* New York: Basic Books, 1976.

Ginsburg, G. P. (Ed.). *Emerging strategies in social psychological research.* New York: Wiley, 1979.

Glass, D. C. *Behavior patterns, stress and coronary disease.* Hillsdale, N.J.: Erlbaum, 1977.

II. THE SPECIAL FIELDS OF PSYCHOLOGY

Glass, D. C., & Singer, J. E. *Urban stress.* New York: Academic Press, 1972.

Gouldner, A. *The coming crisis in Western sociology.* New York: Basic Books, 1970.

Graumann, C. F. Die Scheu des Psychologen vor der Interaktion. Ein Schisma und seine Geschichte. *Zeitschrift für Sozialpsychologie,* 1979, *10,* 284–304.

Haines, H., & Vaughan, G. M. Was 1898 a "great date" in the history of social psychology? *Journal of the History of the Behavioral Sciences,* 1979, *15,* 323–332.

Hale, M., Jr. *Human science and social order: Hugo Münsterberg and the origins of applied psychology.* Philadelphia: Temple University Press, 1980.

Hamlyn, D. W. Behaviour. *Philosophy,* 1953, *28* (No. 105).

Hampden-Turner, C. *Radical man: The process of psycho-social development.* Cambridge, Mass.: Schenkman, 1970.

Hampshire, S. *Thought and action.* London: Chatto & Windus, 1959.

Harré, R. *Social being.* Oxford: Blackwell, 1979.

Harré, R., & Secord, P. F. *The explanation of social behaviour.* Oxford: Basil Blackwell & Mott, 1972.

Hastie, R., Ostrom, T., Ebbesen, E. B., Wyer, R. S., Hamilton, D., & Carlston, D. E. (Eds.). *Person memory: The cognitive basis of social perception.* Hillsdale, N.J.: Erlbaum, 1980.

Heider, F. Attitudes and cognitive organization. *Journal of Personality,* 1946, *21,* 107–112.

Heider, F. *The psychology of interpersonal relations.* New York: Wiley, 1958.

Helmreich, R. Applied social psychology: The unfulfilled promise. *Personality and Social Psychology Bulletin,* 1975, *1,* 548–560.

Hendrick, C. Social psychology as history and as traditional science: An appraisal. *Personality and Social Psychology Bulletin,* 1976, *2,* 392–403.

Hermann, T. *Die Psychologie und ihre Forschungsprogramme.* Göttingen: Hogrefe, 1976.

Hirsch, E. D., Jr. *The aims of interpretation.* Chicago: The University of Chicago Press, 1976.

Hirschman, A. *Exit, voice and loyalty: Responses to decline in firms, organization and states.* Cambridge, Mass.: Harvard University Press, 1970.

Hollis, M. *Models of man: Philosophical thoughts on social action.* Cambridge, England: Cambridge University Press, 1977.

Holt, E. B. The whimsical condition of social psychology, and of mankind. In H. M. Kallen & S. Hook (Eds.), *American philosophy today and tomorrow.* New York: Furman, 1935.

Holzkamp, K. *Kritische Psychologie.* Hamburg: Fischer Taschenbach Verlag, 1976.

Hovland, C. I., Janis, I. L., & Kelley, H. H. *Communication and persuasion.* New Haven: Yale University Press, 1953.

Hudson, L. *The cult of the fact.* New York: Harper Torchbook, 1972.

Israel, J., & Tajfel, H. (Eds.). *The context of social psychology: A critical assessment.* New York: Academic Press, 1972.

Ittelson, W. H. (Ed.). *Environment and cognition.* New York: Seminar Press, 1973.

James, W. *The varieties of religious experience.* New York: Collier, 1961. (Originally published, 1902.)

Jay, M. *The dialectical imagination.* London: Heinemann, 1973.

Jones, E. E., & Davis, K. E. From acts to dispositions. In L. Berkowitz (Ed.), *Advances in social psychology* (Vol. 2). New York: Academic Press, 1965.

Joynson, R. B. Models of man: 1879–1979. In A. J. Chapman and D. M. Jones (Eds.), *Models of man.* London: British Psychological Society, 1980.

Kelley, H. H. Attribution theory in social psychology. In D. Levine (Ed.), *Nebraska symposium on motivation, 1967.* Lincoln: University of Nebraska Press, 1967.

Kelley, H. H. *Causal schemata and the attribution process.* Morristown, N.J.: General Learning Press, 1972.

Kelman, H. C. The rights of the subject in social research: An analysis in terms of relative power and legitimacy. *American Psychologist,* 1972, *27,* 989–1016.

Kessler, S. J., & McKenna, W. *Gender: An ethnomethodological approach.* New York: Wiley, 1978.

Kirsch, I. The impetus to scientific psychology: A recurrent pattern. *Journal of the History of the Behavioral Sciences*, 1976, *12*, 120–129.

Koch, S. Epilogue. In S. Koch (Ed.), *Psychology: A study of a science* (Vol. III). New York: McGraw-Hill, 1959.

Koch, S. Psychology as science. In S. C. Brown (Ed.), *Philosophy of psychology*. London: Macmillan, 1974.

Koch, S. Language communities, search cells, and the psychological studies. In W. J. Arnold (Ed.), *Nebraska Symposium on Motivation, 1975*. Lincoln: University of Nebraska Press, 1976.

Kuhn, T. S. *The structure of scientific revolutions* (2d ed.). Chicago: The University of Chicago Press, 1970. (Originally published, 1962.)

Kvale, S. Dialectics and research on remembering. In N. Datan & H. W. Reese (Eds.), *Life-span developmental psychology*. New York: Academic Press, 1977.

Leary, D. The philosophical development of the conception of psychology in Germany. *Journal of the History of the Behavioral Sciences*, 1978, *14*, 113–121.

Leichtman, M. Gestalt theory and the revolt against positivism. In A. R. Buss (Ed.), *Psychology in social context*. New York: Irvington, 1979.

Lewin, K. *A dynamic theory of personality*. New York: McGraw-Hill, 1935.

Lewin, K. Formalization and progress in psychology. *Studies in Topological and Vector Psychology*, 1940, *1*, 9–42.

Lewin, M. Kurt Lewin's view of social psychology: The crisis of 1977 and the crisis of 1927. *Personality and Social Psychology Bulletin*, 1977, *3*, 159–172.

Lorenz, K. *On aggression*. New York: Bantam, 1967.

Lubek, I. The relatively unknown social psychologies of Gabriel Tarde and sons. Paper presented at the 1979 meeting of the American Psychological Association, New York.

MacCorquodale, K., & Meehl, P. E. On a distinction between hypothetical constructs and intervening variables. *Psychological Review*, 1948, *55*, 95–107.

Mackenzie, B. Darwinism and positivism as methodological influences on the development of psychology. *Journal of the History of the Behavioral Sciences*, 1976, *12*, 330–337.

Mahoney, M. J. *Scientist as subject*. Cambridge, Mass.: Ballinger, 1976.

Marx, L. Reflections on the neo-romantic critique of science. *Daedalus*, 1978, 61–74.

McGuire, W. J. The yin and yang of progress in social psychology: Seven koans. *Journal of Personality and Social Psychology*, 1973, *26*, 446–456.

McHugh, P. On the failure of positivism. In J. D. Douglas (Ed.), *Understanding everyday life*. Chicago: Aldine Press, 1970.

McKeachie, W. J. The decline and fall of the laws of learning. *Educational Researcher*, 1974, *3*, 7–11.

Meacham, J. A. A transactional model of remembering. In N. Datan & H. W. Reese (Eds.), *Life-span developmental psychology*. New York: Academic Press, 1977.

Meehl, P. E. Theoretical risks and tabular asterisks: Sir Karl, Sir Ronald, and the slow progress of soft psychology. *Journal of Consulting and Clinical Psychology*, 1978, *26*, 806–834.

Mertens, W., & Fuchs, H. *Krise der Sozialpsychologie?* Munich: Franz Ehrenwirth Publishers, 1978.

Mishler, E. G. Meaning in context: Is there any other kind? *Harvard Educational Review*, 1979, *49*, 1–19.

Mischel, T. Psychological explanations and their vicissitudes. In W. J. Arnold (Ed.), *Nebraska Symposium on Motivation, 1975*. Lincoln: University of Nebraska Press, 1976.

Mixon, D. Instead of deception. *Journal of the Theory of Social Behaviour*, 1972, *2*, 145–177.

Morawski, J. *Human interest and psychological utopias*. Unpublished doctoral dissertation, Carleton University, 1979.

Mueller, C. G. Some origins of psychology as science. *Annual Review of Psychology*, 1979, *30*, 9–29.

Murchison, C. *Social psychology*. Worcester, Mass: Clark University Press, 1929.

Neisser, U. *Cognition and reality*. San Francisco: Freeman, 1976.

Newcomb, T. M. *The acquaintance process*. New York: Holt, 1961.

II. THE SPECIAL FIELDS OF PSYCHOLOGY

Nisbett, R. E., & Ross, L. *Human inference: Strategies and shortcomings of social judgment*. Englewood Cliffs, N.J.: Prentice-Hall, 1980.

Peters, R. S. *The concept of motivation*. London: Routledge & Kegan Paul, 1958.

Petrinovich, L. Probablistic functionalism. *American Psychologist*, 1979, 34, 373–390.

Piaget, J. *The origins of intelligence in children*. New York: Norton, 1952.

Piaget, J. *Understanding causality* (D. Miles & M. Miles, trans.). New York: Norton, 1974.

Popper, K. R. *Logik des Forschung*. Vienna: Springer, 1935. (Trans. as *The logic of discovery*. London: Hutchinson, 1959.)

Popper, K. R. *The poverty of historicism*. London: Routledge & Kegan Paul, 1957.

Quine, W. V. O. *From a logical point of view*. Cambridge, Mass.: Harvard University Press, 1953.

Reese, H., & Overton, W. Models of development and theories of development. In L. R. Goulet & P. B. Baltes (Eds.), *Life-span developmental psychology: Research and theory*. New York: Academic Press, 1970.

Ricoeur, P. *Freud and philosophy: An essay on interpretation*. New Haven: Yale University Press, 1970.

Rieber, R. W. Wundt and the Americans. In R. W. Rieber (Ed.), *Wilhelm Wundt and the making of scientific psychology*. New York: Plenum, 1980.

Riegel, K. F. The influence of economic and political ideologies upon the development of developmental psychology. *Psychological Bulletin*, 1972, 78, 129–141.

Rodin, J., & Langer, E. J. Long-term effects of a control-relevant intervention with the institutionalized aged. *Journal of Personality and Social Psychology*, 1977, 35, 897–902.

Rychlak, J. F. Psychological science as a humanist views it. In W. J. Arnold (Ed.), *Nebraska Symposium on Motivation, 1975*. Lincoln: University of Nebraska Press, 1976.

Rychlak, J. F. *The psychology of rigorous humanism*. New York: Wiley, 1977.

Samelson, F. History, origin, myth, and ideology: "Discovery" of social psychology. *Journal for the Theory of Social Behavior*, 1974, 4, 217–231.

Samelson, F. Struggle for scientific authority: The reception of Watson's behaviorism, 1913–1920. *Journal of the History of the Behavioral Sciences*, 1981, 17, 399–425.

Sampson, E. E. Psychology and the American ideal. *Journal of Personality and Social Psychology*, 1977, 35, 767–782.

Sampson, E. E. Scientific paradigms and social values: Wanted—a scientific revolution. *Journal of Personality and Social Psychology*, 1978, 36, 1332–1343.

Sarbin, T. R. Contextualism: A world view for modern psychology. In A. W. Landfield (Ed.), *Nebraska Symposium on Motivation: Personal Construct Psychology, 1976*. Lincoln: University of Nebraska Press, 1977.

Schachter, S. The interaction of cognitive and psychological determinants of emotional states. In L. Berkowitz (Ed.), *Advances in Experimental Social Psychology* (Vol. 1). New York: Academic Press, 1964.

Schachter, S., & Singer, J. Cognitive, social and psychological determinants of emotion. *Psychological Review*, 1962, 69, 379–399.

Scheibe, K. E. The psychologist's advantage and its nullification: Limits of human predictability. *American Psychologist*, 1978, 33, 869–881.

Schuler, H. *Ethische Probleme der psychologischer Forschung*. Toronto: Hogrefe, 1980.

Schwartz, B., Lacey, H., & Schuldenfrei, R. Operant psychology as factory psychology. *Behaviorism*, 1978, 6, 229–254.

Seligman, M. E. P. *Helplessness: On depression, development, and death*. San Francisco: Freeman, 1975.

Sherif, M. Crisis in social psychology: Some remarks towards breaking through the crisis. *Personality and Social Psychology Bulletin*, 1977, 3, 368–382.

Shotter, J. *Images of man in psychological research*. London: Methuen, 1975.

Shotter, J. Action, joint action and intentionality. In M. Breuner (Ed.), *The structure of action*. Oxford: Blackwell, 1980.

Silverman, I. The experimenter: A (still) neglected stimulus object. *Canadian Journal of Psychology*, 1971, *15*, 258–270.

Skinner, B. F. *Verbal behavior*. New York: Appleton-Century-Crofts, 1957.

Smith, M. B. Is experimental social psychology advancing? *Journal of Experimental and Social Psychology*, 1972, *8*, 86–96.

Smith, M. B. *Humanizing social psychology*. San Francisco: Jossey-Bass, 1974.

Snyder, C. R., & Fromkin, H. L. *Uniqueness: The human pursuit of difference*. New York: Plenum, 1980.

Sprowls, J. W. Recent social psychology. *Psychological Bulletin*, 1930, 27, 380–393.

Strickland, L. H., Aboud, F. E., & Gergen, K. J. (Eds.). *Social psychology in transition*. New York: Plenum, 1976.

Surkin, M., & Wolfe, A. (Eds.). *An end to political science*. New York: Basic Books, 1970.

Taylor, C. *The explanation of behaviour*. London: Routledge & Kegan Paul, 1964.

Taylor, C. Interpretation and the science of man. *The Review of Metaphysics*, 1971, 25 (No. 1).

Thorngate, W. Possible limits on a science of social behavior. In L. Strickland, F. E. Aboud, & K. J. Gergen (Eds.), *Social psychology in transition*. New York: Plenum, 1976.

Unger, R. M. *Knowledge and politics*. New York: Free Press, 1975.

Walster, E., Walster, G. W., & Berscheid, E. *Equity, theory and research*. Boston: Allyn & Bacon, 1978.

Watson, J. B. *Behaviorism*. Chicago: The University of Chicago Press, 1924.

Wicklund, R. A., & Brehm, J. W. *Perspectives on cognitive dissonance*. Hillsdale, N.J.: Erlbaum, 1976.

Winch, P. *The idea of a social science and its relation to philosophy*. London: Routledge & Kegan Paul, 1958.

Wundt, W. *Lectures on human and animal psychology* (Trans. of 2d ed. by J. E. Creighton & E. B. Titchener). New York: Macmillan, 1894. (Originally published, 1863–1864.)

Wundt, W. *Principles of physiological psychology* (Partial trans. of 5th ed. by E. B. Titchener). New York: Macmillan, 1904. (Originally published, 1874.)

Wundt, W. *Völkerpsychologie* (Vols. 1–10). Leipzig: Engelmann, 1900–1920.

Zinn, H. *The politics of history*. Boston: Beacon Press, 1970.

PART III
SOCIAL CONSTRUCTION AND THE
RELATIONAL SELF

[10]

The Social Constructionist Movement
in Modern Psychology

Kenneth J. Gergen   *Swarthmore College*

ABSTRACT: Social constructionism views discourse about the world not as a reflection or map of the world but as an artifact of communal interchange. Both as an orientation to knowledge and to the character of psychological constructs, constructionism forms a significant challenge to conventional understandings. Although the roots of constructionist thought may be traced to long-standing debates between empiricist and rationalist schools of thought, constructionism attempts to move beyond the dualism to which both of these traditions are committed and to place knowledge within the process of social interchange. Although the role of psychological explanation is rendered problematic, a fully developed constructionism could furnish a means for understanding the process of science and invites the development of alternative criteria for the evaluation of psychological inquiry.

This article attempts to bring into focus the central contours of a contemporary movement of challenging implication. It would be misleading to say either that the movement is of recent origin or that its proponents are legion. The roots of the movement may properly be traced to earlier eras, and one might prefer to speak of a shared consciousness rather than a movement. However, in its current metamorphosis this emerging body of thought contains implications of substantial significance. Not only are broad vistas of inquiry opened for study, but the foundations of psychological knowledge also are thrown into critical relief. When the implications are fully elaborated, it becomes apparent that the study of social process could become generic for understanding the nature of knowledge itself. Social psychology would not stand, in this case, as a derivative of general psychology. Rather, the latter would be viewed as a form of social process, both the grounds and outcomes of which stand to be elucidated by social inquiry. In similar fashion, epistemological inquiry along with the philosophy of science could both give way, or become subsumed by, social inquiry. These are indeed bold conjectures, and as we shall see, to make good on them may require relinquishing much that is sacred. However,

it is the plausibility of these conjectures that I hope to demonstrate in this article while simultaneously clarifying the contours and origins of the social constructionist movement.[1]

The Social Constructionist Orientation

Social constructionist inquiry is principally concerned with explicating the processes by which people come to describe, explain, or otherwise account for the world (including themselves) in which they live. It attempts to articulate common forms of understanding as they now exist, as they have existed in prior historical periods, and as they might exist should creative attention be so directed. At the metatheoretical level most such work manifests one or more of the following assumptions.

1. What we take to be experience of the world does not in itself dictate the terms by which the world is understood. What we take to be knowledge of the world is not a product of induction, or of the building and testing of general hypotheses. The mounting criticism of the positivist–empiricist conception of knowledge has severely damaged the traditional view that scientific theory serves to reflect or map reality in any direct or decontextualized manner (cf. Feyerabend, 1976; Hanson, 1958; Kuhn, 1962/1970; Quine, 1960; Taylor, 1971). How can theoretical categories be induced or derived from observation, it is asked, if the process of identifying observational attributes itself relies on one's possessing categories? How can theoretical categories map or reflect the world if each definition used to link

This article is an elaboration of an invited address to Divisions 8 and 24 delivered at the annual meeting of the American Psychological Association, Anaheim, California, September 1983.

Requests for reprints should be sent to Kenneth J. Gergen, Department of Psychology, Swarthmore College, Swarthmore, Pennsylvania 19081.

[1] Although the term *constructivism* is also used in referring to the same movement (cf. Watzlawick, 1984), this term is also used in reference to Piagetian theory, to a form of perceptual theory, and to a significant movement in 20th century art. The term *constructionism* avoids these various confusions and enables a linkage to be retained to Berger and Luckmann's (1966) seminal volume, *The Social Construction of Reality.*

category and observation itself requires a definition? How can words map reality when the major constraints over word usage are furnished by linguistic context? How is it possible to determine whether competing theories refer to the same entities, without reference to some other theory not contained in those under comparison? If each theoretical proposition depends for its intelligibility on an array of related propositions, what aspect of the propositional network would be challenged by a disconfirmation of any single proposition? These and other telling questions have largely gone unanswered, and the lack of answers has left the empirical sciences without a viable logic of justification (Weimer, 1979).

Running counterpoint with this developing doubt has been a steadily intensifying concern with the constraints over understanding engendered by linguistic convention. Wittgenstein's (1963) *Philosophical Investigations* must be viewed as seminal in this regard. By asking such questions as where does an individual feel grief or happiness, could a person have a profound feeling in one second, and can the features of hope be described, Wittgenstein brought into poignant clarity the extent to which the use of mental predicates is convention bound. His work has served to inspire an impressive array of philosophic studies into the linguistic constraints governing the use of such concepts as mind (Ryle, 1949), intention (Anscombe, 1976), sense data (Austin, 1962b), and motivation (Peters, 1958). Such inquiry has also elucidated a variety of important problems created through the reification of the language. In effect, many classic problems both in psychology and philosophy appear to be products of linguistic entanglement; with clarity concerning the nature and functions of the language the problems may often be decomposed.

Social constructionism has been nurtured by the soil of such discontent. It begins with radical doubt in the taken-for-granted world—whether in the sciences or daily life—and in a specialized way acts as a form of social criticism. Constructionism asks one to suspend belief that commonly accepted categories or understandings receive their warrant through observation. Thus, it invites one to challenge the objective basis of conventional knowledge. For example, in Kessler and McKenna's (1978) investigation of the social construction of gender, the attempt is made to break down the seemingly incorrigible fact that there are two genders. By examining the variations in the way differing cultures and subcultural groups understand gender, the referents for the terms *man* and *woman* are obscured. Possibilities are opened for alternative means of understanding gender differences or of abandoning such distinctions altogether. In Averill's (1982) extensive work on emotion one is forced to question the

assumption that anger is a biological state of the organism and is invited to consider it as a historically contingent social performance. Sarbin (1984) extended this line of thinking to the entire array of emotional terms. Emotions are not objects "out there" to be studied, ventured Sarbin; emotion terms acquire their meaning not from real-world referents but from their context of usage.

Similar kinds of critiques have been launched against the taken-for-granted character of suicide (Atkinson, 1977), beliefs (Needham, 1972), schizophrenia (Sarbin & Mancuso, 1980), altruism (Gergen & Gergen, 1983), psychological disorder (Garfinkel, 1967), childhood (Kessen, 1979), domestic violence (Greenblat, 1983), menopause (McCrea, 1983), and situational causes (Gergen & Gergen, 1982). In each case, the objective criteria for identifying such "behaviors," "events," or "entities" are shown to be either highly circumscribed by culture, history, or social context or altogether nonexistent.

2. The terms in which the world is understood are social artifacts, products of historically situated interchanges among people. From the constructionist position the process of understanding is not automatically driven by the forces of nature, but is the result of an active, cooperative enterprise of persons in relationship. In this light, inquiry is invited into the historical and cultural bases of various forms of world construction. For example, historical investigation has revealed broad historical variations in the concept of the child (Aries, 1962), of romantic love (Averill, 1985), of mother's love (Badinter, 1980), and of self (Verhave & van Hoorne, 1984). In each case constructions of the person or relationships have undergone significant change across time. In certain periods childhood was not considered a specialized phase of development, romantic and maternal love were not components of human makeup, and the self was not viewed as isolated and autonomous. Such changes in conception do not appear to reflect alterations in the objects or entities of concern but seem lodged in historically contingent factors. Ethnographic study yields much the same conclusion. Conceptions of psychological process differ markedly from one culture to another (see Heelas & Lock's 1981 edited volume). Accounts of emotion among the Ifaluk (Lutz, 1982), of identity among the Trobrianders (Lee, 1959), of knowledge among the Illongot (Rosaldo, 1980), and of the self among the Maori (Smith, 1981) all serve as challenges to the ontology of mind in contemporary Western culture. They invite us to consider the social origins of taken-for-granted assumptions about the mind—such as the bifurcation between reason and emotion, the existence of motives and memories, and the symbol system believed to underlie language. They direct our attention to the social, moral, political,

and economic institutions that sustain and are supported by current assumptions about human activity.

Constructionist inquiry has further been directed to the axioms or fundamental propositions underlying descriptions of persons in present-day society (Davis & Todd, 1982; Gergen, 1984a; Ossario, 1978; Semin & Chassein, in press; Shotter & Burton, 1983; Smedslund, 1978). It is first asked whether the folk models of mind within a culture necessarily determine or constrain the conclusions reached within the profession. How can the psychologist step outside cultural understandings and continue to "make sense"? Further, it is asked, are there generic rules governing accounts of human action from which common conventions are derived? Such work is of special interest as it begins to outline the possible constraints over what psychological research can say. If it is possible to isolate propositions or assumptions grounding discourse about persons, then we are furnished with a basis for understanding what psychological theory *must* say if it is to be reasonable or communicable.

3. The degree to which a given form of understanding prevails or is sustained across time is not fundamentally dependent on the empirical validity of the perspective in question, but on the vicissitudes of social processes (e.g., communication, negotiation, conflict, rhetoric). As proposed in this case, perspectives, views, or descriptions of persons can be retained regardless of variations in their actual conduct. Regardless of the stability or repetition of conduct, perspectives may be abandoned as their intelligibility is questioned within the community of interlocutors. Observation of persons, then, is questionable as a corrective or guide to descriptions of persons. Rather, the rules for "what counts as what" are inherently ambiguous, continuously evolving, and free to vary with the predilections of those who use them. On these grounds, one is even led to query the concept of truth. Is the major deployment of the term *truth* primarily a means for warranting one's own position and discrediting contenders for intelligibility (Gergen, 1984b)?

In this vein, Sabini and Silver (1982) have demonstrated how people manage the definition of morality in relationships. Whether an act is defined as envy, flirtaton, or anger floats on a sea of social interchange. Interpretation may be suggested, fastened upon, and abandoned as social relationships unfold across time. In the same way, Mummendey and her colleagues (Mummendey, Bonewasser, Loschper, & Linneweber, 1982) have shown how decisions are reached as to whether an action constitutes aggression. Thus, aggression ceases to exist as a fact in the world and becomes a labeling device for social control. Other investigators (cf. Cantor & Brown, 1981; Harré, 1981; Lalljee, 1981) have dis-

cussed social negotiation processes underlying the attribution of causality to persons' actions. Earlier work on self-identity (Gergen, 1977) has focused on the manner in which self-definition is realigned over time as social circumstances are altered. Communications specialists Pearce and Cronen (1980) have outlined a general theory for the negotiation of reality. Others have concentrated on the family (Reiss, 1981) and the media (Adoni & Mane, 1984) as they contribute to prevailing forms of interpretation.

Much this same line of thinking has been increasingly employed by historians and sociologists of science to understand scientific conduct. For example, Mendelsohn (1977) has argued that the epistemological assumptions of modern science were developed largely as a means of gaining social control. Bohme (1977) has discussed the informal rules used within scientific communities to determine what they count as facts. Investigators such as Latour and Woolgar (1979) and Knorr-Cetina (1981) have carried out participant observation in natural science laboratories—much as anthropologists exploring tribal customs. As they contend, what passes for "hard fact" in the natural sciences typically depends on a subtle but potent array of social microprocesses. In effect, the move is from an experiential to a social epistemology (Campbell, 1969; Sullivan, 1984).

4. Forms of negotiated understanding are of critical significance in social life, as they are integrally connected with many other activities in which people engage. Descriptions and explanations of the world themselves constitute forms of social action. As such they are intertwined with the full range of other human activities. The opening, "Hello, how are you?" is typically accompanied by a range of facial expressions, bodily postures, and movements without which the expression could seem artificial, if not aberrant. In the same way, descriptions and explanations form integral parts of various social patterns. They thus serve to sustain and support certain patterns to the exclusion of others. To alter description and explanation is thus to threaten certain actions and invite others. To construct persons in such a way that they possess inherent sin is to invite certain lines of action and not others. Or to treat depression, anxiety, or fear as emotions from which people involuntarily suffer is to have far different implications than to treat them as chosen, selected, or played out as on a stage.

It is in this vein that many investigators have been concerned with the prevailing images or metaphors of human action employed within the field of psychology. Queries have been raised over the broad social implications of viewing persons as machines (Shotter, 1975), as self-contained individuals (Sampson, 1977, 1983), or as economic bargainers in social relations (Wexler, 1983). Attacks have also been levied against the damaging effects on children of the prevailing constructions of the child's mind (Walkerdine, 1984), the sexism implicit in investigation that assumes the superiority of universal principles in moral decision making (Gilligan, 1982), the effects of theories of cognitive mechanism in their implicit unconcern with material circumstances in society (Sampson, 1981), and the anomic effects of psychological assessment in organizations (Hollway, 1984).

Social Constructionism in Historical Perspective

The significance of the constructionist movement is more fully appreciated against the backdrop of history. Although a full treatment of the relevant background is beyond the scope of this article, it does prove useful to understand constructionism in relation to two major and competing intellectual traditions. These traditions can largely be distinguished in terms of basic epistemological orientations or models of knowledge. On the one hand, thinkers such as Locke, Hume, the Mills, and various logical empiricists in the present century have traced the source of knowledge (as mental representation) to events in the real world. Knowledge copies (or should ideally copy) the contours of the world. This *exogenic perspective* (Gergen, 1982) thus tends to view knowledge as a pawn to nature. Proper knowledge maps or mirrors the actualities of the real world. In contrast, philosophers such as Spinoza, Kant, Nietzsche, and various phenomenologists have tended to adopt an *endogenic perspective* regarding the origins of knowledge. In this case, knowledge depends on processes (sometimes viewed as innate) endemic to the organism. Humans harbor inherent tendencies, it is said, to think, categorize, or process information, and it is these tendencies (rather than features of the world in itself) that are of paramount importance in fashioning knowledge.

The exogenic-endogenic antinomy has also played a major role in the history of psychological theory. As I have outlined elsewhere (Gergen, 1982), early German theorists often wrestled in vain with means of cementing the two perspectives. The attempt of classical psychophysical research to plot the precise relationship between external and internal worlds is but one case in point. As psychology developed in the United States, guided as it was by both pragmatist and positivist philosophy, it took on a strong exogenic character. Behaviorism (along with neobehaviorism) placed (and continues to place) the major determinants of human activity in the environment. If the organism is to adapt successfully, it is claimed, its knowledge must adequately represent or reflect that environment. Until recently the en-

dogenic perspective failed to flourish on American soil. A handful of Gestalt psychologists, with their emphasis on autochthonous tendencies of perceptual organization, and a stalwart band of phenomenologists virtually prevented the orientation from otherwise perishing.

Yet, within the past two decades we have witnessed what appears to be a major reversal in emphasis. The endogenic perspective has returned in full force in the guise of cognitive psychology. The seeds for this evolution in social psychology were planted by Kurt Lewin, whose central concern with the psychological field was essentially a holdover from continental rationalism. In the hands of his students this emphasis reinstituted itself in such concepts as social (as opposed to physical) reality (Festinger, 1954), the social comparison process (Festinger, 1954), motivated perception (Pepitone, 1949), emotions as perceived (Schachter, 1964), and cognitive dissonance (Festinger, 1957). The centrality of this work in social psychology also served to hone the sensibilities of subsequent generations of researchers. Concerns with logical inference, cognitive schemata, information storage and retrieval, and cognitive heuristics have all extended the Lewinian premise: Human action is critically dependent on the cognitive processing of information, that is, on the world as cognized rather than the world as it is. Of course, much the same shift in explanatory emphasis has taken place within psychology more generally. The contours of the "cognitive revolution" are widely recognized.

Yet, it is my view that in spite of the richness of conceptualization and the profundity of its heritage, the endogenic perspective has not yet achieved full ascendency—nor can it in principle. There is much to be said on this account, but again a brief sketch is necessitated. First, cognitivism has not yet—neither in social psychology nor in psychology more generally—overturned the exogenic perspective because the exogenic perspective forms the metatheoretical basis of the science itself. That is, the contemporary conception of psychological science is a by-product of empiricist or exogenic philosophy—committed as it has been to rendering an account of objective knowledge of the world. The experimental psychologist thus sets out to employ methods for establishing objective knowledge about cognitive processes. To the extent that the investigator claims to achieve an accurate representation of the world (thus rendering support for exogenics), it threatens the view that it is the world as represented (cognized) rather than the world in itself which is of importance. In seeking objective truth (that which is true independent of subjective appraisal) the cognitive researcher thus denigrates the importance of the very processes he or she seeks to elucidate. The exogenic basis of the scientific activity undermines the validity of the endogenic theories under examination.

Nor, would it seem, can cognitivism ultimately achieve hegemony in psychological discourse. This may be anticipated in part by the example furnished by the history of the philosophy of knowledge. This history has been one of continuous and unresolved disputation between exogenic (or empiricist, in this context) and endogenic (rationalist, idealist, phenomenological) thinkers. Essentially, the history of the philosophy of knowledge can largely be written in terms of a continuous series of pendulum swings. We have witnessed the conflict between Plato's pure forms of knowledge versus Aristotle's concern with the role of sensory experience; between the authority granted to experience by Bacon, Locke, and Hume versus the rational capacities granted to the mind by Descartes, Spinoza, and Kant; between the emphasis placed by Schopenhauer and Nietzsche on will and passion in the generation of knowledge, and the attempts of logical positivists to ground all knowledge in observables. What is to prevent the same historical trajectory in psychology? We have most recently witnessed in the cognitive revolution a shift from an exogenic to an endogenic perspective. As the inherent flaws of cognitivism are once again revealed in future psychological work, are we again to anticipate a return to some form of (suitably enlightened) environmentalism? (Gibsonian affordance theory [Gibson, 1979] may already be foreshadowing the new swing.) And such problems are sure to emerge. For example, when cognitivism is extended to its natural conclusion it reverts into an unhappy and unacceptable solipsism. And, cognitivism remains perennially unable to resolve such thorny problems as the origin of ideas or concepts and the manner in which cognitions influence behavior (cf. Gergen, 1985). Compelling explanations for how cognitions could either be "built up" from experience or genetically programmed remain to be fashioned. Nor have theorists been able to solve the Cartesian dilemma of explaining how "mind stuff" can influence or dictate discrete bodily movements.

It is against this backdrop that one can appreciate the emergence of social constructionism. Rather than recapitulating yet again the movement of the pendulum, the challenge (for many) has been to transcend the traditional subject–object dualism and all its attendant problems (cf. Rorty, 1979) and to develop a new framework of analysis based on an alternative (nonempiricist) theory of the functioning and potentials of science. This movement begins in earnest when one challenges the concept of knowledge as mental representation. Given the myriad of insolubles to which such a concept gives rise, one is moved to consider what passes as knowledge in human affairs. At least one major candidate is that of linguistic rendering. We generally count as knowledge that which is represented in linguistic propositions—stored in books, journals, floppy disks, and the like. These renderings, to continue an earlier theme, are constituents of social practices. From this perspective, knowledge is not something people possess somewhere in their heads, but rather, something people do together. Languages are essentially shared activities. Indeed, until the sounds or markings come to be shared within a community, it is inappropriate to speak of language at all. In effect, we may cease inquiry into the psychological basis of language (which account would inevitably form but a subtext or miniature language) and focus on the performative use of language in human affairs.[2]

As we have seen, analyses of the social constructionist variety have been devoted to such broad topics as gender, aggression, mind, causality, person, self, child, motivation, emotion, morality, and so on. Typically the concern has been with the language forms that pervade the society, the means by which they are negotiated, and their implications for other ranges of social activity. In such endeavors social psychologists begin to join hands, as well, with a new range of disciplines. Rather than looking toward the natural sciences and experimental psychology for kinship, an affinity is rapidly sensed with a range of what may be termed *interpretive disciplines*, that is, disciplines chiefly concerned with rendering accounts of human meaning systems (cf. Rabinow & Sullivan, 1979). On the most immediate level, social constructionist inquiry is conjoined with ethnomethodological work (cf. Garfinkel, 1967; Psathas, 1979) with its emphasis on the methods employed by persons to render the world sensible, and with much dramaturgical analysis (cf. Goffman, 1959; Sarbin & Scheibe, 1983) and its focus on the strategic deployment of social conduct. Similarly, treatments of the social basis of scientific knowledge, including the history and sociology of knowledge, become relevant (Knorr, Krohn, & Whitley, 1981; Knorr-Cetina & Mulkay, 1983). Anthropological inquiry acquires a renewed interest for psychology. Of special interest is the work of symbolic anthropologists concerned with the construction of the world, including persons, developed in non-Western cultures (cf. Geertz, 1973; Shweder & Miller, 1985). Similarly, psychology gains a temporal dimension as its analyses become articulated with historical research in the

[2] If the emphasis is shifted, much cognitive research becomes relevant to constructionist pursuits. Research on social prototypes, implied personality theory, attributional schemata, the concept of intelligence, and the like do not, from the present standpoint, inform us about another world—namely, an internal, cognitive one. Rather they might elucidate the nature of social discourse and thus raise interesting questions about the function of such terms in scientific and social life.

constructionist mode (Nowell-Smith, 1977; White, 1978). And, psychology stands to gain much by opening consideration on literary theory, including accounts of metaphor (Lakoff & Johnson, 1980), narratology (Genette, 1980), and the deconstruction of meaning (Culler, 1982). Such work informs as to the means by which various linguistic figures or tropes serve to organize or guide the attempt to "describe" reality.

Constructionism and the Problematics of Psychological Explanation

Thus far we have considered grounding assumptions of the constructionist orientation, along with its historical roots and contemporary emergence. It remains now to touch upon the implications of constructionism both for the character of psychological inquiry and for the nature of science more generally. With regard to psychology the implications are far reaching, and many years will be required before they are fully explored. To appreciate the arguments at issue consider the typical constructionist analysis of psychological processes or mechanisms. In Averill's (1982) hands the concept of anger is largely cut away from a deterministic physiology and becomes a form of social role; anger as a term thus does not refer to a mental state but constitutes part of the role itself. In a related analysis (Mills, 1940), doubt is cast on the concept of motivation as a primal power capable of moving people to action, and the focus shifts to people's talk about their motives and its social implications. The mind (Coulter, 1979) becomes a form of social myth; the self-concept (Gergen, 1985) is removed from the head and placed within the sphere of social discourse. In each case, then, what have been taken by one segment of the profession or another as "facts about the nature of the psychological realm" are suspended; each concept (emotion, motive, etc.) is cut away from an ontological base within the head and is made a constituent of social process. In agreement with Wittgenstein's (1963) later analyses, one ceases to view mental predicates as possessing a syntactic relationship with a world of mental events; rather, as Austin (1962a) and other post-Wittgensteinians have proposed, such terms are cashed out in terms of the social practices in which they function.

From this perspective, then, all psychological theorizing and the full range of concepts that form the grounds for research become problematic as potential reflectors of an internal reality and become themselves matters of analytic interest. Professional agreements become suspect; normalized beliefs become targets of demystification; "the truth" about mental life is rendered curious. Or, in a slightly different light, the contemporary views of the profession on matters of cognition, motivation, perception,

information processing, and the like become candidates for historical and cross-cultural comparison. From the constructionist perspective they often constitute a form of ethnopsychology, historically and culturally situated, institutionally useful, normatively sustained, and subject to deterioration and decay as social history unfolds.

As is clear, constructionism will inevitably confront strong resistance within psychology more generally. It forms a potential challenge to traditional knowledge claims; psychological research itself is placed in the uncomfortable position of a research object. Yet for social analysts the shift is one of heady proportion. No longer would social inquiry confront the threat of becoming a derivative enterprise—merely elaborating the social implications of more fundamental psychological processes. Rather, what is taken to be psychological process at the very outset becomes a derivative of social interchange. The explanatory locus of human action shifts from the interior region of the mind to the processes and structure of human interaction. The question "why" is answered not with a psychological state or process but with consideration of persons in relationship. Few are prepared for such a wrenching, conceptual dislocation. However, for the innovative, adventurous and resilient, the horizons are exciting indeed.

Constructionism and the Character of Science

Although many will find it difficult to relinquish the use of psychological mechanisms, structures, and processes as major explanatory vehicles, this loss may be coupled with a challenge of no small consequence. The challenge is essentially that of grappling with a new conception of knowledge. To appreciate the point it should be realized that problems inherent in both the endo- and exogenic orientations are also deeply engrained in the contemporary conception of scientific knowledge and its acquisition. In particular, the empiricist assumptions that form the undergirding rationale for research in psychology (and virtually all contemporary science) are drawn chiefly from the exogenic intellectual tradition. This orientation, with its emphasis on knowledge as an internal representation of the state of nature, is manifestly apparent in the traditional attempt to establish scientific knowledge through processes of empirical verification and falsification. However, if constructionism is to transcend the exogenic–endogenic antinomy, and the interminable conflict it has thus far spawned, then it must also eschew the empiricist account of scientific knowledge. As it abandons the subject–object dichotomy central to disciplinary debate, so must it challenge dualism as the basis for a theory of scientific knowledge. What is confronted, then, is the traditional,

Western conception of objective, individualistic, ahistoric knowledge—a conception that has insinuated itself into virtually all aspects of modern institutional life. As this view is increasingly challenged one must entertain the possibility of molding an alternative scientific metatheory based on constructionist assumptions. Such a metatheory would remove knowledge from the data-driven and/or the cognitively necessitated domains and place it in the hands of people in relationship. Scientific formulations would not on this account be the result of an impersonal application of decontextualized, methodological rules, but the responsibility of persons in active, communal interchange.

Elsewhere, the contours of this emerging metatheory have been referred to as *sociorationalist* (Gergen, 1982; Gergen & Morawski, 1980). In this view the locus of scientific rationality lies not within the minds of independent persons but within the social aggregate. That which is rational is the result of negotiated intelligibility. For social thinkers the further development of the metatheory should be of especially high priority. For, if the character of sociorationalist process is among the focal concerns of the social investigator, then the critical task of understanding the generation and evolution of knowledge falls centrally to scholars within the social sphere. Much philosophic inquiry—including the philosophy of science—thus falls subject to social constructionist analysis. To a certain degree philosophers of science are already aware of this prospect. In recent years philosophic inquiry into foundations of scientific knowledge has waned. Confidence in empiricist assumptions has largely been eroded, and there is no obvious contender on the horizon (Bernstein, 1978).[3] Such inquiry has become increasingly replaced by historical analysis. Kuhn's (1962/1970) seminal treatise on revolutions in scientific knowledge is essentially a historical account, and much subsequent discussion of rationality and progress in science has largely proceeded on historical as opposed to philosophic grounds. Such history is essentially social, and its elaboration requires close attention to processes of human interchange. It remains, however, for social analysts more generally to become aware of the pivotal position that they might legitimately occupy.

Thus far feminist thinkers have been among those most acutely aware of such possibilities. For feminists, the empiricist orientation to knowledge

has not generally been a congenial perspective—advocating as it does manipulation, suppression, and alienation of those one wishes to understand (Jaeger, 1983). Further, from the feminist perspective, empiricist science seems to have been oft employed by males to construct views of women that contribute to their subjugation (Bleier, 1984; Weisstein, 1971). Both the process and the products of empiricist science have thus come under attack. As a result many feminists have searched for alternative forms of understanding—both of science and of other human beings. Constructionism, because of its emphasis on the communal basis of knowledge, processes of interpretation, and concern with the valuational underpinnings of scientific accounts, has been an attractive alternative. Thus, feminists have been frontrunners in employing interpretive research strategies (Acker, Barry, & Esseveld, 1983; Bowles, 1984), documenting the scientific construction of gender (Morawski, in press), demonstrating the pragmatic uses of constructionist inquiry (Sassen, 1980), and exploring the foundations for constructionist metatheory (Unger, 1983).

Yet, the possibility of an alternative theory of knowledge can hardly demand broad appeal. The investments in and sense of security fostered by the enduring traditions are profound. Acute misgivings can be anticipated within these circles regarding criteria of knowledge and the companionate problem of appropriate methodology. Traditional empiricism holds experience to be the touchstone of objectivity; hypotheses are said to be confirmed or challenged by virtue of sense data. Yet, from the constructionist viewpoint, both the concepts of experience and sense data are placed in question. From what grounds do they derive their truth warrants? Are the so-called "reports of one's experience" not linguistic constructions guided and shaped by historically contingent conventions of discourse? Yet, although casting doubt on the process of objective warranting, constructionism offers no alternative truth criteria. Accounts of social construction cannot themselves be warranted empirically. If properly executed, such accounts can enable one to escape the confines of the taken for granted. They may emancipate one from the demands of convention. However, the success of such accounts depends primarily on the analyst's capacity to invite, compel, stimulate, or delight the audience, and not on criteria of veracity. Required, then, are alternative criteria for evaluating knowledge claims—criteria that might reasonably take into account existing needs for systems of intelligibility, limitations inherent in existing constructions, along with a range of political, moral, aesthetic, and practical considerations.

By the same token, social constructionism offers no "truth through method." In large degree the

---

[3] Recent interest has been generated in a "realist" alternative to empiricist metatheory (Bhaskar, 1978; Manicas & Secord, 1983). However, although opposed to the Humean basis of scientific explanation, realist philosophy of science shares with empiricism a range of fundamental assumptions. It thus suffers from most of the criticisms lodged against empiricism.

sciences have been enchanted by the myth that the assiduous application of rigorous method will yield sound fact—as if empirical methodology were some form of meat grinder from which truth could be turned out like so many sausages. Yet, as analysts such as Quine, Taylor, Hanson, and Feyerabend have shown, such enchantment is of doubtful merit. Previous security is without firm foundation. For one seeking such security social constructionism will scarcely be palatable. Yet this is not to imply that constructionism eschews investigative methods. Whether rendering the conduct of organisms intelligible or demystifying existing forms of understanding, research methods can be used to produce "objectifications" or illustrations useful in advancing the pragmatic consequences of one's work. In this sense it would seem that virtually any methodology can be employed so long as it enables the analyst to develop a more compelling case. Although some methods may hold the allure of large samples, others can attract because of their purity, their sensitivity to nuance, or their ability to probe in depth. Such assets do not thereby increase the "objective validity" of the resulting constructions. However, like vivid photographs or startling vignettes drawn from daily life, when well wrought they may add vital power to the pen.

Others may eschew the constructionist orientation for what appears to be its rampant relativism. Yet, as we have seen, the attempts to justify objective foundations for knowledge have yet to furnish reason for optimism. One might well argue that the scientist's claims to privileged knowledge have served as mystifying devices within the society more generally. Constructionism offers no foundational rules of warrant and in this sense is relativistic. However, this does not mean that "anything goes." Because of the inherent dependency of knowledge systems on communities of shared intelligibility, scientific activity will always be governed in large measure by normative rules. However, constructionism does invite the practitioners to view these rules as historically and culturally situated—thus subject to critique and transformation. There is stability of understanding without the stultification of foundationalism. Further, unlike the moral relativism of the empiricist tradition, constructionism reasserts the relevance of moral criteria for scientific practice. To the extent that psychological theory (and related practices) enter into the life of the culture, sustaining certain patterns of conduct and destroying others, such work must be evaluated in terms of good and ill. The practitioner can no longer justify any socially reprehensible conclusion on the grounds of being a "victim of the facts"; he or she must confront the pragmatic implications of such conclusions within society more generally.

Should the challenge of developing an alternative metatheory be accepted, a variety of interesting changes may be anticipated in the character of professional life. The problem of forging a compelling account of the social genesis of knowledge is not inconsequential. New theoretical tools are required—concepts that lie between the problematic explanatory domains of psychology and sociology. The functions of language, both as a system of reference and as a form of social participation must be elaborated. A general account must be furnished of the social dimensions of natural science, social science, and philosophy. The demarcation (if any) between science and nonscience must be carefully examined. The extent to which scientific accounts may be (if ever) corrected or modified through observation must be assessed. In effect, an array of challenging problems will be confronted, problems that are essentially conceptual rather than empirical. For such tasks dialogue is essential between psychologists and like-minded colleagues in sociology, anthropology, history, philosophy, and literary studies. Should such dialogue occur, we might reasonably anticipate the development of new theoretical departures, metatheory for a new conception of science, and a general refurbishment of intellectual resources.

REFERENCES

Acker, J., Barry, K., & Esseveld, J. (1983). Objectivity and truth: Problems in doing feminist research. *Women's Studies International Forum, 4,* 423–435.
Adoni, H., & Mane, S. (1984). Media and the social construction of reality. *Communication Research, 11,* 323–340.
Anscombe, G. E. M. (1976). *Intention.* Oxford, England: Blackwell (Original work published 1957)
Aries, P. (1962). *Centuries of childhood: A social history of family life.* New York: Vintage.
Atkinson, J. M. (1977). *Discovering suicide: Studies in the social organization of sudden death.* London: Macmillan Press.
Austin, J. L. (1962a). *How to do things with words.* Cambridge, MA: Harvard University Press.
Austin, J. L. (1962b). *Sense and sensibilia.* London: Oxford University Press.
Averill, J. (1982). *Anger and aggression.* New York: Springer-Verlag.
Averill, J. (1985). The social construction of emotion: With special reference to love. In K. J. Gergen & K. E. Davis (Eds.), *The social construction of the person.* New York: Springer-Verlag.
Badinter, E. (1980). *Mother love, myth and reality.* New York: Macmillan.
Berger, P., & Luckmann, T. (1966). *The social construction of reality.* Garden City, NY: Doubleday.
Bernstein, R. (1978). *The restructuring of social and political theory.* Philadelphia: University of Pennsylvania Press.
Bhaskar, R. (1978). *A realist theory of science* (2nd ed.). Atlantic Highlands, NJ: Humanities Press.
Bleier, R. (1984). *Science and gender, a critique of biology and its theories on women.* New York: Pergamon.
Bohme, G. (1977). Cognitive norms, knowledge interests and the constitution of the scientific object. In E. Mendelsohn & P. Weingart (Eds.), *The social production of scientific knowledge.* Dordrecht, The Netherlands: Reidel.

Bowles, G. (1984). The use of hermeneutics for feminist scholarship. *Women's Studies International Forum, 7,* 185–188.

Campbell, D. (1969). Ethnocentrism of disciplines and the Fish-scale model of omniscience. In M. Sherif & C. W. Sherif (Eds.), *Inter-disciplinary relationships in the social sciences* (pp. 140–152). Chicago: Aldine.

Cantor, D., & Brown, J. (1981). Explanatory roles. In C. Antaki (Ed.), *The psychology of ordinary explanations* (pp. 221–242). London: Academic Press.

Coulter, J. (1979). *The social construction of the mind.* New York: Macmillan.

Culler, J. (1982). *On deconstruction.* Ithica, NY: Cornell University Press.

Davis, K. E., & Todd, M. J. (1982). Friendship and love relationships. In K. Davis (Ed.), *Advances in descriptive psychology* (Vol. 2, pp. 79–122). Greenwich, CT: JAI Press.

Festinger, L. (1954). A theory of social comparison processes. *Human Relations, 7,* 117–140.

Festinger, L. (1957). *A theory of cognitive dissonance.* Evanston, IL: Row, Peterson.

Feyerabend, P. K. (1976). *Against method.* New York: Humanities Press.

Garfinkel, H. (1967). *Studies in ethnomethodology.* Englewood Cliffs, NJ: Prentice-Hall.

Geertz, C. (1973). *Interpretation of cultures.* New York: Basic Books.

Genette, R. (1980). *Narrative discourse.* Ithaca, New York: Cornell University Press.

Gergen, K. J. (1977). The social construction of self-knowledge. In T. Mischel (Ed.), *The self, psychological and philosophical issues.* Oxford, England: Blackwell.

Gergen, K. J. (1982). *Toward transformation in social knowledge.* New York: Springer-Verlag.

Gergen, K. J. (1984a). Aggression as discourse. In A. Mummendey (Ed.), *Social psychology of aggression* (pp. 51–68). New York: Springer-Verlag.

Gergen, K. J. (1984b) *Warranting voice and the elaboration of the self.* Paper presented at the Wales Conference on Self & Identity, Cardiff, Wales.

Gergen, K. J. (1985). Theory of the self: Impasse and evolution. In L. Berkowitz (Ed.), *Advances in experimental social psychology.* New York: Academic Press.

Gergen, K. J., & Gergen, M. M. (1982). Form and function in the explanation of human conduct. In P. Secord (Ed.), *Paradigms in the social sciences* (pp. 127–151). Beverly Hills, CA: Sage.

Gergen, K. J., & Gergen, M. M. (1983). The social construction of helping relationships. In J. D. Fisher, A. Nadler, & B. DePaulo (Eds.), *New directions in helping* (Vol. 1, pp. 144–163). New York: Academic Press.

Gergen, K. J., & Morawski, J. (1980). An alternative metatheory for social psychology. In L. Wheeler (Ed.), *Review of personality and social psychology* (pp. 326–352). Beverly Hills: Sage.

Gibson, J. J. (1979). *The ecological approach to visual perception.* Boston: Houghton Mifflin.

Gilligan, C. (1982). *In a different voice.* Cambridge, MA: Harvard University Press.

Goffman, E. (1959). *The presentation of self in everyday life.* New York: Doubleday.

Greenblat, C. S. (1983). A hit is a hit is a hit . . . Or is it? In R. J. Finkelhor, R. J. Gelles, G. T. Hotaling, & M. A. Straus (Eds.), *The dark side of families: Current family violence research* (pp. 132–158). Beverly Hills, CA: Sage.

Hanson, N. R. (1958). *Patterns of discovery.* London: Cambridge University Press.

Harré, R. (1981). Expressive aspects of descriptions of others. In C. Antaki (Ed.), *The psychology of ordinary explanations* (pp. 139–156). London: Academic Press.

Heelas, P., & Lock, A. (Eds.). (1981). *Indigenous psychologies.* London: Academic Press.

Hollway, W. (1984). Fitting work: Psychological assessment in organizations. In J. Henriques, W. Hollway, C. Urwin, V. Louze, & V. Walkerdine (Eds.), *Changing the subject* (pp. 26–59). London: Methuen.

Jaeger, A. (1983). *Feminist politics and human nature.* New York: Rowman & Allanheld.

Kessen, W. (1979). The American child and other cultural inventions. *American Psychologist, 34,* 815–820.

Kessler, S., & McKenna, W. (1978). *Gender: An ethnomethodological approach.* New York: Wiley.

Knorr, K. D., Krohn, R., & Whitley, R. (Eds.). (1981). *The social process of scientific investigation.* Dordrecht, The Netherlands: Reidel.

Knorr-Cetina, K. D. (1981). *The manufacture of knowledge.* Oxford, England: Pergamon.

Knorr-Cetina, K. D., & Mulkay, M. (1983). *Science observed.* Beverly Hills, CA: Sage.

Kuhn, T. S. (1970). *The structure of scientific revolutions* (2nd rev. ed.). Chicago: University of Chicago Press. (Original work published 1962)

Lakoff, G., & Johnson, M. (1980). *Metaphors we live by.* Chicago: University of Chicago Press.

Lalljee, M. (1981). Attribution theory and the analysis of explanations. In C. Antaki (Ed.), *The psychology of ordinary explanations* (pp. 119–138). London: Academic Press.

Latour, B., & Woolgar, S. (1979). *Laboratory life, the social construction of scientific facts.* Beverly Hills, CA: Sage.

Lee, D. (1959). *Freedom and culture.* New York: Prentice-Hall.

Lutz, C. (1982). The domain of emotion words in Ifaluk. *American Ethnologist, 9,* 113–128.

Manicas, P. T., & Secord, P. E. (1983). Implications for psychology of the new philosophy of science. *American Psychologist, 38,* 399–413.

McCrea, F. B. (1983). The politics of menopause: The "discovery" of a deficiency disease. *Social Problems, 31,* 111–123.

Mendelsohn, E. (1977). The social construction of scientific knowledge. In E. Mendelsohn & P. Weingart (Eds.), *The social production of scientific knowledge.* Dordrecht, The Netherlands: Reidel.

Mills, C. W. (1940). Situated actions and vocabularies of motives. *American Sociological Review, 5,* 904–913.

Morawski, J. (in press). The measurement of masculinity and femininity: Engendering categorical realities. *Journal of Personality.*

Mummendey, A., Bonewasser, M., Loschper, G., & Linneweber, V. (1982). It is always somebody else who is aggressive. *Zeitschrift für Sozialpsychologie, 13,* 341–352.

Needham, R. (1972). *Belief, language & experience.* Chicago: University of Chicago Press.

Nowell-Smith, P. H. (1977). The constructionist theory of history. *History and Theory, Studies in the Philosophy of History, 16,* 4.

Ossario, P. (1978). *What actually happens.* Columbia: University of South Carolina Press.

Pearce, W. B., & Cronen, V. E. (1980). *Communication, action and meaning.* New York: Praeger.

Pepitone, A. (1949). Motivation effects in social perception. *Human Relations, 3,* 57–76.

Peters, R. S. (1958). *The concept of motivation.* London: Routledge & Kegan Paul.

Psathas, G. (1979). *Everyday language.* New York: Irvington.

Quine, W. V. O. (1960). *Word and object.* Cambridge, MA: M.I.T. Press.

Rabinow, P., & Sullivan, W. (Eds.). (1979). *Interpretive social science: A reader.* Berkeley: University of California Press.

Reiss, D. (1981). *The family's construction of reality.* Cambridge, MA: Harvard University Press.

Rorty, R. (1979). *Philosophy and the mirror of nature.* Princeton, NJ: Princeton University Press.

Rosaldo, M. (1980). *Knowledge and passion, Ilongot notions of self and social life.* Cambridge, England: Cambridge University Press.

Ryle, G. (1949). *The concept of mind*. London: Hutchinson.

Sabini, J., & Silver, M. (1982). *The moralities of everyday life*. London and New York: Oxford University Press.

Sampson, E. E. (1977). Psychology and the American ideal. *Journal of Personality and Social Psychology, 35*, 767–782.

Sampson, E. E. (1981). Cognitive psychology as ideology. *American Psychologist, 36*, 730–743.

Sampson, E. E. (1983). Deconstructing psychology's subject. *Journal of Mind and Behavior, 4*, 135–164.

Sarbin, T. R. (1984, August). *Emotion: A contextualist view*. Invited address delivered at the meeting of the American Psychological Association, Toronto, Ontario, Canada.

Sarbin, T. R., & Mancuso, J. C. (1980). *Schizophrenia: Medical diagnosis or verdict?* Elmsford, NY: Pergamon.

Sarbin, T. R., & Scheibe, K. E. (Eds.). (1983). *Studies in social identity*. New York: Praeger.

Sassen, G. (1980). Success anxiety in women: A constructivist interpretation of its social significance. *Harvard Educational Review, 50*, 13–24.

Schachter, S. (1964). The interaction of cognitive and physiological determinants of emotional state. In L. Berkowitz (Ed.), *Advances in experimental social psychology* (Vol. 1, pp. 49–81). New York: Academic Press.

Semin, G. R., & Chassein, J. (in press). The relationship between higher order models and everyday conceptions of personality. *European Journal of Social Psychology*.

Shotter, J. (1975). *Images of man in psychological research*. London: Methuen.

Shotter, J., & Burton, M. (1983). Common sense accounts of human action: Descriptive formulations of Heider, Smedslund, & Ossorio. In L. Wheeler (Ed.), *Review of personality and social psychology* (Vol. 4, pp. 272–296). Beverly Hills, CA: Sage.

Shweder, R. A., & Miller, J. (1985). The social construction of the person: How is it possible? In K. J. Gergen & K. E. Davis (Eds.), *The social construction of the person*. New York: Springer-Verlag.

Smedslund, J. (1978). Bandura's theory of self-efficacy: A set of common sense theorems. *Scandinavian Journal of Psychology, 19*, 1–14.

Smith, J. (1981). Self as experience in Maori culture. In P. Heelas & A. Lock (Eds.), *Indigenous psychologies* (pp. 145–160). London: Academic Press.

Sullivan, E. V. (1984). *A critical psychology*. New York: Plenum.

Taylor, C. (1971). Interpretation and the sciences of man. *Review of Metaphysics, 25*(1).

Unger, R. K. (1983). Through the looking glass: No wonderland yet! (The reciprocal relationship between methodology and models of reality). *Psychology of Women Quarterly, 8*, 9–32.

Verhave, R., & van Hoorne, W. (1984). The temporalization of the self. In K. J. Gergen & M. M. Gergen (Eds.), *Historical social psychology* (pp. 325–346). Hillsdale, NJ: Erlbaum.

Walkerdine, V. (1984). Developmental psychology and the child-centered pedagogy. In J. Henriques, W. Hollway, C. Urwin, V. Louze, & V. Walkerdine (Eds.), *Changing the subject* (pp. 153–202). London: Methuen.

Watzlawick, P. (Ed.). (1984). *The invented reality*. New York: Norton.

Weimer, W. B. (1979). *Notes on the methodology of scientific research*. Hillsdale, NJ: Erlbaum.

Weisstein, N. (1971). Psychology constructs the female. In V. Gornick & B. K. Moran (Eds.), *Women in sexist society* (pp. 96–104). New York: Basic Books.

Wexler, P. (1983). *Critical social psychology*. Boston: Routledge & Kegan Paul.

White, H. (1978). *Tropics of discourse*. Baltimore, MD: Johns Hopkins University Press.

Wittgenstein, L. (1963). *Philosophical investigations* (G. E. M. Anscombe, Trans.). New York: Macmillan.

[11]

European Journal of Social Psychology, Vol. 19, 463–484 (1989)

Social Psychology and the Wrong Revolution

KENNETH J. GERGEN
*Department of Psychology,
Swarthmore College,
Swarthmore, PA. 19081,
U.S.A.*

Abstract

Many social psychologists take increasing comfort in cognitive explanations of human action. This paper first attempts to demonstrate that cognitively based formulations not only delimit the possibilities for social understanding, but create a range of intractable conceptual problems. If real world events are reduced to cognitive representations of the world, then social events cease to exist for the discipline as legitimate foci of concern. Further, once the reality of cognition is granted, there is no conceptual means of viably explaining either the origins or acquisition of cognitive categories (schemas, representations, etc.), or the relationship between cognition and action. The paper then goes on to argue that the cognitive revolution in psychology blinds the discipline to the far more pervasive revolution occurring elsewhere in the intellectual world, that of social epistemology. When cognition is replaced by language as the major means for representing the world, then the individual is replaced by the social relationship as the central focus of concern. Theory and research within the framework of social epistemology are reviewed and their implications discussed.

INTRODUCTION

It is widely agreed that during the past several decades psychological study in general has undergone a major transformation. This tranformation is often described as a 'cognitive revolution' (Baars, 1986). What is meant by the term cognitive revolution varies from one context to another. Some feel it is a shift in emphasis from black-box behaviourism to a neo-behaviourist concern with internal processes; others see it as an alteration from 'bottom-up' models of human functioning to 'top down' theories; still others view it as a shift from environmentalist conceptions of behaviour to nativist. While all these views capture important elements of the transformation, it is finally clear that the cognitive revolution has meant a radical reduction of inquiry to a small range of explanatory constructs. And it is the operation of these constructs (e.g. schemas, attention, memory, heuristics, accessibility and the like) that takes procedural precedence over human activity itself. For, as the cognitive perspective proposes, human activity is largely a derivative of

0046-2772/89/050463-22$11.00
© 1989 by John Wiley & Sons, Ltd.

Received February 1989

cognitive process. If we wish to understand such activity, it is the activating mechanism that demands the attention.

Social psychologists have hardly been immune to this more general revolution in psychology. Indeed, one might say that the work of Kurt Lewin and his protegees (namely Festinger, Schachter, and Kelley) played a substantial role in its development. For, how could one resist the strong and insistent message conveyed by this early work, to whit, 'It is not the world in itself that determines human action but the way in which the world is perceived'? For Festinger (1954) it was not 'physical reality' but 'social reality' that determined the course of social comparison. And in his later theory of cognitive dissonance (Festinger, 1957), it was a purely cognitive demand for consistency to which broad-ranging (and often aberrant) patterns of behaviour were traced. For Schachter (1964) emotions ceased to exist as events sui generis, and became the result of cognitive labelling. And for Kelley (1983) the attribution of causality became a function of a series of mental heuristics. These themes were critical in much of the classic work on person perception (Heider, 1958), attribution theory (*cf.* Jones and Davis, 1965), and research on emotion (Zillmann, 1978). As texts by Eiser (1980) and Fiske and Taylor (1984) also demonstrated, the cognitive orientation could be extended successfully to include most of the major literature in attitude change, altruism, bargaining, attraction, and equity. To further fortify the revolution, a new, and unifying theoretical language (one based primarily on the metaphor of the mind as computer) has also emerged in what are often considered the glamour areas of social cognition: prejudice (*cf.* Hamilton and Rose, 1987), social schemata (Cantor and Mischel, 1979), person memory (Hastie, *et al.* 1980), accessibility (Higgins, King, 1981), stereotypes (Hamilton and Rose, 1980) and social inference (Nisbett and Ross, 1980). And to fix the revolution in the European context, one finds that the major areas of intergroup relations and social representation—which initially invited concern with social phenomena in themselves are being slowly reconceptualized as forms of cognitive inquiry.

To be sure, the cognitive revolution has been a major intellectual and empirical achievement. It has succeeded in opening a broad vista of exciting and challenging inquiry. It has raised a host of new and interesting questions, and furnished creative solutions to problems of long-standing. However, as I hope to demonstrate in what follows, for social psychologists this revolution must be considered but a temporary waystation en route to an autonomous and fully genuine form of social psychoogy. As I will argue, we are in great danger of getting off at the wrong revolution. For, as will become evident, not only are there major problems intrinsic to the cognitive perspective, but there is yet another transformation taking place within the intellectual world. As many believe, this movement is of far greater scope and portent than that embodied in the cognitive foray. Of greatest importance, it is a revolution in which social psychology is beginning to play a coloratura role. After examining a number of critical shortcomings of the cognitive orientation, we can explore this emerging domain of social epistemology.

THE PROBLEMATICS OF COGNITIVE EXPLANATION

As is the case with any major intellectual movement, misgivings have begun to emerge on a variety of fronts. The historically oriented have begun to experience a form of deja vu: recalcitrant problems from the period of early mentalism reappear and remain unsolved within contemporary cognitivism (Grumann and Sommer, 1984). An increasingly vocal minority claim that insufficient attention has been given to the emotions along with basic motives. Like Freud before, it is maintained that the cognitive system must be motivated if it is to function at all. And thus, cognition is but a pawn to more fundamental psychological wellsprings. Searle (1984) has demonstrated shortcomings in the view that cognitive systems (modelled on the computer) could ever explain human communication. Sampson (1981) has taken the cognitive orientation to task for its suppression of real world problems. Costall and Still (1987) have published a variety of essays probing the problems of the cognitive orientation. Coulter's (1983) volume carries out a Wittgensteinian attack on the concept of cognition. And, even within cognitivist ranks a serious split is developing between those holding fast to traditional psychological concepts against those arguing that such misleading 'folk ideas' must be replaced by fully biological (Churchland, 1979) and computational models (Stich, 1983).

Yet, it is to another range of problems that I wish to devote my present remarks, problems inherited from the Western tradition of understanding itself. For, it seems to me, that as one extends the logical implications of a cognitive commitment, one confronts a series of inescapable cul de sacs. And, until we press beyond the tradition in which cognitivism is submerged, not only will we continue to spin in the recycling of old waste, but we shall fail to achieve a genuine social psychology. There are three of these problems that deserve special attention.

The disappearance of the social world

At the outset let us consider the range of phenomena to which one might hope social psychology would be adequate. For example, we might hope that the field would render interesting and significant accounts of social conflict, cooperation, intimacy, conformity, social influence, social movements, aggression, peace, power, oppression, revolution, and the like. In effect, we wish the discipline to speak to major issues confronting the society, and to offer insights and possible guidance toward improved social forms. But now let us examine the fate of these various phenomena as one dons the lens of cognitivism. As we saw, the primary injunction of the cognitivist is that it is not the world as it is that determines action, but one's cognition of the world. Thus, for example, an influence attempt is not an influence attempt unless the recipient perceives it to be such; a hostile attack must be interpreted in this way if it is to evoke an aggressive reaction; groups do not exist unless they are perceived to exist by the membership. The result of this line of argument, when extended, is that there are no influence attempts, hostile attacks, groups, and the like in and of themselves. If one lived in a culture where no one perceived anything that counted as an hostile attack, there simply would be no hostile attacks in that world. Social events, then, are granted existence only by virtue of the perceiver's category system. To put it another way, the cognitive perspective reduces the social world to a projection or an artifact of the individual cognizer (see also Graumann, 1988). There is no group worth studying in itself (to answer Steiner's 1974 query), for 'groupness' is essentially an attribute projected onto the social world by the individual. And so is the fate of all other so-called 'social phenomena'.

At this point many are inclined to shrug their shoulders, and conclude that cognitive reductionism may be unfortunate but it is simply a fact of life; who can deny that it is the world as perceived rather than the world as it is to which we respond. Yet, let us examine the logical implications of such a conclusion. For, if we continue to reduce the world as it is to the world as mentally represented, there ceases to be a 'real world' in which the individual operates. And by implication, there ceases to be a subject matter for the science. For, how can we excuse the scientist from the same argument? Are not scientists, too, locked into their own conceptual or perceptual systems, expressing only their subjectivities rather than accurate representations of the way things are? As we see, when cognitivism is extended there is no real world, no science, and essentially nothing that we could call knowledge. The cognitive account lapses into solipsism.

Is there any means of escaping this infelicitous conclusion? I do not believe so insofar as social psychology remains committed to a dualistic metaphysics. That is, the field has unwittingly fallen heir to a Cartesian world view in which a strong distinction is made between a knowing subject and an object of knowledge, mind reflecting material, consciousness mirroring nature. In the past we have more or less taken the distinction for granted; it represents part of the sedimented common sense of the discipline — and indeed the culture more generally. Yet, what is the warrant for such a distinction; on what ground is it to be justified? Certainly not on the ground of objectivity, for indeed the very concept of objectivity as it is currently used (i.e. mind accurately reflecting nature) already grants the distinction. In effect, it is a metaphysical leap; there are no evidential ground by which it is demanded. And indeed, if one is sensitive to a long line of conceptual critiques, from Wittgenstein (1963), Ryle (1949), and Austin (1962), through Rorty (1978), one may wish to escape it altogether. The next two points will amplify this admonition.

The impasse of origin

Understandably, most cognitivists have wished to stop short of the conclusion of solipsism. Instead, they have forged ahead to posit a real world (surely a real world cannot be denied), and then treated the relation between the real and the cognized world as a problem to be explored empirically. In effect, the conceptual impasse is replaced (or let us say suppressed) by an empirical challenge. In this context the preeminant research question is, of course, how to account for mental representation. How does the real world inform the cognitive world? How does our repository of internal thoughts, concepts, schemata and the like become built up from experience? How is it that they come to reflect the world in such a way that the organism is adaptive? In effect, how are we to account for the origin of cognitive contents? Without answers to these questions, cognition remains locked within a private world.

A variety of solutions to such problems have been proposed; all suffer a similar fate. At the outset, one confronts a variety of reinforcement accounts of concept development. Such accounts have been popular within general psychology since the publication of Hull's (1920) classic work on concept attainment. Such theories typically, though not exclusively, cast the concept learning process into the metaphor of the hypothesis text. Thus, for example, Restle (1962) described a variety of hypothesis testing strategies of concept attainment, each based on the assumption that concepts are learned through environmental success and failure. Similarly, Bower and Trobosso (1964) view concepts as depending, at least in part, on error signals from the environment. In Levine's (1966) work, correct responses are emphasized as opposed to errors. In a model placing greater emphasis on cognitive mediation Simon and Kotovsky (1963) proposed that one forms an hypothesis about the sequential pattern to which he or she has been exposed and then tests the adequacy of the hypothesis against subsequent exposures. More directly germane to social psychology, Epstein (1980) has proposed that the self-concept is developed in much the same manner as scientific theory, it thus comes to reflect the results of hypothesis testing and is corrected through falsification.

Yet, let us examine further, for if it is our perception of the world rather than the way itself to which we respond, how could the process of reinforcement (or hypothesis testing) get underway? If our perception of the world is 'schema driven', as it is said, how could we recognize when our predictions met with success? To be specific, in order for reinforcement (correct outcomes, errors, or other forms of environmental feedback) to correct or modify one's concept, the individual must already possess a conceptual repertoire. At a minimum, two forms of conceptual would have to be in place, the one specific and the other more general. On the specific level, the individual must possess an hypothesis or a criterial concept for which reinforcement or feedback would be relevant. One must possess an hypothesis or conceptual structure, such as, 'I am a good or bad X' in order for environmental feedback to function as a corrective or verifying device. Without such a conceptual forestructure, there is nothing the individual would be asking for the environment, no information for which he/she would be searching. On a more general level, the reinforcement model also requires that the individual possess a prior concept of reinforcement classes. If one cannot conceptualize an event as a 'success', or an 'error', then he/she simply remains uninformed. If children cannot distinguish between a 'parental admonishment' and the remainder of the booming, buzzing confusion, if they possess no preliminary concepts of what the utterances 'good' and 'bad' could mean, then environmental feedback of these sorts would fail to extend their conceptual repertoire.

Yet, as is quickly discerned, it is precisely the origins of these various conceptual predilections that theories designed to explain. For after all, from whence the various concepts making up the hypothesis one wishes to test, and how does the child come to acquire concepts of admonishment and praise? In effect, reinforcement accounts fail to offer a satisfactory explanation of conceptual development, because reinforcement (or hypothesis testing) cannot function without a conceptual structure already intact.

A major alternative to reinforcement theories in psychology may be termed 'cognitive mapping' in form. As a class, such accounts generally presume that unconstrained observation of the external world will enable the individual to develop conceptual templates, cognitive representations or other mental systems that capture important features of the real world. This is essentially the position taken by Fiske and Taylor (1984) in their summary of the current literature on schema development. As they conclude, 'schemata change as they develop out of repeated exposures with instances. Schemata become more abstract, more complex, and often more moderate. They also seem to become more organized and compact, which frees up the capacity to notice discrepancies and to assimilate exceptions without altering the schema' (p. 178) Such views are also implied by most pattern recognition models in psychology. The most well developed theory of this variety is Rosch's (1978) 'natural category' formulation. From Rosch's perspective cognitive categories increasingly accommodate themselves to the contours of reality. As Rosch proposes, through the observation of objects in the real world, people become acquainted with the structure of real-world attributes. They observe that such attributes are not randomly distributed, but appear in recurring, structural combinations. Thus, for example, certain creatures have wings, beaks, feathers and claws. Continued exposure to such a configuration of commonly associated features lends itself to the formation of the natural category, 'bird'. Ultimately, then, exposure to real-world events produces a cognitive map or environmentally valid form of mental representation.

Interestingly, the precise details by which mental mapping occurs have not been elaborated. The process by which the individual searches the environment, registers certain configurations, disregards others, creates hypotheses about co-occurrences, moves logically from discriminate sensations to general abstractions, and so on—all critical to

468   _Kenneth J. Gergen_

the ultimate intelligibility of mapping theory—are left opaque. Yet as the preceding analysis suggests, it is precisely the nature of the process by which the individual builds up categories from experience that is problematic. In particular, the theorist again confronts the problem of understanding how the individual would come to recognize the features, objects or configurations of events of the world at the outset. How would it be possible to recognize the features of a particular configuration without a preliminary concept of these features? For example, how does one come to recognize feathers, beaks, wings, and so on, all features which enter into the generation of the natural category 'bird'? Must one not already possess a category system in which such features are rendered sensible and discriminant in order for recognition to occur? From whence this category system? Further there is no salvation in arguing that these attributes are themselves built up from exposure to their sub-features or attributes. For such a rebuttal would simply place the critical question at one step remove. How would these features be recognized? In effect, to solve the problem of how people come to have concepts of birds and other 'natural occurrences', Rosch must ultimately rely on the existence of uninterpreted, uncategorized inputs into the cognitive system. But, if inputs only count or are significant to the individual insofar as they are cognized (interpreted, labelled, categorized, etc.) then such entries into the mental system are nonsensical. They simply would not register as identifiable events.

Faced with such stultifying dilemmas, there are many thinkers of recent decades who have been tempted to fall back on some form of nativist explanation of category development. Extending a tradition traceable at least to Kant's positing of _a priori_ categories, the attempt has been to argue that humans must be genetically equipped to make certain basic distinctions. For Kant, human nature enables the individual to comprehend space, time, causality, and other elementary aspects of the world. In a similar manner, Chomsky (1968) has more recently proposed that the individual must possess an innate knowledge of language. And, as Gibson (1979) and his followers propose, our categories for understanding the world are in fact representations of the world, for if they were not, the human species would have long ago perished. Natural selection has essentially left us with a set of cognitive constructs that are adapted to the world as it must be.

Yet, substantial problems also inhere in the nativist orientation to concept origin. It is difficult to imagine that genetic preparedness could furnish more than a rudimentary set of conceptual orientations (e.g. causality, time). Yet, even if these are admitted it is difficult to see how the further array of concepts typically available to the individual could be derived. Given certain kinds of distinctions, how are other developed? If one is genetically programmed to distinguish between 'God save the king' and everything else, on what grounds are distinctions among elements of the 'everything else' to be made? Correspondingly, it is difficult to square the nativist account with the immense and ever growing vocabulary of human affairs. New concepts are daily media occurrences; it is absurd to count them as hard-wired and equally problematic to view them as environmentally derived. And too, the leap to a nativist position can be nothing more than metaphysical. For, if we are programmed for the reception of certain kinds of events and not others, then we should never be able to question the adequacy of our beliefs. We would never register those events that would demonstrate to us the limitations of our capacities. Our system of understanding would not be subject to empirical refutation.

The impasse of action

Thus far we find that within the cognitive arena there is no means of deriving cognitive structure from the nature of the world, no means of inserting into mental space the particulars of the objective realm. We must now press on to ask about the relationship between cognition and subsequent behaviour. How are we to comprehend the influence of cognition on human action? It was often said of the early cognitivist, Edward Tolman, that his theory of cognitive maps was problematic in that it left the organism, 'lost in thought'. No means was provided of generating action from cognition. Has this fundamental problem now been solved? With an eye cast toward the history of philosophy, one might suspect that it has not. As philosophers since Descartes have unsuccessfully pondered, how is mind able to influence matter or physical movements? How can a realm without spatio-temporal coordinates cause changes in a second realm that does possess these features?

Yet, there are additional problems that surface more distinctly in present-day cognitive inquiry. The first concerns the movement from the realm of abstract concepts to the concrete realm of action. Concepts or mental categories are traditionally viewed as abstractions from reality. They are not thus eidetic images of the world, but categories into which events are placed according to a specified range of criteria. As many commentators put it, cognition is that process through which experience is organized; often it is added that this organization is propositional in form. Yet, if concepts, schemata and the like are abstract in form, one rapidly confronts the question of how such knowledge may be put to behavioural use. How does the individual employ a system of abstractions for generating concrete or particularized actions? Attempts to answer this question lead us into a conceptual swamp no less penetrable than that confronted in the case of origins. Let us explore.

Consider the individual who cognizes himself as a 'friendly person' and wishes to place this concept into action. How would he determine what constitutes a 'friendly' action on any particular occasion? The concept of 'friendly person' is fully mute in this respect. The abstraction does not in itself recommend or specify any particular set of bodily movements (e.g. 'extend the right hand forward from the body at a velocity of 20 kph...') Virtually any movement of the body may be considered friendly or unfriendly depending on the confluence of circumstances. This problem appears to yield to solution if one resorts at this point to a second-order construct or rule, namely one that prescribes the exact character of 'friendly actions' on various occasions. This second-order construct (possibly viewed as a hierarchical substructure of the more general class, 'friendly') might inform the individual, 'On occasions of meeting a friend, a smile and a greeting represent friendly behaviour'. Yet, as we readily discern, this second order rule is also in the abstract form; it too leaves important questions of particulars unanswered. It tells us nothing of what counts in the concrete situation as 'meeting a friend', it fails to tell us what form of bodily, action constitutes a 'smile' or a 'greeting', What is now requried is a third-order construct or rule, one that informs the individual what these concepts mean in the concrete instance. Such a construct might inform one that a 'friend' is one who 'gives you support' and that 'smiling' is a matter of 'turning the corners of the mouth in the upward direction'. Yet, how is the individual now to determine what constitutes 'support' on any occasion, and what it means in terms of bodily movements to 'turn the corners of the mouth upward?' Such instructions are, after all, abstractions without specified particulars.

As rapidly discerned, the problem of applying conceptual knowledge to concrete circumstances casts one back upon subsidiary conceptualizations (application rules), which must themselves be defined in terms of still other coneptualizations (rules), and so on in an infinite regress. There is no place at which the conceptual meaning can be defined in other than conceptual terms—thus no exit to the range of unconceptualized particulars. Nowhere does abstract or conceptual thought enable one to make derivations to the realm of concrete action. One is essentially left to rove the dictionary of the mind, as it were, continuously defining concepts in terms of other concepts in terms of other concepts. In large degree this problem is a companion to the conundrum of origin. In this context we found that there is no way to drive from any given object in the world any particular conceptualization or mental category. Real world particulars do not demand that any particular conceptualization be made of them. In the same way, once within the conceptual realm, there is no means of defining what would count as a concrete instantiation of the mental category. Real world particulars are not themselves part of the mental make-up; only their conceptual representations are.

Let us consider a second major problem confronting the theorist who wishes to move from cognition to action. Here we must ask how an immobile structure, such as the concept or schema can produce a mobile action. Concepts in themselves seem to be inert—typically portrayed as forms of structure. Thus, to hold oneself to be 'happy-go-lucky' fails in itself to motivate one to action; it simply operates as a container of knowledge. Or more dramatically, one might interpret a given situation as one of 'grave danger' from which rapid exit was essential for preserving life. However, there is nothing within this conceptual portrayal that demands or causes any particular form of action. Even should the individual conclude, 'I must run', there is nothing in the conceptual appraisal itself that would generate movements of the body. Once armed with a particular array of concepts, then, what finally moves the individual to action?

To avoid this problem, some have found it more plausible to posit additional psychological sources of motivation. It is these sources that move the individual to action, as it is often held, while concepts or schemas furnish the direction or criteria for action. Or, in the more popular vernacular, we have our desires, wants, and needs and we use our knowledge of the world to help us obtain our ends. Yet, let us examine more closely. First, should the cognitive theorist admit that cognition was driven by a motivational system, then motives replace cognition as the critical focus of study. In this case, cognitions would become 'mere derivatives', and motives the centre of scientific importance. To move in this direction would be to give up the game. There is a second problem in adding a motivational source. How is it that motives and cognitions work together? How, for example, does the conceptual system know what the motives wish to achieve, what constitute the goals of our desires? Would the conceptual system not have to possess a means of registering the state of the motivational system? Yet, if the conceptual system is top-down in nature—if it is the perception of the desire rather than the desire itself that counts—then is desire not effectively removed from the scene? Does it not disappear as an instigating device in the same way that 'real groups' or 'real relationships' were obliterated in the earlier analysis? A consideration of motivation leads us to additional problems. For how is it that motivation can operate without some means of (1) identifying the goal that it is attempting to achieve, and (2) holding this goal in place for a sufficient duration that action can be sustained across time? Yet, if we grant to the motivational source these kinds of capabilities, it rapidly becomes clear that we have created yet a second domain of cognition. That is, we have endowed motives with the ability to recognize and retain information. We now have not one cognitive system within the individual but two. The theoretical edifice begins to buckle under the strain of its own weight.

THE SECOND REVOLUTION: SOCIAL EPISTEMOLOGY

We have now encountered major conceptual impediments to a cognitive account of human activity. As suggested earlier, the major difficulties with the cognitive orientation in psychology are derivative of more general problems inhering in dualistic metaphysics. When a real world is to be reflected by a mental world, and the only means of determining the match is via the mental world, then the former will always remain opaque and the relationship between the two inexplicable. Yet, there is another revolution afoot within the intellectual world, one that not only enables these hoary problems to be abandoned, but opens the way to genuine (as opposed to derivative) social inquiry. It is a revolution that sweeps across various sectors of the history of science (Kuhn, 1970; Feyerabend, 1976), the philosophy of social science (Taylor, 1971; von Wright, 1971), the sociology of knowledge (Latour and Woolgar, 1979; Knorr-Cetina, 1981), literary theory (Fish, 1980; Norris, 1983), communications theory (Cronen, Pearce and Tomm, 1985) social anthropology (Marcus and Fischer, 1984; Clifford, 1983) the philosophy of history (White, 1978) and feminist studies (Harding, 1986; Keller, 1985). The recent emergence of the journal *Social Epistemology*, also underscores the interdisciplinary character of these concerns. Unfortunately, because of the relative insularity of social psychological research from the remainder of the intellectual world, it is a revolution that has been slow to materialize within our own discipline. As we shall see, exciting vistas have begun to open but the potential has scarcely been realized.

There are many ways in which this more general revolution may be made intelligible. At the same time it is too early in the proceedings to furnish a tidy and broadly supportable rationale. There is an extended dialogue taking place across disciplines and the variegated voices hardly speak with the same accent. However, somewhere toward the centre of this colloquy is what may be viewed as the emergence of a social as opposed to a dualist epistemology. That is, the locus of knowledge is no longer taken to be the individual mind but rather, to inhere in patterns of social relatedness. This fundamental shift and its significance for social psychology can be understood in terms of three interdependent arguments.

From mind to language

Let us first suspend concern with the unyielding problems of how mind and world are related. We need not cast these concerns aside indefinitely. Rather, if we bracket such issues for the time being, we are free to labour in an orchard where the fruits lie within more immediate grasp. And, once we have enjoyed the offerings we may return to the initial difficulties with a freshened perspective. In particular, let us shift the point of concentration from mind and world to the relationship between words and world. Let us shift attention from 'the propositions in our heads' to the propositions in our written and spoken language. In this case we may put aside murky questions about how schemas, prototypes, memories, motives and the like operate, and focus on the

way our words are imbedded within our life practices. This move prepares us for yet
another. For language is inherently an outcome of social interchange. Should an
individual possess a language that was soley private, it would not by common
standards be considered a language. It would fail to communicate. Communication
requires the coordinated actions of at least two persons. Should these proposals seem
reasonable for the moment, then we are positioned to conclude that what we take to be
knowledgeable propositions about the world are essentially the outcome of social
relatedness. What we take to be knowledge bearing propositions are not achievements
of the individual mind, but social achievements.

From accuracy to practice

The critical question posed by a dualist epistemology is how the mind comes to reflect
the nature of the real world. Until this question can be answered, there is no means of
determining when an individual has acquired accurate knowledge, or determining
which of several competing accounts best approximates the truth. In effect, standards
of truth depend on answering what we have seen to be a set of seemingly insoluble
problems. One might even be suspicious at this point about how the sciences (or those
of high rank within the culture more generally) can speak so piously of truth and
objectivity when the conceptual underpinnings of such terms are so fundamentally
enfeebled. Yet, by shifting our focus from mind to language, our initial move in the
present sequence, the nature of such concerns, shift dramatically. For, in this case we
need not ask how language comes to form an accurate picture of the world. Indeed,
such a question seems misleading from the outset. For, extending Saussure's thesis,
why should we suppose that there is any set of sounds or markings that is uniquely
suited to mirror or reflect any 'slice of reality?' There is no reason to argue that
whatever this is before me is any more a 'table' than it would be to designate it with any
series of nonsense syllables. Or, to bring the argument to its more dramatic
conclusion, once the shift has been made from mind to language, we find that it is no
more or less objective to call this a table than it is a lamp post or Leon Festinger. For,
as we see, what we happen to call things on any given occasion is not a matter of
fidelity with the world as it is; it is rather a matter of which particular social
relationships we wish to coordinate successfully.

Another way of phrasing the case, here following Wittgenstein, is to say that the
language we use in referring is not a picture of the world but an implement for carrying
out social practices. Thus, if I am talking with my young nephew I might refer to 'the
blue ball'; if I were with my artist friends I would call it an 'indigo ball'. for my
colleague in physiological psychology I would only be acceptable if I announced that
the ball had no colour at all. For after all, colour is (in his practice) an experience of
light at various wavelengths reflecting on the retina. This does not render the scientist
any more accurate in his judgements than it does the six-year-old; it is simply to say
that each individual uses terms that are more or less adequate to a series of practices in
which he/she is engaged. One must be careful at this point not to confuse this
argument with the instrumentalist view of science—a view that valorizes scientific
terms in the degree to which they are useful in the process of prediction and control.
From the present standpoint, language is not a system that makes predictions. Theories
in themselves fail to predict events (the same arguments made above against the
possibility of deriving action from concepts applies). Rather, what we take to be

predictions are built into social practices. Scientific theories do not derive their utility from their capacity to store useful information about the world and to make it available for future predictions. Rather, such theories derive their utility from their position within the practices of the scientific community. They enable the members of such communities to coordinate their actions one with another (Gergen, 1988c).

From validity to utility

As one moves from individual to social epistemology questions of truth and objectivity recede into obscurity. If what is meant by an objectively valid report is that it derives from an accurate registering of the real world by the experiential world, then the concept of 'objective validity' ceases to be sacred. Rather, concepts of truth and objectivity may largely be viewed as rhetorical devices. They are, for example, useful in rendering praise or allocating blame. We reward a child for 'telling the truth' not because he has accurately reported on the state of his sensory neurons, but because his report accords with our adult conventions. When we prize the medical specialist who discovers a fatal illness just in time for remedy, it is not because she has seen the body for what it is. Rather, she has carried out a series of practices (along with socially agreeable modes of indexing) that eventuate in what we conventionally call 'the prolonging of life'.

This outcome generates a new domain of concern for the social epistemiologist, that of human values, In the case of dualist epistemology, concern with ethics, morals, and ideology became secondary (and for many, discarded altogether). The critical problem was whether the individual was accurately registering the world as it is; whether the perceiver happended to like or loathe what he/she saw was irrelevant to the process of acquiring knowledge. And, in fact, such value investments were typically considered inimical to objectivity. In contrast, for the social epistemologist the accounts that are made of the world are embedded in social practices. Each account will render support to certain social practices and threaten others with extinction. Thus, a critical question to be put to various account of the world is what kinds of practices do they support? Do they enable us to live in ways we feel valuable or are they threatening to social patterns held dear? Thus, for the social epistemologist a major question to be asked of, let us say, Skinnerian behaviour theory, is not whether it is objectively valid. Rather, one would ask, if we adopt the theoretical language proposed in this domain, in what ways would our lives be enriched or impoverished? Would we wish to abandon the various practices in which terms such as 'intention', 'freedom' and 'dignity' are central constituents? And if a negative reply to such questions can be articulated, one may well wish to develop an alternative account of human action.

FORMS OF EXPLORATION: THE FOCUSED PROGRAMME

What forms of inquiry are invited by this shift from a personal to a social epistemology? Are there exemplars that would enable one to see how these various abstractions are cashed out in scientific practice? In treating these issues it is first necessary to distinguish between what may be termed the 'focused' as opposed to the 'extended programme' of inquiry. That is, if one adopts the social perspective, there are certain lines of inquiry that are specifically invited. They are endeavours carried out in terms of the epistemological stance itself, that extend its presumptions, and treat its terms (for all practical purposes) as is they reflected the world as it is. Yet, because concerns with truth have been replaced with issues of intelligibility, the social perspective does not demand that all inquiry be carried out in its terms. It also invites the scholar to explore and extend any form of intelligibility that he/she finds meaningful. More will be said about the extended programme shortly. However, let us first consider inquiry in the focused domain.

As indicated earlier, the vast share of relevant scholarship has taken place in related disciplines, such as sociology, anthropology, history, philosophy and literary studies. Reference to some of this work has been provided. However, there is also emerging within contemporary psychology a rapidly expanding body of literature that is coherent with the social epistemological standpoint. This work generally falls within one of three domains.

Social and reflexive critique

Because the shift to the social perspective also brings with it a renaissance of concern with values and ideology, the social analyst is invited to speak out on matters heretofore bordering on the unprofessional (for science, it is said, 'deals in facts, not values'). Much of this critical concern has been focused on the sciences themselves. For in their claims to superiority in matters of objective truth, the sciences are viewed as dangerously mystifying. And the problem is all the more severe inasmuch as most psychologists themselves seem either disinterested or blind to the social political implications of simply 'telling it like it is' (Ibanez, 1983).

Thus far such critique within psychology has primarily been voiced by critical and feminist psychologists. The critical wing, drawing sustenance from Marx's early attack on the seeming value neutrality of Capitalist economic theory, and spurred by the later writings of Habermas (1975) and Holzkamp (1976) has been vigorous and far reaching. Plon's (1974) critique of conflict research, Wexler's (1980) proposal for a 'critical social psychology', and edited volumes by Armistead (1974), Larsen (1980) and Ingelby (1980) all provide relevant exemplars. Feminist thinkers have also seen within much psychological research implicit assumptions of male superiority. Such critique has gone much further than pointing to the lack of gender comparisons in much psychological research, along with the associated belief that theories of the male psyche are virtually universal. For example, Gilligan (1982) has shown how Kohlberg's theory of moral development unthinkingly places the male mode of moral decision-making at a 'superior stage of development' than the female preference. Other investigators have gone on to demonstrate how androcentric biases have not only permeated theories of human action, but empiricist metatheory and methodological practices as well (Wilkinson, 1986; Morawski, 1987; Unger, 1988; Gergen, 1988).

Although critical and feminist critiques have been among the most concerted, critical inquiry is hardly limited to these domains. Apfelbaum and Lubek (1976) have shown how mainstream research in conflict resolution 'renders invisible' the plight of various minorities and the particular forms of injustice to which they are subjected. Both Furby (1979) and Stam (1987) have articulated the ideological biases underlying locus of control research. Sampson (1978, 1988) has developed a series of powerful arguments against the ideology of 'self-contained individualism' unwittingly furthered by most forms of psychological theory. Deese (1984) has shown how many popular conceptions in contemporary psychology obliterate the presumptions underlying democratic forms of governance. Wallach and Wallach (1983) have argued that much psychological theory sanctions selfishness. And Schwartz (1986) has shown how theories based on the presumption that human action is motivated by a maximization of gains foster the very kinds of activities that they predict.

Because its messages are often painful and its grounds poorly understood, such lines of inquiry have hardly been embraced (let alone read) by the rank and file researcher. However, the importance of such work can hardly be underestimated. Both in terms of the new modes of expression offered to the profession, and in terms of its sensitizing of the discipline to the social and political impact of its 'objective reports', such work represents a vital and important development. The major needs at this point are for an expansion in the range of voices represented in this endeavour, an expansion of targets to include broad social patterns and the broadscale institutionalization of the form (e.g. courses, journals etc.) The new journal, *Psych Critique* represents an important first step in these directions.

Configurations of content

The most lively area of research within the limited programme is that concerend with people's present constructions of the world. Such work typically falls under the rubric of 'social constructionism'. The popularity of such research is due in part to the relative ease with which it can be conducted (e.g. paper and pencil measures or interviews often suffice), and its close association with research in social cognition and social representation. Thus, researchers across these areas agree that it is vital to explore how people construct the world around them, and that such constructions are intimately related to patterns of action. However, where cognitivists (Forgas, 1981) will claim they are assessing states of cognition, and social representationists vascillate between social and cognitive explanations, social constructionists are more likely to speak in terms of shared modes of discourse. While dualists of cognitive stripe confront a range of difficulties (see above) in explaining how cognitive categories are acquired or produce action, constructionists will view the relationship between discourse and patterns of action as conventional. That is, discourse is but a single component of more complex patterns of action. The relationship among components is a product of social practice in the sense that certain phrases (e.g. 'I love you', 'I'm so happy', 'This is serious') are normally accompanied by particular sets of facial expressions and body postures if they are to be effective in the normal processes of social coordination. Social constructionists also view such research as particularly important in its emancipatory function. Such research is not only used to undermine the common sense or taken for granted realities, but to open the way for change.

In this latter mode, for example, Kessler and McKenna (1978) have used a wide variety of sources to show the defeasibility of the common sense assumption that there are two genders. Semin and his colleagues (Semin and Chassein, 1985; Semin and Krahe, 1987) have demonstrated the dependency of scientific formulations of personality on common belief systems within the culture. Kitzinger (1987) demonstrates how liberalist constructions of lesbiansim undermine the radical implications of lesbian lifestyles, and contribute to continued homophobia. Other relevant work has focused on the construction of human sexuality (Tiefer, 1987), the educational process (Dann, in press), alcoholism (Furnham and Lowik, 1984),

476   *Kenneth J. Gergen*

physical illness (Pennebaker and Epstein, 1983), forms of personal relationship (Davis and Roberts, 1985), mental processes (Coulter, 1979), and personal sincerity (Silver and Sabini, 1985).

It is also in this domain that social constructionist inquiry bears close affinity with research in social representation. In its original Durkheimian phase, social representation was defined as 'The elaborating of a social object by the community for the purpose of behaving and communicating' (Moscovici, 1963, p. 251). In this sense, there is little important difference between social construction and social representation. And, even though Moscovici (1984) has more recently given a cognitive reformulation of social representation (see Jahoda, 1988; Parker, 1987 and McKinlay and Potter, 1987 for critiques) much of the associated research has continued within the initial frame. Thus, for example, Herzlich's (1973) inquiry into views of health and illness, Jodelet (1984) on images of the body, Carugati (in press) on the construction of intelligance, Chombart DeLauwe (1984) on the cultural conceptualization of the child, Gilly (1980) on representations of student-teacher relationships, Livingstone (1987) on television relationships, Weimer, Wagner and Kruse (1987) on man–woman relationships, and others (see Farr and Moscovici's 1984 summary) all focus on the shared public understandings extant within the culture.

For the cognitively oriented psychologist, the typical presumption is that contemporary research is of universal implication. That is, if 'fundamental' processes of cognition are being tapped, one is making a contribution for all time (or at least until human genetics are altered). For this reason, there is but a secondary interest in the localized cognitive styles of other cultures and historical periods. In contrast, for the social constructionist, there is an acute sensitivity to the perspectives of other peoples and times. For, as the investigator demonstrates variations in perspectives, the effect is to break the hold of the common sense realities of contemporary culture. It is to deconstruct local ontologies, and thereby free the individual from the constraints of existing convention. Averill's research on anger (1982) is an excellent examplar. For, in contemporary culture (including the sciences) there is a strong tendency to consider the emotions as biological in origin and determining in their effects. Yet, by surveying patterns of behaviour in a variety of cultures, Averill is able to demonstrate that what we take to be biological givens are essentially cultural constructions. Anger takes the form of a performance, it may be carried out well or poorly, or it may be abandoned as a technique of relating. This conclusion is amplified in the work of Lutz (1988) on the social construction of emotion. Other incursions into cultural variations in the construction of the person include those of Shweder and Miller (1985), Rosaldo (1980), and Kirkpatrick (1985). Edited volumes by Heelas and Lock (1981), Carrithers, Collins and Lukes (1985), Gergen and Davis (1985) and Harré (1986) contain a range of additional explorations.

In addition to energizing interest in other cultures, the constructionist orientation has added a significant new element to historical psychology. For in the same way that historical variations in construction remind us of the 'thrown condition' of our focal realities, historical incursions are also effective. Perhaps most prominent in this domain has been an extensive line of investigation into the historical dependency of both child development and the cultural definition of the child. The work of van den Berg (1961) and Aries (1962) was groundbreaking in this case. More recently Kessen has concluded his historical analysis with the view that, 'the child is essentially and eternally a cultural invention and... the variety in the child's definition is not the removable error of an incomplete science' (p. 815, 1979). Kessen's perspective is additionally supported by a variety of reviews of developmental conceptions over history (Kagan, 1983; Borstelman, 1983) and by a variety of studies comparing constructions of the child across cultures (cf. Goodnow, 1984; Harkness and Super, 1983). The implications of such work are also vastly expanded by additional inquiry into the historical vicissitudes in concepts of aging (Schutze, 1983), love and passion (Averill, 1985; Luhman, 1987), sense of smell (Corbin, 1986), and mother love (Badinter, 1980). In each case, such research invites a reflexive reconsideration of our contemporary commitments and sensitivity to alternative possibilities.

The construction of social pattern

A third major focus of inquiry is on social processes themselves. Such inquiry has benefited greatly from Garfinkel's (1967) pioneering work on ethnomethodology (methods for generating and sustaining common sense conceptions), Goffman's (1959, 1963) many insights into the micro-social order, and Harré's various contributions (1979, with 'Secord, 1972) to an ethogenic social psychology. One of the centrally compelling features of such work has been its shift in the locus of interest and explanation from the internal or psychological realm to the domain of interaction. Interest in psychological processes within single individuals is replaced by a concern with interdependencies, jointly determined outcomes, or 'joint action' (in Shotter's (1980) terms.) Although not always breaking with the individualistic perspective, much social psychological research into self-presentation and impression management (see edited volumes by Schlenker (1985) and Tedeschi (1981), social accounting (Shotter, 1984; Semin and Manstead, 1983; Antaki, 1981; Burnett, McGhee and Clarke, 1987), the social construction of emotion (Wagner, 1988), and interaction episodes (Marsh, Rosser, and Harré, 1978; Forgas, 1979) has centred on the domain of social interdependency. Mummendey (1984) and her colleagues have explored a variety of ways in which aggression emerges as a product of interaction, as opposed to the dispositions of single persons. Felson (1984) has nicely demonstrated the importance of such a view for understanding various criminal offences. Inquiry into collective memory (Middleton and Edwards, 1989; Shotter, 1989) further demonstrates the possibility or redefining psychological processes as social ones.

Additionally exciting vistas of study have been opened by recent incursions into discourse processes. In their lively introduction to the topic, Potter and Wetherell (1987) demonstrate wideranging ways in which conversational interchange constructs and creates social patterns. Billig's (1987) volume, *Arguing and Thinking* offers a new perspective on attitude change, by removing the process from the head and placing it in the interactional or discursive context. Smedslund's (1985) research into the ordinary language conventions governing the intelligibility of psychological theory (and thus rendering it non-empirical) has raised issues of critical importance. Much of my own recent work has focused on psychological discourse. In this case the attempt has been first to explore various sources — most especially pragmatic and linguistic —of the ways we have of characterizing our mental states (Gergen, 1985, 1988a). Second, inquiry has been made into the way various literary devices — such as narrative and metaphor — constrain the ways in which we can characterize the mind (Gergen and Gergen, 1988; Gergen, In press). Additional attention has been given to the way in which conventional definitions govern what we can say about the relationship between mind and world (Gergen, 1988b).

These various enterprises hardly exhaust the possibilities of the focused programme. Particularly invited at this juncture are explorations into means of conceptualizing interaction patterns and processes. The vast share of the Western vocabulary of understanding is individual in character, calling attention to individual traits, mechanisms, dispositions and the like. Much in need are concepts that are oriented around interaction — that account for the simultaneous actions of two or more persons. In effect, the special demand is for a relational vocabulary of understanding (see also Ibanez, 1985). It is this vocabulary of social relatedness that also hold greatest promise for solving the array of problems put to the cognitivist at the outset of this paper. As earlier proposed, the cognitive revolution effectively obliterates concern with genuinely social process. Yet, from the standpoint of social epistemology intelligibility about the world is a derivative of persons in relationship. The invitation is, then, for the social psychologist to treat social relatedness (as opposed to isolated minds) as a reality of preeminent significance. And it is within the context of social interchange that the problems of origins and effects would be treated. The question of the origins of mental categories we found principally insoluble. However, once we abandon cognitive categories as critical to understanding human action, and replace such categories with discourse, we are prepared to treat the question of origins anew. We might inquire, for example, into the pragmatic functions of language in various social settings. As Wittgenstein proposed, words function much as tools; if this metaphor is adopted it would suggest that new terms emerge within relationships as a function of practical exigency. The grounds for examining the relationship between thought and action, an insoluble problem in the cognitivist perspective, also yields to alternative solutions. As cognitive categories are replaced by terms in discourse, one is invited to abandon the presumption of causal connection. That is, we might usefully consider the relationship between discourse and action not one of cause and effect, but rule governed or conventional. Discourse is, after all, only one form of action, and not a central fount from which all actions flow. Thus, the relationship between words and other movements of the body is not unlike the relationship between a handshake and a smile. On occasions of greeting, it is simply more felicitous that the two accompany each other.

Finally, the constructionist orientation invites experimentation with new forms of scientific discourse. For, we as scientists are also engaged in forms of social construction — fashioning frames of discourse for living lives. If this is our task, rather than that of fashioning verbal mirrors, then we need no longer be constrained by the arrid and deadening conventions currently governing writing. We have now reached the stage where our conventions of professional writing are so rarefied and barren of rhetorical efficacy that we can scarcely tolerate ingesting the literature of our own guild. Needless to say, we can little anticipate the interest of others. If we are to construct the world, we might usefully consider forms that enliven, compel, or unsettle.

TOWARD DETENTE: THE EXTENDED PROGRAMME

The various endeavours described thus far are all consistent with the earlier outlined suppositions of a social epistemology. They serve to elaborate and extend this form of discourse and to supply vivifying examples or applications. In many cases what traditionally passes for empirical research has been used to carry out these tasks. At this point the querrelous reader may wish to enter. If social epistemology abandons claims to truth — indeed, the very concept of truth as traditionally conceived — then is it not incoherent to use various empirical methods of research? The reply is that such methods do not function as warrants for the truth of the propositions which they serve. Constructionist endeavours of the kind outlined above are not important because they are true or false; their significance is derived from the social and intellectual utility of viewing social life in this way. They offer a significant alternative to many contemporary ways of constructing the world, and thereby offer new alternatives for action. So called 'empirical' research is essentially rhetorical in its function. It furnishes an effective way of lending literary force to the various accounts. It imparts a means of translating the abstract theoretical language into the argot of daily life and rendering that life anew.

It is this orientation to empirical research that, in the end, opens the way to a detente between the social epistemologist and social psychologist of traditional stripe. If the function of theories is to picture the world as it is, the competition between theories approximates a zero-sum game. If one theory is accurate, then discrepant voices are simply wrong. In this sense, the competition between radical behaviourism and cognitivism, for example, is a fight to the death. The two theories cannot both be true simultaneously. And so it is in contemporary social psychology that the terrain is dotted with warring and hostile camps with dialogue across encampments at a minimum. Yet, when one enters the world of social epistemology such warfare proves unnecessary. The game is not zero-sum, and truth is not the arbiter among domains. Rather, each form of theoretical intelligibility — cognitive, behaviourist, phenomenological, psychoanalytic, and the like — provides the culture with discursive vehicles for carrying out social life. As the number of theoretical intelligibilities is expanded within the profession, so are the symbolic resources of the culture at large.

In this sense the earlier critique of the cognitive programme is not intended as lethal. It is primarily an attempt to demonstrate certain conceptual chasms, and thereby curb the imperious thrust of the movement As indicated, the movement has had much to offer in the way of new and interesting insights into individual action. However, to the extent that it becomes a prevailing voice, the discipline loses its capacities to enrich the culture. It seems essential that we avoid reducing the social world to the psychological. This is so because such reduction not only ensures that the discipline will remain a subsidiary derivative of general psychology. It will also prevent the development of a truly social vocabulary of understanding — and thus curtail and constrain our forms of relatedness.

REFERENCES

Antaki, C. (1981). *The Psychology of Ordinary Explanations of Social Behaviour.* Academic Press, London.
Apfelbaum, E. and Lubek, I. (1976). 'Resolution vs. revolution? the theory of conflicts in question'. In: Strickland, L., Aboud, F. and Gergen, K. (Eds) *Social Psychology in Transition*, Plenum, New York.
Aries, P. (1962). *Centuries of Childhood: A Social History of Family Life*, Vintage, New York.
Armistead, N. (1974). *Reconstructing Social Psychology*, Penguin, Baltimore, MD.

480   *Kenneth J. Gergen*

Austin, J. L. (1962). *How To Do Things With Words*, Oxford University Press, New York.
Averill, J. R. (1985). The social construction of emotion: With special reference to love'. In: Gergen K. J. and Davis, K. E. (Eds) *The Social Construction of the Person*, Springer-Verlag, New York.
Averill, J. R. (1982). *Anger and Aggression*, Springer-Verlag, New York.
Baars, B. J. (1981). *The Cognitive Revolution in Psychology*, Guilford Press, New York.
Badinter, E. (1980). *Mother Love, Myth and Reality*, Macmillan, New York.
Billig, M. (1987). *Arguing and Thinking*, Cambridge University Press, London.
Borstelman, L. J. (1983). Children before psychology: Ideas about children from antiquity to the late 1800s'. In: Mussen, P. H. (Ed.) *Handbook of Child Psychology Vol. 1: History, Theory and Methods*, 4th edn, Wiley, New York.
Bower, G. and Trabosso, T. (1964). *Attention in Learning*, John Wiley & Sons, New York.
Burnett, R., McGhee, P. and Clarke, D. (1987). *Accounting for Relationships*, Methuen & Co. London.
Cantor, N. and Mischel, W. (1979). 'Prototypes in person perception'. In: Berkowitz, L. (Ed.) *Advances in Experimental Social Psychology*, Academic Press, New York.
Carrithers, M., Collins, S. and Lukes, S. (1985). *The Category of the Person*, Cambridge University Press, Cambridge.
Carugati, F. (In press). 'The social representation of intelligence and its development'. In Semin, G. and Gergen, K. (Eds) *Everyday Understanding: Social and Scientific Implications*. Sage, London.
Chombart de Lauwe, M. J. (1984). 'Changes in the representation of the child in the course of social transmission'. In: Farr, R. M. and Moscovici, S. (Eds) *Social Representations*, Cambridge University Press, Cambridge.
Chomsky, N. (1968). *Language and Mind*, Harcourt, Brace and World, New York.
Clifford, J. (1983). 'On ethnographic authority', *Representations*, 2: 132-143.
Corbin, A, (1986). *The Foul and the Fragrant*, Harvard University Press, Cambridge.
Costall, A. and Still, A. (1987). *Cognitive Psychology in Question*, St. Martin's Press, New York.
Coulter, J. (1979) *The Social Construction of the Mind*, Macmillan, New York.
Coulter, J. (1983). *Rethinking Cognitive Theory*, St. Martin's Press, New York.
Cronen, V. E., Pearce, W. B. and Tomm, K (1985). 'A dialectical view of personal change'. In: Gergen, K. G. and Davis, K. E. (Eds) *The Social Construction of the Person*, Springer-Verlag, New York.
Dann, H. D. (In press). Subjective theories: A new approach to psychological research and educational practice'. In: Semin, G. and Gergen, K. J. (Eds) *Everyday Understanding: Social and Scientific Understanding*, Sage, London.
Davis, K. E. and Roberts, M. K. (1985). 'Relationships in the real world: The descriptive psychology approach to personal relationships'. In: Gergen, K. J. and Davis, K. E. (Eds) *The Social Construction of the Person*, Springer-Verlag, New York.
Deese, J. (1984). *American Freedom and Social Sciences*, Columbia University Press, New York.
Eiser, J. R. (1980) *Cognitive Social Psychology*, MacGraw-Hill, New York.
Epstein, S. (1980). 'The self-concept, a review and the proposal of an integrated theory of personality'. In: Staub, E. (Ed.) *Personality: Basic Issues and Current Research*, Prentice-Hall, Englewood Cliffs, NJ.
Farr, R. and Moscovici, S. (1984). *Social Representations*, Cambridge University Press, Cambridge.
Felson, R. B. (1984). 'Patterns of aggressive interaction'. In: Mummedey, A. (Ed.) *Social Psychology of Aggression*, Springer-Verlag, Heidelberg.
Festinger, L. (1954). 'A theory of social comparison processes', *Human Relations*, 7. 117-140.
Festinger, L. (1957). *A Theory of Cognitive Dissonance*, Row, Peterson, Evanston, IL.
Feyerabend, P. K. (1976). *Against Method*, Humanities Press, New York.
Fish, S. (1980). *Is There a Text in this Class?* Harvard University Press, Cambridge, MA.
Fiske, S. and Taylor, S. (1984). *Social Cognition*, Addison-Wesley Publishing, Menlo Park, CA.
Forgas, J. (1981). *Social Cognition*, Academic Press, New York.
Forgas, J. (1979). *Social Episodes. The Study of Interaction Routines*, Academic Press, New York.

Furby, L. (1979). 'Individualistic bias in studies of locus of control'. In: Buss, A. (Ed.) *Psychology in Social Context*, Halstead Press, New York.

Furnham, A. and Lowik, V. (1984). 'Lay theories of the causes of alcoholism', *British Journal of Medical Psychology*, 57: 319–332.

Garfinkel, K. (1967) *Studies in Ethnomethodology*, Prentice-Hall, Englewood Cliffs, NJ.

Gergen, K. J. (1985). 'Social pragmatics and the origin of psychological discourse'. In. Gergen, K. J. and Davis, K. E. (Eds) *The Social Construction of the Person*, Springer-Verlag, New York.

Gergen, K. J. (1988a). 'If persons are texts'. In: Messer, S. B., Sass, L. A. and Woolfolk, R. L. (Eds.) *Hermeneutics and Psychological Theory*, Rutgers University Press, New Brunswick, New York.

Gergen, K. J. (1988b). 'Knowledge and social process'. Bar-Tal, D. and Kruglanski, A. (Eds) *The Social Psychology of Knowledge*, Cambridge University Press, Cambridge.

Gergen, K. J. and Gergen, M. (1988), 'Narrative and the self as relationship'. In: Berkowitz, L. (Ed.) *Advances in Experimental Social Psychology*, Vol. 21. Wiley, New York.

Gergen, K. J. (1988c). 'The concept of progress in psychological theory'. In Baker, W., Mos, L., Rappard, H. and Stam, H. *Recent Trends in Theoretical Psychology*, Springer-Verlag, New York.

Gergen, K. J. (In press b). 'Metaphors of the social world'. Leary, D. (Ed.) *Metaphors in the History of Psychology*, Cambridge University Press, Cambridge.

Gergen, K. J. and Davis, K. E. (1985). *The Social Construction of the Person*, Springer-Verlag, New York.

Gergen, M. (1988). *Feminist Structures of Knowledge*, New York University Press, New York.

Gibson, J. J. (1979). *The Ecological Approach to Visual Perception*, Houghton-Mifflin, Boston.

Gilligan, C. (1982). *In a Different Voice. Psychological Theory and Women's Development*, Harvard University Press, Cambridge, MA.

Gilly, M. (1980) *Maitres-eleves: Roles Institutionnels et Representations*. Presses universitaires de France, Paris.

Goffman. E. (1963). *The Presentation of Self in Everyday Life*, Doubleday & Co., New York.

Goodnow, J. J. (1984). 'Parents' ideas about parenting and development: A review of issues and recent work'. In: Lamb, M. E., Brown, A. L. and Rogoll, B. (Eds) *Advances in Developmental Psychology*, Lawrence Erlbaum, Hillsdale, NJ.

Graumann, C. F. (1988) 'Der Kognitivismus in der Sozialpsychologie — Die Kehrseite der "Wende"', *Psychologische Rundschau*, 39. 83-90.

Graumann, C. F. and Sommer, M. (1984). 'Schema and inference. Models in cognitive social psychology' In: Royce, R. R. and Mos, L. P. (Eds) *Annals of Theoretical Psychology*, Vol. 1, Plenum Press, New York.

Habermas, J. (1975). *Legitimation Crisis*, Beacon Press, Boston.

Hamilton, D. and Rose, T. (1980). 'Illusionary correlation and the maintenance of stereotypic beliefs', *Journal of Personality and Social Psychology*, 39: 832-845.

Harding, S. (1986), *The Science Question in Feminism*. Cornell University Press, Ithica, NY.

Harkness, S. and Super, C. (1983). 'The cultural construction of child development', *Ethos*, 11, (4): 222-231.

Harré, R. (1979). *Social Being: A Theory for Social Psychology*, Blackwell, Oxford.

Harré, R. (1986). 'The Social Construction of Emotion, Blackwell, Oxford.

Harré, R. and Secord, P. (1972). *The Explanation of Social Behaviour*, Blackwell, Oxford.

Hastie, R., Ostrum, T., Ebbeson, E., Wyer, R., Hamilton, D. and Carlston, D. (Eds) (1980). *Person Memory: The Cognitive Basis of Social Perception*, Erlbaum, Hillsdale.

Heelas, P. and Lock, A. (1981). *Indigenous Psychologies*, Academic Press, London.

Heider, F. (1958). *The Psychology of Inter-Personal Relations*, Wiley, New York.

Henriques, J., Hollway, W., Urwin, C., Venn, C. and Walkerdine, V. (1984). *Changing the Subject*, Methuen & Co. Ltd., London.

Herzlich, C. (1973). *Health and Illness: A Social Psychological Analysis*, Academic Press, London.

Higgins, E. and King, G. (1981). 'Accessibility of social constructs: Information processing consequences of individual and contextual variability', In: Cantor, N. and Kihlstrom, J. (Eds) *Personality, Cognition and Social Interaction*, Erlbaum, Hillsdale, NJ.

Holzkamp, K. (1976) *Kritische Psychologie*, Fischer, Taschenbuch-Verlag, Hamburg.

482   *Kenneth J. Gergen*

Hull, C.L. (1920). 'Quantitative aspects of the evolution of concepts: An experimental study', *Psychological Monographs*, **28**: 123-125.
Ibanez, T. (1983). 'Los efectos politicos de la psicologia social', *Cuadernos de Psicologia*, **11**: 95-106.
Ibanez, T. (1985), 'La psicologia social: En busca del paradigma perdido? *Cuadernos de Psicologia*, **1**: 59-78.
Ingelby, D. (1980). *Critical Psychiatry: The Politics of Mental Health*, Pantheon, New York.
Jahoda, G. (1988). Critical notes and reflections on social representations'. *European Journal of Social Psychology*, **18**: 195-209.
Jodelet, D. (1984). 'The representation of the body and its transformations'. In. Farr, R. and Moscovici, S. (Eds) *Social Representations*, Cambridge University Press, Cambridge.
Jones, E. E. and Davis, K. E. (1965). 'From acts to dispositions'. In: Berkowitz, L. (Ed.) *Advances in Experimental Social Psychology*, Vol, 2, Academic, New York.
Kagan, J. (1983). 'Classifications of the child', P. H. (Ed.) *Handbook of Child Psychology, Vol. I, Theory and Methods*, Wiley, New York.
Keller, E. F. (1985), *Reflections on Gender and Science*, Yale University Press, New Haven.
Kelley, H. H. (1983). 'Love and commitment', In: Kelley, H. H., Bersheid, E., Christensen, A., Harvey, J. H., Levinger, G., McClintock, E., Peplau, L. A. and Peterson, D. R. (Eds) *Close Relationships*, Freeman, New York.
Kessen, W. (1979). 'The American child and other cultural inventions', *American Psychologist*, **34**: 815.
Kessler, S. and McKenna, W. (1978). *Gender: An Ethnomethodological approach*, Wiley, New York.
Kirkpatrick, J. (1985). 'How personal differences can make a difference', In: Gergen, K. J. and Davis, K. E. (Eds) *The Social Construction of the Person*, Springer-Verlag, New York.
Kitzinger, C. (1987). *The Social Construction of Lesbiansim*, Sage, London.
Knorr-Cetina, K. D. (1981). *The Manufacture of Knowledge*, Pergamon, Oxford.
Kruse, L., Weiner, E. and Wagner, F. (1988). What men and women are said to be: Social Representation and Language. *Journal of Language and Social Psychology*, **7**: 3-4, 243.
Kuhn, T. S. (1970). *The Structure of Scientific Revolution*, (2nd revised edn) University of Chicago Press, Chicago IL. (Original published 1962).
Larsen, K. S. (1980). *Social Psychology: Crisis or Failure*, Institute for Theoretical History, Monmouth, OR.
Latour, B, and Woolgar, S. (1979). *Laboratory Life, the Social Construction of Scientific Facts*, Sage, Beverly Hills, CA.
Levine, M. (1966). 'Hypothesis behaviour by humans during discrimination learning', *Journal of Experimental Psychology*, **71**, 331-336.
Livingstone, M. (1987), 'The representation of personal relationships in television drama: realism, convention and morality', In: Burnett, R., McGhee, P. and Clarke, D. (Eds) *Accounting for Relationships*, Methuen & Co., London.
Luhman, N. (1987). *Love as Passion*, Harvard University Press, Cambridge.
Lutz, C. (1986). 'The anthropology of emotions', *Annual Anthropology Reviews*, **15**: 405-436.
Lutz, C. (1988) *Unnatural Emotions*. University of Chicargo Press, Chicago, Ill.
Marcus, G. E. and Fischer, M. E. (Eds) (1984). *Anthropology as Cultural Critique*. University of Chicago Press, Chicago, Ill.
Marsh, P., Rosser, E. and Harré, R. (1978). *The Rules of Disorder*, Routledge & Kegan Paul, London.
McKinlay, A. and Potter, J. (1987). 'Social representations: A conceptual critique', *Journal for the Theory of Social Behaviour*, **17**: 471-488.
Middleton, D. and Edwards, D. (1989) (Eds) *Collective Remembering*, Sage, London.
Morawksi, J, (1987). 'After reflection: Psychologist uses of history', In. Stam, H., Rogers, T. and Gergen, K. (Eds) *The Analysis of Psychological Theory*, Hemisphere, Washington, DC.
Moscovici, S. (1963). 'Attitudes and opinions', *Annual Review of Psychology*, **14**: 231-260.
Moscovici, S. (1984). 'The phenomenon of social representations'. In: Farr, R. and Moscovinci, S. (Eds) *Social Representations*, Cambridge University Press, London.
Mummendey, A. (1984). *Social Psychology of Aggression*, Springer-Verlag, Heidelberg.
Nisbitt, R. and Ross, L. (1980). *Human Inference: Strategies and Shortcoming of Human Judgment*, Prentice-Hall, Englewood Cliffs, NJ.

Norris, C. (1983). *The Deconstructive Turn*, Methuen, New York.

Parker, I. (1987). 'Social representations: Social psychology's (mis) use of sociology', *Journal for the Theory of Social Behaviour*. 17: 447–470.

Pennebaker, J. and Epstein, D. (1983). 'Implicit psychophysiology: Effects of common beliefs and indiosyncratic physiological responses on symptom reporting', *Journal of Personality*, 3: 468–496.

Plon, M. (1974). 'On the meaning of the notion of conflict and its study in social psychology', *European Journal of Social Psychology*, 4: 389–436.

Potter, J. and Wetherell, M. (1987). *Discourse and Social Psychology*. Sage, Beverly Hills.

Restle. F. A. (1962). 'The selection of strategies in cue learning' *Psychological Review*, 69: 320–343.

Rorty, R. (1978) *Philosophy and the Mirror of Nature*, Princeton University Press, Princeton, NJ.

Rosaldo, M. (1980). *Knowledge and Passion, Ilongot Notions of Self and Social Life*, Cambridge University Press, Cambridge, MA.

Rosch, E. (1978). 'Principles of categorization'. In: Rosch, E. and Lloyd, B. B. (Eds) *Cognition and Categorization*, Erlbaum, Hillsdale, NJ.

Ryle, G. (1949). *The Concept of Mind*, Hutchinson, London.

Sampson, E. E. (1978). 'Scientific paradigms and social values', *Journal of Personality and Social Psychology*, 36: 1332–1343.

Sampson, E. E. (1981). 'Cognitive psychology as ideology', *American Psychologist*, 36: 730–743.

Sampson, E. E. (1983). 'Deconstructing psychology's subject', *Journal of Mind and Behavior*, 4: 135–164.

Sampson, E. E. (1988). 'The debate on individualism', *American Psychologist*, 43: 15–22.

Schachter, S. (1964). 'The interaction of cognitive and physiological determinants of emotional state'. In: Berkowitz, L. (Ed.) *Advances in Experimental Social Psychology*, *Vol. 1*, Academic, New York.

Scheman, N. (1983). 'Individualism and the objects of psychology', In: Harding, S. and Hintikka, M. (Eds) *Discovering Reality*, D. Reidel Publishing, Dordrecht.

Schlenker, B. (1985). *The Self and Social Life*, McGraw-Hill, New York.

Schulze, Y. (1986). 'Die gute mutter. Zur geschichte des normativen musters', *Mutterliebe*, Kleine-Verlag, Bielefeld.

Schwartz, B. (1986). *The Battle for Human Nature*, Norton, New York.

Searle, J. (1984). *Minds, Brains and Science*, Harvard University Press, Cambridge.

Semin, G. and Chassein, J. (1985). 'The relationship between higher order models and everyday conceptions of personality', *European Journal of Social Psychology*, 15: 1–16.

Semin, G. and Krahe, B. (1987). 'Lay conceptions of personality: eliciting tiers of a scientific conception of personality', *European Journal of Social Psychology*, 17: 199–209.

Semin, G. and Manstead, A. S. (1983). *The Accountability of Conduct*, Academic Press, London.

Shotter, J. (1980). 'Action, joint action and intentionality'. In: Brenner, M. (Ed.) *The Structure of Action*, Blackwell, Oxford.

Shotter, J. (1984). *Social Accountability and Selfhood*, Blackwell, Oxford.

Shotter, J. (1989). 'Remembering and forgetting as social institutions', In. Middleton D. and Edwards, D. (Eds) *Collective Remembering*, Sage, London.

Shweder, R. A. and Miller, J. G. (1985). 'The social construction of the person: How is it possible?' In: Gergen, K. J. and David, K. E. (Eds) *The Social Construction of the Person*, Springer-Verlag, New York.

Simon, H. A. and Kotowsky, K. (1963). 'Human acquisition of concepts for sequential patterns', *Psychological Review*, 70: 534–546.

Silver, M. and Sabini, J. (1985). 'Sincerity: Feelings and constructions in making a self', In: Gergen, K. J. and Davis, K. E. (Eds) *The Construction of the Person*, Springer-Verlag, New York.

Smedslund, J. (1985). 'Necessarily true cultural psychologies'. In: Gergen, K. J. and Davis K. E. (Eds) *The Social Construction of the Person*, Springer-Verlag, New York.

Stam, H. (1987). 'The psychology of control: A textual critique' In: Stam, H. J., Rogers, T. B. and Gergen, K. J. (Eds) *The Analysis of Psychological Theory*, Hemisphere Publishing, Washington, DC.

484   *Kenneth J. Gergen*

Steiner, I. (1974). 'Whatever happened to the group in social psychology? *Journal of Experimental Social Psychology*, 10: 94–108.
Taylor, C. (1971). 'Interpretation and the sciences of man', *the Review of Metaphysics*, 1: 25.
Tedeschi, J. (1981). *Impression management theory and social psychological research*. New York: Academic Press.
Tiefer, L. (1987). Social constructionism and the study of human sexuality. In: Shaver, P. and Hendrick, C. (Eds) *Sex and gender*. Beverly Hills: Sage.
Unger, R. K. (1983). Through the looking glass: No wonderland yet! *Psychology of Woman Quarterly*, 8: 9–32.
van den Berg, J. H. (1961). *The changing nature of man*. NY: Norton.
von Wright, G. H. (1971). *Explanation and understanding*. Ithica, NY: Cornell University Press.
Wagner, H. L. (Ed.) (1988). The social context of emotion. Special edition of the *British Journal of Social Psychology*, 27.
Wallach, M. and Wallach, L. (1983). *Psychology's sanction for selfishness*. San Francisco: W. H. Freeman and Co.
Wexler, P. (1983). *Critical social psychology*. Boston, MA: Routledge, Kegan & Paul.
White, H. (1978). *Tropics of discourse*. Baltimore, MD: Johns Hopkins University Press.
Wilkinson, S. (1986). *Feminist social psychology*. Philadelphia, PA: Open University Press.
Wittgenstein, L. (1963). *Philosophical investigations*. (G. Anscombe, trans.) NY: MacMillan.
Zillmann, D. (1978). 'Attribution and misattribution of excitatory reactions.'. In: Harvey, J. H., Ickes, W. J. and Kidd, R. F. (Eds) *New Directions in Attribution Research, Vol. 2*, Erlbaum, Hillsdale, NJ.

Chapter 4

Aggression as Discourse

Kenneth J. Gergen

To speak is simultaneously to engage in world construction. This is so in two major senses, the first implicative and the second pragmatic. In the former sense, world construction depends on the fact that language serves not as an arrangement of sounds, but as a system of symbols. To qualify as symbols, linguistic entities must imply a realm of referents; not to do so would be to lose identity as language. Thus to engage in the production of language is typically to forge an implicit commitment to a realm of referents not contained within the language itself. In effect, the act of speaking invites the listener to accept an independent ontological system. At the same time, language also has a pragmatic, or what Austin (1962a) has called a performative, aspect. That is, it is much like moving a rook in chess, holding someone in an embrace, or looking disinterested while under attack. It is itself a form of social intercourse. And, as performance, it frequently has social effects. Depending on the language one employs, another may admit defeat, profess deep love, or even kill. One's words are thus active constituents in a world of ongoing social interchange (Searle, 1970).

That language does imply an ontology, or serve to objectify, is not particularly controversial, so long as it is possible to establish linkages between the system of symbols and a range of relevant particulars. Typically such linkages are established through a process of ostensive definition, that is, through demonstrating or setting the experiential context for word usage. In using the word "cat", the mother may point to a small furry object with four legs and thereby establish the referent for the term; as the term is used in the presence of a variety of furry creatures over time, the child essentially learns that the term can refer to a range of objects. As Quine (1960) has made clear, the precise qualities of the referents may remain obscure; the referents for the term may essentially comprise a "fuzzy set" (in this case both literally and figuratively). Yet, through the process of ostensive identification, the world created through language may be treated, for all practical purposes, as possessing a reality independent of the language itself. By the same token, it is this process of ostensive definition that furnishes the major basis for the practical deployment of the language. Such phrases as, "You have jam on your nose," "Your check has arrived," or "Your house is on fire," have important consequences, primarily because of the rough state of affairs that they symbolize.

For purposes of clarity those linguistic descriptors linked to the realm of immediate observables (for some persons at some time) can be said to rely on *direct ostensive grounding*.[1] Such terms may be contrasted with two additional types of descriptors, the first of special importance to much natural science inquiry, and the second, as we shall see, of paramount importance to the understanding of aggression. Those descriptors subject to *indirect ostensive grounding* gain their immediate legitimacy through their linkages to other descriptors; however, this secondary tier of descriptors is itself subject to direct ostensive grounding. Thus, for example, the term "gravity" does not refer directly to any event or set of events in particular. However, the term is linked to sets of descriptors that are themselves ostensively grounded. To say that "the ball falls to the earth" may through common practice be tied to a fuzzy set of observable events (widespread agreement can generally be obtained as to whether a ball is or is not falling to the ground). To say that the ball's movement is the "result of gravitational force" is to establish a linguistic context for the usage of the term "gravity." When one is permitted by ostensive definition to say "the ball is falling," one also has warrant to speak of gravity. Descriptors subject to indirect ostensive grounding may prove problematic when the common linking practices (either from the indirect to the direct descriptor or from the latter to the realm of experience) are either too flexible or conflicting. However, with sufficient negotiation, it should be possible, in principle, to reach general agreement that indirect descriptors could be challenged or corrected by observation. If dropped objects suddenly begin to "ascend into space," the common theory of gravity might well be subject to emendation.

Yet, there is a third class of descriptors that are more problematic in character. The grounding of these terms is based neither on direct nor ostensive grounding, but on equivalence functions within the language itself. That is, the descriptive terms are legitimated through reference to other linguistic integers. In effect, they are *linguistically grounded*. This grounding essentially depends on a system of equivalency functions, or rules that determine the conditions under which the descriptors may appropriately be used. The rules essentially indicate a range of words that, together, would function as the equivalent of the descriptor in question. In the most primative case, these integers may simply serve as synonyms of the descriptor. Consider, for example, the descriptor "obedient," as in "Richard is an obedient man." One is hard put to locate a set of spatiotemporal constituents of the term "obedient"; the term simply does not derive its warrant for usage from any particular arrangement of the muscles, skeleton, neurons, and so on. Richard may presumably be defined as obedient regardless of the displacement of limbs, facial muscles, etc. However, the term is made intelligible because it is tied through equivalence rules to other integers in the language. If one is asked

---

1 The process by which words become defined through the referencing of observables is extensively described by Rommetveit (1968).

what is meant by the sentence, "Richard is an obedient man," for many purposes it would be sufficient to answer that he obeys orders, follows the rules, and avoids displays of autonomy. Fundamentally, such terms are the functional equivalents of obedience; if asked to produce a synonym for these terms, obedience would be a prime candidate. The equivalency system is essentially closed with regard to external or "real-world" grounding. In the same way, the term "heaven" gains legitimacy. Although the term itself has no spatiotemporal co-ordinates of common access, pervasive equivalency rules enable us to understand it as "the dwelling place of God." The latter phrase is similarly without referential exit to observables, but the user of the phrase may be successfully understood as speaking about "heaven."

This third class of linguistically grounded descriptors is both as problematic as it is essential within social life.[2] Such descriptors are problematic because they carry with them all the pragmatic force of the preceding classes, but without the same warrant. For example, in the case of ostensive grounding, one may warn, "You should leave at once; the building is on fire," and, if the advice is not heeded, the consequences may be lethal. The pragmatic consequences of the message are independent of the language itself. Employing the same linguistic form one might warn, "You should leave this place at once or you will go to hell." This utterance may carry with it the same pragmatic force as the warning of fire. Yet one is hard put in this case to link the travels to hell with a range of observables. The term "hell" is treated as an ontological equivalent to "fire." Although the latter is no more or less "real" than the former, the latter term can be linked to observables in a way that often has practical advantages. The term "hell" can only be grounded in other language. Its pragmatic power is essentially borrowed.

In general, it may be proposed that the social effects ("perlocutionary," in Austin's terms) of descriptive terms is derived in major part from the extent to which the ontological system implied by the descriptors is linked in a practical way with ongoing events. If the language can be ostensively defined, either directly or indirectly, such definitions can furnish the basis for informed and adaptive action. Terms with direct and indirect ostensive grounding should thus have considerable power in daily affairs. Yet, utterances such as, "You will go to hell if you don't ...," and "Richard is very unhappy today," may also have important social consequences, and these utterances cannot be ostensively grounded. In some degree the power of such linguistically grounded descriptors may be derived from their formal similarity to the ostensive descriptors. Yet, this dependency must be viewed as partial. It is not that the threat of hell has lost its force in much of contemporary society because of the slowly emerging realization that its warrant is solely linguistic. Rather, much of the pragmatic force of such descriptors is derived from common practices of social sanctioning. In many sectors of society a man who is told that his conduct will take him to hell is wise to change

---

2 Elsewhere (Gergen, 1982) I have tried to demonstrate that most descriptions of human action are linguistically, and not empirically, grounded and that, given the particular character of the denotative process, it could scarcely be otherwise.

his ways, not because of this particular likelihood, but because of the social dis-approval he is otherwise likely to incur. In Pennsylvania Dutch culture, a man who engages in "sinful" activity may be systematically shunned by an entire community; no one in the community may be allowed to speak with him or in any other way acknowledge his existence. Similarly, if a friend tells you her mother has just died and you announce that you are feeling happy about it, her dismay will not be the result of an ontological breach, but a social one. It is a breach in the social rules of emotional utterances that may result in the broken friendship. In effect, linguistically grounded descriptors may often serve impor-tant social functions, and their warrant and significance in the culture should properly be traced to these functional bases.

Aggression as Linguistically Grounded

Common discourse on aggression is world constructing in both of the previously described modes. Sentences such as, "The Russians are guilty of aggression in Afghanistan," "American culture is highly aggressive," "Patterns of human ag-gression are similar to those in various animal communities," and "There is a positive relationship between ambient temperature and aggression," first imply an ontology. It follows from such utterances that included in the inventory of en-tities making up the world are various forms of behavior, one of which is aggres-sion. Certain people at certain times display this behavior, and such behavior is different in its fundamental character from behaviors which are not aggressive. Such utterances also possess a variety of pragmatic implications. To say that the Russians or the Americans display aggression, for example, is to have different implications for how they are to be treated than if their behavior under such cir-cumstances were described as "self-protective," "energetic," or "idealistic." The pragmatic interests served by the scientific use of the term aggression have been explored elsewhere by Lubek (1979).

The uses to which the term aggression is put in the above instances might pass without interest if the term were subject either to direct or indirect ostensive grounding. If such grounding were accomplished, then to say that the Americans are aggressive people would have much the same ontological status as saying, "There is no snow on Mount Fuji." Spatiotemporal reorderings should be possi-ble in both instances. In the case of Mount Fuji, independent observers should all be able to reach agreement regarding the existence of snow; photographic re-cordings might also be employed, or inferences could be made from various in-dicators of temperature and precipitation. This is not to presume the indepen-dent existence of snow, but it is the case that by virtue of observation, broad agreement can easily be reached regarding the relevance or adequacy of the term snow. Yet, what are the spatiotemporal exemplars of the term aggression? At what velocity should the body be moving? At what angle should the left femur be extended? What adjustments must be made by stretch reflexes, and at what rate should sodium ions flow into the neurons for an action to qualify as ag-gression? All such questions are without answers, it would appear, because the term aggression is not one of those descriptors linked ostensively to ongoing events.

If the term aggression does not refer to a range of spatiotemporal particulars, then to what does it refer? Perhaps the most adequate answer to this question is furnished by those most deeply invested in developing behavioral indicators of aggression, namely behavioral scientists. Interestingly this issue has been fraught with conflict since the concerted study of aggression began in the 1930s. In their groundbreaking treatise, Dollard, Doob, Miller, Mowrer, and Sears (1939) defined aggression as "an act whose goal-response is injury to an organism" (p. 11). Yet, although it was wrought within the behaviorist framework, investigators were quick to see that this definition was, in fact, nonbehavioral. That is, its ultimate reference was the "goal-response," an internal or psychological construct used to earmark the directionality of behavior. To correct this state of affairs, Buss (1961) later proposed to define aggression as "a response that delivers noxious stimuli to another organism" (p. 1). However, this definition drew extensive fire (cf. Bandura and Walters, 1963; Feshbach, 1964; Kaufmann, 1970), in large measure because it failed to take account of the motive of the actor. As it was argued, Buss' definition would allow the actions of a surgeon or a dentist to be termed aggressive, as would any accidental act resulting in another's pain or death. In light of these criticisms, Buss later altered his definition to "the attempt to deliver noxious stimuli, regardless of whether it is successful" (1971, p. 10). However the term "attempt" again reinstated the psychological referent for aggression. In one form or another, the psychological instigation to aggression has served as the critical locus of definition in almost all subsequent treatments of the topic (cf. Berkowitz, 1962; Baron, 1977).[3] Even in Zillmann's (1979) extensive (44 pages) and highly behavioristic account of the concept of aggression, it is concluded that the term refers to "Any and every activity by which a person *seeks* to inflict bodily damage or physical pain ..." (p. 33, italics added). "To seek" is, after all, a state of intent, rather than an activity subject to public observation.

While sometimes embarrassing, the fact that aggression as a theoretical construct generally refers to an internal or hypothetical realm has hardly proved lethal to the research endeavor. Often the fact is simply ignored, and investigation proceeds just as if the term refers to a series of observable events in nature. Various behaviors, such as delivering shock to another person or striking a plastic doll, are simply said to be aggressive and no attempt is made to explicate or examine the underlying motivational base of research participants. However, certain investigators have attempted to remain consistent with the definitional presuppositions. In these cases it is generally advanced that the term aggression has *indirect* grounding in observables. As it is said, aggression is a hypothetical con-

---

3 One significant exception is Bandura (1973), who defines aggression as "behavior that results in personal injury and in destruction of property" (p. 4). However, in an attempt to avoid the kinds of attack leveled against Buss' early work, Bandura adds the promise that "social judgment" must determine which acts are to be labeled aggression. This latter proviso creates as many problems as it solves, for any act may be subject to myriad interpretations, and, thus, what counts as "research on aggression" falls victim to whose definitional tastes prevail.

struct and, although such constructs are not subject to direct observation, one may develop reliable indicators of its presence of absence. For example, when an individual verbalizes his motives (e. g., "Yes, I was trying to kill him"), when the action is accompanied by forethought, or when physiological measures indicate a heightened state of arousal, then it may be more justifiably argued that the behavior in question is aggression and not something else (e. g. altruism, religious worship, etc.). In effect, the term aggression does not refer directly to these measures, but its definition is, in part, linked to observables (e. g., aggression is that which is indicated by a statement of intent, physiological arousal, and so on, which statements are then linked to observables).

But let us examine more closely this resort to the argument for indirect, ostensive grounding. Do behavioral scientists of this persuasion have a proper analogy with the physical sciences, such that the term aggression functions much like those of gravity, atoms, and magnetic force? It would not appear so. This contention becomes clear when one attempts to specify the realm of observables to which the indirect indicators refer. For example, what is the ostensive anchoring for a statement of intent? At first glance, it appears that a "statement of intent" refers to just that, an individual's observable utterances. But does it? If such utterances were recorded with a sound spectrograph, and the results of this instrumentation compared with various other utterances produced by the individual, would it be possible to differentiate between utterances indicating an intention to aggress, as opposed to other states or intentions? Clearly, the answer is no. A statement of intent to do harm, in terms of its properties as sound, will look like many other sounds emitted by the person. Similarly, if the statement, "I meant to kill him," were analyzed in terms of its phonemic properties, its syllabic order, or its grammaticality, one could scarcely identify whether the statement was an indicator of an aggressive intent or some other. This is to say that it is not the physical properties of the utterance, "I meant to kill him," to which the descriptive phrase "statement of intent" refers. The speaker could issue such words in a shout or a whisper, in script or cursive, in Hebrew or Sanskrit, in proper grammatical form or in slang, and it would still make little difference as to the judgment of intent.

Then to what does this latter range of descriptors, such as statement of intent, refer? If such descriptor are not themselves ostensively grounded, then what are their referents? As it is rapidly surmised, such descriptors bear a strong family resemblance to the term aggression itself. That is, they appear to have ostensive anchors, but this appearance is a misleading product of the tendency to confer ontic status on the world implied by words. When the veil of objectification is rent, we find again that such descriptors refer to other psychological states. That is, one is not, after all, interested in the physical properties of such descriptors, but in the underlying meaning, motive, intention, and the like. One is not concerned with the physical properties of the utterance, "I meant to . . .," but with the speaker's *intention* in saying these words – for example, whether he or she was "trying" to give an accurate picture of an intentional state, prevaricating, speaking out of a trancelike stupor, or the like. In the same way, it is not the individual's statements regarding his or her hostility or indicators of physiological arousal that are ultimately significant in determining whether an action was aggressive, but, rather, what these indicators signify about the psychological conditions under which they were produced. A statement of hostility can, after all, be used to mislead, and an accomplished liar can control his or her state of physiological arousal, even when exposed to a lie detector.

One might pursue the possibility of developing measures that could ostensively define measures of these particular states. However, as this procedure is implemented, it is soon realized that one has entered an infinite regress in which every indicator of a psychological state (e. g., meaning, intention, conceptual system, motive, etc.) is itself defined in terms of other psychological states. To measure the meaning behind the statement, "I intended to . . .," would itself require an interpretation of the psychological state necessary to produce the behavioral outcome. In terms of the distinctions developed earlier, this is to say that all statements about aggression, along with a broad range of other person descriptors, are neither directly nor indirectly grounded in observables. Rather, they are linguistically grounded; their definition is exhausted by an inventory of the linguistic contexts in which they are embedded.

The Structural Unpacking of Aggression Discourse

What does the preceding analysis indicate for the study of aggression? First, it seems clear that the concept of aggression should be "deontologized"; that is, the assumption that the term stands in referential relationship to an array of spatiotemporal events must be discarded. In this case one also finds reason to question the function of what has been understood to be empirical research on the genesis of, the conditions giving rise to, the psychological basis for, the physiological inputs to, or behavioral consequences of aggression. Given the lack of worldly events to which such study might be addressed, how is one to consider the outcomes of such work? At the same time, the present analysis indicates the propitiousness of at least two lines of alternative inquiry. The first is closely related to the earlier discussion of the pragmatic aspects of language. As we have seen, language is an important implement for altering or sustaining social pattern; when part of an ongoing discourse, the term aggression can often be a potent instrument of influence or control. Inquiry is invited, then, into the pragmatics of the language of aggression. How is this particular construction of persons to be achieved in the social sphere and with what effects? From whence is its power in social interchange derived? Openings into these issues have been made in other contributions to the present volume. For example, Mummendey, Linneweber, and Löschper (this volume) describe social factors that enter into the negotiation of whether an act is deemed aggressive. And Ferguson and Rule (this volume) and Tedeschi (this volume) explore various normative considerations that may bear on whether an act is labeled aggressive.[4]

---

4 See also Rommetveit's (1979) discussion of "metacontracts" among participants in the determination of meaning, along with Blakar's (1979) inquiry into language as a means to social

The second major thrust of exploration suggested by the present analysis is into what may be termed the grammar of aggression, that is, the rules or conventions governing common discourse about aggression. As we find, aggression is essentially an integer in a language system. Thus, the constraints over what may be said about aggression do not lie in the realm of observation, but in the system of conventions for speaking about it. We cannot easily say about aggression that it goes backward, or travels in circles, is influenced by spirits, or is a form of compulsion. In Austin's (1962a) terms, such utterances violate common "felicity conditions" for speaking about aggression. However, in most social contexts we can say that aggressive tendencies vary in their intensity, that people often aggress because they are frustrated, or that some cultures are more aggressive than others. None of these pronouncements is warranted by virtue of common observation; such warrants are embedded within the common conventions of language use. This is to say that the limits to what science may "discover" about aggression as "a phenomenon" are, for the most part, already lodged within the common conventions of discourse. To elucidate these conventions is to begin to apprehend the limits of what science may generate as "knowledge about aggression." Study of these conventions also serves emancipatory functions, for to gain cognizance over the conventional basis for accepted truth is to remove dependency on such conventions and to invite the creative development of alternatives.

It is to the latter of these programs of inquiry that our major attention will now be given. Later we shall touch on the implications of this analysis for the pragmatics of aggression. The focal attempt at this point is to lay bare certain suppositions embedded within common discourse concerning aggression. This analysis must necessarily proceed with caution, for there are no commonly accepted and well-honed techniques presently available for this purpose. The present analysis does benefit from a variety of preceding inquiries. Within ordinary language philosophy, disquisitions on the language of mind (Ryle, 1949), motivation (Peters, 1958), sense data (Austin, 1962b), emotion (Kenny, 1963), and the like furnish potent demonstrations of the significance of contextual clarification for philosophic inquiry. As Shotter & Burton (1983) have shown, there is also within Heider's (1958) formulation of naive psychology an implicit grammar for action accounting, one that furnishes a rudimentary logic underlying explanations for human behavior more generally. More recently, Smedslund (1978, 1980) has laid out a series of axiomatic definitions of human action from which an indefinite number of theoretical propositions could follow. As Smedslund argues, such propositions are not subject to empirical assessment once the initial definitions are accepted, even when treated as empirical by the scientific establishment. Further, Ossorio (1978) has ambitiously attempted to furnish a set of fundamental dimensions required by linguistic practices in distinguishing human actions from each other. Additionally helpful are the attempts of Ossorio

---

power, and Pearce and Cronen's (1980) analysis of the social management of meaning. The work of Garfinkel (1967) and others within the ethnomethodological tradition (cf. Psathas, 1979) is also germane.

(1981) and Davis and Todd (1982) to develop a *paradigm case* method for determining the set of ordinary language criteria relevant to the use of a given concept.[5]

The method developed for present assessment may be termed *structural unpacking*. It is essentially a formalized rendering of the linguistic conventions necessary or essential for deploying a descriptive term. In this particular case the task is to specify the linguistic conditions commonly pertaining to the deployment of the integer, aggression. It is to convert to a formal structure what is commonly taken to be intelligent discourse about aggression. To speak of the result as a structure is not to link the present analysis with the kind of structuralist inquiries undertaken by Levi-Strauss, Lacan, and others within the French structuralist tradition. In most respects the foundational rationale for the present undertaking is in contention with the universalist leanings inherent in much structuralist writing. Rather, the term structure is used in the present case to call attention to the pervasive character of many current conventions. It is to catch what are essentially evolving patterns of discourse in a single stopframe.

The process of structural unpacking proceeds through the posing of criterial questions for usage of the descriptor in question. Each question attempts to determine a criterion that would enable the common user of the language to distinguish between the appropriateness of using the descriptor in question, as opposed to a range of alternative terms. To consider the structural unpacking of the term apple, a criterial query concerning color would enable most persons to sort between apple and a wide range of competitors. Similarly, the criterial question of "edibleness" would permit one to distinguish between the appropriateness of using the term apple, as opposed to a wide variety of alternatives (e. g., airplanes, hats, stones). As additional criterial queries are posed, the conditions under which it is possible to call an object an apple are progressively narrowed. As criteria of color, shape, size, taste, and so on are added, one gains increasing clarity concerning the linguistic conditions under which it is appropriate to employ the term apple and no other term.

As should be apparent, this form of analysis leaves a certain degree of latitude for the investigator, as there are no definitive rules for what criterial queries may be posed. Thus the investigator is thrust back on his or her own familiarity with the language or must consult other language users. Further, such analyses may be viewed as approaching, rather than reaching, completion over time. There is no obvious means of determining when all possible queries have been established, and, given the continuous evolution of language usage, it may also be supposed that differing criteria may become appropriate over time (e. g., the criterion "city" would presently include "The Big Apple"). Finally, many descriptors are essentially polysemous, that is, they are embedded within several differing structures. For example, the descriptor "cool" is employed in at least two,

---

5 Significant foundational work for the present undertaking is also represented in the contributions of Burke (1945), Mills (1940), and Scott and Lyman (1968). And, of course, Wittgenstein's (1980) inquiries into the philosophy of psychology must be considered seminal to all of the above.

quite distinct language contexts. Criterial queries must be sensitive to such structural differentiation.[6]

With this sketch in mind, we may proceed with the structural unpacking of aggression. Although there are differing structures in which this descriptor is featured, let us presently confine ourselves to the structure that seems implicit in most psychological research, in much policy making, and in many contexts of daily life. As an initial criterion, it seems clear that the term is used as a descriptor primarily when talk is about *animate,* as opposed to *inanimate,* beings. That is, the criterion of animation separates aggression from a huge number of other descriptors. Thus we cannot (except metaphorically) speak of the table or the clock as aggressing; we can speak of aggression in humans, primates, insects, and even in the plant kingdom. Although this criterion may appear of scant significance for an initial cutting device, there are two noteworthy implications. First, implied by the process of structural unpacking is the possibility of ultimately developing a taxonomy of structure. Similar to Levi-Strauss's elucidation of structure through the principle of homology, by separating terms according to criteria of broad consequence, family resemblances among descriptors may become apparent and functional or pragmatic equivalencies clarified. Thus, for example, the term *aggression* shares certain characteristics with terms like *love* and *respect;* this class of descriptors is essentially reserved for animate beings. Further, this initial criterion appropriately recognizes and extends the distinction developed within the philosophy of social science between action and behavior (cf. Taylor, 1964). As argued in this domain, descriptions of human action necessarily make certain presumptions that pertain to human beings, but not to inanimate objects. Those descriptors used in the natural sciences are thus inappropriately and misleadingly extended to human action. Sense cannot be made of human action, as the behaviorists believed, by employing a language reducible to physics. As the present analysis suggests, however, the prerequisite distinction among descriptors should be that of animate vs inanimate, and not human vs nonhuman. Much of the language for person description is equally applicable to other animal beings.

As a second orienting criterion, it seems clear that the term *aggression* falls into a class of terms used in discourse about *interdependent,* as opposed to *independent,* activity. That is, contemporary conventions generally prevent one from employing the term aggression to communicate about the conduct of a sole individual. One simply cannot aggress unless there is a target for his or her actions. In this regard, *aggression* is structurally similar to terms like *dancing, cooperating, helping,* or *ruling.* The descriptor is functionally dissimilar to terms such as *singing, painting,* or *exercising* – each of which may be applied to the activities of a single animate being. As this distinction indicates, the warrantability of using aggression as a descriptor can depend on characterization of at least two actors. Constraints over the use of the term may be traced both to talk about the actor and the recipient.

Given this latter bifurcation, let us first consider the simpler case, that of the

---

6 See Rommetveit (1979) for discussion of the differential contexualizations of single words.

recipient or potential victim. What must be the case in speaking of the victim of the action if the actor is to be termed aggressive? There would appear to be two major requirements. First, the recipient must derive *pain*, as opposed to *pleasure*, from the actor's conduct. If it were said of the recipient that, although he seemed to be in pain, secretly he enjoyed the actor's behavior, it would be inappropriate to speak of the behavior as aggression. (It might, for example, be viewed as sadomasochistic.) Second, the recipient's pain must be understood as *undeserved* (unjust, inappropriate), as opposed to *deserved* (just, appropriate). If the actor's behavior causes pain and the recipient is deserving, we would not meaningfully call the action aggression. Rather, it would be more appropriate to use such terms as punishment, retaliation, self-defense, correctional action, moral training, teaching, or the like. The use of the descriptor *aggression* may require additional characterizations of the recipient, but for present purposes we may consider these criteria as orienting and foundational.

In turning to the actor (the potential aggressor), three essential conditions are apparent. First, it must be said of the act that it was *intentional*, as opposed to *unintentional*. One cannot thus speak of an unintentional aggressive act. If a hunter believes he is shooting a bear and fells a colleague, it would not be said of the act that it was aggressive. However, if it were said of the same action that the hunter intended to slay his fellow, it would be quite appropriate to describe the action as aggression. Second, the aim of the intention must be that of delivering *pain* or harm to another (or others), as opposed to *pleasure*. Thus, if the agent said of her caustic criticism that it was intended to help the recipient correct his miserable ways and once again find happiness, it could not appropriately be said that she aggressed; rather, it might be said that she was teaching a bitter lesson or taking his future in her hands. And finally, it must be said that the actor's conduct is *unjust* or inappropriate, as opposed to *just* or proper. Even though it may be said of a hangman that he intends to deliver harm to another, it would not typically be said that his conduct is aggressive. Rather, he is doing his duty, serving the public, or helping to dispense justice. If the same individual were to hang someone not deemed a villain by society, his actions might be called wantonly aggressive.

Thus far a series of seven criteria have been proposed, each of which appears stipulative with respect to discourse on aggression. These seven criteria have been collected in Figure 4.1. As proposed, virtually all of these criteria must be either implicit or explicit as one speaks of an act as aggressive. Let us term this array of criteria a *structural nucleus*. Its nucleic property derives from the fact that, at least in the ideal case, virtually all the indicated properties, and only these properties, must be assumed. For purposes of defining aggression the set is complete and autonomous within itself. (Further analysis would surely reveal necessary additions to the nucleus, but for purposes of the present analysis the seven criteria will prove sufficient.) It should further be noted that the terms of the nucleus are essentially redundant. That is, once an action has been called aggressive all of the constituent features of the nucleus can be employed felicitously in speaking of the actor and the recipient. Or, once the actor and the recipient have been described in these terms, no new information is added by calling the action aggressive.

62   Kenneth J. Gergen

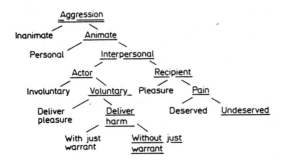

Fig. 4.1. Structural nucleus for aggression

Yet, while the structural nucleus lays out the warranting conditions for the term aggression, the schema must be expanded in an essential way. The predicate aggression may figure in many accounts of action in which the definitional equivalents do not occur. It may properly be said, for example, that, "The man was angry and therefore aggressed," while "He was happy and therefore aggressed" borders on cultural nonsense. To use the term "angry" in the preceding context is thus to increase the probability of describing the action as aggressive, while the term "happiness" inhibits the ascription. Yet, neither anger nor happiness is a constituent element of the structural nucleus. Likewise, if it were said that, "Mary criticized her friend Martha," one would be less inclined to view this criticism as aggression than if Martha was said to be Mary's enemy. In effect, the probability of employing the term aggression depends not only on placing it within the context of its definitional nucleus, but on additional attributes of the linguistic context, as well. The task that now confronts us is how to account for these latter effects in terms of the structural analysis proposed here.

To answer this query let us return to examine the relationship between the *primary term* in the nucleus "aggression" and the *secondary terms* on which it relies for its definition. This relationship is of one to many, in the sense that the primary integer requires a set of greater than one in order for parity or identity to be achieved. Thus, the secondary terms possess the meaning "aggression" only when employed as a group. However, this leaves open the definition or meaning of the secondary integers in isolation. As is quickly seen, the meaning of these terms is also subject to structural unpacking. That is, each of the single terms comprising the secondary integers in the preceding analysis may be viewed as a primary predicate within a separate structural nucleus. The "intention," "harm," "just," "animate," and so on stand subject to the same unpacking procedure as did aggression. Each possesses secondary equivalencies that serve to define or to establish the warrant over its usage. The exposition of this relationship between primary and secondary terms, the latter of which stand in a primary to secondary relationship with still further terms, and so on, may be viewed as *vertical unpacking*.

The major integer in question (i. e., aggression) is featured as the vertex of the network and is accompanied by a descending order of related structural nuclei.

Vertical unpacking may be contrasted with the process of *horizontal unpacking*. In this case, attention is drawn to the fact that each of the secondary integers in the initial nucleus may also be featured as a secondary integer in a range of other nuclei. Thus, for example, the term unjust, which partially contributes to what is meant by the term aggression, is also a secondary integer in a variety of other nuclei. If it were said of a person, "He underpaid his workers," the descriptor "underpaid" would be partially defined by the secondary term unjust. Similarly such descriptors as cheating, exploiting, and oppressing would undoubtedly contain the term unjust as a part of the secondary retinue. It follows from this line of reasoning that each structural nucleus possesses conventionally based and overlapping attachments to a range of other nuclei, both in the horizontal and vertical dimension, and these to still others. In effect, each structural nucleus is a constituent of an interrelated (and indefinitely extended) complex.

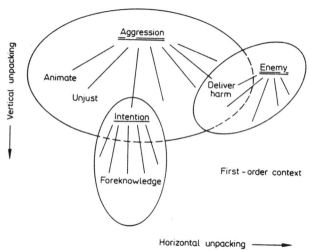

Fig. 4.2. Constituents of the aggression nucleus as embedded in other nuclei

A partially unfolded schematic of the broader linguistic context of the aggression integer is featured in Figure 4.2. For present purposes let us focus attention on the relationship between the aggression nucleus and several structures to which it is immediately related. We may term these immediately attached nuclei, both within the horizontal and vertical planes, nuclei of the *first-order context*, inasmuch as the secondary terms of the structural nucleus in question are either defined by, or are featured within, these nuclei. Now, if the term aggression is made more or less probable, depending on whether secondary integers within its own nucleus are employed in a descriptive account, then the use of these secondary integers may be appropriately governed by the occurrence of the various terms within the first-order context. To illustrate, in the vertical dimension a critical criterion of whether an individual possesses an intention to act is whether he or she has *foreknowledge* of results. If it is said that a person did not know his or her actions would have a particular effect, it could not properly be said that the effect was intentional. Thus, to say that an individual had no foreknowledge indirectly affects the warrantability of calling the person aggressive. To move now in the horizontal direction, it was said that aggression was partially defined by the criterion of delivering harm. Yet, within the first-order context we find the integer "delivering harm" is also featured as a secondary integer of other nuclei. For example, the definition of "enemy" would undoubtedly include, as a definitional criterion, the delivery of harm, and not benefit; in contrast, to be a friend is, by definition, to be someone to whom benefit, rather than harm, is given. Given these linkages, it becomes more appropriate to say that criticism of an enemy is aggressive, while criticism of a friend is not.

As we may conclude, whether or not one is permitted to speak of an individual or group as aggressing depends not on the physical characteristics of the action in question, but on the linguistic context in which the term is embedded. This context is not only composed of the secondary predicates (e. g., intention, delivering harm, unjust) that go into defining aggression by conventional standards, but also by the context in which these predicates are embedded. Thus, when an individual uses terms within the broader context (either horizontal or vertical), such terms influence the likelihood of one's making sense with terms in the primary context. Whether descriptive terms in the context have less warranting power than the constituents of the nucleus itself, or whether those in the vertical dimension have more power than those in the horizontal, remain interesting questions for future inquiry. The major purpose of this treatment has been to furnish an analytic account of the linguistic grounding of person descriptors in general, and aggression in particular.

On the Negotiation of Aggression

A distinction was initially drawn between two ways in which language creates reality, the first by objectification and the second by pragmatic deployment. Although analytically separate, these modes of world construction are closely related. One's ability to achieve social effects depends on the structure of objectifications, and this structure is realized only within the nexus of pragmatic encounter. It is to the former of these dependencies, that of pragmatics on structure, to which we must at last turn, not only because it saves the previous analysis from becoming an arid formalism, but because the major focus of this volume is on aggression as social process. It seems clear from the present analysis that virtually all social patterns stand vulnerable to the ascription of aggression; likewise, virtually any other predicate within the vocabulary of person description can be used to account for what is taking place. As argued, the selected descriptor tells us virtually nothing about the features of the ongoing movements; it in no way reflects the state of nature. Rather, the selection of descriptors may principally be viewed as a performative, or an integer within a flexible though partially structured social sequence. In the fashion of Putnam (1978) or Habermas (1971), one might wish to argue that person description is quintessentially "interest relevant" in this respect. However, to speak of the interests, designs, or intentions underlying the selection of descriptive terms is once again to enter the structural labyrinth.

Rather than being drawn into futile conjecture about purpose, interest, or intent, it seems more fruitful to scan the sorts of rhetorical structures in which the term aggression most frequently figures. That is, we may ask what follows "logically." (in terms of conventional sense-making) if an individual or group is said to be aggressive. What else is one then permitted to say or do?[7] Although there are a number of possibilities, at least one of the most commonly employed sequences is terminated in punishment. As we have seen, by common definition, aggression is an unjust action. And within common language conventions, unjust or unfair acts are deserving of retribution. They may be set aright by punishing the agent. Thus, to attribute aggression commonly furnishes one with the right, if not the duty, to bring harm to the actor. And these reciprocal acts, because they achieve justice, are not easily subject to the ascription of aggression. More generally, then, to call an act aggressive is to generate a right to control or punish the agent and to do so in a way that is in itself not subject to retribution.

Given the attempt to attribute aggression to a person or a group, the outcomes of the structural unpacking process prove highly informative. Such outcomes first inform one of the range of linguistic integers that must be invoked if the ascription is to be justified or sustained. If one is to explain why an action is to be distinguished as aggression, as opposed to a host of competitors, structural unpacking specifies how this must be done. First, it may be anticipated that the adversary will draw from the range of secondary constituents of the definitional nucleus. For example, one attempting to demonstrate how the Russian presence in Afghanistan is an act of aggression might wish to argue that acts of violence were perpetrated against the people (bringing harm), such attacks were planned (intention), the Russians lacked legal or moral right to invade (injustice), and so on. Although it might first appear that these various elaborations furnish a factual warrant for calling the Russians aggressive, a more sensitive analysis reveals that for purposes of ascription, this elaboration adds no new information. That is, once the act has been termed aggressive, all the components hold true by definition. To say that the act is aggressive *because* it brings harm, is intentional, and so on is essentially to say that the act is aggressive because it is aggressive. Or, in terms of literary analysis, statements regarding intention, injustice, and so on serve as tropes, or figurative substitutes, for aggression.

As the earlier analysis also makes clear, the attempt to justify or sustain the ascription of aggression will not be limited to employing terms from the structural nucleus alone. Rather, the adversary may also usefully draw predicates from the first-order context, both horizontal and vertical. For example, one may draw from the vertical context in trying to demonstrate the validity of intention (in

---

7 It is not, thus, as Grice (1957) and Searle (1970) propose, that the fundamental goal of the listener is to determine what the speaker *intended* him or her to understand by a sentence. Rather, as indicated here, the task faced by the listener is to assess the *action consequences* (including linguistic) that would result, should the sentence be accepted.

the primary nucleus) by maintaining that the Russians knew in advance that bloodshed would be required. In this case the adversary would essentially be citing a definitional component (possessing cognizance) that contributes to the definition of what it is to have an intention. Or, to draw from the horizontal context, one might argue that the Russians were not traditional friends of the Afghans or decided unilaterally to invade the country. The former use of the term "not friends" gives conventional warrant to the criterion of "harm-doing" in the primary nucleus; to speak of "invasion" is to increase the warrant for "unjust" in the primary nucleus, as to invade is, within a particular definitional nucleus, an unjust act. Again we see that the resort to terms in the first-order context does not add essential information to the ascription. All such terms are redundant with the ascription of aggression. The justification is essentially a rhetorical one, amounting to a multiplicity of overlapping assertions.

Yet, in cases of ascribing aggression it is often difficult to obtain univocal agreement. Others may be engaged in differing ascriptional projects, most particularly if they are the targets of the initial labeling. As Mummendey and her colleagues (Mummendey, Bornewasser, Löschper, & Linneweber, 1982) have said, "It's always somebody else who is aggressive." And with good reason. As we have seen, the ascription of aggression renders one vulnerable to punishment. At this juncture the results of the structural unpacking process again take on a predictive function. In this case they inform one of the linguistic grounds upon which negotiation is likely to occur. It is useful in this case to view the participants in such negotiations as ontological adversaries, each attempting to vindicate a particular reality while vitiating that of the opponent.[8] Thus, the supporter for the Russian presence in Afghanistan might first assert an alternative definition of the situation (e. g., self-defense, giving support to a teetering government) and then demonstrate the invalidity of the elements of the structural nucleus and its relatives within the first-order context. The attempt might thus be to show how the common Afghan is experiencing no harm, but is being aided, that the governing power has extended an invitation to Russia, and that there was no intention to do harm to the nation – in each case undermining one of the definitional supports for the aggression ascription. Or, a tactical move may be made within the first-order context. It may be maintained (vertical context level) that the warfare has been conducted against rebel forces attempting to overthrow the justly constituted government, and thus the act is not unjust. And, within the horizontal context it might be ventured that Russia has considered itself an ally and protector of its close neighbor, thus undermining the validity of the "harm-doing" constituent of the primary nucleus. In effect, each adversary may be expected to move from one sector of the aggression nucleus to the associated context to sustain a given position regarding the act.

---

8 For a relevant analysis of the negotation of conflicting metaphors, see Lakoff and Johnson (1980).

Summary

This chapter attempts to lay the groundwork for understanding discourse on aggression. As it is shown, the term itself is defined by, or can be equated with, a set of criterial attributes. The term and its attributes are termed a structural nucleus. Further unpacking reveals that each criterial attribute is embedded within still other nuclei. Such terms may figure as predicates to be defined by further attributes within a nucleus or as defining characteristics for still other predicates. It is further proposed that virtually all that may sensibly be said about aggression, whether in the conduct of science or social relationships more generally, can be derived from the full unpacking of the language conventions. As proposed, such language conventions cannot, in principle, be corrected or corroborated by observation of human behavior.

References

Austin, J. L. *How to do things with words*. New York: Oxford University Press, 1962. (a).
Austin, J. L. *Sense and sensibilia*. London: Oxford University Press, 1962. (b).
Bandura, A. *Aggression. A social learning analysis*. Englewood Cliffs, N. J.: Prentice-Hall, 1973.
Bandura, A., & Walters, R. H. *Social learning and personality development*. New York: Holt, Rinehart & Winston, 1963.
Baron, R. A. *Human aggression*. New York: Plenum, 1977.
Berkowitz, L. *Aggression: A social psychological analysis*. New York: McGraw-Hill, 1962.
Blakar, R. M. Language as a means of social power. In R. Rommeteveit & R. M. Blakar (Eds.), *Studies of language, thought and verbal communication*. London: Academic Press, 1979.
Burke, K. *A grammar of motives*. New York: Prentice Hall, 1945.
Buss, A. H. *The psychology of aggression*. New York: Wiley, 1961.
Buss, A. H. Aggression pays. In J. L. Singer (Ed.), *The control of aggression and violence: Cognitive and physiological factors*. New York: Academic Press, 1971.
Davis, K. E., & Todd, M. J. Friendship and love relationships. In K. E. Davis & T. Mitchell (Eds.), *Advances in descriptive psychology* (Vol. 2). Greenwich, England: JAI Press Inc., 1982.
Dollard, J., Doob, L. W., Miller, N. E., Mowrer, O. H., & Sears, R. R. *Frustration and aggression*. New Haven, Conn.: Yale University Press, 1939.
Feshbach, S. The function of aggression and the regulation of aggressive drive. *Psychological Review*, 1964, *71*, 257–272.
Garfinkel, H. *Studies in ethnomethodology*. Englewood Cliffs (NJ): Prentice Hall, 1967.
Gergen, K. J. *Toward transformation in social knowledge*. New York: Springer, 1982.
Grice, H. P. Meaning. *Philosophical Review*, 1957, *64*, 377–388.
Habermas, J. *Knowledge and human interest*. Boston, Mass.: Beacon Press, 1971.
Heider, F. *The psychology of interpersonal relations*. New York: Wiley, 1958.
Kaufmann, H. *Aggression and altruism: A psychological analysis*. New York: Holt, Rinehart & Winston, 1970.
Kenny, A. *Action, emotion & will*. London: Routledge & Kegan Paul, 1963.
Lakoff, G., & Johnson, M. *Metaphors we live by*. Chicago: University of Chicago Press, 1980.
Lubek, I. A brief social psychological analysis of research on aggression in social psychology. In A. R. Buss (Ed.), *Psychology in social context*. New York: Irvington, 1979.
Mills, C. W. Situated actions and vocabularies of motive. *American Sociological Review*. 1940, *5*, 904–913.
Mummendey, A., Bornewasser, M., Löschper, G., & Linneweber, V. It is always somebody else who is aggressive. A plea for a social psychological perspective in aggression research. *Zeitschrift für Sozialpsychologie*, 1982, *13*, 177–193.

68   Kenneth J. Gergen

Ossorio, P. G. *"What actually happens."* Columbia, S. C.: University of South Carolina Press, 1978.

Ossorio, P. G. Outline of descriptive psychology for personality theory and clinical applications. In K. E. Davis (Ed.), *Advances in descriptive psychology* (Vol. 1). Greenwich, Conn.: JAI Press, Inc. 1981.

Pearce, W. B., & Cronen, V. E. *Communication, action and meaning: The creation of social realities.* New York: Praeger, 1980.

Peters, R. S. *The concept of motivation.* London: Routledge & Kegan Paul, 1958.

Psathas, G. (Ed.) *Everyday language: studies in ethnomethodology.* New York: Irvington, 1979.

Putnam, H. *Meaning and the moral sciences.* London: Routledge & Kegan Paul, 1978.

Quine, W. V. O. *Word and object.* Cambridge, Mass.: M. I. T. Press, 1960.

Rommetveit, R. *Words, meanings and messages.* New York: Academic Press, 1968.

Rommetveit, R. Deep structure of sentences versus message structure. In R. Rommetveit and R. M. Blakar (Eds.), *Studies of language, thought and verbal communication.* London: Academic Press, 1979.

Ryle, G. *The concept of mind.* London: Hutchinson, 1949.

Scott, M. B., & Lyman, S. Accounts. *American Sociological Review,* 1968, *33,* 46–62.

Searle, J. R. *Speech acts: An essay in the philosophy of language.* London: Cambridge University Press, 1970.

Shotter, J., & Burton, M. Common sense accounts of human action: The descriptive formulations of Heider, Smedslund, & Ossorio. In L. Wheeler (Ed.), *Review of personality and social psychology* (Vol. 4). Beverly Hills, Calif.: Sage, 1983.

Smedslund, J. Bandura's theory of self-efficacy: A set of commonsense theorems. *Scandinavian Journal of Psychology,* 1978, *19,* 1–14.

Smedslund, J. Analysing the primary code. In D. Olson (Ed.), *The social foundations of language: Essays in honour of J. S. Bruner.* New York: Norton, 1980.

Taylor, C. *The explanation of behavior.* London: Routledge & Kegan Paul, 1964.

Wittgenstein, L. *Remarks on the philosophy of psychology* (Vols. 1 & 2). Oxford: Basil Blackwell, 1980.

Zillmann, D. *Hostility and aggression.* Hillsdale, N.J.: Lawrence Erlbaum, 1979.

[13]

©1990 The Institute of Mind and Behavior, Inc.
The Journal of Mind and Behavior
Summer and Autumn 1990, Volume 11, Numbers 3 and 4
Pages 353 [107] – 368 [122]
ISSN 0271-0137
ISBN 0-930195-05-1

Therapeutic Professions and the Diffusion of Deficit

Kenneth J. Gergen

Swarthmore College

The mental health professions operate largely so as to objectify a language of mental deficit. In spite of their humane intentions, by constructing a reality of mental deficit the professions contribute to hierarchies of privilege, reduce natural interdependencies within the culture, and lend themselves to self-enfeeblement. This infirming of the culture is progressive, such that when common actions are translated into a professionalized language of mental deficit, and this language is disseminated, the culture comes to construct itself in these terms. This leads to an enhanced dependency on the professions and these are forced, in turn, to invent additional terms of mental deficit. Thus, concepts of infirmity have spiraled across the century, and virtually all remaining patterns of action stand vulnerable to deficit translation. Required within the professions are new linguistic formulations that create a reality of relationships without evaluative fulcrum.

How may I fault thee? Let me count the ways. . .

Impulsive personality	*Low self-esteem*
Malingering	*Narcissism*
Reactive depression	*Bulimia*
Anorexia	*Neurasthenia*
Hysteria	*Hypochondriasis*
Mania	*Dependent personality*
Psychopathia	*Frigidity*
Peter Pan syndrome	*Voyeurism*
External control orientation	*Authoritarianism*
Anti-social personality	*Transvestism*
Exhibitionism	*Agoraphobia*
Seasonal affective disorder. . .	

My central concern in this paper is with the effects of the mental health professions on the quality of cultural life. Judging from my many colleagues,

---

Requests for reprints should be sent to Kenneth J. Gergen, Ph.D., Department of Psychology, Swarthmore College, Swarthmore, Pennsylvania 19081.

students and friends engaged in therapeutic practices, I believe there is a strong and genuine commitment to a vision of human betterment. Further, although research results are interminably equivocal, I am convinced that at least from the standpoint of many who seek help, the therapeutic community plays a vital and humane role in cultural life. Yet, my concern in the present offering is with the paradoxical consequences of the prevailing vision of human betterment, and the pervasive dependency of people on these professions for improving their lot. For, there is reason to believe that in the very efforts to furnish effective means of alleviating human suffering, there are important respects in which mental health professionals simultaneously generate a network of increasing entanglements for the culture at large. Such entanglements are not only self-serving for the professions, but add exponentially to the existing sense of deficit. After exploring this progressive infirming of the culture, its causes and proliferating effects, I shall open discussion on possible alternatives to the existing condition.

Mental Language: Reified or Relational

In order to appreciate the nature and magnitude of the problems at stake, a prelude is required. In particular, a distinction must be drawn between existing views of the vocabulary of mind. We commonly employ such terms as "thinking," "feeling," "hoping," "fearing," and the like referentially. That is, we use such terms as if they depicted or reflected actual occurrences. The statement, "I am angry," is intended, by common convention, to describe a state of mind, differing from other states such as joy, embarrassment or ecstasy. The vast majority of therapeutic specialists proceed in much the same manner. Therapists listen for hours to people's accounts in an attempt to ascertain the quality and character of their "inner life" — their cognition, emotions, unarticulated fears, conflicts, illogicalities, blind spots, repressions, "the world as they experience it," and so on. As it is typically presumed, the individual's language provides a vehicle for "inner access" — revealing or setting forth to the professional the character of the not-directly-observed. And, as it is further reasoned, this task is essential to the therapeutic outcome — whether for reasons of furnishing the therapist with information about the problem domain (thus leading to remedial actions on the therapist's part), or for the client-provoking self-insight and clarification, enhancing the sense of autonomy or self-control, instigating a process of catharsis, reducing guilt and so on.

Whether in the therapeutic context or daily life, the presumption that the language of the mind reflects, depicts or refers to actual states may be termed *reificationist*. That is, such an orientation treats as real (as ontological existants) that to which the language seems to refer. As otherwise put, it is to engage in the *fallacy of misplaced concreteness*, treating as concrete the putative object rather than the sign. Certain readers will protest at this juncture at the demotion of what they believe to be a referential language (referring to actual states) to the status of reifying device. They may argue that, "It simply is the case that I have mental states, and when I say I am angry I do so because my state of mind is different from when I am sad or sexy. I speak of anger to reflect real states of anger." However, lest such resistance render the reader insensitive to all that follows, it is useful to make a rapid tour through the groves of intractable problems generated by a realist view of psychological language:

1. How can consciousness turn in upon itself to identify its own states? How can experience become an object to itself? Can a mirror reflect its own image?

2. What are the characteristics of mental states by which we can identify them? By what criteria do we distinguish, let us say, among states of anger, fear and love? What is their color, size, shape, or weight? Why do none of these attributes seem quite applicable? Because our observations of the states prove to us that they are not?

3. How can be we certain when we identify such states correctly? Could other processes (e.g., repression, defense) not prevent accurate self-appraisal? (Perhaps anger is eros after all.)

4. By what criterion could we judge that what we experience as "certain recognition" of a mental state is indeed certain recognition? Would not this recognition require yet another round of self-assessments, the results of which would require additional processes of internal identification, and so on in an infinite regress?

5. Although we may all agree in our use of mental terms (that we experience fear, ecstasy, or joy, for example, on particular occasions) how do we know that our subjective experiences resemble each other? By what process could we possibly determine whether my "fear" is equivalent to yours? How then do I know I possess what everyone else calls "fear"?

6. How are we to account for the disappearance from the culture of many mental terms popular in previous centuries, along with the passing fashions in mental terminology of the present century? (Whatever happened to melancholy, sublimity, neuralgia, the inferiority complex, and the adolescent identity crisis?) Have the words disappeared because such processes no longer exist in mortal minds?

7. How are we to account for the substantial differences in psychological vocabulary from one culture to another? Did we once have the same mental events as the primitive tribesman, for example, the emotion of *fago*, described by Lutz (1988) in her studies of the Ifaluk? Have we lost the capacity to experience this emotion? Is it lurking there within the core of our being, buried beneath layers of Westernized, industrialized acculturation?

Mental realists have yet to furnish viable and compelling answers to any of these perennial conundrums. Thus, although we need not go so far as to doubt that "something is going on" when we report a mental state, to treat the reports as descriptions, pictures or maps of identifiable events is essentially to reify the existing language practices.

Let us contrast the reificationist orientation to mental language with yet another. Following Wittgenstein (1963) in this case, let us abandon the view of mental language as a referential picture of inner states, and consider such language as a constituent feature of social relationships. That is, we may venture that psychological language obtains its meaning and significance from the way in which it is used in human interaction. Thus, when I say "I am unhappy" about a given state of affairs, the term "unhappy" is not rendered meaningful or appropriate according to its relationship to the state of my neurons or my phenomenological field. Rather, the report plays a significant social function. It may be used, for example, to call an end to a set of deteriorating conditions, enlist support and/or encouragement, or to invite futher opinion. Both the conditions under which the report can be used and the functions it can serve are also circumscribed by social convention. The phrase, "I am deeply sad" can be satisfactorily reported at the death of a close relative but not the demise of a spring moth. A report of depression can secure others' concern and support; however it cannot easily function as a farewell, an invitation to laughter, or a commendation. In this sense mental language is more like having a nine iron when shooting from a sandtrap than possessing a mirror of the interior, more like a strong grip between trapeze artists than a map of inner conditions. We shall call this orientation to mental language *relational,* in its emphasis on the use of mental language within ongoing relationships.

(It should be noted that the relational view of mental discourse does not commit one to a "skin deep" view of such language. Rather, mental terms are only constituent parts of full blown action patterns – patterns that may engage one fully. To "do anger" properly, for example, may require an enormous recruitment of bodily resources – with mental language playing but a minor part in the performance. For a more extended account, see Gergen and Gergen, 1988.)

Invitations to Infirmity

The pervasive stance toward psychological language in Western culture is decidedly reificationist. We generally accept persons' accounts of their subjective stats as valid (at least for them). If sophisticated, we may wonder if they are fully aware of their feelings, or have been misled in an attempt to protect themselves from what is "really" there. And, if scientific in bent, we may wish to know the distribution of various mental states (e.g., loneliness, depression) in the society more generally, the conditions under which they occur (e.g., stress, burnout), and the means for their alleviation (e.g., the comparative efficacy of differing therapies). However, we are unlikely to question the existence of the reality to which such terms seem to refer; and because the prevailing ontology of mental life remains generally unchallenged, we seldom inquire into the utility or desirability of such terms in daily life. If the language exists because the mental states exist, there is little reason to ask about preferences. To do so would be tantamount to asking whether we approve the roundness of the world.

Yet, if we view psychological discourse from a relational perspective, the language of the mind loses its rhetorical capacity as "truth bearing." One cannot claim rights to language use on grounds that existing terms "name what there is." Rather, significant questions are invited concerning the functions of existing terminologies in maintaining or changing the patterns of cultural life. What are the effects on human relationships of the prevailing vocabularies of the mind? Given our goals for human betterment, do these vocabularies facilitate or obstruct? And, most important for present purposes, what kinds of social patterns are facilitated (or prevented) by the existing vocabulary of psychological deficit? How do the terms of mental health professions, terms such as "neurosis," "cognitive dysfunction," "depression," "post-traumatic stress disorder," "character disorder," "repression," "narcissism" and so on, function within the culture more generally? Do such terms lend themselves to desirable forms of human relationship, should the vocabulary be expanded, are there more promising alternatives? There are no simple answers to such questions; however, neither is there at present a prevailing dialogue concerning such issues. My purpose here is not so much to develop a final answer as to generate a forum for continuing discussion.

Grounds for such discussion have been laid in several relevant arenas. In a range of pointed volumes Thomas Szasz (1961, 1963, 1987) has demonstrated that concepts of mental illness are not demanded by observation. Rather, he proposes they function much as social myths, and are used (or misused, from his perspective) largely as means of social control. Sarbin and Mancuso (1980) echo these arguments in their focus on the concept of schizophrenia as a social construction. Similarly, Ingelby (1980) has demonstrated the ways in which categories of mental illness are socially negotiated so as to serve the values or ideological investments of the profession. Kovel (1980) proposes that the mental health professions are essentially forms of industry that operate largely in the service of existing economic structures. Feminist thinkers have also explored the ways in which nosologies of illness, diagnosis and treatment have all been biased in favor a patriarchal system (Brodsky and Hare-Mustin, 1980; Hare-Mustin and Marecek, 1988).

Let us extend the implications of such discussions to consider the functioning of mental deficit language in social life. Again, there is much to be said on this matter, and not all of it is critical. On the positive side, for example, the vocabulary of the mental health professions does serve to render the alien familiar, and thus less fearsome. Rather than viewing non-normative activities as "the work of the devil" or "frighteningly strange," for example, they are given professional labels, signifying that indeed, they are perfectly reasonable by scientific standards. At the same time, this professional transformation of the unusual invites one to replace repugnance with more humane reactions — sympathetic reactions of the kind displayed toward the physically ill. Further, because the mental health professions are allied with science, and science appears to be a progressive or problem solving activity, such labels also invite a hopeful attitude toward the future. One need not labor under the belief that today's strangeness is forever.

For most of us these represent improvements of the present vocabulary of mental deficit over predecessors of yore. Yet, optimism on such matters is hardly merited. For there is a substantial "down side" to existing intelligibilities, and as I shall hope to demonstrate later in this paper, these problems are of continuously increasing magnitude. As an opening to the problem, we must consider the functioning of mental deficit vocabularies in engendering and facilitating each of the following processes.

Social Hierarchy

Although attempting to occupy a position of scientific neutrality, it has long been recognized that the helping professions are premised on certain assumptions of the cultural good (Hartmann, 1960; Masserman, 1960). Professional visions of "healthy functioning" are suffused with cultural ideals of personhood (London, 1986; Margolis, 1966). In this context we find, then, that mental deficit terms operate as evaluative devices, demarking the position of individuals along culturally implicit dimensions of good and bad. We may often feel a degree of sympathy for the person who complains of being incapacitated by depression, anxiety, or a Type A personality. However, such sympathies may often be tinged with a sense of self-satisfaction, for the complaint simultaneously casts us into a position of superiority. In each case the other reveals a failure — insufficient buoyancy, levelheadedness, calm, control — and thereby defines others as superior in these regards. While such results may seem inevitable, even desirable as a means of sustaining cultural values, it is vital to realize that (1) the existence of the terms invites such rituals of degradation (Goffman, 1961), and (2) other vocabularies could carry out the same descriptive work without such perjorative effects.

This is to say, that the existence of a vocabulary of deficit is akin to the availability of weapons; their very presence invites certain patterns of action, in this case the creation of implicit hierarchies. The greater the number of criteria for mental well-being, the greater number of ways in which one can be rendered superior (or inferior) in comparison to others. Further, the same events can be indexed in other ways, with far different outcomes. Through skilled language use one might reconstruct depression as "psychic incubation," anxiety as "heightened sensitivity," and Type A freneticism as "Protestant work ethic." Such use of language would either reverse or erase the existing hierarchies.

Reduced Interdependency

Because mental deficit terms imply the existence of "problems in need of attention," and the mental health professions are accorded a certain degree of expertise on such matters, the use of the vocabulary contributes to the institutionalization of treatment. In the same way that attributing teenage criminality to economic deprivation, deteriorated family conditions, or lack of recreational outlets would each have different behavioral or policy implications, attributing non-normative actions to mental deficits suggests that professional help is required. Yet, when such help is sought, the discussion of "the problem" is removed from its generating context and reestablished within the professional sphere. Or, in other terms, the mental health professions appropriate the process of realignment that would naturally occur in the non-professional context. One may venture that processes of natural realignment are often slow, anguished, brutal, or befuddled, and that life is too short and too precious to "wait and see." However, the result nevertheless is that problems otherwise requiring concerted participation of organically related persons are removed from their ecological niche. Marriage partners carry out more intimate communication with their therapists than with each other, even saving significant insights for revelation in the therapeutic hour. Parents discuss their children's problems with specialists, or send problem children to treatment centers, and thereby reduce the possibility for authentic (unselfconscious) communication with their offspring. Organizations placing alcoholic executives in treatment programs thereby reduce the kind of self-reflexive discussions that would elucidate their contribution to the problem. In each case, tissues of organic interdependency are injured or atrophy.

Self-Enfeeblement

Because of their reifying capacities, mental deficit terms are essentialist in character. That is, they operate so as to establish the essential nature of the person being described. They designate a characteristic of the individual perduring across time and situation, and which must be confronted if the person's actions are to be properly understood. The result of deploying mental deficit terms is thus to inform the recipient that "the problem" is not circumscribed, limited in time and space to a particular domain of his/her life, but that it is fully general. He or she carries the deficit, like a cancer, from one situation to another, and like a birthmark or a fingerprint, as the textbooks say, the deficit will inevitably manifest itself. In effect, once people understand their actions in terms of mental deficits, they are sensitized to the problematic potential in all their activities, the ways in which they are infected or diminished. The weight of "the problem" now expands manyfold; it is as inescapable as their own shadow. The sense of enfeeblement becomes complete.

There are other lamentable repercussions of mental deficit language. As existentialist theorists argue, because such language is embedded in a deterministic worldview, in which persons' actions are caused by their essences, people cease to experience their actions as voluntary (Bugenthal, 1965). They feel their actions to be outside the realm of choice, inevitable and unchangeable, unless they place themselves – dependently – in professional hands. Further, as Sparks (1989) has proposed, by conceptually placing problems within the personality structure of the individual, professionals suggest to people that their problems are virtually intractable.

The Process of Progressive Infirmity

It is a central contention of the present paper that problems of the preceding variety are not simply pervasive in modern culture; rather, they are expanding exponentially within the present century. This process of progressive infirmity now requires attention. The concept of neurosis did not originate until the mid-18th century. (Had such problems simply escaped general notice for so many centuries?) In 1769 William Cullen, a Scottish physician, elucidated the four major classes of *morbi nervini*. These included *Comota* (reduced voluntary movements, with drowsiness or loss of consciousness), the *Adynamiae* (diminished involuntary movements), *Spasmi* (abnormal movement of the muscles), and *Vesaniae* (altered judgment without coma) [see Lopez-Pinero's 1983 account]. Yet, even in 1840, with the first official attempt in the United States to tabulate mental disorder, categorization was crude. It proved satisfactory, indeed to use only a single category, in which idiotic and insane persons were grouped together (Spitzer and Williams, 1985). At present, the American Psychiatric Association's 1987 *Diagnostic and Statistical Manual of Mental Disorders*, third edition, revised [DSM-III-R] lists some 200 categories of mental disorder. Many additional "problematic behaviors" (e.g., stress, burnout, erotomania, etc.) are discussed and treated within the profession more generally. As the language of psychological deficit has expanded, so have we increased the culture's hierarchies of discrimination, damaged the naturalized patterns of interdependence, and expanded the arena of self-deprecation. In effect, as the language of deficit has proliferated, so has the culture become progressively infirmed.

On the optimistic side, one might propose that the increase in the language of deficit reflects an incremental sharpening of our capacities to distinguish among the existing array of psychological states and conditions. However, such a proposal grows from the same reificationist soil that proved so barren in our initial proceedings. There is little sense to be made of the supposition that the enormous proliferation in the language of psychological deficit represents a refinement in linkages between discourse and the mental world as it really is. How then are we to account for the proliferation of such language and the consequent infirming of the culture? Here again the relational view of language becomes useful, for as we consider the functions of discourse in human relationships it is possible to discern a pattern of formidable consequence. In particular, we may locate a cyclical process which, once activated, operates to expand the domain of deficit discourse in ever increasing degrees. We are not dealing, then, with an accidental surge in such discourse, but with a systematic process that feeds upon itself to engender an exponentially increasing infirmity.

For analytic purposes the cycle of progressive infirmity may be broken into four major stages. In actual practice, events in each of these stages may be confounded, with temporal ordering seldom smooth, and with exceptions at every turn. However for purposes of clarity, the cycle of progressive infirmity may be outlined as follows:

Deficit Translation

Let us view the situation of mental health professionals in the following way: they confront a client group whose lives are managed in terms of a common or everyday discourse. Because life management seems impossible in terms of everyday understandings individuals in the client group seek professional help. Or, in effect, they seek advanced (more objective, discerning, etc.) forms of understanding. In this sense it is incumbent upon the professional to (1) furnish an alternative discourse (theoretical framwork, nosology, etc.), and (2) translate the problem as presented in the daily language into the uncommon language of the profession. In terms of the preceding this means that problems understood in the profane or marketplace language of the culture must be translated into the sacred or professional language of mental deficit. A person whose habits of cleanliness are excessive by common standards becomes an "obsessive compulsive," one who rests the morning in bed becomes "depressive," one who feels he is not liked is redefined as "paranoid," and so on. (An extended treatment of the way in which the client's childhood memories are reformulated by the psychoanalyst in terms of Freudian theory of psychosexual development is furnished by Spence, 1982.) For the client such translations may be essential, for not only do they assure that the professional is doing a proper job, but that the problem is well recognized or understood within the profession.

Cultural Dissemination

The mental health professional generally follows a scientific mode of analysis in which the attempt is to establish systematic ontologies or inclusive categories for all that exists within a given domain (e.g., animal or plant species, tables of chemical elements). The DSM-III-R is perhaps the most apt exemplar within the field of mental health, in its attempt to reduce all existing problems to a systematic and finite array of categories. The result of this mode of procedure, however, is to universalize existing problems. It is to inform the client that his/her problem is but an isolated instance of a larger class. Other instances in the class may thus be presumed. It is partly for this reason that pressures are created for a broad dissemination of mental deficit language. In the same way that signs of breast cancer, diabetes or venereal disease should become common knowledge within the culture, so should citizens be able to recognize symptoms of stress, alcoholism, and depression. Thus, mental deficit information is featured in undergraduate curricula, popular magazines, television programming, newspaper features, and the like. (Because of the exotic and self-relevant character of such information, there is also a broad audience for such materials.) The result is, however, a continuous insinuation of the professional language into the sphere of daily relationships.

Cultural Construction

As intelligibilities of deficit are disseminated into the culture at large, they become absorbed into the common language. They become part of "what everybody knows" about human behavior. In this sense, terms such as neurosis, stress, alcoholism and depression are no longer "professional property." They have been "given away" by the profession to the public. Terms such as split personality, identity crisis, PMS (pre-menstrual syndrome) and mid-life crisis also enjoy a certain degree of popularity. And, as such terms make their way into the cultural vernacular, they become available for the construction of everyday reality. Shirley is not simply "too fat"; she has "obese eating habits"; Fred doesn't simply "hate gays," but is "homophobic"; and so on.

Nor is such construction limited to the redefinition of problems already recognized. That is, as deficit terms become increasingly available for making the social world intelligible, that world becomes increasingly populated by deficit. Events which passed unnoticed become candidates for interpretation; events once viewed as "good and proper" can now be reconceptualized as problematic, and in the extreme case recognized symptoms come to serve as cultural models. (Consider the spread of "bulimia" once it was recognized as a "common problem.") Once such terms as "stress" and "occupational burn-out" enter the commonsense vernacular, they become lenses through which any working professional can reexamine his/her life and find it wanting. What was valued as "active ambition" can now be reconstructed as "workaholic"; the "smart dresser" can be redefined as "narcissistic"; and the "autonomous and self-directed man" becomes "defended against his emotions." Furnish the population with hammers of mental deficit, and the whole world needs pounding.

Vocabulary Expansion

As individual actions are increasingly identified in terms of mental deficit terminology, so does the culture generate a new wave of candidates for professional help. Counseling, weekend self-enrichment programs, and programs of personality refurbishment may represent a first line of dependence; all allow people to escape the uneasy sense that they are "not all they should be." Others may seek more direct means of help for their "eating disorders," "incest victimization," or "post traumatic stress disorders." At this point, however, the stage is set for the final revolution in the cycle of progressive infirmity. For as the layperson approaches the profession with a now-appropriated professional discourse, the role of the professional is threatened. If the client has already identified the problem accurately, and knows (as in many cases) what is commonly to be done at the professional level, then the window of professional expertise is increasingly closed. (The worst case scenario would be that people learn to diagnose and treat themselves within their family and friendship circles, thus rendering the professional redundant.) In this way there is a constant pressure placed upon the professional to "advance" understanding, to spawn "more sophisticated" terminology, and to generate new insights and forms of therapy. It is not that the shift in emphasis from classic psychoanalysis to neo-analysis to object relations, for example, is required by an increasingly sensitive understanding of mental dynamics. Indeed, each wave sets the stage for its own recession and replacement; as therapeutic vocabularies become common sense the therapist is propelled into new modes of departure. The ever-shifting sea of therapeutic fads and fashions is no mere defect in the profession; rapid change is virtually demanded by a public whose discourse is increasingly "psychologized."

Progressive Infirmity: No Exit?

A recent circular invited participation in a San Diego conference on theory, research and treatment of addiction. As the circular announced, "Addictive behavior is arguably the number one health and social problem facing our country today." Among the "addictions" to be discussed were exercise, religion, eating, work, and sex. New domains of behavior now enter the ledger of deficit, subject to broad concern and professional treatment. The construction of infirmity expands again, and there is no principled means of termination. When the culture is furnished a language of mental deficit, and persons are increasingly understood in these ways, an increasing population of "patients" is created. This population, in turn, forces the profession to expand its vocabulary and thus the array of mental deficit terms available for cultural use. More problems are constructed, more help sought, and the array of deficit terms again presses forward. Again, one can scarcely view this cycle as smooth and undisrupted. Some schools of therapy remain committed to a single vocabulary; others have little interest in dissemination; some professionals attempt to speak with clients only in the "common language," and many popular concepts within the culture lose currency over time. Rather, we are speaking here of a general drift, an historical tendency of the kind, for example, that enables American psychiatric discourse to move from the restricted domain of a single journal (The *American Journal of Insanity*) in the mid-1800s to a three volume handbook – with over 50 chapters – a century later that has made therapeutic training an essential part of pastoral preparation, and that has made clinical psychology one of the fastest growing professions of the century.

I am in no way attempting to allocate blame for this trajectory. For the most part it is a necessary byproduct of the earnest and humane attempt to enhance the culture's life quality. With certain variations in the logic of the cycle, it is not unlike the trajectories spawned by both the medical and legal professions – toward increased medical needs on the one hand and the increased forms of litigation on the other. However, to the extent that the mental health professions are concerned with cultural life quality, discussion of progressive infirmity should become focal. Are there important limitations on the above arguments; are there signs of a leveling effect; are there means of reducing the proliferation of an enfeebling discourse?

I have no ready remedy in hand for the termination of the cycle. However, I do feel that the same logic that enables such a cycle to be articulated does invite a dialogue from which solutions might be derived. For, as we have seen, progressive infirmity is favored by the reificationist assumption of mental language. It is when we believe that the words for mental deficit stand in a referential relationship to processes or mechanisms in the head that the problem begins. It is when we believe that people actually possess mental processes such as repression, for example, that we can comfortably characterize them as repressed. At the outset, then, some form of generalized reeducation in the functions of language might be favored.

Of course it is absurdly optimistic to believe that either the formal or informal educational processes could significantly alter the picture theory of language, and the companionate assumption of mind-body dualism, both so central to Western tradition. More promising is the development of alternative vocabularies within the mental health profession, vocabularies that (1) do not trace problematic behavior to psychological sources within single individuals, and (2) ultimately erase the concept of "problem behavior" itself. I am speaking here first of the development of a vocabulary of relatedness that would come to equal the rhetorical power of individualized language in making the social world intelligible. We have innumerable terms for characterizing individuals; and when confronting the social world we rapidly and securely fall back on this vocabulary. For example, we see an individual acting in a particular way, and we can scarcely avoid characterizing these actions as outward signs of inner states of depression, fear, anxiety and the like. The individualized form of accounting is ready at hand. It is far more difficult, however, to view such behavior as indicative of processes of relatedness, signs of particular forms of interaction. Such conclusions are not conceptually impossible; we simply have little vocabulary at hand for making the world intelligible in this way. While we have a highly nuanced vocabulary of individual players we are virtually inarticulate regarding the games in which they are embedded. With an adequate vocabulary in hand, we might reconstruct depression as a constituent part of a relational form. In the same way that a serve is essential for the game of tennis, and the consumption of a wafer for Catholic mass, so are "depressed actions" essential constituents of certain kinds of interaction sequences (see Gergen and Gergen, 1988). The same kind of translation could be undertaken with the full body of psychological terminology available for common use.

The impetus toward relational intelligibilities is already manifest in the mental health professions. Harry Stack Sullivan's emphasis on the embeddedness of symptoms in interpersonal relations represented an important beginning. In varying degrees the work of theorists in family systems, second order cybernetics, social ecology, stragetic therapy, contextual therapy, and therapeutic communication processes (see Hoffman's 1981 summary) all extend and elaborate a relational perspective. For many social practitioners the language of mental deficit also stands inadequate, and means are sought to generate understandings of individuals-in-relationship (Kirk, Siporin, and Kutchins, 1989). And too, these ventures share much with present theorizing in social constructionism, discourse processes, parent-child interaction, conversational management, ethnomethodology, and organizational management. With cooperative efforts across these otherwise isolated endeavors, the possibilities for new and significant forms of intelligibility seem enormous.

With the development of relational intelligibilities may ultimately come the demise of the category "problem behavior" itself. As we come to see human actions as embedded within larger units, parts of wholes, such actions cease to be "of themselves." There are no problem behaviors independent of arrangements of social interdependency. However, we need not capitulate to, the presently alluring move of shifting blame from individual to group. (The concept of "dysfunctional family" or "perverse triangle," for example, simply sets the stage for a new cycle of impairment.) For, it is also clear from a relational standpoint that the language of evaluation, blame, and thus problematics is born of relatedness; such language functions so as to coordinate the activities of individuals around ends they signify as valuable. Thus, the labeling of actions as in some way "problematic" is itself an outcome of relational process. In this way we see that there are no intrinsic or essential "goods" or goals to which individuals or groups should necessarily strive. There are only goods and goals (and concomitant failures) within particular systems of understanding. The professional need not be concerned, then, with "improvement" as a real-world challenge. (Depressive activity, for example, is not inherently problematic, and may serve an important function in maintaining the well-being of a group from its standpoint.) Rather, the emphasis may appropriately shift to enhancing consciousness of the larger system of interdependencies in which such evaluations are generated, and the capacity of relationships for coordinated integration into the larger network.

References

American Psychiatric Association. (1987). *Diagnostic and statistical manual of mental disorders* (third edition, revised). Washington, D.C.: Author.

Brodsky, A.M., and Hare-Mustin, R.T. (1980). *Women and psychotherapy: An assessment of research and practice.* New York: Guilford.

Bugenthal, J.F.T. *The search for authenticity.* New York: Hold, Rinehart & Winston.

Gergen, K.J., and Gergen, M.M. (1988). Narrative and the self as relationship. In L. Berkowitz (Ed.), *Advances in experimental social psychology* (pp. 17–56). New York: Academic Press.

Goffman, E. (1961). *Asylums: Essays on the social situation of mental patients and other inmates.* Garden City, New Jersey: Doubleday.

Hare-Mustin, R., and Marecek, J. (1988). The meaning of difference: Gender theory, postmodernism and psychology. *American Psychologist, 43,* 455–464.

Hartmann, H. (1960). *Psychoanalysis and moral values.* New York: International Universities Press.

Hoffman, L. (1981). *Foundations of family therapy.* New York: Basic.

Ingleby, D. (1980). Understanding mental illness. In D. Ingleby (Ed.), *Critical psychiatry: The politics of mental health* (pp. 23–71). New York: Pantheon.

Kirk, S., Siporin, M., and Kutchins, H. (1989). The prognosis for social work diagnosis. *Social Casework: The Journal of Contemporary Social Work, 70,* 295–304.

Kovel, J. (1980). The American mental health industry. In D. Ingleby (Ed.), *Critical psychiatry: The politics of mental health* (pp. 72–101). New York: Pantheon.

THE DIFFUSION OF DEFICIT 367 [121]

London, P. (1986). *The modes and morals of psychotherapy*. New York: Hemisphere Publishing.

Lopez-Pinero, J.M. (1983). *Historical origins of the concept of neurosis* [D. Berrios, Translator]. Cambridge: Cambridge University Press.

Lutz, C. (1988). *Unnatural emotions*. Chicago: University of Chicago Press.

Margolis, J. (1966). *Psychotherapy and morality*. New York: Random House.

Masserman, J. (1960). *Psychoanalysis and human values*. New York: Grune and Stratton.

Rose, N. (1985). *The psychological complex*. London: Routledge & Kegan Paul.

Sarbin, T.R., and Mancuso, J.C. (1980). *Schizophrenia: Medical diagnosis or moral verdict?* Elmsford, New York: Pergamon.

Sparks, P. (1989). *Causal attributions of personality*. Unpublished doctoral dissertation, Oxford University.

Spence, D. (1982). *Narrative truth and historical truth*. New York: Norton.

Spitzer, R.L., and Williams, J.B. (1985). Classification of mental disorders. In H.L. Kaplan and B.J. Sadock (Eds.), *Comprehensive textbook of psychiatry* (pp. 580-602). Baltimore: Williams & Wilkins.

Szasz, T.S. (1961). *The myth of mental illness: Foundations of a theory of personal conduct*. New York: Hoeber-Harper.

Szasz, T.S. (1963). *Law, liberty and psychiatry: An inquiry into the social uses of mental health practices*. New York: Macmillan.

Szasz, T.S. (1987). *Insanity: The idea and its consequences*. New York: John Wiley.

Wittgenstein, L. (1963). *Philosophical investigations* [G. Anscombe, Translator]. New York: Macmillan.

[14]

NARRATIVE AND THE SELF AS RELATIONSHIP

Kenneth J. Gergen

DEPARTMENT OF PSYCHOLOGY
SWARTHMORE COLLEGE
SWARTHMORE, PENNSYLVANIA 19081

Mary M. Gergen

DEPARTMENT OF PSYCHOLOGY
PENNSYLVANIA STATE UNIVERSITY
DELAWARE COUNTY CAMPUS
MEDIA, PENNSYLVANIA 19063

> We belong to the sound of the words
> we've both fallen under.
>
> (Pat Benatar)

I. Introduction

This is a story about stories —and most particularly, stories of self. Most of us begin our encounters with stories at our parents' knees. Through fairy tales, folk tales, legends, and myths we receive our first organized account of human action. Stories continue to absorb us as we read novels, biography, and history; they occupy us at the movies, the theater, and before the television set. And, possibly because of this intimate and longstanding acquaintanceship, stories also serve as a critical means by which we make ourselves intelligible within the social world. We tell extended stories about our childhoods, our relations with family members, our years at school, our first love affair, the development of our thinking on a given subject, and so on. We also tell stories about last night's party, this morning's class, or lunch with a companion. We may even create a story to relate how we cut ourselves while shaving or scorched the breakfast muffins. In each case, we use the story form to identify ourselves to others and to ourselves. So prevalent is the story process in western culture that Bruner (1986) has gone as far as to suggest a genetic proclivity for narrative understanding. Whether biologically prepared or not, one can scarcely underestimate the importance of stories in our lives and the extent to which they serve as vehicles for rendering selves intelligible.

Yet, to say that we use stories to make ourselves comprehensible does not go far enough. Not only do we tell our lives as stories, but there is a significant sense in which our relationships with each other are lived out in narrative form. The ideal life, Nietzsche proposed, is one which corresponds to the ideal story; each act is coherently related to all others and there is nothing to spare (Nehamas, 1986). More cogently, Hardy (1968) has written, "we dream in narrative, daydream in narrative, remember, anticipate, hope, despair, believe, doubt, plan, revise, criticize, construct, gossip, learn, hate and love by narrative" (p. 5). Elaborating this view, MacIntyre (1981) proposes that enacted narratives form the basis of moral character. The present analysis stops short of saying that lives *are* narrative events (and here we are in agreement with Mink, 1970). Stories are, after all, forms of accounting, and it seems misleading to equate the account with its putative object. However, narrative accounts are embedded within social action. Events are rendered socially visible through narratives, and they are typically used to establish expectations for future events. Because of the immersion of narrative in the events of daily life, these events will become laden with a storied sense. Events will acquire the reality of "a beginning," "a climax," "a low point," "an ending," and so on. People will live out the events in such a way that they and others will index them in just this way. This is not to say, then, that life copies art, but rather, that art becomes the vehicle through which the reality of life is generated. In a significant sense, then, we live by stories—both in the telling and the doing of self.

In this article we shall attempt to explore the nature of stories, both as they are told and lived in social life. We shall begin with an examination of story form— or more formally, the structure of narrative accounts. We shall then turn to the manner in which narratives of the self are constructed within social life and the uses to which they are put. As our story advances it shall become increasingly clear that narratives of the self are not fundamentally possessions of the individual; rather they are products of social interchange—possessions of the socius. This analysis will set the stage for a discussion of lived narrative. Here we shall propose that the traditional concept of individual selves is fundamentally problematic. What have served as individual traits, mental processes, or personal characteristics can promisingly be viewed as constituents of relational forms. The form of these relationships is that of the narrative sequence. Thus, by the end of our story we shall find that the individual self has all but vanished into the world of relationship.

II. Self-Narratives

A. THE STRUCTURE OF SELF-NARRATIVE

Writers of fiction, philosophy, and psychology have frequently portrayed human consciousness as a continuous flow. One does not confront a series of segmented snapshots, as it is said, but an ongoing process. Similarly, in our experience of self and others we seem to encounter not a series of discrete, endlessly juxtaposed moments, but goal-directed, coherent sequences. As many historiographers have suggested, accounts of human action can scarcely proceed without temporal embedding. To understand is indeed to place events within a context of preceding and subsequent events. To bring the matter home, one's view of self in a given moment is fundamentally nonsensical unless it can be linked in some fashion with one's own past. Suddenly and momentarily to see oneself as "aggressive," "poetic," or "out of control," for example, would seem whimsical or mysterious. However, when aggression follows longstanding and intensifying antagonism, it is rendered sensible. In the same way, being poetic or out of control can be comprehended when placed in the context of one's personal history. It is just this point which has led a number of commentators to conclude that understanding of human action can proceed on none other than narrative grounds (MacIntyre, 1981; Mink, 1970; Gergen, 1984a).

We shall employ the term *self-narrative* (Gergen & Gergen, 1984) to refer to the individual's account of the relationship among self-relevant events across time. In developing a self-narrative the individual attempts to establish coherent connections among life events (Cohler, 1979; Kohli, 1981). Rather than seeing one's life as simply "one damned thing after another," the individual attempts to understand life events as systematically related. They are rendered intelligible by locating them in a sequence or "unfolding process" (deWaele & Harré, 1976). One's present identity is thus not a sudden and mysterious event, but a sensible result of a life story. As Bettelheim (1976) has argued, such creations of narrative order may be essential in giving one's life a sense of meaning and direction.

Before embarking on this analysis a word must be said about the relationship between the concept of self-narrative and related theoretical notions. In particular, the concept of self-narrative bears an affinity with a variety of constructs falling generally within the domains of cognitive, rule–role, and dramaturgical theory. However, there are significant distinctions. The concepts of rule (Harré & Secord, 1972), narrative grammar (Mancuso & Sarbin, 1983), scripts (Schank & Abelson, 1977), story schema (Mandler, 1978), and predictability tree (Kelly & Keil, 1985) have all been used to account for the psychological basis for understanding and/or directing sequences of action across time. That is, theorists in each of these cases have tended to focus on psychological structures that enable people to understand or organize inputs into narrative structures or to interrogate the relevant rule, grammar, script, or schema for indications of proper or appropriate conduct. In contrast to these accounts, we view self-narratives as properties of social accounts or discourse. Narratives are, in effect, social constructions, undergoing continuous alteration as interaction progresses. The individual in this case does not consult an internal narrative for information. Rather, the self-narrative is a linguistic implement constructed by people in relationships and employed in relationships to sustain, enhance, or impede various actions. It may be used to indicate future actions but it is not in itself the basis for such action. In this sense, self-narratives function much as histories within society do more generally. They are symbolic systems used for such social purposes as justification, criticism, and social solidification.

If our initial concern is with narratives of the self, we require a working definition of the narrative. How is this form of social accounting to be differentiated from others? This issue is far more than definitional. Narrative forms of explication are a frequent means of generating what we take to be true or accurate accounts of self. Whether it is a matter of revealing one's early experiences or relating events of the day, one is typically attempting to furnish an accurate reflection of the happenings in one's life. As it is usually assumed, such accounts are event driven. That is, the story ideally operates as a mirror to nature: the character of events drives the character of the story. Yet, as inquiries by Loftus (1979), Wegner, Giuliano, and Hertel (1985), and Spence (1982) indicate, what is remembered and how events are structured is vitally dependent on the social processes in which people are immersed. Memory is not so much an individual as it is a social process. In the present context, conventions of narrative construction furnish just such influences. Thus, an explication of the rules or elements of proper story telling establish the criteria for what we take to be truthful accounts. As we understand the restrictions on how we tell stories about ourselves, we confront the limits of potential for "truth telling." If we do not wish to become unintelligible, we cannot tell stories that break the rules of proper narrative. To go beyond the rule is to engage in tales told by idiots. Thus, rather than being driven by facts, we find that truth telling in this instance is largely governed by a forestructure of conventions for narrative construction.

There has been a variety of attempts to outline the components of the well-formed narrative. They have occurred within domains of literary criticism (Frye, 1957) semiotics (Propp, 1968; Rimmon-Kenan, 1983), historiography (Mink, 1970; Gallie, 1964), and certain sectors of social science (Labov, 1981; Sutton-Smith, 1979; Mandler, 1984). The present attempt draws much from these various analyses. It synthesizes a variety of common agreements, excludes certain distinctions that seem peripheral (e.g., perspective, characterization), and adds ingredients necessary to understand why stories possess a sense of direction and drama. In our view, the following components appear to be especially important to the construction of intelligible narrative in contemporary western culture.

a. The Establishment of a Valued End Point. In order to count as an acceptable story one must first establish "the point" of the story, an event to be explained, or "a point" on the informal level. The selected end point, typically saturated with value, is understood to be desirable or undesirable. For example, the end point may be the protagonist's well-being ("how I narrowly escaped death"), the discovery of something precious ("how we fell in love"), personal loss ("how I lost the debate") and so on. As MacIntyre (1981) has written, "Narrative requires an evaluative framework in which good or bad character helps to produce unfortunate or happy outcomes" (p. 456). We have few tales about how leaves are scattered in the wind or sands swirled in the ocean tides, primarily because these outcomes have no common cultural value. As it is also seen, this initial rule for the well-formed narrative immediately introduces a nonobjective ingredient. The shared values of the interlocutors determine what is counted an appropriate end point, and such values cannot be derived from events in themselves.

b. Selection of Events Relevant to the Goal State. Once a goal is established it serves to dictate the kinds of events that can subsequently figure in the account. The myriad candidates for "eventhood" are greatly reduced by the establishment of the end point or goal; narrative structure prevents the telling of "the whole truth." An intelligible story is one in which events are selected that serve to make the goal more or less probable. Thus, if one's story is about the winning of a soccer match ("how we won the game"), the kinds of events that are relevant are those that bring the goal closer or make it more distant (e.g., "Tom's first kick bounced off the goal, but with a thrust of his head he was able to deflect the ball into the net"). Only at the risk of inanity would one introduce into the story of a soccer match a note on 15th century monastery life or a hope for future space travel.

c. The Ordering of Events. Once a goal state has been established and events are selected relevant to the achievement or loss of this state, the events are typically placed in an ordered arrangement. As Ong (1982) indicates, the bases for such order (e.g., importance, interest value, recency) may change with history. However, perhaps the most widely used contemporary convention of ordering is that of linear, temporal sequence. For example, certain events are said to occur at the beginning of the football match and these precede events that are said to take place toward the middle and the end. It is tempting to say that the sequence of related events should match the sequence in which the events actually occurred. However, this would be to confuse the rules of intelligible rendering with what is the case. Temporal ordering is, after all, a convention, which employs an internally coherent system of signs; its features are not required by what is the case. Rather, the system may be applied or not to what is the case depending on one's purposes. Clock time may not be effective, for example, if one wishes to speak of one's "experience of time passing in the dentist's chair"; nor is it adequate if one wishes to describe relativity theory in physics. That yesterday preceded today is a conclusion demanded by rules of rhetoric.

d. Establishing Causal Linkages. By contemporary standards the ideal narrative is one in which the events preceding the goal state are causally linked. Each event should be a product of that which has preceded. ("Because the rain came we fled indoors." "As a result of his operation he couldn't meet his class.") This is not to subscribe to a narrow, Humean view of causality. Rather, causal accounts are discursive forms in which the specific articulation of one event or series of events is said to require the occurrence of a subsequent event. What may be included within the acceptable range of causal forms is historically and culturally dependent. Thus, many scientists wish to limit discussions of causality to the Humean variety; social philosophers often prefer to view human action as caused by reason; botanists often find it more convenient to employ teleological forms of causality. Regardless of one's preference in causal models, when events within a narrative are related in an interdependent fashion the outcome approximates more closely the well-formed story.

e. Demarcation Signs.   Most properly formed stories employ signals to indicate a beginning and ending. As Young (1982) has proposed, the narrative is "framed" by various rule-governed devices that indicate when one is entering the "tale world," or the world of the story. "Once upon a time . . .," "Did you hear this one . . .," "You can't imagine what happened to me on the way over here . . .," or "Let me tell you why I'm so happy . . ." would all be signals to the audience that a narrative is to follow. Endings may also be signaled by phrases (e.g., "So now you know what happened . . .") but need not be. Laughter at the end of a joke may indicate the ending of the tale world; often the description of the story's point is sufficient to indicate that the tale world is terminated.

Does it matter whether narratives are well formed in matters of daily living? From what we have said, the use of narrative components would appear vital to creating a sense of reality in one's accounts of self. The social utility of well-formed narrative is revealed in research on courtroom testimony. In their volume *Reconstructing Reality in the Courtroom* Bennett and Feldman (1981) subjected research participants to 47 testimonies that were either genuine accounts of events or totally contrived. Ratings made of the stories revealed that the participants were unable to discriminate between genuine and false accounts. However, an analysis of those accounts believed to be genuine as opposed to false proved interesting: participants made judgments largely according to the approximation of the stories to well-formed narratives. Stories believed to be genuine were those in which events relevant to the end point were dominant and in which causal linkages among elements were more numerous. In further research Lippman (1986) experimentally varied the extent to which courtroom testimonies demonstrated the selection of events relevant to an end point, causal linkages among the events, and diachronic ordering of the events. Testimonies approximating the well-formed narrative in these ways were consistently found to be more intelligible and the witnesses to be more rational. Thus, the self-narratives of daily life may not always be well formed, but under certain circumstances their structure may be critical.

B. VARIETIES OF NARRATIVE FORM

Employing the above rules of narrative structure one can generate a sense of coherence and directionality in one's life. However, theoretical understanding is further enriched if we can classify forms of narrative. If certain sequences are highly shared within the culture then a syllabary of possible selves begins to emerge. In certain respects the question here is similar to that of literary theorists concerned with plot lines. Since Aristotelian times philosophers, literary theorists, and others have attempted to develop a formal vocabulary of plot; as it is often argued, there may be a limited set of fundamental plots of which all stories are manifestations. To the extent that people are engaged in the emplotment of their lives, this would be to place a limit over the range of life stories that could be played out.

In one of the most extensive accounts of plot within the present century Northrup Frye (1957) argues that there are four basic forms of narrative, each of which is rooted in the human experience with nature and most particularly with the evolution of the seasons. Thus, the experience of spring and the uprising of nature gives rise to the *comedy*. In the classic tradition comedy typically involves a challenge or threat which is overcome to yield social harmony. A comedy need not be humorous, even though its ending is a happy one. In contast, the free and calm of summer days give inspiration to the *romance* as a dramatic form. The romance in this case consists of a series of episodes in which the major protagonist experiences challenge or threats and through a series of struggles emerges victorious. The romance need not be concerned with attraction between people. During the autumn, when one experiences the contrast between the life of summer and the death of coming winter, the *tragedy* is born; and in winter, with one's increasing awareness of unrealized expectancies and the death of dreams, the *satire* becomes the relevant expressive form.

Joseph Campbell's (1956) analysis of primitive myth is also helpful in our pursuit of narrative form. As he proposes, there is one "monomyth" from which a myriad of variations has been drawn in primitive mythology. The monomyth, rooted in unconscious psychodynamics, concerns the hero who has been able to overcome personal and historical limitations to reach a transcendent understanding of the human condition. For Campbell, heroic narratives in their many local guises serve vital functions of psychic education. For our purposes, we see that the monomyth carries a form similar to that of the romance. That is, negative events (trials, terrors, tribulations) are followed by a positive outcome (enlightenment).

From these and similar analyses two conclusions can be hazarded. First, we find that what is common to the sequential shift of the tragedy, the comedy, the romance, and the monomyth are progressions toward (or failures in) achieving a given point or goal state. In effect, each of these plot forms can be understood in terms of our preceding analysis of narrative components. However, it also seems clear that these analyses of plot seem unduly restrictive. From the present perspective it is possible to derive a means for understanding the full range of plot variations and to gain a more detailed glimpse into the limit and potentials for self-definition. To elaborate, as we first saw, a story's end point is weighted with value. Thus, a victory, a consummated affair, a discovered fortune, or a prize-winning paper all might serve as valued goal states or story endings. On the opposite end of the evaluative continuum would fall a defeat, a lover lost, a fortune squandered, or a professional failure. Further, we can then view the various events that lead up to the story's end (the selection and ordering of events) as moving one through two-dimensional, evaluative space. As one approaches the valued goal over time, the story line becomes more positive; as one approaches failure, disillusionment, and so on, one moves in the negative direction. All plots, then, may be converted to a linear form with respect to their evaluative shifts over time.

At the most rudimentary level this allows us to isolate three forms of narrative. The first may be described as a *stability narrative*, that is, a narrative that links events in such a way that the individual remains essentially unchanged with respect to evaluative position. As depicted in Fig. 1, we also see that the stability narrative could be struck at any level along the evaluative continuum. At the upper end of the continuum the individual might conclude, for example, "I am still as attractive as I used to be," or at the lower end, "I continue to be haunted by feelings of failure." As can also be seen, each of these narrative summaries possesses inherent implications for the future. In the former case the individual might conclude that he or she will continue to be attractive for the foreseeable future, and in the latter, that feelings of failure will persist regardless of circumstance.

This rudimentary, stability narrative may be contrasted with two others. The individual may link together experiences in such a way that either increments or decrements characterize movement along the evaluative dimension over time. In the former case we may speak of *progressive*, and in the latter, *regressive* narratives (see Fig. 1). For example, the individual might be engaged in a progressive narrative with the surmise, "I am really learning to overcome my shyness and be more open and friendly with people," or a regressive narrative with the thought, "I can't seem to control the events in my life anymore." Directionality is also implied in each of these narratives, with the former anticipating further increments and the latter further decrements.

As should be clear, these three narrative forms, stability, progressive, and regressive, exhaust the fundamental options for the direction of movement in evaluative space. As such they may be considered rudimentary bases for other more complex variants. Theoretically one may envision a potential infinity of variations on these rudimentary forms. However, for reasons of social utility,

NARRATIVE AND SELF AS RELATIONSHIP   25

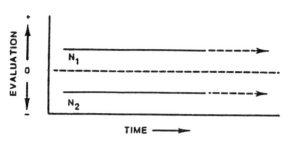

Stability Narrative

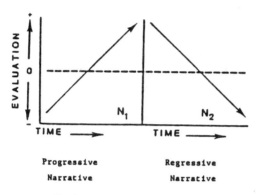

Progressive   Regressive
Narrative   Narrative

Fig. 1.   Rudimentary narrative forms.

aesthetic desirability, and linguistic capability, the culture may limit itself to a truncated repertoire of possibilities. Among this limited set we may place the tragic narrative, which in the present framework would adopt the structure depicted in Fig. 2. The tragedy, in this sense, would tell the story of the rapid downfall of one who had achieved high position. A progressive narrative is thus

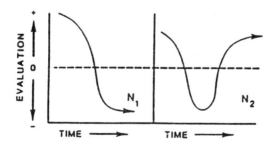

Fig. 2.   Tragic (N_1) and comedy-romance (N_2) narratives.

26   KENNETH J. GERGEN AND MARY M. GERGEN

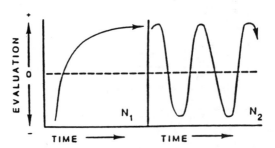

Fig. 3. "Happily-ever-after" (N_1) and romantic saga (N_2) narratives.

followed by a rapid regressive narrative. In this sense both the romance and the comedy (Fig. 2) are the reverse of the tragedy; for both a regressive narrative is followed by a progressive narrative. Life events become increasingly problematic until the denouement, whereupon happiness is rapidly restored to the major protagonists. Further, if a progressive narrative is followed by a stability narrative (see Fig. 3), we have what is commonly known as the happily-ever-after myth, which is widely adopted in traditional courtship. And we also recognize the romantic saga as a series of progressive–regressive phases (Fig. 3). In this case, for example, the individual may characterize his/her past as a continuous array of battles against the powers of darkness. Other narrative forms, including unification myths, communion narratives, and dialectic theory, are considered elsewhere (Gergen & Gergen, 1987; M. Gergen & K. Gergen, 1987).

C. NARRATIVE AND THE CREATION OF DRAMA

Friedrich Nietzsche once advised, "Live dangerously, it is the only time you live at all." These words carry with them an important element of personal validity. For many persons moments of high drama are those that most crystallize one's sense of identity. It is the major victory, the danger withstood, the return of a lost loved one, and so on that furnish one most acutely with a sense of self. Maslow's (1961) studies of peak experiences as identity markers also illustrate the point. At the same time, it must be realized that the capacity of an event to produce drama is largely a function of its place within a narrative. Isolated events in themselves appear limited in their dramatic impact. For example, a film depicting the continuous, random juxtaposition of startling events (a gunshot, a sword waving, a horse jumping a wall, a low-flying aircraft) would soon produce tedium. It is the relationship among events, not the events themselves, that seems chiefly responsible for producing drama. What characteristics of narrative form are necessary, then, to generate what may be termed dramatic engagement?

At the outset, it is helpful to look again at the dramatic arts as a source of insight. In this case, it is of initial interest that one can scarcely locate a theatrical exemplar of the three rudimentary narratives illustrated in Fig. 1. A drama in which all events were evaluatively equivalent (stability narrative) would scarcely be considered drama. Further, a steady but moderate enhancement (progressive narrative) or decrement (regressive narrative) in a protagonist's life conditions would also seem boring. At the same time, it is interesting to observe that the tragic narrative depicted in Fig. 2 bears a strong resemblance to the simpler, but unarousing regressive narrative. How does the tragic narrative, with its powerful dramatic impact, differ from the more rudimentary regressive narrative? Two characteristics seem particularly significant. First, we note that the relative decline in events is far less rapid in the prototypical regressive narrative than it is in the case of the tragic narrative. Whereas the former is characterized by moderate decline over time, the latter organizes events in such a way that decline is precipitous. In this light one may conjecture that the rapidity with which events deteriorate in such classic tragedies as *Antigone, Oedipus Rex,* and *Romeo and Juliet* may be essential to their dramatic impact. More generally, it may be suggested that the rate of change or, more formally, *the acceleration of the narrative slope* constitutes one of the chief components of dramatic engagement.

A second major component is also suggested by the contrast between the regressive and the tragic narratives. In the former case (see Fig. 1) there is unidirectionality in the slope line, whereas in the tragic narrative (Fig. 2) we find a progressive narrative (sometimes implied) followed by a regressive narrative. It would appear to be this "turn of events," or the change in evaluative relationship among events, that contributes to a high degree of dramatic engagement. It is when the hero has almost attained the goal, found his sweetheart, won the crown, and then is brought low, that drama is created. In more formal terms, the *alteration in narrative slope* may be considered a second major component of dramatic engagement.

A final word must be added to this discussion concerning suspense and danger—the sense of high drama one sometimes experiences during an athletic contest, at a meeting where important decisions are being made, during a debate, or while gambling. Such cases seem to elude the foregoing analysis, as they need not entail either acceleration or alteration in the narrative slope. One is fully and continuously engaged with no major changes in the story line. However, closer inspection reveals that the drama of suspense and danger are special cases of the two preceding rules. In both cases the sense of drama depends on the impending possibilities of acceleration or change. One is in suspense, for example, when a victory, an award, a jackpot, and the like may suddenly be awarded. Danger results from confronting the potential for sudden loss, destruction, death, and the like. All such events propel one suddenly toward or away from a valued goal or end point in the narrative sequence. Suspense and danger are thus the result of anticipated narratives.

III. Narrative Form in Two Populations:
An Application

The above analysis not only furnishes a basic vocabulary for describing and differentiating among forms of narrative and their attendant drama, it also speaks to issues of potential selves. As we pointed out, in order to maintain intelligibility in the culture, one's stories of self must employ the commonly accepted rules for narrative construction. Those narrative constructions in broad cultural usage form a set of ready-made intelligibilities; in effect, they offer a range of potentials for the social construction of the self. At first glance it would appear that narrative forms do not impose such constraints. As our analysis makes clear, theoretically the number of potential story forms approaches infinity. Attempts such as those of Frye and Campbell unnecessarily delimit the range of potential story forms. At the same time, it is also clear that there is a certain degree of agreement among analysts in Western culture, from Aristotle to the present, suggesting that certain story forms are more readily employed than others. In this sense, forms of self-narrative may also be constrained. For example, consider the person who characterizes him/herself by means of a stability narrative; life is directionless; it is merely moving in a steady, monotonous fashion neither toward nor away from a goal. Such a person might seem an apt candidate for psychotherapy. Similarly, one who characterized his/her life as a repetitive pattern in which each positive occurrence was followed immediately by a negative occurrence and vice versa would be regarded with suspicion. We simply do not accept such life stories as approximating reality. In contrast, if one could make sense of one's life today as "a long struggle upward," a "tragic decline," or a continuing saga in which one suffers defeats but rises from the ashes to achieve success, we are fully prepared to believe. One is not free simply to have any form of history he or she wishes. Cultures invite certain identities and discourage others.

In this light it is of interest to explore how various American subcultures characterize their life histories. Let us consider two contrasting populations: adolescents and the elderly. In the former case 29 youths between the ages of 19 and 21 were first confronted with the task of charting their life history along a general evaluative dimension (Gergen & Gergen, 1987b). Drawing on their earliest recollections to the present, how would they characterize their state of general well being? The characterizations were to be made with a single "life line" in two-dimensional (age × evaluation) space. The most positive periods of their history were to be represented by displacing the line upward, and negative periods were to be represented in a downward displacement.

What graphic forms might these self-characterizations take? Do young adults generally portray themselves as part of a happily-ever-after story, about to reach a positive plateau on which they can optimistically live out the remainder of their lives? Or, do they characterize themselves as living out a heroic saga, conquering one peril after another? Or more pessimistically, and reflective of recent economic trends, does life only appear to be growing even bleaker after the initially happy years of childhood? To explore such matters, an initial attempt was made to derive the average life trajectory from the data. To this end the mean displacement of each individual's life line from a neutral midpoint was computed at each 5-year interval. By interpolation these means could then be connected graphically to yield an overall life trajectory. The results of this analysis are featured in Fig. 4. As evidenced here, the general narrative form employed by this group of young adults is none of those conjectured above. Rather it is that of the romance. On the average these young adults tend to view their lives as happy at an early age, then beset with difficulty during the adolescent years, but now on an upward swing that promises well for the future. They confronted the foes of adolescence and emerged victorious.

As suggested by the preceding analysis, the self-narrator is free in principle to use any narrative template to account for his/her life. Since life events must themselves be rendered meaningful through narrative, and one must inevitably be selective as to which events are included in a given narrative, one's life experiences do not in themselves dictate the selection of the life story. In this light it is interesting to take account of the content through which this sample justified the use of the romance. Participants in the study were asked to describe the events surrounding the most positive and negative periods in their life line. As these accounts revealed, the content of these events was highly diverse. Positive points might be furnished by success in a school play, experiences with friends, owning a pet, or discovering music, while low periods might result from such wide-ranging experiences as moving to a new town, failing at school,

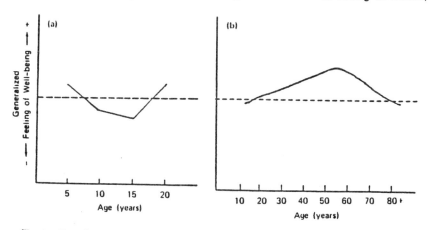

Fig. 4. Narratives of generalized well-being on two samples: (a), young adult; (b), aged.

parental marital problems, and losing a friend. In effect, the crisis in the adolescent period does not appear to reflect any single objective factor in this period. Rather the participants seem to use this given narrative form and employ whatever "facts" they can to justify their selection.

One might conjecture that the typical young adult, when describing his/her life history in brief (for an anonymous audience), employs the narrative form of the typical television drama. Such dramas typically begin on a positive note, an untoward event occurs (competition, theft, threat, challenge, murder, etc.), and the remainder of the hour is spent in bringing matters to a happy conclusion. Such narratives also contain a certain degree of dramatic engagement as the slope line alters direction on at least two occasions and accelerations (or decelerations) can be rapid. An informative contrast to the narrative choice of the young adult group is supplied by a sample of 72 persons ranging in age from 63 to 93 years (M. Gergen, 1980). In this case each respondent was interviewed about his/her life experiences. In one relevant line of questioning the respondent was asked to describe his/her general sense of well-being during various periods of life. When were the happiest days, why did things change, in what direction is life now progressing, and so on. These various responses were coded in a way that would render the results comparable with the young adult sample. The results are also depicted in Fig. 4.

In this case we find that the typical narrative of the older person is that of an inverted rainbow. That is, the young adult years were difficult, but a progressive narrative enabled a peak of well-being to be achieved somewhere between the ages of 50 and 60. However, life since these "golden years" had become less favorable. Aging was seen as a regressive narrative. Such results may seem reasonable, reflecting natural declines in aging. However, let us recall that these narratives are not the products of life itself but constructions of life—and they could be otherwise. It is at this point that one must inquire into the role of the social sciences themselves in fostering the view that the life course is an inverted rainbow. The psychological literature is replete with factual accounts of early "development" and late "decline" (Gergen & Gergen, 1987). To the extent that such views make their way into the public consciousness, they furnish the elderly with little sense of hope or optimism. With different views of what is important in aging—such as those adopted by many Asian cultures—social scientists might furnish constructions of far more positive and enabling potential.

IV. Elaborating the Thesis of Self-Narrative

We have explored basic rules of narrative accounting, common narratives of identity in Western culture, and the dramatic engagement of varying narrative forms. We must now expand and elaborate our theoretical net in three significant ways. First it is important to consider more directly matters of truth and multiplicity in narrative form. We can then turn to the pragmatic basis of narrative accounts, and finally to the process of negotiating such accounts in ongoing relations. With these elaborations in place we can press on to explore lived narratives.

A. TRUTH AND MULTIPLICITY IN NARRATIVE

When Joyce Carol Oates was once challenged to describe her development as an author, she despaired. No single, coherent account seemed to furnish "the truth." Rather, as she lamented, she found herself developing countless miniature stories. "Each angle of vision, each voice, yields . . . a separate writer-self, an alternative Joyce Carol Oates," each of these "contains so small a fraction of the truth, it is untrue" (*New York Times,* July 11, 1982). This account reintroduces a theme of critical importance in understanding narrative constructions. Narratives may be used by novelists to frame compelling stories, but in both science and everyday life they are treated as windows on the truth. When one recounts the party of the previous evening, tells a life story, or furnishes a scholarly account of the rise of slavery, for example, each is typically treated as a candidate for veracity—subject to challenge by others who might have "seen more accurately or objectively." Yet such claims are subject to significant question. We touched on the question of narrative truth in our earlier discussion. Let us now confront it more squarely.

The assumption of truth through narrative rests on two subpropositions: first, that one can be accurate or inaccurate in reporting the facts (the basic building blocks or elements of the narrative), and second, that one can be correct or incorrect with respect to ordering the facts. Space limitations prevent a full discussion of the complexities of objectivity in description. However, there are two arguments that demand brief consideration. The first concerns objectivity in behavioral description. Consider here the critique of the noted historian R. D. Collingwood (1946). As he proposed, historians attempting to account for human activity are not concerned with people's actual bodily movements, that is, their observed activities. Rather, historians furnish accounts of what people are attempting, trying, intending, or thinking they are doing. The history of bodily movements would be an absurdity; we should scarcely be able to understand behavior if it were described in terms of its velocity, direction, and the like. Rather, history is written in terms of the *meanings* assigned to movement. To say that in 1215 King John sealed the Magna Carta at Runnymede makes reference to his intentions and not to the actual movements of pressing wax to parchment. If

John's hands had been pressed to paper by his companions or he had accidentally sealed the document while believing it was some other, one would be disinclined to say that he had sealed the Magna Carta. In effect the description refers not to the spatiotemporal event, but to the intentions underlying the movement. In elaborating Collingwood's argument we have tried to demonstrate that each attempt to discover intentions, meanings, and the like commits the investigator to still further unwarranted beliefs about the mind (Gergen, 1982). To fathom the underlying meaning of one observed behavior we must use other observations, whose meanings are also in need of interpretation. The search for "true meaning" plunges one into an infinite regress. For further discussion of the interpretive basis of social knowledge the reader should consult Gadamer (1976), Gauld and Shotter (1977), Rabinow and Sullivan (1979), and Giddens (1976).

Over and above the problem of describing people's actions, there is the more general problem of relativity in all description. Whether or not a given description of an event is valid depends primarily on the historically situated conventions of a given culture or subculture rather than on the absolute match between word and thing. To illustrate, whether a wooden desk is a solid or not depends on whether the observer is an antique dealer or an atomic physicist; whether a skirt is more accurately described as blue or as colorless depends on whether the observer is the designer or a perceptual psychologist; and whether the earth is flat or round depends on whether one is driving to the supermarket or flying to Stockholm. Each of the competing descriptions has a limited validity for a certain subculture confronting specific tasks. There is no single perspective that has privileged access to "the real truth" (see also Goodman, 1978; Hanson, 1958; Gergen, 1986).

The second relevant proposition, that there is an objective relationship among events, proves equally if not more problematic. As we saw, narratives gain their coherence through the establishment of a goal state. Whether event A (falling from a horse) is better or worse than event B (mounting and galloping into the distance) depends on the end point served. Thus if the protagonist were a heroic marshall in a Western novel, the narrative relationship would be considered progressive; if the protagonist is a heinous villain, the narrative reverts to a regression. Yet the establishment of the goal state in itself is a matter of value. One is ill put to establish value estimations objectively. In effect, narrative relationships are perspectival, and there would appear to be no principled limit over perspective.

Consistent with these views, Donald Spence (1982) has demonstrated the misleading character of the archeological metaphor in psychoanalytic practice. Whereas analysts have traditionally believed they were "exploring the depths of the mental world," or "searching to discover the underlying truths" of the psyche, Spence demonstrates how the discoveries are prefigured in the discourse with which the analysis begins. Rather than disclosing the "historical truth" about the analysand, the analyst and analysand work together to generate a "narrative truth." This narrative truth is a socially constructed one, and its contours will inevitably be determined by the demands of the well-formed story in general and their particular realization in the form of psychoanalytic theory. For many the remaining question is whether the resultant fiction is indeed a convenient one in terms of treatment goals. For analyses of the extent to which scientific theories are themselves guided by literary rules see Potter, Stringer and Wetherell (1984), Landau (1984), and Gergen and Gergen (1987).

B. MULTIPLICITY IN NARRATIVE

As we saw, Joyce Carol Oates found herself confronting a multiplicity of life accounts. Even though it is common practice to speak as if each individual possesses "*a* life story," in fact there would appear to be no *one* story to tell. People appear capable of adopting multiple perspectives and selecting events so as to justify the selected narrative. Common experience in the culture will typically offer the individual exposure to a wide variety of narrative forms, from the rudimentary to the complex. Thus, the individual typically enters relationships with a potential for using any of a wide number of forms. In the same way an experienced skier approaches a steep incline with a variety of techniques for effective descent or a teacher confronts a class with a variety of means for effective communication, so the individual can usually construct the relationship among life experiences in a variety of ways. At a minimum, effective socialization should equip the person to interpret life events as consistencies, as improvements, or as decrements. And, with little additional training, the individual should develop the capacity to envision life as tragedy, comedy, or romantic saga (see also Mancuso & Sarbin, 1983, on "second-order selves").

To illustrate, in our research we have asked participants to draw graphs indicating their feelings of satisfaction over the years in their relationship with their mother, their father, and their academic work. These graph lines pose a striking contrast to the "generalized well-being" account depicted earlier in Fig. 4. In that case the students portrayed their general life course as a "romance"—a positive childhood, followed by an adolescent fall from grace, and capped by a positive retrenchment. However, in the case of both father and mother, participants tended most frequently to select progressive narratives, slow and continuous for the father, but more sharply accelerated in the most recent time period for the mother. Thus, they portrayed their relationships with each parent as showing increasing improvement. Yet, although attending one of the most competitive colleges in the country, the students tended to depict their feeling of satisfaction with their academic work as one of steady decline—a regressive narrative that left them in the present on the brink of dissatisfaction.

Not only do people enter social relationships with a variety of narratives at their disposal, but, in principle, there are no temporal parameters within which events must be related through narratives. That is, one may attempt to relate events occurring over vast periods of time or determine the relationship among events within a brief period. One may find it possible to see his or her life as part of a historical movement commencing centuries ago or as originating in early adolescence. At the same time, the individual may choose to describe as a tragedy that which has unfolded as friends select their positions at the dinner table. We may use the terms *macro* and *micro* to refer to the hypothetical or idealized ends of the temporal continuum within which events are related. *Macronarratives* refer to those events spanning broad periods of time, while *micronarratives* relate events within brief durations. The historian typically excels in the macronarrative, while the comedian who relies on sight gags may be the master of the micronarrative.

Given the capacity to relate events within different temporal perspectives, it becomes apparent that people often engage in the construction of *nested narratives*, or narratives within narratives (see also Mandler, 1984). Thus, they may come to see themselves as part of a long cultural history, but nested within this narrative they may possess an independent account of their development since childhod, and within this account establish a separate portrayal of their life as a professional or the development of their image within the few preceding moments. A man may view himself as bearing the contemporary standard for a race that has struggled for centuries so that he may live (a progressive narrative) and at the same time see himself as one who was long favored by his parents only to disappoint them with increasing frequency as he grew older (the tragic narrative) and simultaneously see how he managed to rekindle the waning ardor of a woman friend on a given evening (the comedy).

The concept of nested narratives raises a variety of interesting issues. To what extent may we anticipate coherence among nested narratives? As Ortega y Gasset (1941) proposed in his analysis of historical systems, "the plurality of beliefs on which an individual, or people, or an age is grounded never possesses a completely logical articulation" (p. 166). Yet, there are many social advantages to "having one's stories agree." To the extent that consistency among narratives is sought, macronarratives acquire preeminent importance. Such narratives seem to lay the foundations within which other narratives are constructed. One's account of an evening with a friend would not seem to dictate one's account of one's life history; however, one's life history does constitute grounds for understanding the trajectory of the evening. To extrapolate, it may be ventured that those people with an extensive background in the history of their culture or subculture, or with an elaborated sense of their place in history, may possess more coherence among narratives than those with a superficial sense of their historical position. Or, placed in a different light, people from a young culture or nation may experience a greater sense of freedom of momentary action than those from cultures or nations with a long and prominent historical narrative. The former may experience a lesser degree of strain to behave in a way that is coherent with the past.

In this light it is interesting to consider recent inquiry into terrorist activity. Typically, terrorists have been viewed as either disturbed, irrational, and potentially psychotic on the one hand, or politically motivated activists on the other. However, based on his examination of Armenian terrorist activity, Tololyan (1987) argues that the terrorist is carrying out the implications of a long-standing culturally sedimented narrative. The narrative begins in A.D. 450 and describes many valorous attempts to protect the Armenian national identity. Such stories of courage, martyrdom, and the pursuit of justice have continued to accumulate over the centuries and are embedded within common Armenian folk culture. To become a terrorist, then, is to engage in a nested narrative—a personalized living out of the implications of one's history.

C. THE PRAGMATICS OF SELF-NARRATIVE

We now see that the individual harbors the capacity for a multiplicity of narrative forms. This multiplicity is favored, in part, by the variegated demands placed upon the individual by the social environment. As Wittgenstein advised, "Think of the tools in a tool-box: there is a hammer, pliers, a screw-driver, a rule, a glue-pot, glue, nails and screws. The functions of words are as diverse as the functions of these objects." Narrative constructions are essentially linguistic tools with important social functions. As one masters the various means of making oneself intelligible through narratives, social capabilities are enhanced. Let us consider a selected number of common functions of various forms of self-narrative.

Consider first the primitive narrative of stability. Although generally void of dramatic value, the capacity of people to identify themselves as stable units has great utility within a culture. One's capacity to act functionally within society depends largely on the stability of social patterns. If others' conduct shifts randomly from one moment to the next one would be rendered helpless. There would be little way of knowing how to achieve any goal (including sustaining life) that depended on others' actions. Thus, much effort is expended by people in establishing recurring or stabilized patterns of conduct and ensuring through various sanctions that they are maintained by others as well. The broad societal demand for stability of conduct finds its functional counterpart in the ready accessibility of the stability narrative. Negotiating social life successfully requires that the individual is capable of making him/herself intelligible as an enduring, integral, or coherent identity. For example, in certain political arenas, it may be of great functional value to present oneself as a "born Southerner, raised in the South, married in the South, and part of its future.'' Or, on the more personal level, to be able to show how one's love, parental commitment, honesty, moral ideals, and so on have been unfailing over time, even when their outward appearances have seemed more contingent, may be of exceptional importance in retaining ongoing relations. In close relationships people often wish to know that others ''are what they seem,'' which is to say that certain characteristics are enduring across time. A major means for rendering such assurance is through the stability narrative.

It is important to note at this point a major way in which the present analysis conflicts with more traditional accounts of personal identity. Theorists such as Prescott Lecky, Erik Erikson, Carl Rogers, and Seymour Epstein have all viewed personal identity as something akin to an achieved condition of the mind. The mature individual, on this account, is one who has ''found,'' ''crystallized,'' or ''realized'' a firm sense of self or personal identity. In general this condition is viewed as a highly positive one and, once achieved, variance or inconsistency in one's conduct may be minimized. However, from the present vantage point, the individual does not arrive at a stabilized state of mind. Rather, he or she develops the capacity for understanding him/herself in this manner and creditably communicating this understanding to others. One does not acquire a state of ''true self'' but a potential for communicating that such a state is possessed.

This latter position becomes fortified when we turn to the social functions of the progressive narrative. On a general level there would appear not only a pervasive need for stability but also a contrasting need for change. The possibility of positive change, or movement in a positive direction, would seem particularly useful as a means of motivating and inviting. For many the possibility of alleviating poor conditions furnishes a chief motivational source. Careers are selected, hardships are endured, and many personal resources (including one's most intimate relations) are sacrificed in the belief that a progressive narrative can be achieved. And, it is clearly of great functional value to be able to construct such narratives for others. The success of many relationships depends importantly on the ability of the participants to demonstrate how their undesirable characteristics have diminished over time—even if they appear to be continuing undaunted. As Kitwood's (1980) research suggests, people make special use of the progressive narrative in early stages of a relationship. In effect, the general investment in positive change is best expressed through a narrative that demonstrates the ascending relationship among events over time.

As should be evident from this analysis. one must be prepared in most relationships to render an account of oneself as both inherently stable and, yet, in a state of positive change. Functioning viably in a relationship often depends on one's ability to show that one has always been the same and will continue to be so and, yet, contrapuntally to show how one is continuing to improve. One must be reliable but demonstrate progress: one must be changing but maintain a stable character. Achieving such diverse ends is primarily a matter of negotiating the meaning of events in relationship to each other. Thus, with sufficient skill one and the same event may figure in both a stability and a progressive narrative. For example, graduation from medical school may be used as evidence that one has always been intelligent and at the same time demonstrate that one is en route to high professional status.

Can a case be made for the social value of regressive narratives? At least one compelling answer to this question is furnished by taking account of the common effects of regressive narratives. In particular, when people are informed of steadily worsening conditions they often attempt to compensate. They strive to offset or reverse the decline through enhanced activity. Through intensification of effort, they attempt to turn a potential tragedy into a comedy. Regressive narratives furnish an important means, then, of motivating people (including oneself) toward achieving positive ends. This means is employed on a national level when a government demonstrates that the steady decline in the balance of payments can be offset only with a grass-roots commitment to purchasing locally manufactured products. The same technique may be employed by the individual in attempting to bolster his or her enthusiasm for a given project: "I am failing at this, if I don't get myself together I'll really be finished."

D. THE SOCIAL EMBEDDING OF SELF-NARRATIVE

Although the object of the self-narrative is the single self, it would be a mistake to view such constructions as the product or possession of single selves. In the reliance on a language system for relating or connecting events one is engaging in an inherently social act. Words acquire communicative capacity by virtue of shared usage. A movement of the hand fails to communicate, for example, unless it has the capacity to be understood by at least one other person. Thus, in understanding the relationship among events in one's life, one relies on discourse that is born of social interchange and inherently implies an audience. Over and above this embedding of narratives in the social sphere, the social basis of narrative construction is amplified in three additional processes: public performance, negotiation, and reciprocation.

As suggested by our earlier analysis narrative accounts are not isolated from daily affairs; they are immersed within processes of ongoing interchange. They serve to unite the past and present and to signify future trajectories (Csikszentmihalyi & Beattie, 1979). To maintain that one has always been an honest person (stability narrative) suggests that one will do what others see as avoiding temptation when it is subsequently encountered. To construct one's past in such a way that one has overcome increasingly greater obstacles to achievement (progressive narrative) suggests that one should treat oneself with a certain degree of public respect. Or, to see oneself as losing one's abilities because of increasing age (regressive narrative) is to suggest to others that one will be less energetic in future dealings. Most important for present purposes, as these behavioral implications are realized in action they become subject to social evaluation. Others can find such actions coherent or contradictory to the self-narratives. And, to the extent that such actions are in conflict with the self-narrative, doubt is cast upon its validity. If others express doubt about one's honesty, suggest that one's pride is unmerited, or find one's reduction in activity unwarranted, revisions are invited in the narrative construction relevant to such action. Thus, as narratives are realized in the public arena, they become subject to social evaluation and resultant molding.

As the individual's actions encounter varying degrees of approbation, the process of negotiation comes to play a prominent role. That is, it becomes increasingly necessary for the individual to explicate the self-narrative in such a way that one's actions seem coherent and connected with each other and with the narrative itself. If faced with others who doubt one's honesty, one can demonstrate how his or her previous actions have been without blemish. Or, one can try to convince others of the validity of the progressive narrative by legitimizing one's pride or the regressive narrative by justifying one's diminished activities. In effect, whether a given narrative can be maintained depends importantly on the individual's ability to negotiate successfully with others concerning the meaning of events in relationship with each other (cf. de Waele & Harré, 1976; Hankiss, 1981).

Active negotiation over narrative form is especially invited under circumstances in which the individual is asked to justify his or her behavior, that is, when one has acted disagreeably with respect to common frames of understanding. However, the process of social negotiation need not be solely a public one. People generally avoid the threat of direct negotiation by taking prior account of the public intelligibility of their actions. They select in advance actions that can be justified on the basis of an intelligible or publicly acceptable narrative. As Murray's (1985a) research on marathon runners indicates, decisions to run typically depended on a privately pondered narrative in which runners reasoned that subjecting themselves to the race would enable them to be "born again," or better people. Perhaps the bulk of the negotiation process is anticipatory or implicit, taking place with an imaginary audience prior to the moment of action. In this way most human interaction can proceed unproblematically.

The social generation of narrative does not terminate with the negotiation process in its explicit and implicit forms. An additional facet of narrative construction throws its interactive basis into vivid relief. Thus far we have spoken of narratives as if solely concerned with the temporal trajectory of the protagonist alone. This conception must now be expanded. The incidents woven into a narrative are not only the actions of the single individual but the actions of others as well. In most instances others' actions contribute vitally to the events to be linked in narrative sequence. For example, in justifying his continuing honesty, the individual may point to an instance in which another person has tempted him; to illustrate one's achievement may depend on showing how another person was vanquished in a particular competition; in arguing that one has lost capabilities he or she may point to the alacrity with which a younger person performed a particular task. In all cases, the action of the other enters as an integral part of one's own actions. In this sense, narative constructions typically require a supporting cast. The implications of this condition are broad indeed.

First, in the same manner that the individual feels that he or she has priority in self-definition, others also feel themselves to have primary jurisdiction over the definition of their own actions. Thus, if the other is present, one's understanding of his/her supporting role cannot easily proceed without his/her acquiescence or agreement that "Yes, that's how it was." If others are not willing to accede to their assigned parts then one can ill afford to rely on their actions within a narrative. If another fails to see his or her actions as "offering temptation," the actor cannot easily conclude that he/she has displayed honesty; if the other can show how he or she was not really vanquished in a given competition, the actor can scarcely use the episode as a stepping stone in a progressive narrative; if the younger person can demonstrate that his or her alacrity was only an apparent one, far overestimating true abilities, then the actor can ill afford to weave the incident into a regressive narrative.

This reliance on others' definition of their actions places the actor in a precarious position. As we have seen, people possess a variety of narrative forms ranging over various periods of time and which stand in various relations to each other in terms of nesting. At the same time members of a supporting cast may choose at any point to reconstruct their actions in opposing ways. Thus, an actor's success in sustaining a given self-narrative is fundamentally dependent on others' willingness to play out certain pasts in relationship to the actor. In Wilhelm Schapp's (1976) terms, each of us is "knitted into" others' historical constructions, as they are into ours.

This delicate interdependence of constructed narratives suggests that a fundamental aspect of social life is a reciprocity in the negotiation of meaning. Because one's narrative constructions can be maintained only so long as others play their proper supporting role, and in turn because one is required by others to play supporting roles in their constructions, the moment any participant chooses to renege, he or she threatens the array of interdependent constructions. For example, an adolescent may reveal to his mother that he believes she has been a "very bad mother," thus potentially destroying her continuing self-narrative as a "good mother." Yet, at the same time, the son risks his mother's reply that she always felt his character was so inferior that he never merited her love. His continuing narrative of "self as good" is thus thrown into jeopardy. A lover may

40   KENNETH J. GERGEN AND MARY M. GERGEN

announce that she has begun to feel her male partner no longer interests her as he once did, thus potentially crushing his stability narrative; however, she does so at the peril of his replying that he has long been bored with her and is happy to be relieved of his lover's role. In such instances the parties in the relationship each pull out their supporting roles, and the result is a full degeneration of the narratives to which they contribute. In effect, our ontological security is a matter of public domain. For further discussion of narratives of relationship the reader may consult M. Gergen and Gergen (1987a).

V. Lived Narratives as Relational Scenarios

Thus far our analysis has been focused on social accounts—how it is people engage in the process of making themselves (and others) intelligible in ongoing relationships. However, as this analysis has unfolded, so has the explanatory fulcrum subtly shifted. At the outset, we could speak of self-narratives as a form of social accounting engaged in by individuals in the presence of others. However, as our analysis has progressed, it has become increasingly clear that the process of story telling is not the act of an autonomous and independent actor. First, we found that the actor's capacities for intelligibility are embedded within a sociohistorical context; in the telling of a story the actor is relying on certain features of a preexisting social order. In this sense it would be plausible to say that the culture is speaking through the actor, using the actor to reproduce itself. Further, we found that self-narratives depend on the mutual sharing of symbols, socially acceptable performances, and continued negotiation. Finally, we found that narratives typically require the interweaving of identities and, thus, the support of others within the social sphere of interaction. In these various senses, then, the telling of the story is not so much the act of an independent individual as the result of a mutually coordinated and supportive relationship. As we now shift our attention to lived narratives, the self as independent entity disappears and is replaced by fully relational forms. Let us explore.

Just as people make use of narrative form in making themselves intelligible to others, they also engage in life activities that represent the conventionalized instantiations of these intelligibilities. For example, in order to tell the story of how one overcame a handicap to rise to success should require that one be able to gain others' agreement that certain configurations count as "a handicap," others as "success," and so on. Although narrative accounts in no way map or mirror the world, they are typically embedded in a series of life events that furnish them with an undergirding sense of verisimilitude. In effect, people frequently live out sequences of activity with a sense of storyhood. One senses life improving, relations breaking down, a leveling of strife, and so on. Accompanying these actions and the concomitant attempt to make them intelligible is often a sense of drama (or its lack). As one generates intelligibility, so life becomes dramatically saturated. Indeed, without this sense of dramatic engagement born of narrative, life might seem both flavorless and empty.

Yet, in the same way that narrative accounting is essentially a product of relationships—rather than isolated, social atoms—so are lived narratives. One can scarcely live out a story in social isolation—even if others are geographically removed. Indeed, there is an important sense in which the very meaning of an individual's actions from moment to moment is derived from the manner in which they are embedded within ongoing relationships. We speak of persons as having motives, beliefs, understandings, plans, and so on, as if these are properties of individual selves. Yet, how is it that we formulate these expressions? If your arm is raised above your head there is little that may be said about your motives. Your action is merely a spatiotemporal configuration. In contrast, if another person were before you, crouching and grimacing, suddenly it becomes possible to speak of you as aggressive, oppressive, or ruthless. If the other were a child standing on tiptoes, arms outstretched, his ball lodged in a tree above your head, it would be possible to characterize you as helpful or nurturant. Additional configurations of the other might yield the conclusion that you were playful, obedient, protective, proud, and so on. Note that your movement is similar in each case, yet it is possible to characterize yourself—until the relational context is articulated. Similarly, the other person's movements have little bearing on our description until they are seen within the context of your conduct. In effect, what we label as individualized characteristics—aggressiveness, playfulness, altruism, and the like—are primarily products of joint configurations (see also Shotter's 1984 discussion of *joint-action*).

As we see, the discourse of relationship represents a vastly unarticulated subtext upon which rests the text of individual selves. The pragmatic question is whether we can articulate this subtext. Can we bring into the foreground that which has remained obscured? It is as if we have at our disposal a rich language for characterizing rooks, pawns, and bishops but have yet to discover the game of chess. The present question is thus whether we can redefine qualities of self in such a way that their derivation from the whole is made clear. Can we develop a language of understanding in which there are not powerful, helpful, intelligent, or depressed selves, for example, but in which these characterizations are derivative from more essential forms of relationship? Can we define the games in which the characteristics of self are rooted? Let us use the emotions as the test case.

A. EMOTIONS AS CONSTITUENTS OF RELATIONAL FORMS

Traditionally the emotions have been viewed as private experiences or possessions of the individual. It is individuals who have emotions, who are struck or driven by their emotions, and who may or may not give expressions to their emotions. Yet, this view of emotion is tied strongly to the biological view of human conduct. As theorists from Darwin (1872) to Plutchik (1980) contend, the human organism is biologically equipped with a delimited number of emotional potentials. When activated, these biologically based patterns may be discovered anatomically or biochemically, and they carry with them certain experiential and behavioral correlates. Yet, in spite of its common-sense appeal, the biological view has ceased to command the attention of many social scientists. Critics have argued that it is difficult to reconcile the biological view with much anthropological research. As such inquiry consistently demonstrates, both the vocabulary of the emotions and the patterns of what might be viewed as emotional expression vary dramatically from one culture or historical period to another (Lutz, 1985; Harkness & Super, 1985). For example, as demonstrated by Averill (1982), patterns of what Westerners call "hostility" are scarcely found in many cultures, and bizarre patterns (such as "running amok") are wholly unknown in Western culture. Given a common biological heritage, it is difficult for the biologically oriented scientist to explain why there is not a greater similarity in emotional patterning. Biological expressions of thirst, hunger, and procreative impulses are easily demonstrated; why are the emotions not amenable to similar demonstration?

Of equal importance, there is broad agreement among many theorists that biological reductionism robs emotions of their most vital element—a psychological meaning. Thus, it is argued, if the human body were stimulated to act in a way that one might define as rage, the person would not be experiencing or expressing "real rage," but rather a "sham rage." Similarly, if a drug is administered that creates euphoria, this state of happiness is not viewed as authentic, but drug induced. Real states of emotion, by common usage, are suffused with social meaning. There is an object of one's rage and a justification for its expression; one is happy for a reason and this happiness is expressed to certain people and not to others. To abstract the emotion from its social meaning is to reduce the person to automaton status, personlike but not fundamentally human (DeRivera, 1984).

Discontented with the biological view, many recent investigators have turned to cognitive-based explanations of emotion. The potential power of cognitive explanations initially became apparent with Schachter's two-factor theory of emotion and its experimental realization by Schachter and Singer (1962). As Schachter argued, there was little to distinguish among emotions on a biological basis. All emotions seemed to be accompanied by a state of generalized arousal; the same arousal could thus serve as the basis for virtually any emotion. Which emotion was experienced depended on one's cognitive assessment or labeling, and this assessment depended on environmental cues. Subsequent investigators have located a variety of shortcomings in the Schachter and Singer research

(Reisenzein, 1983), and still others have found that generalized arousal does not seem essential for persons to claim emotional experiences. There has been a resulting tendency for recent cognitive theorists thus to reduce emotion to cognition—that is, to redefine emotion in terms of the application of cognitive schemata.

Yet, for many the cognitive replacement for biological reductionism falls short of the mark. For the more traditional, it flies in the face of a longstanding dichotomy between rationality and emotionality; it prematurely abandons phenomenologically compelling distinctions among experiences. Further, to reduce the human being to a rational decision maker seems to make the same mistake as biological reductionism: humanity loses important dimensions (Sabini & Silver, 1985). In particular, cognitive reductionism seems to rob humanity of one of its most significant features: the capacity for valuing existence. There is something more to life than cognitive processing, as it is said, and this "something more" is possibly more significant for one's life satisfaction than rational processing. Indeed rational processing would seem to operate in the service of one's values, preferences. or feelings. Unless one cares about a given end, there is little function for reasoning powers. "Caring" is a matter of the heart—that is, the emotions.

There is also a variety of important conceptual problems inhering in the assumption of cognitive categories or schemata, some of which have been outlined elsewhere (Gergen, 1984b). Without recapitulating the arguments, their major thrust has been to demonstrate the intractable difficulties deriving from the assumption that understanding is a conceptually (or schematically) based process. If this position is embraced there is no explanatory means available for understanding either how the conceptual repertoire can be expanded or how concepts could ever give rise to action. In effect, there is significant reason to question the cognitive program more generally (see also Coulter, 1983; Ryle, 1949).

Against this backdrop, many theorists have shifted their attention in a third direction, namely toward viewing emotion as a form of social performance. It is this view that is most fully elaborated in Averill's work on hostility and on romantic love (Averill, 1982, 1985; see also Armon-Jones, 1985). As Averill argues, emotions may be viewed as "transient social roles," or syndromes of action for which various cognitive and physiological processes are recruited for effective execution. This position has a variety of advantages. It absorbs the many cross-cultural studies of variation in emotional patterning. It erases the problem of determining how many emotions there are, while recognizing the possibility that there may be different physiological patterns for various kinds of emotional performances (thus avoiding the naiveté of the "general arousal" assumption). Further, it does not reduce the human being to a one-dimensional cognizer. For some the metaphor of emotions as performance is not altogether a happy one, suggesting as it does that emotions are "play acted" or the result of superficial staging. However, such criticism depends on the extension of the metaphor beyond what Averill and other constructionists intend. Emotional performances can be dead serious.

From the present standpoint, the performance orientation to emotions seems the most promising alternative available. However, it possesses one significant shortcoming: in its present form it remains individualistic in its premises. That is, it adopts the traditional view that emotions are possessions of single individuals (or performers). Thus, it would follow, one could understand emotions by focusing attention on the actions of single performers. Yet, following the lines of the preceding arguments, spontaneous emotional performance, cut away from historical process, would be nonsensical. For example, if your hostess at a dinner party suddenly bolted from her seat to express hostility or buried her head in her lap and began loudly sobbing, you would undoubtedly be unsettled or abashed. Further, if she could not make it clear how such outbursts were related to a series of preceding and/or anticipated events (essentially a narrative account)—if she announced that she merely felt like such outbursts for no particular reason—you might seriously consider her a candidate for psychiatric assistance. To be intelligible the emotional action must be a constituent of a recognizable narrative. There is good reason, then, to view emotional performances as constituents of larger or more extended patterns of interaction.

B. EMOTIONAL SCENARIOS: THE CASE OF ESCALATING HOSTILITY

With these thoughts in mind we have embarked on a line of research attempting to elucidate the broader scenarios in which emotional expressions are embedded. In effect, we ask as a first step in the research process whether we can identify common interaction sequences in which emotional performances play a critical role. Traditional experimental methodology offers little assistance in this task, as such methods are confined to examining the immediate effects of a given stimulus configuration. They are ill equipped to explore patterns of action which unfold or emerge over longer periods of time (see Gergen, 1984, for a more extended discussion of this point). However, a relevant and intriguing study by Richard Felson (1984) furnishes a useful starting point for our analysis. Felson interviewed 380 male excriminal offenders and mental patients for whom violence had been a problem. Among other things, they were asked to describe an incident in which violence had occurred. In analyzing these narratives Felson discovered that violent actions were not spontaneous, uncontrollable eruptions, but rather, embedded in reliable patterns of interchange. In particular, the typical pattern of interacton was one in which *Person A* violated a social rule or norm (e.g., playing the radio too loud, stepping in front of the line, interrupting others' privacy, etc.). A verbal exchange followed, in which *Person B* typically reproached *A*, blaming and ordering him/her to cease or correct the offensive behavior. *Person A* refused to accept the blame or order, *B* threatened, *A* continued, and then *B* attacked *A*. In effect Felson succeeded in revealing a common interaction scenario or narrative in which physical aggression is a reliable part.

By common standards, the relationship between violence and the emotions is, of course, an intimate one: violence is typically viewed as an expression of hostile emotions. In this sense Felson's research provides a significant illustration of the fruitfulness of viewing emotions as relational components. Further study was thus undertaken to explore scenarios of hostility and violence in normal populations. This exploration was further inspired by the work of Pearce and Cronen (1980) on the management of meaning. As they have pointed out, there are many recurring patterns of interchange that are unwanted by the participants and, yet, willingly repeated. Domestic violence may be a significant exemplar of such *unwanted repetitive patterns* (URPs). That is, neither husband nor wife may want physical violence, but once the pattern (or scenario) has begun, they may feel little choice but to bear on toward its normative conclusion—physical abuse. This view also suggests that under certain conditions hostility and physical violence may be viewed as appropriate, if not desirable. While hostility and violence are typically abhorred in our textbooks and treated as undesirable if not bizarre, such treatments fail to appreciate the contexts of their occurrence. To the participants violence may seem, at a given moment in a scenario, not only appropriate, but morally required.

With these concerns in mind research was designed to elucidate a relational scenario of escalating hostility (Harris, Gergen, & Lannamann, 1987). Often it appears both expected and desired in our culture that people will respond to acts of hostility with hostility; further, each escalation in hostility on the part of one member of a relationship will evoke increased hostility on the part of another. If such a scenario is carried out over time, it would seem that participants might eventually come to see physical aggression as both normal and desirable (see also Coyne's 1976 analysis of depression).

To explore these issues a sample of undergraduates was exposed to unfolding stories involving two-person interaction. At the story's outset one protagonist would mildly criticize the other. The story was interrupted at this point, and the participants were asked to rate the probability, desirability, and advisability of each of a series of behavioral responses. The list of behavioral options ranged from highly conciliatory at the one extreme to physical violence at the other. Thus, for example, the participants read about a young married couple. In the first scene the husband mildly criticized his wife's cooking. The participants then rated a range of options (from embracing and kissing to physical striking) for the wife. After the evaluations were made the participants turned the page to read

46   KENNETH J. GERGEN AND MARY M. GERGEN

that the reaction of the wife had been to escalate the hostility—she responded by
criticizing her husband. Again, the story was halted and ratings made of the
husband's probable reactions to his wife, along with their desirability and advisability. In the next episode it is then found that he becomes harsher in his
comments to his wife, and so on. Eight instances of escalation were thus furnished to participants with evaluations made after each.

Although this article is not the place for a full examination of the findings, the
results depicted in Fig. 5 are exemplary of the general pattern of ratings for each
of the stories and all three measures. Specifically the figure displays the mean
ratings of probability for the most hostile options (combined) and the most
conciliatory options (combined). As can be seen, the rated probability of hostile
options increases over the eight intervals, while the probability of conciliation
options decreases. The results proved highly reliable on a statistical basis and
suggest that we are tapping a highly conventionalized scenario in the culture.

Most interestingly, however, this same pattern of mounting hostility and de-
creasing conciliation is generally revealed in both the ratings of desirability and
advisability. That is, the research participants not only saw the increasing hostility as probable, but they also saw it as appropriate and praiseworthy. While the
participants would never recommend at the outset of the scenario that the husband or wife throw the dinner on the floor, by the end of four exchanges they are
quite willing to endorse this option. The sawtooth trajectory featured in the figure
is the result of the participants' ratings of the husband versus the wife in the
story. The sample (predominantly female) generally endorsed more hostility for
the female than for the male. None of them advised that the husband should
strike the female. Yet, in the second story involving hostile interchanges between
two male students, even physical violence was endorsed.

As such research suggests, when mild hostility is expressed, it seems both

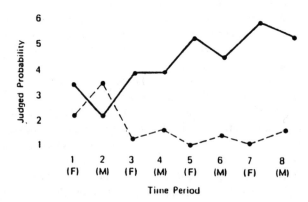

Fig. 5.   Estimated probability of aggressive (—) and conciliatory (- - - -) options in male–female
interchange. F, female; M, male.

appropriate and desirable for the target to respond with hostility as well. And, although neither participant may wish an embittered antagonism, this early exchange invites the participants to engage in a widely shared cultural scenario. Each may righteously attack the other with slightly increasing intensity, and as the scenario unfolds there is little that either can do to change the direction of events. The parallel between such domestic incidents and undertakings at the international level (e.g., Libya and the United States) is remarkable and suggests that a major role for the social sciences is that of creatively developing alternative means of breaking the scenarios before the point of violence (Gergen, 1986).

C. EMOTIONAL SCENARIOS: EXPANDING THE SPECTRUM

Encouraged by these results more recent work has broadened the perspective by exploring the way in which a variety of different emotions—including anger, depression, and happiness—fit within lived narratives. Working with Wendy Davidson, the research strategy in this case has been more open ended than in the foregoing. Rather than trying to elucidate a single pattern, as in the case of escalating hostility, the attempt was to explore the possibility of multiple scenarios. That is, it seemed plausible that any given emotional expression might be embedded in a variety of common sequences or scenarios, just as a given move of the torso might figure in a variety of standard dances or the movement of the arm might be included in a variety of gymnastic routines. This exploratory technique also seemed fruitful in pinpointing differences between effective or desirable scenarios as opposed to ineffectual or failing ones. Following the earlier reasoning, some conventional patterns of interchange lead people in unwanted directions—as in the case of escalating hostility. However, by broadening the range of possible routines, it might be possible to isolate promising as opposed to failing forms of interchange.

The procedure employed in these various cases was identical. An initial group of some 20 undergraduate participants was presented with a vignette in which they were told of a friend who expressed to them one of the several emotions. Typically, for example, the friend was said to be a roommate who entered the room and expressed a given emotion (such as "I am really angry at you," "I'm feeling so depressed," or "I'm so happy"). In each case the research participants were asked how they would respond to the expression. As a result of preliminary analysis it became apparent that such expressions would engender only a single form of reply, that of an inquiry into the cause. In effect, people are scarcely free to reply to a friend's expression of emotion in any way they wish. To remain intelligible by cultural standards, one must inquire into the source. Yet, this inquiry is far more than a cultural formality. In terms of narrative theory more generally, the emotional expression is without sense or definition until it has been placed within a narrative context—that is, supplied with antecedents. The answer to the question "why are you feeling. . ." furnishes the recipient with an indication of what story is being played out. On a more metaphoric level, the answer has the perlocutionary effect of informing the listener what game is being played or what dance is being performed. Without this information the recipient cannot know what further actions on his/her part will be sensible or appropriate. Indeed, in this study, there was no participant who responded to the initial emotional expression with other than a query into cause.

The research participants were then furnished with a prepared reply to the query. The roommate was angry because the target (in this case the research participant) had revealed a failing grade to a mutual friend after pledging secrecy; depression was attributed to a general feeling that nothing was going right, classes were going badly, a recent breakup of a close relationship, no sleep, and so on; happiness was attributed to the general feeling that everything was going well—classes, a close relationship, and so on. The research participants were then asked to indicate how they would reply to this explanation. At this point in the research two rounds of turn-taking (or interacts) had thus been achieved.

This array of partial scenarios was then used as the sample pool to explore a third round of turn-taking. That is, sample protocols were selected at random from the initial pool of interchanges and were presented to a new group of research participants. This group was asked to take the part of the roommate who had initially engaged in the emotional expression, explained why he/she felt this way, and was then confronted by the roommate's response. Special note was made in this case, and later, as to whether participants might feel the scenario was at an end. That is, if they indicated that there wasn't anything more to be said or felt puzzled about what might be added, it was taken as a signal that the scenario was at an end. If such responses occurred, no further inquiries were made. If a response was made, the participants were then asked to supply what they felt would be the likely reaction of their roommate.

Responses at each phase of these scenario samples were then subjected to categorization. With such simplification it was hoped that it would be possible to locate generic scenario forms. As this categorization proceeded it became apparent that at stage of any interchange more than 90% of the responses could reliably be placed into one of three categories. In effect, it appears that at each choice point in the unfolding scenarios, participants typically faced at least three intelligible alternatives. The generality and limits of this pattern remain to be explored.

In order to appreciate the character of the fuller set of findings consider the depiction of the anger scenarios in Fig. 6. The case is particularly interesting in light of the results of the earlier study of escalating hostility. As this schematic makes clear, we first see that the initial interact is composed of the expression of

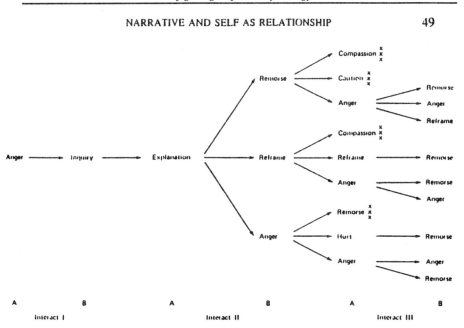

Fig. 6. Emotional scenarios for expressions of anger.

anger and the resultant questioning of the reason. In the second interact the explanation for the anger is given (as described above), and the research participants generated three major options. The most frequently selected option is *remorse* (e.g., "I'm very sorry I hurt your feelings"). The second most frequent reaction is that of *reframing*. The reframing response is one in which the interlocutor attempts to redefine the precipitating event in such a way that anger is no longer appropriate. In the present case, for example, participants tended to use two forms of reframing, the first a plea of ignorance over the wishes that the information remain secret, and the second a claim of positive intent (e.g., "I only did it because I thought it would be helpful to you."). Ranking third in frequency of selection is the response of *anger* (e.g., "Don't you think you're overreacting a bit? It's not such a big deal."). This latter pattern points up an important limitation on the earlier study of escalating hostility. As it appears, while escalation of hostility is a common scenario in our culture, it is neither essential nor necessary (e.g., required biologically). Rather, it is one possible option among several and, at least in the present case, not one which is typically preferred.

As Fig. 6 demonstrates, with the third interact, scenario endings become possible. Participants begin to find a natural break in the exchange. The most favored antecedent of the ending is the expression of remorse in the second interact. If remorse is expressed in this instance, two of the three replies (and the most favored two) lead to the end of the narrative. Remorse is likely to be followed by *compassion* ("That's OK. It really doesn't matter so much, I guess") or by *caution* ("Well, I hope you will never do that kind of thing again."). The reframing reply in the second interact is somewhat less successful in bringing the scenario to an end. Of the three options selected by participants, only the least preferred reaction (that of compassion) succeeds in bringing matters to a conclusion. The most frequent reaction to reframing, however, is an attempt on the part of the emotional person to reframe once again, typically so as to reinstate the validity of the initial claim to anger ("You knew very well it wouldn't help me."). However, a very common reaction to the reframing response is simply more anger. Reframing may be viewed as a form of insult as it challenges the person's capacities for understanding. In any case, if reframing engenders anger the story remains open.

A similar picture emerges when we consider the angry reaction to anger. If this occurs, the most common reply is that of still more anger. In effect, these latter results furnish a partial replication of the above findings on the escalation of hostility.

A more thorough understanding of such patterns can be derived from a brief comparison of the anger scenarios with those involving depression and happiness (Fig. 7 and 8). In the case of depression, reframing, advice, and commiseration are the most common reactions. And, of the subsequent reactions to these moves, all but two options lead to a story ending. Apparently, advice can be an ineffectual reply to depression; when it is used there is at least a small possibility of its leading to an anger response. Whether or not this anger then precipitates a new scenario, that of anger expression (Fig. 6), remains to be explored. Further,

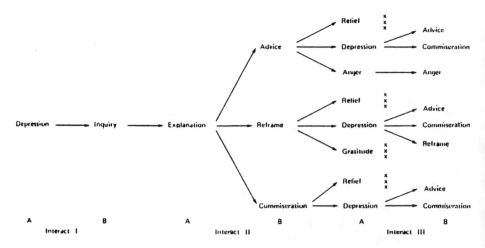

Fig. 7. Emotional scenarios for expressions of depression.

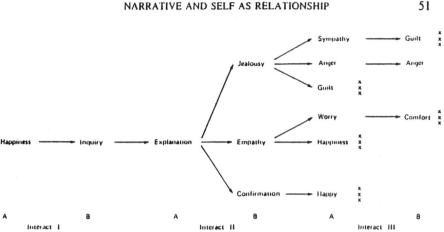

Fig. 8. Emotional scenarios for expressions of happiness.

if one commiserates with depression ("I'm really sorry you feel so bad"), there is a high probability that this response will serve as an invitation for even more intense expressions of depression. The reframing option (e.g., "Oh, things may not be as bad as you see them. Think how lucky you are that . . .") seems most promising at this juncture for bringing the scenario to a conclusion.

With regard to expressions of happiness, the most common reaction by far (70% of the respondents) is that of empathy ("That makes me happy too."). This reply markedly delimits the possible reactions of the initiator, as he/she is univocally seen as ending the story at this point with an expression of happiness. Much the same result occurs if one responds to happiness with confirmation ("That's really great for you.") The story rapidly ends with the initiator's furthered expression of happiness. However, as the figure demonstrates, expressions of happiness are not always such mutually supportive exchanges. In particular, a friend's expression of happiness may, with a slight degree of probability, lead to an expression of jealousy. If this reaction occurs, a range of possible reactions, including guilt, anger, and hurt may emerge, and the narrative remains open.

Although much additional research is invited at this point, the present findings do enable us to draw several tentative conclusions at this point:

1. When a friend engages in what is termed an emotional expression, and there is no apparent context, one will almost invariably reply with a query into cause. In our view this query acts as a prompt for the telling of a narrative that renders the expression intelligible and simultaneously informs one of the forms of scenario that are subsequently permitted.

2. Once the context for the expression has been furnished, most responses to

the expression may be accounted for with as few as three action classifications. These responses, in turn, will reliably yield additional responses on the part of the expressor of the emotion. These replies, as well as subsequent reactions, can be typically accounted for in terms of three action classifications. In effect, we find that while there is latitude in the range of possible scenarios, there are highly reliable patterns within the culture. Emotional expressions may thus be viewed as but one discrete element in more complex cross-time patterns. The mistake of the traditional view of emotions as possessions of individuals appears to be that of decontextualization. The traditional study of emotion has been akin to the study of the forward pass in football or the handshake in greeting; too little account has been taken of the social process which renders such actions meaningful.

3. Endings for emotional scenarios appear almost invariably to include the expression of happy sentiments. No cases were discovered in which a negative emotional state (e.g., anger, jealousy, depression, etc.) served as a proper ending to the scenario. When lived narratives involve emotional expressions, it appears that they are very likely to be stories with happy endings.

4. Although the data are limited, it may be ventured that scenarios commencing with an expression of what may be termed a positive emotion (an emotion that is valued, sought, or prized) are more truncated or less extended than those commencing with a negative emotion. In part, this conclusion is suggested by the above surmise that positive emotional states are essential for scenario endings. However, as the above graphs also demonstrate, even though it is possible to end an anger or a depression scenario within two and a half interacts, they are typically longer in duration. Most scenarios involving the initial expression of happiness are terminated within two interacts.

5. Drawing together these various results and viewing them in the context of our earlier discussion of narrative forms, it appears that the typical emotional scenario approximates the Aristotelian romance or the comedy. As will be recalled, both the romance and the comedy narratives commence on a positive level, the protagonists are then propelled along a descending narrative slope, and the remainder of the story is occupied with reestablishing a positive level (victory or harmony). When the happy or harmonious state is reached the story is complete. The expression of anger and depression thus operate to tilt the lived narrative in the downward direction. Subsequent interacts operate in such a way as to reestablish a positive state. When a positive emotion is expressed at the outset, the subsequent story is likely to be brief, for the expression is one which typically signifies the end of the scenario. All that is required is a form of confirmation.

Clearly the research reported here is only a beginning. There are many interesting and important questions yet to be asked. More emotional forms must be examined; participants other than college students are needed; *in vivo* scenarios are much in need; scenarios must be followed through the full set of iterations; gender differences must be explored; means of avoiding unwanted patterns must be examined. We see, then, new vistas for inquiry into the emotions opening, new options for daily living emerging, and new ways developing for mental health practitioners to approach the emotional expressions of their clients.

VI. Conclusion

Earlier papers (Gergen, 1984a, b) have attempted to demonstrate the promise for social psychology of theory that is both diachronic and relational. In the former case it has been argued that the intense concentration on singular, isolated processes (e.g., dissonance reduction, reactance, self-awareness) has meant a general impoverishment in theories treating extended, cross-time change. In the case of relational theory, the emphasis on stable mechanisms or processes "within the heads" of single individuals (e.g., attitudes, stereotypes, schemas, traits) has inhibited the growth of theory that takes social interdependency to be its major focus. The present treatment of the self has attempted to take steps in both the diachronic and relational direction. To the extent that both self-understanding and social conduct proceed on a narrative basis, the diachronic character of social life is made manifest. To the extent that narratives are socially derived, socially sustained, and require interdependency of action for their execution, the relational quality of human action is realized. In no way is the present treatment conclusive. Rather it has tried to open consideration on the self as relationship by developing an array of conceptual tools, a lexicon of understanding, that brings coherence to the area and to raise sets of problems for future study. Several lines of research have been employed as a means of vivifying the potential of the orientation. In effect, by reconstructing the self in this way we hope that seeds may be planted for a future harvest.

References

Armon-Jones, C. (1985). Presumption, explication and the social construction of emotion. *Journal for the Theory of Social Behavior*, 15 1–22.

Averill, J. R. (1982). *Anger and aggression: An essay on emotion*. New York: Springer-Verlag.

Averill, J. R. (1985). The social construction of emotion. In K. J. Gergen & K. E. Davis (Eds.), *The social construction of the person*. New York: Springer-Verlag.

Bennett, W. L., & Feldman, M. S. (1981). *Reconstructing reality in the courtroom*. New Brunswick, NJ: Rutgers University Press.

Bettleheim, B. (1976). *The uses of enchantment*. New York: Knopf.

Bruner, J. (1986). *Actual minds, possible worlds*. Cambridge, Mass: Harvard University Press.

Campbell, J. (1956). *The hero with a thousand faces.* New York: Meridian (1st published in 1949).

Cohler, B. J. (1979). *Personal narrative and life-course.* Unpublished manuscript, University of Chicago.

Collingwood, R. G. (1946). *The idea of history.* Oxford: Clarendon.

Coulter, J. (1983). *Rethinking cognitive theory.* New York: St. Martin's Press.

Coyne, J. C. (1976). Toward an interactional description of depression. *Psychiatry,* **29** 28–39.

Csikszentmihalyi, M., & Beattie, O. (1979). Life themes: A theoretical and empirical explanation of their origins and effects. *Journal of Humanistic Psychology,* **19,** 45–63.

Darwin, C. (1955). *The expression of emotions in man and animals.* New York: Philosophical Library (originally published in 1872).

DeRivera, J. (1984). The structure of emotional relationships. In P. Shaver (Ed.), *Review of personality and social psychology,* Beverly Hills, CA: Sage.

de Waele, J. P., & Harré, R. (1976). The personality of individuals. In R. Harré (Ed.), *Personality.* Oxford: Blackwell.

Felson, R. S. (1984). Patterns of aggressive social interaction. In A. Mummendey (Ed.), *Social psychology of aggression.* New York: Springer-Verlag.

Frye, N. (1957). *Anatomy of criticism.* Princeton, N.J.: Princeton University Press.

Gadamer, H. G. (1976). *Truth and method.* New York: Seabury.

Gallie, W. B. (1964). *Philosophy and the historical understanding.* London: Chatto & Windus.

Gauld, A., & Shotter, J. (1977). *Human action and its psychological investigation.* London: Routledge & Kegan Paul.

Gergen, K. J. (1982). *Toward transformation in social knowledge.* New York: Springer-Verlag.

Gergen, K. J. (1984a). An introduction to historical social psychology. In K. Gergen & M. Gergen (Eds.), *Historical social psychology.* Hillsdale, NJ: Erlbaum.

Gergen, K. J. (1984b). Theory of the self: Impasse and evolution. In L. Berkowitz (Ed.), *Advances in experimental social psychology* (Vol. 17) (pp. 49–115). New York: Academic Press.

Gergen, K. J. (1986). Correspondence vs. autonomy in the language of understanding human action. In D. Fiske & R. Shweder (Eds.), *Pluralism and subjectivity in social science.* Chicago: University of Chicago Press.

Gergen, K. J., & Gergen, M. M. (1983). Narratives of the self. In T. R. Sarbin & K. E. Scheibe (Eds.), *Studies in social identity.* New York: Praeger.

Gergen, K. J., & Gergen, M. M. (1986). Narrative form and the construction of psychological science. In T. R. Sarbin (Ed.), *Narrative psychology: The storied nature of human conduct.* New York: Praeger.

Gergen, K. J., & Gergen, M. M. (1987a). Narratives of relationship. In M. McGhee, D. D. Clarke, & R. Burnett (Eds.), *Accounting for relationship.* Oxford: Blackwell (in press).

Gergen, M. M. (1980). *Antecedents and consequences of self-attributional preferences in later life.* Unpublished doctoral dissertation, Temple University.

Gergen, M., & Gergen, K. J. (1984). Social construction of narrative accounts. In K. Gergen & M. Gergen (Eds.), *Historical social psychology.* Hillsdale, NJ: Erlbaum.

Gergen, M., & Gergen, K. J. (1987b). The self in temporal perspective. In R. Abeles (Ed.), *Life-span social psychology.* Hillsdale, NJ: Erlbaum.

Giddens, A. (1976). *New rules of sociological method.* New York: Basic Books.

Goodman, N. (1978). *Ways of worldmaking.* Indianapolis, IN: Hackett.

Hankiss, A. (1981). Ontologies of the self: On the mythological rearranging of one's life-history. In D. Bertaux (Ed.), *Biography and society.* Beverly Hills, CA: Sage.

Hanson, N. R. (1958). *Patterns of discovery.* London: Cambridge University Press.

Hardy, B. (1968). Towards a poetics of fiction: An approach through narrative. *Novel,* **2,** 5–14.

Harkness, S., & Super, C. M. (1958). Child-environment interactions in the socialization of affect. In M. Lewis & C. Saarni (Eds.), *The socialization of emotions.* New York: Plenum.

Harré, R., & Secord, P. F. (1972). *The explanation of social behaviour.* Oxford: Blackwell.

Harris, L. M., Gergen, K. J., & Lannamann, J. W. (1987). Aggression rituals. *Communication Monographs, 53,* 252–265.

Kahn, J., Coyne, J. C., & Margolin, G. (1987). Depression and marital disagreement: The social construction of despair. *Journal of Social and Personal Relationships,* in press.

Kelly, M. H., & Keil, F. C. (1985). The more things change . . . : Metamorphoses and conceptual structure.*Cognitive Science,* **9,** 403–416.

Kermode, F. (1967). *The sense of an ending.* New York: Oxford University Press.

Kessen, W. (1979). The American child and other cultural inventions. *American Psychologist, 34,* 815–820.

Kitwood, T. (1980). *Disclosures to a stranger.* London: Routledge & Kegan Paul.

Knudson, R. M. (1985). Marital compatibility and mutual identity confirmation. In W. Ickes (Ed.), *Compatible and incompatible relationships.* New York: Springer-Verlag.

Kohli, M. (1981). Biography: Account, text and method. In D. Bertaux (Ed.), *Biography and society.* Beverly Hills, CA: Sage.

Labov, W. (1981). Speech actions and reactions in personal narrative. In D. Tannen (Ed.), *Analyzing discourse: Text and talk.* Washington, DC: Georgetown University Press.

Laudau, M. (1984). Human evolution as narrative. *American Scientist, 72,* 262–268.

Lippman, S. (1986). *"Nothing but the facts, ma'am": The impact of testimony construction and narrative style on jury decisions.* Unpublished senior thesis, Swarthmore College.

Loftus, E. F. (1979). *Eyewitness testimony.* Cambridge, Mass: Harvard University Press.

Lutz, C. (1985). Cultural patterns and individual differences in the child's emotional meaning system. In M. Lewis & C. Saarni (Eds.), *The socialization of emotions.* New York: Plenum.

MacIntyre, A. (1981). *After virtue.* South Bend, IND.: University of Notre Dame Press.

Mancuso, J. C., & Sarbin, T. R. (1983). The self-narrative in the enactment of roles. In T. R. Sarbin & K. E. Scheibe (Eds.), *Studies in social identity.* New York: Praeger.

Mandler, J. M. (1978). A code in the node: The use of story schema in retrieval. *Discourse Processes,* **1,** 14–35.

Mandler, J. M. (1984). *Stories, scripts and scenes: Aspects of schema theory.* Hillsdale, NJ: Erlbaum.

Maslow, A. H. (1961). Peak-experiences as acute identity experiences. *American Journal of Psychoanlysis,* **21,** 254–260.

Mink, L. O. (1970). History and fiction as modes of comprehension. *New Literary History,* **1,** 541–558.

Murray, K. D. (1985a). Justificatory accounts and the meaning of the marathon as a social event. *Australian Psychologist,* **20,** 62–74.

Murray, K. D. (1985b). Life as fiction. *Journal for the Theory of Social Behavior,* **15,** 189–202.

Nehamas, A. (1986). *Nietzsche, life as literature.* Cambridge, MA: Harvard University Press.

Ong, W. J. (1982). *Orality and literacy.* London: Methuen.

Ortega y Gasset, J. (1941). *History as a system.* New York: Norton.

Pearce, W. B., & Cronen, V. (1980). *Communication, action and meaning.* New York: Praeger.

Plutchik, R. (1980). A general psychoevolutionary theory of emotion. In R. Plutchik & H. Kellerman (Eds.), *Emotion, theory, research and experience.* New York: Academic Press.

Potter, J., Stringer, P., & Wetherell, Y. (1984). *Social texts and context.* London: Routledge & Kegan Paul.

Propp, V. (1968). *Morphology of the folktale.* Texas: University of Texas Press.

Rabinow, P., & Sullivan, W. M. (1979). *Interpretive social science reader.* Berkeley, Ca: University of California Press.

Reisenzein, R. (1983). The Schachter theory of emotion: Two decades later. *Psychological Bulletin,* **94,** 239–264.

56   KENNETH J. GERGEN AND MARY M. GERGEN

Rimmon-Kenan, S. (1983). *Narrative fiction: Contemporary poetics*. London: Methuen.

Ryle, G. (1949). *The concept of mind*. London: Hutchinson.

Sabini, J., & Silver, M. (1982). *The moralities of everyday life*. New York: Oxford Univ. Press.

Sarbin, T. R. (1968). A preface to a psychological analysis of the self. In C. Gordon & K. J. Gergen (Eds.), *The self in social interaction*. New York: Wiley.

Schachter, S. & Singer, J. L. (1962). Cognitive, social and physiological determinants of emotional state. *Psychological Review*, 69, 379–399.

Schank, R. C., & Abelson, R. P. (1977). *Scripts, plans, goals and understanding*. Hillsdale, NJ: Erlbaum.

Schapp, W. (1976). In *Geschichten verstrickt zum Sein von Mensch und Ding*. Wiesbaden: Heymann.

Shotter, J. (1984). *Social accountability and selfhood*. Oxford: Blackwell.

Spence, D. P. (1982). *Narrative truth and historical truth*. New York: Norton.

Sutton-Smith, B. (1979). Presentation and representation in fictional narrative. *New Directions for Child Development*, 6, 53–66.

Tololyan, K. (1987). Cultural narrative and the motivation of the terrorist. *Journal of Strategic Studies*, in press.

Wegner, D. M., Gialiano, T., & Hertel, P. T. (1985). Cognitive interdependence in close relationships. In W. Ickes (Ed.), *Compatible and incompatible relationships*. New York: Springer-Verlag.

Young, K. (1982). Edgework: Frame and boundary in the phenomenology of narrative. *Semiotica*, 41, 277–315.

[15]

PART IV

REFLECTION AND RECONSTRUCTION

11

Beyond Narrative in the Negotiation of Therapeutic Meaning

Kenneth J. Gergen and John Kaye

I have reached no conclusions, have erected no boundaries
shutting out and shutting in, separating inside
    from outside: I have
    drawn no lines:
        as
manifold events of sand
change the dunes' shape that will not be the same shape
tomorrow,

so I am willing to go along, to accept
the becoming
thought, to stake off no beginnings or ends, establish
        no walls

                  A.R. Ammons, *Carson's Inlet*

When people seek psychotherapy they have a story to tell. It is
frequently the troubled, bewildered, hurt, or angry story of a life or
relationship now spoiled. For many it is a story of calamitous events
conspiring against their sense of well-being, self-satisfaction, or
sense of efficacy. For others the story may concern unseen and
mysterious forces insinuating themselves into life's organized
sequences, disrupting and destroying. And for still others it is as if,
under the illusion of knowing how the world is or ought to be, they
have somehow bumped up against trouble for which their favored
account has not prepared them. They have discovered an awful
reality that now bleeds all past understandings of survival value.
Whatever its form, the therapist confronts a narrative – often
persuasive and gripping; it is a narrative that may be terminated
within a brief period or it may be extended over weeks or months.
However, at some juncture the therapist must inevitably respond to

this account, and whatever follows within the therapeutic procedure will draw its significance in response to this account.

What options are available to the therapist as recipient of a narrated reality? At least one option is pervasive within the culture, and sometimes used as well within counseling settings, social work interviews, and short-term therapies. It may be viewed as the *advisory option*. For the advisor, the client's story remains relatively inviolate. Its terms of description and forms of explanation remain unchallenged in any significant way. Rather, for the advisor the major attempt is to locate forms of effective action 'under the circumstances' as narrated. Thus, for example, if the individual speaks of being depressed because of failure, means are sought for re-establishing efficacy. If the client is rendered ineffectual because of grief, then a program of action may be suggested for overcoming the problem. In effect, the client's life story is accepted as fundamentally accurate for him or her, and the problem is to locate ameliorative forms of action within the story's terms.

There is much to be said on behalf of the advisory option. Within the realm of the relatively ordinary, it is most obviously 'reasonable' and most probably effective. Yet, for the more seriously chronic or deeply disturbed client, the advisory option harbors serious limitations. At the outset, there is little attempt to confront deeper origins of the problem or the complex ways it is sustained. The major concern is in locating a new course of action. Whatever the chain of antecedents, they simply remain the same – continuing to operate as threats to the future. Further, little attempt is typically made to probe the contours of the story, to determine its relative utility or viability. Could the client be mistaken, or defining things in a less than optimal way? Such questions often remain unexplored. In accepting 'the story as told,' the problem definition also remains fixed. As a result the range of possible options for action remains circumscribed. If the problem is said to be failure, for example, the relevant options are geared around means for re-establishing success. Other possibilities are thrust to the margins of plausibility. And finally, in the chronic or severe case, the location of action alternatives too often seems a superficial palliative. For one who has been depressed, addictive, or self-destructive for a period of years, for example, simple advice for living may seem little more than whispering in the wind.

In the present chapter we wish to explore two more substantial alternatives to the advisory option. The first is represented by most traditional forms of psychotherapy and psychoanalytic practice. In its reliance on various neo-Enlightenment assumptions dominant in the sciences of the present century, this orientation toward narrative may be viewed as *modernist*. In contrast, much thinking within the *postmodern* arena forms a powerful challenge to the modernist conception of the narrative, and in doing so opens new modes of therapeutic procedure. This latter orientation is well represented by the various constructionist contributions to the present volume. However, as the present chapter unfolds, we wish to develop dimensions of the constructionist orientation not currently emphasized in the existing analyses. In effect, we wish to press beyond narrative meaning in the making of lives.

Therapeutic Narratives in Modernist Context

Much has been written about modernism in the sciences, literature, and the arts, and this is scarcely the context for thorough review.[1] However, it is useful to consider briefly a set of assumptions that have guided activities in the sciences and the allied professions of mental health. For it is this array of assumptions that have largely informed the therapeutic treatment of client narratives. The modernist era in the sciences has been one committed, first of all, to the empirical *elucidation of essences*. Whether it be the character of the atom, the gene, or the synapse in the natural sciences, or processes of perception, economic decision making, or organizational development in the social sciences, the major attempt has been to establish bodies of systematic and objective knowledge. Such knowledge should, it is reasoned, enable the society to make increasingly accurate predictions about cause and effect relations, and thus, with appropriate technologies in place, to gain mastery over the future. For the modernist, the good society can be erected on the foundations of empirical knowledge.

Empirical knowledge is communicated, of course, through scientific languages. These languages, if they have been well grounded in observation, are said to reflect or to map the world in so far as we can know it. Narratives are essentially structures of language, and in so far as narratives are generated within the scientific milieu they can, on the modernist account, function as conveyors of objective knowledge. Thus, the narratives of the novelist are labeled as 'fiction,' and are considered of little consequence for serious scientific purposes. People's narratives of their lives, what has happened to them and why, are not necessarily fictions. But, as the behavioral scientist proclaims, they are notoriously inaccurate and unreliable. Thus, they are considered of limited value in understanding the individual's life, and far less preferable than the empirically based accounts of the trained scientist. It is thus that the narrative accounts of the scientist are accorded the highest credibility, and are set apart from the markets of entertainment and everyday interaction as 'scientific theories.' From the 'Big Bang' theory of the Earth's origins to evolutionary theory within the natural sciences, and from Piagetian theory of rational development to theories of economic recession and cultural transmission in the social sciences, scientific narratives are structured stories of how things come to be as they are.[2]

The mental health profession today is largely an outgrowth of the modernist context and shares deeply in its assumptions. Thus from Freud to contemporary cognitive therapists, the general belief is that the professional therapist functions (or ideally should function) as a scientist. By virtue of such activities as scientific training, research experience, knowledge of the scientific literature, and countless hours of systematic observation and thought within the therapeutic situation, the professional is armed with knowledge. To be sure, contemporary knowledge is incomplete, and more research is ever required. But the knowledge of the contemporary professional is far superior to that of the turn-of-the-century therapist, so it is said, and the future can only bring further improvements. Thus, with few exceptions, therapeutic theories (whether behavioral, systemic, psychodynamic, or experiential/humanist) contain explicit assumptions regarding (1) the underlying cause or basis of pathology, (2) the location of this cause within clients or their relationships, (3) the means by which such problems can be diagnosed, and (4) the means by which the pathology may be eliminated. In effect, the trained professional enters the therapeutic arena with a well-developed narrative for which there is abundant support within the community of scientific peers.

It is this background that establishes the therapist's posture toward the client's narrative. For the client's narrative is, after all, made of the flimsy stuff of daily stories – replete with whimsy, metaphor, wishful thinking, and distorted memories. The scientific narrative, by contrast, has the seal of professional approval. From this vantage point we see that the therapeutic process must inevitably result in the slow but inevitable replacement of the client's story with the therapist's. The client's story does not remain a freestanding reflection of truth, but rather, as questions are asked and answered, descriptions and explanations are reframed, and affirmation and doubt are disseminated by the therapist, the client's narrative is either destroyed or incorporated – but in any case replaced – by the professional account. The client's account is transformed by the psychoanalyst into a tale of family romance, by the Rogerian into a struggle against conditional regard, and so on.

170　Reflection and Reconstruction

It is this process of replacing the client's story with the professional that is so deftly described in Donald Spence's *Narrative Truth and Historical Truth*. As Spence surmises, the therapist

> is constantly making decisions about the form and status of the patient's material. Specific listening conventions . . . help to guide these decisions. If, for example, the analyst assumes that contiguity indicates causality, then he will hear a sequence of disconnected statements as a causal chain; at some later time, he might make an interpretation that would make this assumption explicit. If he assumes that transference predominates and that the patient is always talking, in more or less disguised fashion, about the analyst, then he will 'hear' the material in that way and make some kind of ongoing evaluation of the state of the transference. (1982: 129)

Such replacement procedures do have certain therapeutic advantages. For one, as clients gain 'real insight' into their problems, the problematic narrative is thereby removed. The client is thus furnished an alternative reality that holds promise for future well-being. In effect, the failure story with which the client entered therapy can be swapped for a success story. And, similar to the advisory option outlined earlier, the new story is likely to suggest alternative lines of action – forming or dissolving relationships, operating under a daily regimen, submitting to therapeutic procedures, and so on. There are new, and more hopeful, things to do. And too, by providing the client a scientific formulation, the therapist has played the appointed role in a long-standing cultural ritual in which the ignorant, the failing, and the weak seek counsel from the wise, superior, and strong. It is indeed a comforting ritual to all who will submit.

Yet, in spite of these advantages, there is substantial reason for concern. Major shortcomings have been located in the modernist orientation to therapy. The scientific community has long been skeptical of the knowledge claims pervasive in the mental health professions. As it is held, mental health practitioners have little justification for their claims to knowledge of pathology and cure. Critics have also inveighed against traditional forms of therapy for their excessive concern with the individual. As it is argued, such theories are blind to the broad cultural conditions in which psychological difficulties may be significantly connected (see, for example, Kovel, 1980). Feminist critics have grown increasingly vocal in such attacks, noting that many 'female disorders' are inappropriately traced to the female mind and are the direct result of the oppressive conditions of the female in society (see, for example, Hare-Mustin and Marecek, 1988). Others have been deeply unsettled by the pathologizing tendencies of the profession. From the modernist standpoint, deviant or aberrant behavior is traced to mental pathologies, and it is the task of the mental health profession – like the medical profession – to identify and treat such disorders. Yet, in accepting such assumptions the profession acts so as to objectify mental illness – even when there are many alternative means of interpreting or understanding the same phenomena (see, for example, Gergen, 1991).

Over and above these problems, there are additional shortcomings in the modernist orientation to client narrative. There is, for one, a substantial imperious thrust to the modernist approach. Not only is the therapist's narrative never placed under threat, but the therapeutic procedure virtually ensures that it will be vindicated. In Spence's terms, 'the search space [within therapeutic interaction] can be infinitely expanded until the [therapist's] answer is discovered and . . . there is no possibility of finding a negative solution, of deciding that the [therapist's] search has failed' (1982: 108). Thus, regardless of the complexity, sophistication, or value of the client's account, it is eventually replaced by a narrative created before the client's entry into therapy and the contours over which he or she has no control.

It is not simply that therapists from a given school will ensure that their clients come away bearing beliefs in their particular account. By implication (and practice) the ultimate aim of most schools of therapy is hegemonic. All other schools of thought, and their associated narratives, should succumb. Psychoanalysts wish to eradicate behavior modification; cognitive-behavioral therapists see systems therapy as misguided, and so on. Yet, the most immediate and potentially injurious consequences are reserved for the client. For in the end, the structure of the procedure furnishes the client a lesson in inferiority. The client is indirectly informed that he or she is ignorant, insensitive, woolly-headed, or emotionally incapable of comprehending reality. In contrast, the therapist is positioned as all-knowing and wise – a model to which the client might aspire. The situation is all the more lamentable owing to the fact that in occupying the superior role, the therapist fails to reveal any weaknesses. Nowhere are the wobbly foundations of the therapist's account made known; nowhere do the therapist's personal doubts, foibles, and failings come to light. And the client is thus confronted with a vision of human possibility that is as unattainable as the heroism of cinematic mythology.

The modernist orientation suffers as well from the fixedness of the narrative formulations. As we have seen, modernist approaches to therapy begin with an a priori narrative, justified by claims to a scientific base. Because it is sanctioned as scientific, this narrative

172   Reflection and Reconstruction

is relatively closed to alteration. Minor modifications may be entertained, but the system itself bears the weight of established doctrine. In the same way biologists seldom question the basic stipulations of Darwinian theory, and psychoanalysts who question the foundations of psychoanalytic theory are placed in professional peril. Under these conditions the client confronts a relatively closed system of understanding. It is not only that the client's own reality will eventually give way to the therapist's, but all other interpretations will also be excluded. To the extent that the therapist's narrative becomes the client's reality, and his or her actions are guided accordingly, life options for the client are severely truncated. Of all possible modes of acting in the world, one is set on a course emphasizing, for example, ego autonomy, self-actualization, rational appraisal, or emotional expressiveness, depending on the brand of therapy inadvertently selected. Or to put it otherwise, each form of modernist therapy carries with it an image of the 'fully functioning' or 'good' individual; like a fashion plate, this image serves as the guiding model for the therapeutic outcome.

This constriction of life possibilities is all the more problematic because it is decontextualized. That is, the therapist's narrative is an abstract formalization – cut away from particular cultural and historical circumstances. None of the modernist narratives deals with the specific conditions of living in ghetto poverty, with a brother who has AIDS, with a child who has Down's syndrome, with a boss who is sexually abusive, and so on. In contrast to the complex details that crowd the corners of daily life – which are indeed life itself – modernist narratives are virtually content-free. As a result, these narratives are precariously insinuated into the life circumstances of the individual. They are, in this sense, clumsy and insensitive, failing to register the particularities of the client's living conditions. To emphasize self-fulfillment to a woman living in a household with three small children and a mother-in-law with Alzheimer's is not likely to be beneficial. To press a Park Avenue attorney for increased emotional expressiveness in his daily life is of doubtful assistance.

Therapeutic Realities in Postmodern Context

The literature on postmodernist culture is rapidly accumulating, and again this is an inappropriate juncture for a full review.[3] However, it is useful to emphasize a single contrast with modernism, one of central significance to the concept of knowledge, science, and therapy. Within the postmodernist wings of the academy, major attention is now devoted to the process of representation, or the means by which 'reality' is set forth in writing, the arts, television, and so on. As it is generally agreed, criteria of accuracy or objectivity are of questionable relevance to judging the relationship between representation and its object. There is no means of arraying all the events in the 'real world' on one side and all the syllables of the language on the other, and linking them in one-to-one fashion, such that each syllable would reflect an isolated atom of reality. Rather, in the case of writing, each style or genre of literature operates according to local rules or conventions, and these conventions will largely determine the way we understand the putative objects of representation. Scientific writing, then, furnishes a no more *accurate* picture of reality than fiction. The former accounts may be embedded in scientific activity in a way that the latter are not. However, both kinds of accounts are guided by cultural conventions, historically situated, which largely determine the character of the reality they seek to depict.

This reconsideration of representation does not thus reduce the importance of scientific narrative. Rather, in two major ways it shifts the site of its significance. First, rather than such narratives retaining the status of 'truth telling' – thus claiming to be predictive aids to survival – they gain their importance as constitutive frames. That is, such narratives constitute reality as one kind of thing rather than another, as good or evil in certain respects as opposed to others. And in doing so, they furnish the rational grounds or justifications for certain lines of conduct as opposed to others. Thus, if we believe with socio-biologists that human action is primarily governed by genetically based urges, the way we carry out daily life is likely to be different than if we believe, with learning psychologists, that people's actions are infinitely malleable. Each account, once embraced, invites certain actions and discourages others. Scientific narratives gain their chief significance, then, in terms of the forms of life which they invite, rationalize, or justify. They are not so much reflections of life already lived as they are the progenitors of the future.

The postmodern shift from the object of knowledge to its representation also relocates the grounds for justification. On the modernist account, scientific descriptions are the product of single individuals – scientists whose patient skills of observation yield insights for all. Individual scientists, then, are more or less authoritative, more or less knowledgeable about the world as it is. From the postmodern perspective, the factual warrant is removed from the scientist's narrative. The scientist may 'know how' to do certain things (what we might call, for example, 'atomic fusion'), but that scientist does not 'know that' what is being done *is*

174   *Reflection and Reconstruction*

'atomic fusion.' What, then, gives the scientist the right to speak with authority? In the same way that the conventions of writing permit things to be said in one way and not others, so the social conventions of the scientific community bestow on its members the right to be authoritative. That is, the scientist only speaks with justifiable assuredness within the community of those who honor those particular ways of speaking. Or to put it otherwise, scientific representations are products of the community of scientists – negotiating, competing, conspiring, and so on. Within a postmodern frame what we take to be knowledge is a social product.

This context of thought furnishes major challenges to the modernist conception of scientific narrative, and most cogently, to the modernist orientation to therapy. At the outset it removes the factual justification of the modernist narratives of pathology and cure, transforming these accounts into forms of cultural mythology. It undermines the unquestioned status of the therapist as scientific authority, with privileged knowledge of cause and cure. The therapist's narratives thus take their place alongside the myriad other possibilities available in the culture, not transcendentally better but perhaps different. And significant questions must be raised with the traditional practice of replacing the client's stories with the fixed and narrow alternatives of the modernist therapist. There is no justification outside the narrow community of like-minded therapists for battering the client's complex and richly detailed life into a single, pre-formulated narrative, a narrative that may be of little relevance or promise for the client's subsequent life conditions. And finally, there is no broad justification for the traditional status hierarchy that both demeans and frustrates the client. The therapist and client form a relationship to which both bring resources and in terms of which the contours of the future may be carved.

It is this postmodern context of thought which informs most of the contributions to the present volume. There is within these chapters a broad abandonment of the traditional narratives of therapy – at least as furnishing reliable and scientifically based accounts of pathology and cure. There is a pervasive abnegation of the role of the therapist as superior knower, standing above the client as an unattainable model of the good life. There is, instead, a strong commitment to viewing the therapeutic encounter as a milieu for the creative generation of meaning. The client's voice is not merely an auxiliary device for the vindication of the therapist's pre-determined narrative, but serves in these contexts as an essential constituent of a jointly constructed reality. In virtually all these chapters the emphasis, then, is on the collaborative relationship between client and therapist as they strive to develop forms of narrative that may usefully enable the client to move beyond the current or continuing crisis.

We strongly endorse these explorations into constructionist forms of practice. We stand as strong admirers and supporters of these efforts to realize the potential of postmodern thought. At the same time, however, the broad implications of the present endeavors are far from clear. We stand at a point of embarcation: a radical departure from traditional assumptions about knowledge, persons, and the nature of 'the real' is at hand. Substantial deliberation and experimentation will be required before the results can be assayed, and even then we shall have but additional fuel for a conversation that should ideally have no end. It is in this spirit that we wish in the remainder of this chapter to bring a sharper focus on the therapeutic narrative in postmodern context. For it is our surmise that current discussions of the construction of meaning in therapy still retain significant vestiges of the modernist world-view. And, if the potentials of postmodernism are to be fully realized, we must ultimately press beyond narrative construction. The ultimate challenge, as we see it, is not so much that of trans-forming meaning, but transcending it. To appreciate this possibility, it is first necessary to explore the pragmatic dimension of narrative meaning.

Narration and Pragmatic Utility

Narrative accounts in modernist frame were to serve as representa-tions of reality – true or false in their capacity to match events as they occurred. If the accounts were accurate they also served as blueprints to adaptive action. Thus, in the therapeutic case, if the narrative reflected a recurring pattern of maladaptive action, one could begin to explore alternative ways of behaving. Or, if it captured the formative processes for a given pathology, palliatives could be prescribed. Within its knowledge frame, the therapist's narrative prescribed a better way of living. For most therapists entering the post-empiricist era, the modernist concern with accuracy is no longer compelling. Narrative truth is to be distin-guished from historical truth, and when closely examined, even the latter is found to be an impostor. What then is the function of narrative reconstruction? Most existing accounts point to the potential of such reconstructions to re-orient the individual, to open new courses of action that are more fulfilling and more adequately suited to the individual's experiences, capacities and proclivities. Thus, the client may alter or dispose of earlier

176   *Reflection and Reconstruction*

narratives, not because they are inaccurate, but because they are dysfunctional in his or her particular circumstances.

Yet, the question must be raised, in precisely what way(s) is the narrative to be 'useful.' How does a language of self-understanding guide, direct, or inform lines of action? Two answers to this question pervade post-empiricist camps at present, and both are problematic. On the one side is the metaphor of *language as a lens.* On this account, a narrative construction is a vehicle through which the world is seen. It is through the lens of narrative that the individual identifies objects, persons, actions, and so on. As it is argued, it is on the basis of the world as seen, and not on the world as it is, that the individual determines a course of action. Yet, to take this position is to view the individual as isolated and solipsistic – simply stewing in the juices of his or her own private constructions. The possibilities for survival are minimal, for there is no means to escape the encapsulation of the internal system of construals. Further, such an account buys a range of notorious epistemological problems. How, for example, does the individual develop the lens? From whence the first construction? For if there is no world outside that which is internally constructed, there would be no means of developing or fashioning the lens. It is simply self-vindicating.[4] And why, in the final analysis, should we believe that language is a lens, that the sounds and markings employed in human interchange are somehow transported into the mind to impose order on the perceptual world? The argument seems poorly taken.

The major alternative to this view holds the narrative construction to be an *internal model*, a form of story that can be interrogated by the individual as a guide to identity and action. Again, there is no brief for the truth of the model; it operates simply as an enduring structure that informs and directs action. Thus, for example, a person who features himself as a hero whose feats of bravery and intelligence should prevail against all odds, finds life unworkable. Through therapy he realizes that such a view not only places him in impossible circumstances but works against close feelings of intimacy and interdependence with his wife and children. A new story is worked out in which the individual comes to see himself as a champion not for himself, but for his family. His heroism will be gained through their feelings of happiness, and will thus depend as well on their assessments of circumstances and potentials. It is this transformed image that is to guide subsequent actions. While there is a certain wisdom to this position, it is again problematic. Stories of this variety are in themselves both idealized and abstract. As such they can seldom dictate behavior in complex, on-going interaction. What does the new story of self say, for example, about the best reaction to his wife's desires for him to spend fewer hours at work and more with the family, or how should he respond to a new job offer, challenging and profitable, but replete with risk? Stories as internal models are not only bare of specific information, but they remain static. The individual moves through numerous situations and relationships – a parent dies, a son is tempted by drugs, an attractive neighbor acts seductively, and so on. Yet, the narrative model remains inflexible – unbending and often irrelevant.

There is a third way of understanding narrative utility and, in our view, it is more conceptually and pragmatically adequate than the prevailing alternatives. The generative metaphor in this case is supplied in Wittgenstein's *Philosophical Investigations* (1953). As Wittgenstein compellingly argues, words gain their meaning not through their capacity to picture reality, but through their use in social interchange. We are engaged, then, in *games of language*, and it is by virtue of their use within these games that words acquire meaning. Thus, for example, what can be said about an emotion such as fear is not determined by 'the fact of fear,' but by the conventions of emotion talk in Western culture. I may say that fear is *strong* but not *sultry*, that it is *subsiding* but not *sedentary*. This is not because fear, as an object of observation, is just this way and not that. Rather, it is because of the limited ways of talking we have inherited from the past. Yet, language games for Wittgenstein are embedded within broader *forms of life*, or to extend the metaphor, *life games*. This is to say that the forms of interchange in which words are embedded, and which give them their value, are not limited to the linguistic realm alone. Such interchanges may include all our actions, along with various objects in our surroundings. Thus to count oneself as angry not only requires the use of certain words within the language games, but certain bodily actions (grinding or gritting the teeth, for example, rather than grinning) that constitute the forms of life in which the language game is embedded. To engage in anger, then, is to participate in a form of cultural dance; failing to take one's place in the dance is to fail at being angry.[5]

With this metaphor in place, let us return to the case of self-narratives. Stories about oneself – one's failures and successes, one's limits and potentials, and so on – are essentially arrangements of words (often conveyed with associated movements of the body). They are, in this sense, candidates for meaning within one or more games of language, one or more cultural dances. If they are to have utility, it is within the confines of a particular game or dance. Utility is to be derived from their success as moves within these arenas – in terms of their adequacy as reactions to previous moves or as instigators to what follows. Consider, for example, a story of failure – how one came to be lethargic and immobile. As we have seen, the story is neither true nor false in itself; it is simply one construction among many. However, as this story is inserted into various forms of relationship – into the games or dances of the culture – its effects are strikingly varied. If a friend has just related a story of great personal success, one's story of failure is likely to act as a repressive force, and alienate the friend who anticipated a congratulatory reaction. If, in contrast, the friend had just revealed a personal failure, to share one's own failings is likely to be reassuring and to solidify the friendship. Similarly, to relate one's story of lethargy and immobility to one's mother may elicit a warm and sympathetic reaction; to share it with a wife who worries each month over the bills may produce both frustration and anger.

To put it otherwise, a story is not simply a story. It is also a situated action in itself, a performance with illocutionary effects. It acts so as to create, sustain, or alter worlds of social relationship. In these terms, it is insufficient that the client and therapist negotiate a new form of self-understanding that seems realistic, aesthetic, and uplifting within the dyad. It is not their dance of meaning that is primarily at stake. Rather, the significant question is whether the new shape of meaning is serviceable within the social arena outside these confines. How, for example, does the story of oneself as 'hero of the family group' play for a wife who dislikes her dependent status, a boss who is a 'self-made woman,' or a rebellious son? What forms of action does the story invite in each of these situations; what kinds of dances are engendered, facilitated, or sustained? It is evaluation at this level that seems most crucial for the joint consideration of therapist and client.

Transcending Narrative

The focus on the pragmatics of narrative performance sets the stage for the critical argument of the present chapter. As we have seen, for many making the postmodern turn in therapy, the narrative continues to be viewed as either a form of internal lens, determining the way in which life is seen, or an internal model for the guidance of action. In light of the preceding discussion of pragmatics, these conceptions are found lacking in three important respects. First, each retains the *individualist* cast of modernism, in that the final resting place of the narrative construction is within the mind of the single individual. As we have reconsidered the utility of the narrative, we have moved outward – from the individual's mind to the relationships constituted by the narrative in action. Narratives exist in the telling, and tellings are constituents of relational forms – for good or ill. Secondly, the metaphors of the lens and the internal model both favor *singularity in narrative*; that is, both tend to presume the functionality of a single formulation of self-understanding. The individual possesses 'a lens' for comprehending the world, it is said, not a *repository* of lenses; and through therapy one comes to possess 'a new narrative truth,' it is often put, not a *multiplicity* of truths. From the pragmatic standpoint, the presumption of singularity operates against functional adequacy. Each narrative of the self may function well in certain circumstances, but lead to miserable outcomes in others. To have only a single means of making self intelligible, then, is to limit the range of relationships or situations in which one can function satisfactorily. Thus, for example, it may be very useful to 'do anger' effectively, and to formulate accounts to justify such activity. There are certain times and places in which anger is the most effective move in the dance. At the same time, to be over-skilled or over-prepared in this regard – such that anger is virtually the only means of moving relationships along – will vastly reduce one's relationships altogether. From the present perspective, narrative multiplicity is vastly to be preferred.

Finally, both the lens and the internal model conceptions favor belief in or *commitment to narrative*. That is, both suggest that the individual lives *within* the narrative as a system of understanding. One 'sees the world in this way,' as it is said, and the narrative is thus 'true for the individual.' Or the transformed story of self is 'the new reality;' it constitutes a 'new belief about self' to support and sustain the individual. Again, however, as we consider the social utility of narrative, belief and commitment become suspect. To be committed to a given story of self, to adopt it as 'now true for me,' is vastly to limit one's possibilities of relating. To believe that one *is successful* is thus as debilitating in its own way as believing that one *is a failure*. Both are only stories after all, and each may bear fruit within a particular range of contexts and relationships. To crawl inside one or the other and take root is to forgo the other, and thus to reduce the range of contexts and relationships in which one is adequate.

To frame the issue in another way, postmodern consciousness favors a thoroughgoing relativism in expressions of identity. On the metatheoretical level it invites a multiplicity of accounts of reality, while recognizing the historically and culturally situated

180   Reflection and Reconstruction

contingency of each. There are only accounts of truth within differing conversations, and no conversation is privileged. If the therapist adopts such a view on the metatheoretical level, it would be an act of bad faith to abandon it on the level of practice. Thus, for the postmodern practitioner a multiplicity of self-accounts is invited, but a commitment to none. It encourages the client, on the one hand, to explore a variety of means of understanding the self, but discourages a commitment to any of these accounts as standing for the 'truth of self.' The narrative constructions thus remain fluid, open to the shifting tides of circumstance – to the forms of dance that provide fullest sustenance.

Can such a conclusion be tolerated? Is the individual thus reduced to a social con artist, adopting whatever posture of identity gains the highest pay-off? Certainly, the postmodern emphasis is on flexibility of self-identification, but this does not simultaneously imply that the individual is either duplicitous or scheming. To speak of duplicity is to presume that there is a 'true expression' of self that could otherwise be available. Such a view is quintessentially modern, and thus abandoned. One may interpret one's actions as duplicitous or sincere, but these ascriptions are, after all, simply components of different stories. Similarly, to presume that the individual possesses private motives, and a rational calculus of self-presentation is again to sustain the modernist view of the self-contained individual. From the postmodern vantage point, the relationship takes priority over the individual self. That is, selves are only realized as a byproduct of relatedness. It is not independent selves who come together to form a relationship, but particular forms of relationship that engender what we take to be the individual's identity. Thus, to shift in the form and content of self-narration from one relationship to another is neither deceitful nor self-serving. Rather, it is to honor the various modes of relationship in which one is enmeshed. It is to take seriously the multiple and varied forms of human connectedness that make up a life. Adequate and fulfilling actions are only so in the terms of criteria generated within the various forms of relationship themselves.

The questions persist. Does the postmodern constructionist abandon that cherished possession in Western culture, personal identity? The answer is 'yes' if what is meant by identity is the story told, the action taken, the part played. However, if one is willing to press beyond these *products* to the underlying *process* in which they are realized, it is still possible to retain a view of individual animation. James Carse (1986) provides a useful metaphor in his meditation on finite and infinite games. As he proposes, there are finite games, the purpose of which is to win, and these may be compared with the infinite game in which the purpose is to continue to play. The rules are different for each finite game; it is only by knowing the rules that one knows what the game is. However, in the infinite game the rules change in the course of play, when players agree that the play may be threatened by a finite outcome – a victory of some players and a defeat of others. In Carse's terms, 'Finite players play within boundaries; infinite players play with boundaries. . . . Finite players are serious; infinite players are playful.' In this vein, self-narration takes place within the confines of the finite game. Each portrayal of self operates within the conventions of a particular relationship. However, we may yet retain our place in the infinite game – beyond narrative. If there is identity at this level, it cannot be articulated, laid out for public view in a given description or explanation. It lies in the boundless and inarticulable capacity for relatedness itself.

Therapeutic Moves

In the light of the above, it should be clear that we reject the simple adoption of narrative reconstruction or replacement as a guiding metaphor for psychotherapy. We would argue, rather, for embedding the emphasis on narrative and narrative thinking in a broader concern with the generation of meaning via dialogue. This involves a reconception of the relativity of meaning, an acceptance of indeterminacy, the generative exploration of a multiplicity of meanings, and the understanding that there is no necessity either to adhere to an invariant story or to search for a definitive story. 'Re-authoring' or 'restorying' seems to us a first-order therapeutic approach, one which implies the replacement of a dysfunctional master narrative with a more functional one. At the same time this result carries the seeds of a prescriptive rigidity – one which might also serve to confirm an illusion that it is possible to develop a set of principles or codes which can be invariantly applied irrespective of context. It is this very rigidity which is arguably constitutive of the difficulties people experience in their lives and relationships. Just as psychotherapists may be restrained by a limiting code, so people who experience their lives as problematic seem trapped within a set of limiting precepts, behavioral codes, and constitutive conventions. Acting from these conventions, they are not only restrained from alternate punctuations but can become imprisoned in painful transactional patterns with those around them.

Heinz von Foerster has made the acute observation that we are

182   *Reflection and Reconstruction*

blind until we see that we cannot see. If language provides the matrix for all human understanding, then psychotherapy may be aptly construed as 'linguistic activity in which conversation about a problem generates the development of new meanings' (Goolishian and Winderman, 1988: 139). Put differently, psychotherapy may be thought of as a process of *semiosis* – the forging of meaning in the context of collaborative discourse. It is a process during which the meaning of experience is transformed via a fusion of the horizons of the participants, alternative ways of punctuating experience are developed, and a new stance toward experience evolves. A crucial component of this process may inhere not only in the alternative ways of understanding generated by the discourse but also in the different order of meaning which concurrently emerges when our eyes are opened to seeing our blindness.

To help another toward an orientation that comes from seeing that we cannot see implies, first, a release from the tyranny of the implied authority of governing beliefs. Given the linguistic constitution of our world models, this requires in turn (1) a transformative dialogue in which new understandings are negotiated together with a new set of premises *about* meaning; and (2) the evocation of an expectant attitude toward the as yet unseen, the as yet unstoried, the 'meaning ahead of the text' (Ricoeur, 1971). In terms of Bateson's (1972) distinctions between levels of learning, it is a move beyond learning to replace one punctuation of a situation with another (Level 1), to learning new modes of punctuation (Level 2), to evolving what Keeney (1983: 159) calls 'a change of the premises underlying an entire system of punctuation habits' (Level 3). It is a progression from learning new meanings, to developing new categories of meaning, to transforming one's premises about the nature of meaning itself.

For any of these transformations to occur, a context needs to be established which facilitates their emergence. At the outset we are in full accord with Anderson and Goolishian's (this volume) emphasis on creating a climate where clients have the experience of being heard, of having both their point of view and feelings understood, of feeling themselves confirmed and accepted. It involves an endeavor to understand the client's point of view, to convey an understanding of how it makes sense to the person given the premises from which the viewpoint arises. At the same time this does not imply an acceptance or confirmation of the client's premises. It implies rather a form of *interested inquiry* which opens the premises for exploration.

This receptive mode of inquiry – with its openness to different ways of punctuating experience, readiness to explore multiple perspectives and endorse their coexistence – can, to the extent that it is experienced by the other, trigger a changed stance toward experience. By the same token it can liberate participants in therapy from an immersion in limiting constructions of the world. This is because the experiencing of receptivity – of openness to experience, together with a readiness to adopt multiple perspectives and accept the relativity of meaning itself – comprises a change in perspective.

Various ways in which a therapist can contribute to the re-forming of experience are amply illustrated throughout this book. Additional attention must be drawn, however, to the role that can be played in therapy by the exploration of experience from multiple perspectives, by sensitizing another to the relational context in which behavior is situated, and by a thorough *relativizing* of experience. Toward this end, the troubled person can be invited, *inter alia*: to find exceptions to their predominating experience; to view themselves as prisoners of a culturally inculcated story they did not create; to imagine how they might relate their experience to different people in their lives; to consider what response they invite via their interactional proclivities; to relate what they imagine to be the experience of others close to them; to consider how they would experience their lives if they operated from different assumptions – how they might act, what resources they could call upon in different contexts, what new solutions might emerge; and to recall precepts once believed, but now jettisoned.

These are but a few examples of means by which people can be enabled to construct things from different viewpoints, thus liberating them from the oppression of limiting narrative beliefs and relieving the resulting pain. In this way those turning to us in times of trouble may come to transcend the restraints imposed by their erstwhile reliance on a determinate set of meanings and be freed from the struggle than ensues from imposing their beliefs on self and others. For some, new solutions to problems will become apparent, while for others a richer set of narrative meanings will emerge. For still others a stance toward meaning itself will evolve; one which betokens that tolerance of uncertainty, that freeing of experience which comes from acceptance of unbounded relativity of meaning. For those who adopt it, this stance offers the prospect of a creative participation in the unending and unfolding meaning of life.

184   *Reflection and Reconstruction*

I will try
to fasten into order enlarging grasps of disorder, widening
scope, but enjoying the freedom that
Scope eludes my grasp, that there is no finality of vision,
that I have perceived nothing completely,
that tomorrow a new walk is a new walk.

A.R. Ammons, *Carson's Inlet*

Notes

1. For additional discussions of modernism, see Berman, 1982; Frisby, 1985; Frascina and Harrison, 1982; and Gergen, 1991.
2. See Sarbin's (1986) useful volume on narrative psychology.
3. Additional discussions of postmodernism may be found in Connor, 1989; Gergen, 1991; Harvey, 1989; and Silverman, 1990.
4. For additional critique of 'the lens of cognition,' see Gergen, 1989.
5. For further discussion of narratives of the self, see Gergen and Gergen, 1988.

References

Bateson, G. (1972) *Steps to an Ecology of Mind*. New York: Ballantine.
Berman, M. (1982) *All that's Solid Melts into Air: the Experience of Modernity*. New York: Simon & Schuster.
Carse, J.P. (1986) *Finite and Infinite Games*. New York: Macmillan.
Connor, S. (1989) *Postmodernist Culture*. Oxford: Basil Blackwell.
Frascina, F. and Harrison, C. (1982) *Modern Art and Modernism*. London: Open University Press.
Frisby, D. (1985) *Fragments of Modernity*. Cambridge: Polity Press.
Gergen, K.J. (1989) 'Social psychology and the wrong revolution', *European Journal of Social Psychology*, 19: 731–2.
Gergen, K.J. (1991) *The Saturated Self*. New York: Basic Books.
Gergen, K.J. and Gergen, M.M. (1988) 'Narrative and the self as relationship', in L. Berkowitz (ed.), *Advances in Experimental Social Psychology*, vol. 21. New York: Academic Press. pp. 17–56.
Goolishian, H. and Winderman, L. (1988) 'Constructivism, autopoiesis and problem determined systems', in V. Kenny (ed.), 'Radical constructivism, autopoiesis and psychotherapy', special issue of *Irish Journal of Psychology*, 9 (1): 130–43.
Hare-Mustin, R. and Marecek, J. (1988) 'The meaning of difference: gender theory, postmodernism and psychology', *American Psychologist*, 43: 455–64.
Harvey, D. (1989) *The Condition of Postmodernity*. Oxford: Basil Blackwell.
Keeney, B.P. (1983) *Aesthetics of Change*. New York: Guilford Press.
Kovel, J. (1980) 'The American mental health industry', in D. Ingleby (ed.), *Critical Psychiatry: The Politics of Mental Health*. New York: Pantheon.
Parker, D. (1990) *The Mighty World of Eye: Stories/Anti-Stories*. Brookvale, NSW: Simon & Schuster.
Ricoeur, P. (1971) 'The model of the text: meaningful action considered as text', *Social Research*, 38: 529–62.

Sarbin, T. (ed.) (1986) *Narrative Psychology.* New York: Praeger.

Silvermann, H.J. (1990) *Postmodernism – Philosophy and the Arts.* New York: Routledge.

Spence, D. (1982) *Narrative Truth and Historical Truth.* New York: Norton.

Wittgenstein, L. (1953) *Philosophical Investigations.* New York: Macmillan.

Name Index